Seinfeld
FAQ

Seinfeld FAQ

Everything Left to Know About the Show About Nothing

Nicholas Nigro

APPLAUSE
THEATRE & CINEMA BOOKS
An Imprint of Hal Leonard Corporation

Published in 2015 by Applause Theatre and Cinema Books
An Imprint of Hal Leonard Corporation
7777 West Bluemound Road
Milwaukee, WI 53213

Trade Book Division Editorial Offices
33 Plymouth St., Montclair, NJ 07042

Except where otherwise specified, all images are from the author's personal collection.

The FAQ series was conceived by Robert Rodriguez and developed with Stuart Shea.

Printed in the United States of America

Book design by Snow Creative Services

Library of Congress Cataloging-in-Publication Data

Nigro, Nicholas J.
  Seinfeld FAQ : everything left to know about the show about nothing / Nicholas Nigro.
    pages cm
  Includes bibliographical references and index.
  ISBN 978-1-55783-857-5
1. Seinfeld (Television program)—Miscellanea. I. Title.
  PN1992.77.S4285N54 2014
  791.45'75—dc23
                                                                        2014027918

www.applausebooks.com

To my father, Nicholas Nigro, who could never get enough of *Seinfeld*, and who proved that the show transcended generations

Contents

Acknowledgments

Foremost, I'd like to thank my agent, June Clark, for pitching me for this project and for helping me achieve my original dream as a writer—to author a "television" book. And not just any TV book—one about the greatest sitcom of all time! Also, thanks to the fine, always helpful editors at Applause, Marybeth Keating and Jessica Burr, who walked me through this multi-layered endeavor. I would also like to acknowledge the superb job of copy editors Lon and Debra Davis. They demonstrably improved the manuscript with their knowledge of the subject matter and attention to detail.

Special thanks are in order to my brother, Thomas Nigro, who accompanied me on a *Seinfeld* Reality Tour of our own, which began at Times Square and culminated at Tom's Restaurant on Broadway and 112th Street. As we crisscrossed the city entirely on foot—in one afternoon—he snapped many fine photos of *Seinfeld*'s New York. Thanks, too, to the incomparable Kenny Kramer for his contributions and the invitation to join him on his tour, which I look forward to in the future.

There are so many *Seinfeld* aficionados who shared with me their unique insight into the show and, in some instances, images from their personal collections. Many thanks to Joe Nigro, Remy Joseph D'Esposito, Rosanne D'Esposito, Ed Kallawasser, Patrick Downes, Stephen Spinosa, Peter Spadafino, Leon Hodes, Bill Hlubik, Ann Lynch, Sol Ives, Mike "Red" Lee, Gerald T. Mannion, Tony Trenga, Davis Herron, Norman Metter, "The Contest" expert Matt Laufer, Greg Vreeland, "Disciplinarian" Bill Cleary, Samuel Turk, Chris Winch, and, last but not least, John Roach, who thoroughly entertained me with his spot-on impersonations of Jerry, George, Kramer, and—believe it or not—Elaine, too.

Seinfeld
FAQ

Part I
In the Beginning

And Now for Something Completely Different

Postmodern Television

From *Seinfeld*'s humble beginnings, co-creator Larry David insisted that the show's scripts be absent of any trace of pathos or sentimentality. "No hugging" and "no learning" on a *Seinfeld* set were likewise part of David's unbending credo. Under no circumstances would *Seinfeld* characters become wiser, more thoughtful, and more compassionate human beings as the series progressed. They would not ever address the hot-button political issues of the day—at least not in any serious manner—nor make some larger, socially invaluable contributions to the society at large. It is this curiously detached approach to the ways and means of situation comedy that immediately distinguished the show and set it apart from its predecessors both old and newer. No prior sitcom dared present to a television audience an ensemble of neurotic, self-centered, thirty-something characters with dubious morals—jerks, if you will—who, on top of all that, called Manhattan's Upper West Side home.

As the 1970s dawned, America was still mired in an unpopular war in Southeast Asia; civil rights and women's rights movements were making conspicuous headway; and a spanking new environmental awareness assumed center stage as well. It was in this tumultuous snapshot in time that the American sitcom, too, underwent a comprehensive metamorphosis and suddenly—and without fair warning—began to mirror the uneasy, conflicted, but always-animated social reality that ruled the day. Throughout the 1950s and 1960s, the American sitcom remained, by and large, true to its roots by steering clear of contentious societal issues. Sitcoms' abiding missions were to be humorous distractions from the rough and tumble goings-on in the wider world. They were not conceived, nor written, with the intention of tackling the momentous issues making news, or the serious problems transpiring behind closed doors in American homes or on the streets of American neighborhoods.

Indeed, the first half of the 1970s—which was actually a continuation of the culturally sea-changing late 1960s—bore witness to a rather comprehensive purge of old-style sitcoms and variety shows. Once immensely popular comic stalwarts like Jackie Gleason and Red Skelton, for example, disappeared altogether from the primetime lineup. Notoriously, CBS canceled en masse its rural-based shows, starting with *Petticoat Junction* (1963–1970). Pat Buttram, who played unctuous snake oil salesman Mr. Haney on *Green Acres* (1965–1971), complained that the network, in one fell swoop, cast asunder every show with a tree in it, including *The Beverly Hillbillies* (1962–1971), *The Andy Griffith Show* spin-off *Mayberry R.F.D.* (1968–1971), and *My Three Sons* (1960–1972). It little mattered that they were still holding their own in the ratings. Even the venerable Lucille Ball, who'd starred in a sitcom virtually uninterrupted since 1951—when Harry Truman was president—came across as a little too juvenile and silly for the socially conscious 1970s. Her last show, *Here's Lucy* (1968–1974), was the successor of *I Love Lucy* (1951–1957), *The Lucy-Desi Comedy Hour* (1957–1960), and *The Lucy Show* (1962–1968).

Replacing the aforementioned shows and their ilk was mostly a new breed of sitcom that was seen as cutting edge and socially relevant. There were still exceptions like *The Brady Bunch* (1969–1974). Its exceptionalism, as it were, is precisely what drove its show's star, Robert Reed, to distraction. Nonetheless, even *The Brady Bunch* planted a pack of cigarettes in son Greg's jacket, which made for a lesson-packed episode.

The larger purpose behind the considerable change in content was to attract younger, more urban viewers and, of course, make important statements along the way. Sexual matters, for one, were no longer taboo on network television. When *All in the Family* debuted as a midseason replacement on CBS in January 1971—with its lead character a working-class bigot with racial epithets aplenty on the tip of his tongue—it was admittedly something of a culture shock. The 1970s sitcom formula outwardly insisted on characters who were groundbreaking—at least as far as television was concerned—in some evident way. *The Mary Tyler Moore Show* (1970–1977), for instance, revolved around the life and times of a single working woman on her own in the cold, cruel world of Minneapolis-St. Paul. This seemingly innocuous premise was, in fact, groundbreaking in 1970 when the show premiered. Mary Tyler Moore was no longer Laura Petrie from *The Dick Van Dyke Show* (1961–1966). *Good Times* (1974–1979) depicted a family living in a Chicago housing project—the ghetto—with all its inherent problems. *M*A*S*H* (1972–1983) was set in a Korean army hospital and married laughs with the horrors of war. Sitcoms of that era like *Maude* (1972–1978), *One Day at a Time* (1975–1984), and *Alice* (1976–1985) combined comedy with solemn life issues, such as abortion, drug abuse, and male chauvinism. Shows like *Sanford and Son* (1972–1977), *Chico and the Man* (1974–1978), and *The Jeffersons* (1975–1985) brought additional minority characters and, along with them, minority-specific issues to primetime audiences. *Chico and the Man*'s Freddie Prinze was television's first Chicano actor in a starring vehicle. And Redd Foxx's Fred Sanford and LaWanda Page's Aunt Esther weren't averse to using the N-word on occasion. This sort of thing was, in fact, tolerated in the freer, less-afraid-of-words early and mid-1970s.

By the late 1970s, however, the 1960s in-your-face *zeitgeist* was a relic of the past, and it was reflected in the obvious change in tone and tenor of primetime sitcoms. Gone were the more overt heavy hand and in-the-moment nature of so much of early- and mid-1970s programming, which regularly tackled pressing issues of the day and referenced current events. This is precisely why so many of the sitcoms from that time period come across as hopelessly dated all these years later. Allusions to Vietnam, Women's Lib, and Watergate ring no bells with younger views, who consider the 1990s—let alone 1970s—ancient history. Nevertheless, the sitcoms that defined the 1980s didn't exactly back step into the *Ozzie and Harriet–Leave It to Beaver* 1950s. While they certainly jettisoned some of the edge that defined the first half of the 1970s, they nonetheless remained socially relevant and frequently addressed issues of concern for young and old alike. *The Cosby Show* (1984–1992), for example, portrayed an upper-middle-class African-American family living in a tony Brooklyn neighborhood. That hadn't happened before in Sitcomland.

Even when taking into account the life issue–oriented and socially conscious thrust that swept over the American sitcoms in the 1970s and 1980s, they nonetheless employed the same general playbook of their small screen progenitors. From the 1950s through the 1980s, primetime situation comedies typically revolved around families in family settings—usually the home but not always. Hit shows like *M*A*S*H* and *Cheers* (1982–1993), for instance, were set in a fictional army camp in Korea and fictional Boston bar, respectively, but a case could be made that the soldiers, doctors, and nurses at the 4077th Mobile Army Surgical Hospital and the Cheers bar patrons were ipso facto family units. The popular *Taxi* (1978–1983), starring Judd Hirsch, mostly played out in a garage with a group of disparate taxi drivers hanging around and discussing their lives' highs and lows. They were, nonetheless, a family unit, with the aforementioned Judd Hirsch, who played Alex Reiger, the obvious father figure and voice of reason among the diverse ensemble. In addition, sitcoms—be it *I Married Joan* (1952–1955), *WKRP in Cincinnati* (1978–1982), or *Charles in Charge* (1984–1990)—rarely deviated from A and B storylines. That is, a main plot thread running through each show, with a less important subplot filling in the blanks.

Then There Was *Seinfeld*

Along came *Seinfeld* with its four leading characters—Jerry, George, Elaine, and Kramer—all single, with incredibly malleable personalities, and very definitely living in the moment. They lead fragmented lives, too, on a whole host of fronts, including in their jobs and relationships. This omnipresent instability had never been part of the sitcom playbook, be it in the staid 1950s or cutting-edge 1970s. *Seinfeld* episodes, too, were frequently about mundane things like waiting for a table at a Chinese restaurant, searching for a car in a shopping mall's parking garage, or purchasing a cake and a bottle of wine for a dinner party. Also, the show was not remotely interested in being socially relevant—quite the contrary, as a matter of fact.

Seinfeld's characters reveled in being indifferent and anti-heroic—in stark contrast with the preponderance of past sitcom characters. Jerry Seinfeld literally ushered in the age of the anti-hero. He came before Tony Soprano. And never before had a sitcom featured a dominant female lead like Elaine Benes, who, without apology, charted her own life course—and God help anyone who got in her way. The icing on the proverbial *Seinfeld* cake is that the show's endings didn't tie up everything in neat "all is well again" bows, which was the pre-*Seinfeld* sitcom modus operandi, even in the grittier 1970s.

Seinfeld's plotting methodologies likewise broke new ground as they involved multiple storylines wending their way through each and every episode. Typically, each of the show's main characters had one or more unique storylines all their own, unfolding in what was—at that juncture—completely at odds with the much less involved plotting of prior sitcoms.

Debuting at the tail end of a decade that touted such popular sitcoms as *Growing Pains* (1985–1992), *The Wonder Years* (1988–1993), *Family Ties* (1982–1989), *Full House* (1987–1995), and *Alf* (1986–1990), *Seinfeld* wasn't exactly an easy sell. Both Jerry Seinfeld and Larry David considered the show's prospects pretty slim. Foremost, their concept had to pass muster with the always skeptical and often timid network executives, who generally prefer the tried and true to the new and offbeat. It had to be given an initial shot at sinking or swimming based on its merits—a not inconsiderable task in the dog-eat-dog world of television—and it came perilously close to being eaten.

When a pilot entitled "The Seinfeld Chronicles" was authorized, shot, and aired on NBC in July 1989, job one was accomplished. But with the ratings being nothing to write home about, and network brass even less enamored with the show than before, the *Seinfeld* phenomenon almost didn't happen. Commenting on the show's inauspicious beginnings, Jerry Seinfeld told *People* magazine: "NBC executives worried that the show didn't appeal to every genus from humans to swamp people."

In fact, were it not for the foresight of a man named Rick Ludwin, executive vice-president of late-night programming, "The Seinfeld Chronicles" might very well have been the be-all and end-all of the show. From his own finite budget—and scuttling a future Bob Hope special in the process—Ludwin financed the production of four more episodes, which are today considered the sum and substance of season one. Despite its rocky start and rather indifferent welcome, he believed the show had untapped potential because of its quirky originality. Rooted in the notion of where standup comedians get their material, the show was conceived by two standup comedians, Jerry Seinfeld and Larry David, with decidedly different approaches to comedy. Their comedic collaboration insisted that the humor inherent in scripts be observational in

Television's Fab Four. Left to right: Michael Richards as Kramer, Julia Louis-Dreyfus as Elaine, Jason Alexander as George, and Jerry Seinfeld as Jerry.

nature while simultaneously doing an end-run around the traditional method of sitcom storytelling.

So, what exactly was *Seinfeld*'s appeal? Why did this very different show gather momentum and grab higher and higher ratings in its first few seasons on its way to becoming both a blockbuster hit and bona fide phenomenon? For answers to these questions, it's worth going to the source: an episode of *Seinfeld* from the fourth season called "The Pitch," in which George comes up with an idea for a sitcom while casually conversing with Jerry, his best friend. What, pray tell, should the show be about? "Just talking," says George confidently.

"The Pitch" subsequently found Jerry and George pitching their idea for "a show about nothing" to NBC honchos. The plotline more or less mirrored the real-life pitch that Jerry Seinfeld and Larry David made for *Seinfeld*, including the butting of heads with recalcitrant and often clueless network executives. Skirting this reality-versus-unreality boundary is at the heart of *Seinfeld* and what makes it so exceptional in the annals of television. It was, though, actually about *something*—a whole lot of *something*, as its lengthy roster of episodes reveals.

After all, Jerry Seinfeld, a standup comedian, played a character named Jerry Seinfeld, a standup comedian. The show's myriad storylines were frequently based on actual events in the writers' lives. Characters, too, were based on real people. Celebrities playing themselves intermingled with Jerry, George, Elaine, and Kramer from time to time. Like no show before it, *Seinfeld* had this uncanny knack for both reflecting and deflecting reality through the funniest collection of fictional characters ever assembled on television.

Traditional Sitcom Rules Don't Apply Here

Via public television in the 1970s, American viewers were afforded the opportunity to watch episodes of the BBC's *Monty Python's Flying Circus*. The sketch comedy in this British show was unlike anything on American television. It smashed to smithereens the traditional rules of how comedy should be played and what its boundaries were. Time and again throughout its five-year run (1969–1974), *Monty Python's Flying Circus* straddled the line between the real and the imaginary and would be dubbed "postmodern," as would the show's American cousin and TV counterpart, *Seinfeld*, some two decades later. Both *Monty Python's Flying Circus* and *Seinfeld* were "completely different" in their unorthodox approaches to comedy when they respectively aired.

For the purposes of this book, postmodernism can be defined as skirting what are considered the cultural norms, societal conventions, and the established power structure that ordains what is expected of us. From soup to nuts, *Seinfeld* indisputably violated the generally accepted sitcom rules. For openers, its thirty-something main characters were not typically concerned with ethical and moral matters. There weren't many standards of decency—of right and wrong—that carried weight with them. They never, ever learned from the error of their ways, or became better and more empathetic human beings as the show progressed.

Kenny Kramer, Larry David's old friend and the inspiration for the Kramer character, described Jerry, George, Elaine, and Kramer thusly to the *New York Observer*: "These are the most shallow, superficial, self-indulgent people—people who mug old ladies, burn down log cabins, break up other couples—think about it! Horrible, despicable human beings. But we see there's a little of us in them, our own dark character."

Indeed, in sharp contrast with the often-syrupy "special" sitcom episodes of the 1980s, *Seinfeld* altered the face of American television—and there was no turning back. "*Seinfeld* is suffused with postmodern themes," wrote Professor Nod Miller of the University of East London. "To begin with, the boundary between reality and fiction is frequently blurred: this is illustrated in the central device of having Jerry Seinfeld play the character Jerry Seinfeld." R. Wesley Hurd, in his essay on "Postmodernism," said: "The commercial and critical success of this show is attributable not only to the genius of its script, character development, and acting, but also to the way the audience identifies with the fragmented, ludicrous, pastiche of 'moments' which make up the characters' lives. *Seinfeld* is uniquely postmodern in its presentation of groundless, malleable character identities. It is also postmodern—as are most TV sitcoms today—in its radical, up-front play with 'moralities' altered at the characters' whim; there is no one morality."

What the show did that no sitcom before it managed to do was place in American living rooms during primetime a group of people who encounter mostly ordinary life situations—the kinds we've all experienced at one time or another—like bringing laundry to the cleaners, waiting in long lines at the movie theater, and riding in airline coach. But it's the gang's reactions to these mundane situations, and the decisions they make while muddling through them, that are uniquely postmodern. They are typically outside of the mainstream—way, way outside of it. The beauty of *Seinfeld* is that we not only howl heartily at their unorthodox antics, we also await with bated breath the outcomes of their various tribulations. Through all the madcap mayhem, we can simultaneously identify with Jerry, George, Elaine, and Kramer—even if we aren't quite like them—and marvel at their materialistic ways, unmitigated narcissism, and adolescent behavior.

Now, perhaps *Seinfeld* didn't—all by its lonesome—usher in the postmodern sitcom on American television. *Married . . . with Children*, which debuted on the then-new FOX network in 1987, two years before the *Seinfeld* pilot was taped, has been called postmodern for its portrayal of family life. No prior American sitcom family had been seen in such a dim light as the Bundys—Al, Peggy, Bud, and Kelly. And, too, debuting in 1989, the same year "The Seinfeld Chronicles" aired, was *The Simpsons*, another FOX show, this one concerning an über-dysfunctional cartoon family that bore little resemblance to the Hanna-Barbera production *Wait Till Your Father Gets Home* (1972–1974). That primetime cartoon family, the Boyles, dealt head-on with the generation gap that became oh-so-conspicuous in the late 1960s and early 1970s, but postmodern it wasn't. That is, the Boyle family and the Simpson family had very little in common.

Seinfeld, nevertheless, is considered the leader of the postmodern pack because its four main characters were completely unattached and rudderless. Among the popular television sitcoms that followed in *Seinfeld*'s postmodern wake are the animated *Family Guy* (1999–present), *Arrested Development* (2003–present), *The Office* (2005–2013 [U.S. version]), *30 Rock* (2006–2013), and *Modern Family* (2009–present).

Finding Humor in the Strangest Places

There was very little the *Seinfeld* writers wouldn't touch—and this, too, was a defining moment in American television and a bona fide sitcom mold buster. The show's unrelentingly unsentimental satire boldly went where no other show had gone before. *Seinfeld* was perfectly willing to mine humor from other people's misfortunes and completely disregard the growing trend toward political correctness in society, where getting offended and outraged at everything and anything—even comedy—had become par for the course.

A young man with Severe Combined Immunodeficiency (SCID), who is living in a plastic bubble in the *Seinfeld* episode "The Bubble Boy," is hilariously funny. When one of Kramer's Junior Mint candies accidentally drops into Elaine's ex-boyfriend's opened body cavity—while Jerry and Kramer are in a hospital observing a live operation in the episode "The Junior Mint"—we laugh, even if we wouldn't think it very funny if it had been dropped into us. An old lady being mugged for a loaf of marble rye bread by Jerry in the episode "The Rye" is not a particularly amusing circumstance on a police blotter, but it is a laugh riot on *Seinfeld*. Really, there isn't anything inherently entertaining about a handicapped woman in a wheelchair spiraling out of control because

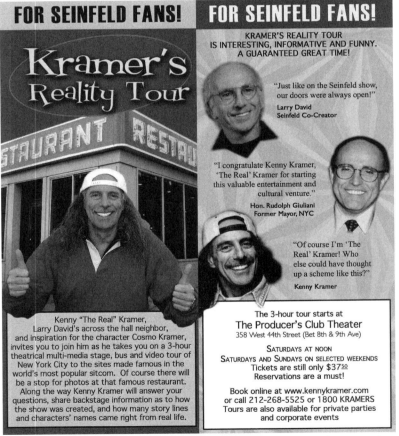

To this day, Kenny Kramer, the inspiration for the Cosmo Kramer character, gives *Seinfeld* Reality Tours in New York City. His bus tour is parodied in "The Muffin Tops," with Cosmo Kramer as the impresario of the "Peterman Reality Tour."

Courtesy of Kenny Kramer

of faulty brakes—courtesy of it having been purchased by George and Kramer to save a few bucks in the episode "The Handicap Spot"—but on *Seinfeld* the spectacle is hilarious. George frantically running from a small kitchen fire and mowing down children, a clown, and an elderly woman with a walker—to make his escape in the episode "The Fire"—might not be so comical in a real-life situation, but on *Seinfeld* it seems both natural and hysterical.

Jerry, George, Elaine, and Kramer personified a postmodern honesty and cold-heartedness that prior sitcoms steadfastly avoided. Even a show like *Roseanne* (1988–1997)—a contemporary sitcom that aired during the *Seinfeld* years—climaxed along traditional sitcom lines. Characteristically coarse and cynical throughout the episodes, *Roseanne* invariably wrapped things up with Dan (John Goodman) and Rosie (Roseanne Barr) pledging their undying love for each other and happy that all was well once more. "All's well that end's well" was certainly not part of the *Seinfeld* script. There were funny endings, yes, but no hugs and no kisses—and not a scintilla of sap.

Warren Littlefield, head of NBC Entertainment during *Seinfeld*'s halcyon years—and the man who offered Jerry Seinfeld five million dollars an episode to return for a tenth season—said at the time: "A decade ago, sitcoms consisted of seven scenes. *Seinfeld* turned each episode into a small film using twenty to thirty scenes and weaving five to seven storylines simultaneously. It was one of the first comedies built for a contemporary audience who could keep up with the numerous stories and quick scenes. It's smart and respects the intelligence of the audience."

Too Postmodern for Some

Predictably, such a groundbreaking show with self-centered, callous characters who do lots of terrible things to lots of people, without feeling much (if any) remorse, was not going to appeal to everybody. As the show became immensely popular and the gang's escapades were the talk of the town, *Seinfeld* critics were loaded for bear. Leon Wieseltier, literary editor at the *New Republic*, branded the show "the worst, last gasp of Reaganite, grasping, materialistic, narcissistic, banal self-absorption." The *New York Times*' Maureen Dowd, who's got an opinion on most everything, called *Seinfeld* part of "the what's-in-it-for-me times that allowed Dick Morris and Bill Clinton to triumph." One would surmise from such critiques that *Seinfeld* was advocating certain behaviors, and that Jerry, George, Elaine, and Kramer were somehow written as role models. And that's the last thing show creators Jerry Seinfeld and Larry David had in mind.

2

Birth of a Notion

"The Show About Nothing"

When a sitcom pilot entitled "The Seinfeld Chronicles" debuted on Wednesday night, July 5, 1989, few in the viewing audience could have ever imagined the impact the show would have on both television and the abiding popular culture. Top NBC executives were anything but enthralled with this very distinctive brand of sitcom but reluctantly gave it a shot—albeit not much of one—by ordering four more episodes. This paltry number, by the way, represents the smallest quantity of shows ever ordered for a sitcom's inaugural season.

The Patron Saint of *Seinfeld*

With programming whiz kid Brandon Tartikoff sniffing that the show's concept was "too New York" and "too Jewish" to succeed, the future prospects of *Seinfeld* were considered suspect from the get-go. Even studio audience members who watched "The Seinfeld Chronicles" live weren't sold on the show's merits. They offered opinions that raised numerous red flags with network bigwigs, who worry at the drop of a hat anyway, and who are inclined to paint doomsday scenarios of anything "outside the box." Sentiments like these were commonplace: "You can't get too excited about two guys going to the laundromat"; "Jerry needs a stronger supporting cast"; and "Why are they interrupting the standup for these stupid stories?" Jerry himself was perceived as "powerless" and "naïve."

Despite the network's initially gloomy prognostications, creators Jerry Seinfeld and Larry David would eventually see their brainchild—renamed *Seinfeld* because of a competing show on ABC called *The Marshall Chronicles*—succeed and become both a blockbuster hit and cultural phenomenon. But it could very easily have never happened. Television writer and producer Phil Rosenthal noted that Rick Ludwin, a young programming executive with genuine foresight, was the man chiefly responsible for *Seinfeld* being born in the first place, and for the show not dying a premature death. Like so many first volleys before it, it very nearly ended up in the overcrowded pilot-episode graveyard—television's equivalent of Potter's field.

Rosenthal, creator and executive producer of the CBS hit sitcom *Everybody Loves Raymond* (1996–2005), wrote in the *Chicago Tribune*: "Without Ludwin,

Seinfeld is one of those rare shows that one can watch over and over again, even if one knows the episodes' myriad plotlines backward and forward. The *Seinfeld* Scene It game combines trivia questions and clips from the series on DVD.

there would have been no *Seinfeld*. He commissioned the pilot, took money out of his specials budget to keep the show alive, and oversaw the program for its entire run." Indeed, monies that were slated to produce two one-hour variety specials for the network were budgeted for *Seinfeld*—one starring eighty-four-year-old comic legend Bob Hope. Warren Littlefield, who headed NBC Entertainment during the 1990s when *Seinfeld* reigned supreme, concurred. "Rick goes down as an NBC patron saint," he said. (NBC reportedly grossed over two hundred million dollars in annual profits from *Seinfeld*, which had Littlefield and other network suits atwitter.)

The *Seinfeld* Embryo

In 1976, at the tender age of twenty-two, Jerry Seinfeld appeared on an HBO special starring put-upon, hangdog comedian Rodney Dangerfield. A mere five years later, he performed on the crown jewel of late-night television, *The Tonight Show Starring Johnny Carson*. As he garnered more and more national exposure via further appearances on *The Tonight Show* as well as *Late Night with David Letterman*, *The Merv Griffin Show*, and other television venues, the NBC network VIPs took a real shine to the young comedian. After hosting *Jerry Seinfeld: Stand-Up Confidential* on HBO in 1987, an hour-long broadcast that blended standup with sketch comedy, the suits appreciated his potential even more.

The fact that Jerry Seinfeld's standup bits were simultaneously very popular and very clean—in other words: television fodder—had them wondering if the comedian could develop an idea for a possible primetime sitcom. "NBC asked

Art imitates life. Jerry and George, just like Jerry and Larry, pitch a "show about nothing" in this esteemed New York City locale.   *Photo by Thomas Nigro*

if I had any ideas for a show, and I said no," Seinfeld recalled in DVD commentary. "Then, a month or two later, I bumped into Larry David at one of the clubs in New York and I was telling him about the meeting. We were walking around near one of those little Korean fruit stands that they have in New York, buying some late-night groceries, and we were making fun of some of the products there. Larry said, 'You know, this is what the show should be: just two comedians making fun of stuff, walking around, talking.'"

Indeed, *Seinfeld* was originally described by a Castle Rock Entertainment press release as an "innovative comedy which explores the question, 'Where do comedians get their material?'" Castle Rock, which is owned by Warner Bros., is the company that produced the show and controls its licensing, etc., in perpetuity. Believe it or not, *Seinfeld* was never pitched or described as a "show about nothing." Considering that the phrase was a joke employed in an episode many years later, Jerry Seinfeld expressed bewilderment at its staying power during a Reddit.com "Ask Me Anything" Q&A. "Larry [David] and I to this day are surprised that it caught on as a way that people describe the show," he mused, "because to us it's the opposite of that."

The Odd Couple

To say that Jerry Seinfeld's standup material and stage presence were at odds with Larry David's would be the understatement of the century. David's brand of humor on the club scene was notoriously edgy, cynical, and frequently dark. He was the master of the madcap while performing—mercurial and impulsive—in sharp contrast with Seinfeld's decidedly composed, well-prepared act.

Divorced from environmental activist Laurie David (producer of *An Inconvenient Truth*, an Academy Award–winning documentary on the effects of global warming) after fourteen years of marriage, and the father of two daughters, David was asked by *Rolling Stone* magazine about the possibility of remarrying at some point in the future. "It would be a silly thing to do," he answered straightaway. "Why would I want that contract? I already have kids. The best situation is being a single parent. The best part about it is that you get time off, too, because the kids are with their mom—so it's the best of both worlds." This is Larry David's patented unsentimental world view and, really, his approach to humor in a nutshell. It proved fundamental to the *Seinfeld* concept and was liberally infused into the show's scripts through season seven.

Among David's multiple writing credits on the show was "The Contest," which won him a Primetime Emmy Award. That particular episode, which features Jerry, George, Elaine, and Kramer in the challenge of a lifetime—of who can go the longest without masturbating—was bestowed the number-one spot on *TV Guide*'s 2009 list of television's "Top 100 Episodes of All Time"—no small accomplishment. Courtesy of its pioneering plotline, the episode was, not surprisingly, steeped in controversy. Upon reviewing the script, the nervous Nellies at NBC naturally had the jitters, but let it run as written because the M-word was never once uttered, although euphemisms galore were,

The Not Necessarily Top Ten *Seinfeld* Episodes

10. "The Soup Nazi," which spawned an unforgettable, oft-repeated catchphrase, "No soup for you!"

9. "The Puffy Shirt," which introduced both a "low-talker" and a shirt that's now ensconced in the Smithsonian's National Museum of American History.

8. "The Outing," where Jerry and George were presumed to be a gay couple—"not that there's anything wrong with that!"

7. "The Yada Yada," which breathed new life into an old expression, "Yada, yada."

6. "The Bubble Boy," where George played Trivial Pursuit with a boy in a bubble and literally burst said bubble during a contentious row over a misprint on an answer card.

5. "The Muffin Tops," where Elaine's former boss, Mr. Lippman, opened up a shop that peddled only the tops of muffins.

4. "The Opposite," where George did the exact opposite of his every natural instinct and turned his life completely around, including getting a job with the New York Yankees.

3. "The Jimmy," which introduced a guy who curiously and repeatedly referred to himself in the third person.

2. "The Marine Biologist," where George uncharacteristically exhibited an act of courage and saved a whale in distress.

1. "The Contest," which featured the gang attempting to abstain from masturbation—although the "M" word was never uttered—in a fierce battle of wills.

including "master of your domain," which immediately became part and parcel of the ever-growing *Seinfeld* lexicon.

Conversely, Jerry Seinfeld's stock-in-trade was wry and observational humor, which likewise became essential to the *Seinfeld* brand. There were never any F-bombs or gratuitous raunchiness in his standup routines. He earned laughs the old-fashioned way and continues employing the same playbook to this day. In the Reddit.com Q&A, a questioner noted that Seinfeld employed an acronym—"A. H."—for a certain cuss word, even when typing his response on a keyboard. In contrast with Larry David's more pessimistic and disdainful comic material, Seinfeld's jokes were more on the plane of: "I was the best man at the wedding. If *I'm* the best man, why is she marrying *him*?" and "Men want the same thing from their underwear that they want from women—a little bit of support and a little bit of freedom."

While the Jerry Seinfeld and Larry David creative marriage was considered something of a Hollywood odd couple, it was nonetheless an unbeatable synergy of comedic genius that exhibited a willingness to mine the ordinariness of everyday life and everyday problems with characters highly adept at the urban art of deceit and perfidy. "I like taking the worst qualities that a person has and trying to make something funny out of it," David quipped on the *Seinfeld* DVD commentary. "Doesn't everybody do terrible things and have terrible thoughts? Just by trying to be as funny as you can, you're going to deal with a lot of things that are real—so the show's really about *something*. The whole thing about the show being about nothing is ridiculous."

With the notable exception of Rick Ludwin, the NBC network executives were somewhat perplexed when they viewed "The Seinfeld Chronicles." (The pilot episode was originally entitled "Stand Up," then "Good News, Bad News.") It was not quite what they expected. *What, pray tell, were they expecting?* After they grudgingly consented to a so-called first season of *Seinfeld*—four measly episodes—Warren Littlefield offered suggestions on how to improve the show's overall concept and reach a larger demographic. (The pilot had scored a 10.9 in the Nielsen ratings and an audience share of 19, which reflected the percentage of television sets tuned into the show.) For one, Littlefield wanted Jerry and Elaine to be an item—engaged in the series. This way, they could eventually get married, which would, of course, attract a big audience. *Yada, yada, yada.* Essentially, he wanted the show to adopt a more traditional sitcom formula. But *Seinfeld* wasn't *Rhoda*. Larry David refused to knuckle under, and his co-creator, Jerry Seinfeld, backed him up to the hilt. Their united stance in refusing to tinker with the essence of what made the show different was an act of courage because it could very easily have meant that the *Seinfeld* debut was also its swan song.

Behind the *Seinfeld* Allure

Sure, *Seinfeld* was postmodern—a palpably different kind of sitcom than what was on television at the time, and totally unique when compared with virtually everything that came before it. But very few of us were tuning in to the show because it had been dubbed "postmodern," because, for one, very few of us knew what the term meant—or, for that matter, cared what it meant. No, there was something else at play—something perhaps a little easier to relate to—as to why the show caught on as it did with the primetime television viewers.

Where, though, was the appeal in *Seinfeld*'s four chief protagonists, who were, individually, the embodiment of the anti-hero? We didn't really care—one way or the other—if said characters met with hardship or got knocked around by life's slings and arrows. The true lure of *Seinfeld*—and why it not only amassed increasingly healthy ratings over the first few years but became the talk of the town as well—was its uncanny ability to make chicken soup out of chicken feathers. Here's the secret: unlike prior sitcoms dating back to the 1950s, *Seinfeld* unearthed meaning from the seemingly meaningless. Week after week, we gleefully tuned in to watch the *Seinfeld* troupe engage in what they considered the ordinary, humdrum slog otherwise known as life. We, though, knew better, identified with it all, and came to the conclusion that the ordinary, humdrum slog—common to us all—is actually rather extraordinary on some higher level. Jerry, George, Elaine, and Kramer confirmed this time and again.

Episodes of *Seinfeld*, remember, didn't typically deal with super-important happenings in the main characters' lives. The pre-*Seinfeld* sitcom almost invariably revolved a central plotline involving a "big deal," of sorts. The *Seinfeld* gang could just as easily be found going out to dinner, visiting a friend, or venturing home from a baseball game. *Seinfeld* somehow elevated the commonplace, which at once struck an important chord and collective funny bone with an ever-expanding and extraordinarily loyal viewership.

3

Characters with Character

An Ensemble Is Born

Comedian Jerry Stiller, who played the volatile, eccentric Frank Costanza, has called Jerry Seinfeld, Jason Alexander, Julia Louis-Dreyfus, and Michael Richards "the best comedy ensemble since the Marx Brothers." There was, however, a casting process that could very well have produced a different result. And the question that is always asked is: Could *Seinfeld* have been *Seinfeld* without the actors who will be forever remembered for their roles as Jerry, George, Elaine, and Kramer? One thing is certain: the show would not have been the same without them.

Calling All Kramers

In an interview with EmmyTVLegends.org, *Seinfeld* producer George Shapiro said that the very first member of the show cast—outside of Jerry Seinfeld, a given—was Michael Richards in the Kessler role for the show's pilot episode. Larry David was familiar with Richards's work from *Fridays* (1980–1982), a late-night sketch comedy show in which they had both appeared as regulars. Shot live, *Fridays* was ABC's attempt to capture some of the magic of *Saturday Night Live* (1975–present) on rival network NBC. *Fridays* ran for fifty-four episodes, from 1980 through 1982. Shapiro recalled that Richards finished up his audition while standing on his head. NBC executive Brandon Tartikoff, who was on hand, quipped, "Yeah, if you want to go for funny." Other actors who auditioned for the Kessler-Kramer role were Larry Hankin, Steve Vinovich, and Tony Shalhoub. Shalhoub went on to star as San Francisco detective Adrian Monk in the long-running USA network series *Monk* (2002–2009).

By George, I Think We've Found Him

The character of George Costanza was the next one cast. Paul Shaffer, David Letterman's bandleader, claims in his 2009 memoir, *We'll Be Here for the Rest of Our Lives*, and in interviews that he was offered the part. "The receptionist took

You can't see one without thinking of the others. The gang in 1997, showing off their Screen Actors Guild Awards for Outstanding Performance by an Ensemble in a Comedy Series.   *Paul Smith/ Featureflash/ Shutterstock.com*

a message: 'Jerry Seinfeld called. He's getting his own show,'" he remembered. "'He wants you to be his sidekick. You don't even have to audition.' And I was kind of overwhelmed, and I said: 'Jerry Seinfeld. What kind of show could he possibly get?'" Shaffer admitted that he didn't even return the call because he had so many other things on his plate at the time. It's hard to envision Paul Shaffer, even with his shiny baldpate, as George Costanza.

Before Jason Alexander, David Alan Grier auditioned for the role of George. Grier, an African-American comedian, would have no doubt supplied viewers with a vastly different George than Jason Alexander's portrayal of the neurotic character. After getting bypassed for the role, Grier did all right for himself when he landed a job on the no-holds-barred sketch FOX network comedy show *In Living Color*, on which he appeared in 142 episodes, from 1990 through 1994.

Believe it or not, the raspy-voiced Steve Buscemi also auditioned for the George part. The actor sported a thick head of hair at the time, which would have been quite a contrast from the increasingly bald George Costanza as played by the increasingly bald Jason Alexander. Buscemi has since appeared in a string of television shows and movies, including *Miller's Crossing* (1990), *Fargo* (1996), and *The Big Lebowski* (1998). He also had recurring roles on the HBO series *The Sopranos* (1999–2007), as Tony Blundetto, and *Boardwalk Empire* (2010–2014), as Nucky Thompson. Other actors considered as possible George Costanzas were Danny DeVito, Nathan Lane, Kevin Dunn, Larry Miller, and Brad Hall, Julia Louis-Dreyfus's husband.

When Jason Alexander was asked to audition for the role he was living in New York City and working in the theater. With little enthusiasm, he completed a taped audition for the folks in Los Angeles who were casting the show. "To my mind, it was just a courtesy read," Alexander recalled in the show's DVD commentary. "They were just putting actors on video. I can't even tell you whose office it was. Because I think it was just like they called some poor, schnooky New York casting director and said, 'Just put this list of people on tape.' And I never thought that I'd get a job from it, so I made a very broad choice of doing a kind of Woody Allen approach to the material . . . and a very broad-based New York accent . . . and glasses that I didn't wear at the time. I knew no one and nothing connected with the show, so I was just relying on blind instinct."

In the EmmyTVLegends.org interview, George Shapiro remembered the initial reaction upon seeing Jason Alexander's taped audition: "Everybody said, 'That's *him*—that's George Costanza!' It was absolutely amazing. He did come in and read later on to seal the deal."

Goodbye Claire, Hello Elaine

In the original casting, Lee Garlington won the role as Claire, the waitress in Pete's Luncheonette. When the show was given a make-or-break four-show shot after the pilot aired, it was decided to do away with Claire and recast the female lead character as Elaine Benes. The network insisted the male-centric show have a strong female lead, or it was no dice. Actresses who auditioned for the role included Patricia Heaton, who ultimately went on to play Debra Barone on CBS's *Everybody Loves Raymond*, and Megan Mullally, who landed the role of Karen Walker on NBC's *Will & Grace*. Both were very popular long-running series. Rosie O'Donnell, of whom Larry David thought highly, tried out for the Elaine part, too, but in the end lost out to Julia Louis-Dreyfus, who was just perfect for the role. Larry David had worked with Louis-Dreyfus while both were with *Saturday Night Live* several years earlier, and he knew what she could do with the character. After missing out on the *Seinfeld* role, O'Donnell found her niche and became the "Queen of Nice" for a time on her highly rated daytime talk show, *The Rosie O'Donnell Show*. She also appeared as a regular for a contentious spell on *The View*, Barbara Walters's much-discussed morning talk show, and returned for a contentious encore in 2014. In addition, O'Donnell has popped up in many television shows and movies along the way, including playing herself on Larry David's *Curb Your Enthusiasm* (2000–2011).

Frank and Morty

Before there was Jerry Stiller in the role of Frank Costanza, there was Tony Award–winning actor John Randolph. Before there was Barney Martin in the role of Morty Seinfeld, there was veteran character actor and writer Phil Bruns. Both Randolph and Bruns appeared in only one episode—the former in "The Handicap Spot," and the latter in "The Stakeout." For syndication of the series, the scenes with John Randolph were re-shot with Jerry Stiller. It was deemed appropriate to do this because fans had become so accustomed to his high-octane portrayal of Frank. The Phil Bruns scenes were not, however, re-shot with Barney Martin.

While John Randolph had a long and distinguished acting career, Larry David, Jerry Seinfeld, and company concluded that the part of George's father merited a stronger comedic flair—a certain zaniness that Stiller could deliver better than anyone else. Randolph, too, was seventy-eight years old and tired looking when he appeared as Frank Costanza. In watching "The Handicap Spot" all these years later—a classic episode with the characters at their hilariously callous best—it's evident that the writers had not yet conceived the definitive Frank Costanza. Frank was grumpy, yes, but hardly frenetic and far from unreasonable. He was even involved in charity work and received an award for his philanthropy. This was not the Frank Costanza of subsequent episodes—not by a long shot. So, even when one watches the re-shot scenes in "The Handicap Spot," with Jerry Stiller instead of John Randolph, it's very strange to see, given how the character's personality dramatically changed after this episode. Phil Bruns, meanwhile, was not brought back to reprise his Morty Seinfeld role because the show's creators were looking for someone who could portray him with a little more bite—and they found him in veteran character actor and former New York City police detective Barney Martin.

Estelle Harris and Liz Sheridan played the characters of Estelle Costanza and Helen Seinfeld, respectively, for the entire series. Harris appeared in a total of twenty-six episodes, while Sheridan appeared in twenty-one episodes during the series' nine-year run.

Since the series finale in 1998, John Randolph, Phil Bruns, and Barney Martin have passed away: Randolph, in 2004, at the age of eighty-eight; Martin, in 2005, at the age of eighty-two; and Bruns, at the age of eighty, in 2012.

Hello Newman, Goodbye Newman, Hello Again Newman

The character of Newman, as played so wonderfully by Wayne Knight, was originally conceived as an African-American man, the son of Jerry's landlord, and Kramer's distressed and suicidal friend. Two actors, Tim Russ and William Thomas Jr., auditioned for the part, which was intended as a one-shot guest role in the episode "The Revenge." Thomas got the job and his scene was filmed,

Due to a misunderstanding with a "low-talker," you have to wear an embarrassing puffy shirt on national television.

Move back one space, and next time make sure you get the correct information.

What distinguished *Seinfeld* from its competitors was its penchant for dealing with the ordinary and mining the human condition for laughs. After all, who doesn't know a low-talker? Card from the *Seinfeld* Scene It game.

but it ended up on the cutting-room floor. Larry David ultimately supplied the voice of Newman, who is never seen in the episode. For syndication, Wayne Knight dubbed over David's voice.

As for Wayne Knight, he originally landed the role of Newman, beating out Armin Shimerman and Dan Schneider, both of whom also auditioned. Once again, Newman was not expected to be a recurring character. He would appear in the episode "The Suicide"—period. But Knight's performance as Newman so impressed Jerry Seinfeld and Larry David that they correctly surmised that there was a lot more comedic mileage left in the character. Newman appeared in a total of forty-four episodes, including "The Finale."

Encore Performances

There were many notable recurring characters in *Seinfeld*, including Elaine's rather unconventional boss and fashion catalog guru, J. Peterman, played so marvelously by John O'Hurley. In early 1995 the actor had been cast in the ABC sitcom *A Whole New Ballgame*, which was unceremoniously canceled after only seven episodes. Larry David's office promptly contacted O'Hurley concerning a guest spot on the show. He would play this quirky character prone to erudite long-windedness, which the *Seinfeld* casting people believed was tailor made for his comedic talents.

During the table read, however, O'Hurley admitted to being less than bowled over by the script of the episode. He noted that *Seinfeld* is an extremely funny show that doesn't necessarily read funny because it is not dependent on one-liners and comic zingers—like so many other sitcoms—but labyrinthine stories instead. O'Hurley described the overall *Seinfeld* experience as quite manic, with some endings of episodes not written until the eleventh hour. Shows typically ran over their time constraints, too, leading—alas—to some of Peterman's more voluble monologues being trimmed down. Nonetheless, Peterman was an enormously popular character and brought back in guest spots from 1995 through 1998, for a total of twenty episodes. His very first appearance was in "The Understudy" and his last—like so many others—"The Finale."

Patrick Warburton is another actor who was very well received in his *Seinfeld* guest part. Playing the deadpan David Puddy, Elaine's on-again, off-again boyfriend, he reprised the role and appeared in a total of ten episodes. Warburton recalls being ecstatic when he was asked to audition for what was his favorite show. Little did he realize at the time that David Puddy, New Jersey Devils hockey fan extraordinaire, who loved nothing more than painting his face and body "devil red" for a game, would become an important part of the *Seinfeld* lore.

Danny Woodburn, who played Kramer's little buddy Mickey Abbott, was one more popular guest star. Woodburn described his Mickey character as not stereotypically a little person part, which he greatly appreciated. He immensely enjoyed his appearances in seven *Seinfeld* episodes, including "The Finale."

The roster of characters who were brought back for encores because of their popularity and, in some instances, importance to a season's story arc include Heidi Swedberg as Susan Ross; Len Lesser as Uncle Leo; Richard Herd as Matt Wilhelm; Ian Abercrombie as Justin Pitt; Richard Fancy as Mr. Lippman; Steve Hytner as Kenny Bania; Bob Balaban as Russell Dalrymple; Peter Crombie as "Crazy" Joe Davola; Phil Morris as Jackie Chiles; Sandy Baron as Jack Klompus; Bryan Cranston as Dr. Tim Whatley; Lisa Mende as Carol; and Warren Frost and Grace Zabriskie as Mr. and Mrs. Ross. Each of the aforementioned characters appeared in a minimum of five episodes. Of course, it should also be noted that the character of George Steinbrenner, as voiced by Larry David, appeared in multiple episodes while George Costanza was in his employ with the New York Yankees.

4

Seinfeld Before It Was *Seinfeld*

The "Seinfeld Chronicles" Pilot

If you are a *Seinfeld* aficionado and have never before laid eyes on "The Seinfeld Chronicles," the show's pilot episode, you'll definitely be in for a few surprises. First of all, the pilot is not to be confused with a later episode in the series called "The Pilot," in which Jerry and George's sitcom concept—at long last—sees the light of day. It was the fictional pair's rendering of "The Seinfeld Chronicles."

Seinfeld in Character . . . Not Quite Yet

"The Seinfeld Chronicles" introduces us to standup comedian Jerry Seinfeld playing the part of standup comedian Jerry Seinfeld. Jason Alexander is on board as Jerry's best friend, George Costanza. And Michael Richards is on hand, too, as Jerry's neighbor down the hall, but his character is known as Kessler, not Kramer. This initial name discrepancy occurred because the Kessler character was so overtly based on the real-life Kenny Kramer, Larry David's old friend. The show's creators and the legal team at NBC were understandably skittish about naming a character after a real person without having ironclad permissions in hand. Worth noting is that, in the earliest stages of the script, the character didn't even exist. He was originally Kramer, then Hoffman, and, finally, Kessler for the pilot episode's shooting. Most conspicuously absent in the original casting is Julia Louis-Dreyfus as Elaine Benes.

The female lead—for lack of a better description—in this *Seinfeld* opening salvo is Lee Garlington, who plays Claire, the world-weary waitress at Pete's Luncheonette, Jerry and George's preferred eatery and hangout before Monk's Café. She appears in the opening scene, utters several lines of unmemorable repartee with Jerry and George, and that's the be-all and end-all of her work on *Seinfeld.* The set for the luncheonette is a remnant from *The Muppets Take Manhattan* movie, which premiered in 1984, five years before "The Seinfeld Chronicles."

When the show was first conceived, the Jerry and George characters were both plying the same trade, standup comedy. In fact, George was named

Bennett, and the two buddies commiserated on the vicissitudes of their mercurial profession. Happily, this notion was short-lived and George Costanza was
duly monikered. Rather than being a comedian, George found himself toiling
in the always-unpredictable real estate business. The George Costanza character
was originally described in publicity materials as "intelligent . . . more ill at ease
with himself than Jerry . . . and unhappy with his current career of real estate
sales." Now, the George Costanza that we came to know and love, despite his
untold character flaws, certainly merited a more lively description than that.

Most strikingly in the pilot is George's general demeanor. He's a whole
lot more confident than the character that would evolve—or devolve, as it
were—throughout the series. Despite the aforementioned publicity accounting
of the George character, Jerry is plainly less secure than George in "The Seinfeld
Chronicles," and actually values his advice. George is nonetheless neurotic and
comes across as blatantly Woody Allen–esque, with a decidedly whiny quality.
Jason Alexander readily admitted that when he first auditioned for the part of
George, he more or less played him as Woody Allen, which is very evident in the
pilot episode as well. On the other hand, the character of Kessler is portrayed
by Michael Richards as downright confused and almost incoherent—more
a grubby airhead than manic "hipster doofus." Jerry, George, and Kessler's
personalities would, of course, develop and noticeably change when the series
was picked up and additional episodes were filmed. Kessler's character overhaul
got him a new name as well.

Character flip-flopping and major alterations like this are commonplace
with television series that are sold as a result of their pilot episodes. In fact,
the pilot and early episodes are frequently dress rehearsals for the finished
product. Characters develop and even markedly change until it's determined
what works and what will afford writers the very best—and in sitcoms, the very
funniest—storylines. In the first several episodes of the sitcom *The Munsters*
(1964–1966)—starring Fred Gwynne, Al Lewis, and Yvonne De Carlo—Herman
is undeniably the respected man of the house and rather savvy on top of that. He
is looked up to, which is fitting for a man who is said to be nine feet tall. It's old
Grandpa, Dracula, who is the childish one, prone to throwing temper tantrums
and getting himself into hot water. To make for better (and funnier) television,
Herman, the Frankenstein monster, quickly became the more foolish and
juvenile of the pair. With Jerry and George, too, it fast became apparent who was
better suited to assume the mantle of a self-doubting, uptight worrywart—and
that was Jason Alexander's George Costanza.

And then there's Kessler, the Kramer of the future, in "The Seinfeld
Chronicles." He would slowly but surely evolve into the "hipster doofus" that
made Cosmo Kramer a favorite character and television icon. The seedy loafer
persona of the pilot would vanish altogether. Upon his initial entry into Jerry's
apartment, Kessler pulls a couple of loaves of bread out of his shirt pockets and
asks if Jerry has any meat in his refrigerator. But the pièce de résistance is that
Kessler actually knocks on Jerry's apartment door. In *Seinfeld*'s last season—in

The center of the *Seinfeld* universe: Jerry's apartment. This familiar version differs from the one in "The Seinfeld Chronicles," which had a different color scheme and, instead of the entryway to the bathroom and bedroom (left), had a door that opened directly into the bathroom.   *NBC/Photofest*

the episode "The Betrayal"—Kramer ties up a loose end and addresses the Kessler name discrepancy. We learn, via a flashback sequence, that Kessler was the name on his door buzzer when he first moved into his apartment, and he never removed it. Jerry, who moved into the building afterwards, had no reason to think that his name was anything but Kessler.

A couple of more particulars worth mentioning vis-à-vis Kessler-Kramer is that he had a dog named Ralph and a more traditional hairstyle and sartorial tastes in the pilot episode, all of which went by the wayside in season one. The sprightly canine's sole appearance complemented material from Jerry's standup. In "The Seinfeld Chronicles," Jerry's standup routines are given ample airtime, which was the norm in the show's fledgling years. They were particularly integral to "The Seinfeld Chronicles," which explained the need for Ralph in the episode. In fact, there are four separate scene breaks that feature Jerry performing in a comedy club. These scenes were filmed on a Hollywood sound stage—not, as it appears, in an actual comedy club—with an audience that included paid extras. All the laughs, however, are the genuine articles. (While the initial seasons of *Seinfeld* opened with Jerry doing standup, the "comedy club" stage completely vanished after season two.)

Jerry's apartment, too, in the pilot episode is not quite like the one we all became accustomed to in the subsequent series. For starters, there is no bedroom off the bathroom—it's a studio—and the window scheme is different. Jerry's got a skylight. Also, the exterior shot of the apartment is not the Los Angeles building used throughout *Seinfeld.* Yet another glaring difference between "The Seinfeld Chronicles" and the eventual series is the music, which was written by New Orleans–born composer Jep Epstein. The theme is more along the lines of a traditional sitcom and worlds apart from the *Seinfeld* sound of the series. When the pilot was put into the syndication package, its original music was replaced with the Jonathan Wolff's jazzy bass-riff compositions that *Seinfeld* fans had come to expect. However, with the DVD release of the show, fans can now watch "The Seinfeld Chronicles" in its virgin form, with its original theme music intact.

In the Beginning

The very first *Seinfeld* scene, as it were, that featured character interaction—on the heels of Jerry's standup routine—occurs in Pete's Luncheonette, where Jerry and George are engaged in a lively discussion about the placement of shirt buttons. Jerry notes that the second button on George's shirt is "in no man's land." In one final *Seinfeld* irony, Jerry and George have this very same conversation—word for word—in the last scene of the last episode, "The Finale." They are seated this time around in a jail cell, not a cozy neighborhood eatery.

"The Seinfeld Chronicles," it should be said, contains some classic dialogue in the glorious tradition of the series. Jerry and George, while in a laundromat, engage in some scintillating banter as the latter, becoming increasingly impatient, requests that the former interrupt the washing machine's drying cycle. George reasons that Jerry's clothes are almost certainly dry and are at risk of being over-dried. Jerry, however, believes otherwise—that the machine knows best—and replies: "You see, once something is wet, it's wet. Same thing with dead—like once you die, you're dead, right? Let's say you drop dead and I shoot you. You're not going to die again. You're already dead. You can't over-die. You can't over-dry."

When the green light was given to shoot four more episodes after the less-than-successful premiere of "The Seinfeld Chronicles"—thank you, Rick Ludwin—changes were in the offing. A commitment of four episodes was not exactly a vote of confidence in the sitcom business. It wasn't a season's worth, or even a half-season's worth. But Julia Louis-Dreyfus was in as Elaine Benes and Lee Garlington was out as Claire, the waitress, taking Pete's Luncheonette with her. The network absolutely insisted on a strong female character in the cast—and the Elaine Benes character was arguably the strongest female character in sitcom history.

Speaking to the *Huffington Post*, veteran character actress Lee Garlington reflected with good humor on her one, brief shining moment on *Seinfeld*, and missing out on being a player in the "show about nothing" and the phenomenon that it spawned after her departure. "I think I watched two episodes in ten years just because I had friends on it or something," she said. "It didn't bother me the first five years. But the second five years drove me nuts. I don't know why. I still see Jason [Alexander] regularly. He's best friends with a friend of mine and I've never talked about it with him, but I'm sure for him he's like, 'Oh, poor Lee! Poor Lee!' Oh, it's funny." On the flip side of the coin, Julia Louis-Dreyfus says that she's never seen the pilot episode—and didn't know one existed until after *Seinfeld* went off the air. She says that she has no intention of ever watching it.

Reception

Even if it wasn't quite the show that it would eventually become, the critical consensus was that *Seinfeld*'s first shout struck more than a funny bone or two. It is obvious that creators and writers Jerry Seinfeld and Larry David didn't quite have the show's concept fleshed out. Watching "The Seinfeld Chronicles" is like watching an ongoing comedic experiment. It's easy to see the seeds of a great show in the making. Despite the characters not yet being in character and cutting loose, and the dialogue not being nearly as pointed as it would eventually become, and, too, Julia Louis-Dreyfus not yet a cast member, the pilot episode is nonetheless a must-watch for *Seinfeld* fans. When the show was rerun as part of the first season of four additional episodes, its original Nielsen rating of 10.9 shot up to 13.9. "The Seinfeld Chronicles" is not to be missed or dismissed. It is, after all, where the *Seinfeld* phenomenon took flight.

Part II
The Core Four

5

Jerry Seinfeld

Master of His Domain

Not to be confused with Jerry Seinfeld the standup comedian, Jerry Seinfeld the character on the sitcom *Seinfeld* likewise toils as a standup comedian. Jerry is both the master of observation and the sarcastic aside. Rather offhandedly, he is wont to say (with unmistakable insincerity), "That's a shame," in response to his friends' various trials and tribulations. Jerry, too, is not afraid to make jokes at their expense and frequently does. One example, from "The Old Man":

> George: Jerry, what gives you pleasure?
>
> Jerry: Listening to you. I come in here. I listen to you. I feel better. Your misery is my pleasure.

Jerry Seinfeld: The Character

Jerry is the quintessential New Yorker. He was born, raised, and still resides in the city. Jerry's closest friend is his boyhood pal, George Costanza, whom he met in gym class at John F. Kennedy High School. His parents, Morty and Helen Seinfeld, are retired and now live in the pleasantly warm climes of Florida. In stark contrast with George, who has a very contentious relationship with his mother and father, Jerry gets along reasonably well with his. Nevertheless, he is happy as a clam that they get their mail delivered in the Sunshine State rather than a subway ride away from his front door; pleased, too, that they don't reside in the same area code with no long-distance phone call cost considerations. This arm's length geographic separation is particularly key to the benign nature of their relationship. While Jerry grew up in a traditional Jewish household, he no longer adheres to the faith's rituals, nor does he keep kosher. For instance, he relishes a cup of crab bisque in the episode "The Soup Nazi."

On occasion, Jerry visits his parents at the retirement villages they call home, including Del Boca Vista. In fact, he is renowned in these places and while interacting with residents, invariably unearths material for his standup act. In the episode "The English Patient," Jerry and his dad call upon Del Boca Vista's recently opened physical fitness amenity. Father and son engage in a little back and forth about such vital accoutrements as medicine balls and sweat suits.

Despite ample evidence to the contrary, Morty and Helen Seinfeld don't consider standup comedy a *real job*—a legitimate moneymaking career. Morty, when in the company of his son, always insists on picking up the tab at restaurants—and everywhere else for that matter. In the episode "The Wallet," he has every intention of paying Jerry's $18.50 gas tab, causing the stubborn pair to engage in a rather lengthy disagreement. Jerry once again makes an impassioned case that he makes a fair living and has the financial wherewithal to pay his own bills, but—as always—it falls on deaf ears.

Brooklyn-born Jerry Seinfeld, whose same-name alter ego is the anchor of the show.   *Entertainment Press/Shutterstock.com*

Ironically, Jerry, the professional comedian, is simultaneously the straight man in his circle of friends and incomparable universe. His apartment—5A (formerly mentioned as 411 and 3A) at 129 West 81st Street—is where a great deal of the show's off-the-wall interacting transpires.

In the series pilot, "The Seinfeld Chronicles," Jerry's occupation is "standup comedian." In the *Seinfeld* finale nine years later, he has the very same job and the very same career. Jerry does extremely well, too, in plying his trade and—despite what his parents think—is financially secure. In the episode "The Cadillac," he purchases a new and very expensive Cadillac Fleetwood for them. On the job frontier, he does suffer a temporary layoff while serving the one-year prison sentence imposed on him in the waning minutes of "The Finale." Fortunately, though, we see Jerry—the quintessential pro in his profession—performing standup for his fellow inmates, so we can rest easy in the knowledge that he will remain sharp as a wolf's tooth and not lose his comedic edge while incarcerated. We know, too, that this new home away from home will furnish him with a mother lode of fresh material for future standup routines.

While Jerry experiences relative employment stability and is content with what he does for a living, George, Elaine, and Kramer have difficulty settling into one job and blazing a singular career path. Kramer, in fact, has virtually no job history and his capacity to live like he does and where he does—on pricey Manhattan's Upper West Side—is a mystery to all who know him.

Elaine, Jerry's dear friend and ex-girlfriend, is forever annoyed with the fact that nothing really bad ever seems to happen to him. Jerry dances through life's raindrops with a dexterity that eludes his less fortunate friends. Money concerns don't ever cast their foreboding shadows over his life. His relationships with women, too, are typically brief and rarely interfere with his lifestyle or derail his life train in any demonstrable way. Elaine expresses her incredulity at Jerry's uninterrupted good fortune in "The Rye."

Elaine: You know, one of these days something terrible is going to happen to you. It has to!

Jerry: No, I'm going to be just fine.

Jerry's Book of Etiquette

Among his copious idiosyncrasies, Jerry is notoriously fastidious and is frequently repulsed by the behaviors of his friends, acquaintances, and even perfect strangers. When he learns that Kramer is not wearing any underwear, for instance, the mere notion of this freaks him out. When Kramer withdraws his blood from the blood bank and stores it in Apartment 5A, he once again wreaks havoc on Jerry's mind, body, and spirit. George, meanwhile, is routinely making Jerry queasy by recounting actions such as (in "The Gymnast") urinating in the health club's communal showers and taking a bite of something that had once called home a garbage receptacle. As per this latter deed, Jerry accuses George of crossing the line "that divides man and bum."

In fact, Jerry's cleanliness and penchant for having everything in its right and proper place is noticed by one and all, including his many lady friends. Courtesy of being "thin and neat," he once acknowledged that he is sometimes mistaken for a gay man—*not that there's anything wrong with that.* Jerry trashed a belt of his because it inadvertently touched the side of a urinal. He replaced a shoelace because it made contact with a men's room floor.

While not on the job and performing standup in neat dress clothes, Jerry is typically attired in smartly pressed, clean jeans—no fading or wear marks around the knees—and is invariably wearing bright white sneakers. Throughout the series, he sports forty-nine different pairs, beginning with his fashionable Nike Driving Force in the show's 1989 pilot. Subsequently, Jerry is seen wearing everything from Nike Air Delta Force to Nike Air Cross Trainer to Nike Air Total Max.

Take a close look at Jerry's kitchen countertop and you'll spy his favorite cleaner: Soft Scrub, which kills—to the renowned germophobe's liking—99.9 percent of germs.

Jerry is a firm believer in keeping his cupboards and refrigerator full of all kinds of foods and liquid refreshments. His friends—particularly Kramer—take full advantage of his exhaustive shopping habits. Among the products that Jerry has on hand at one time or another are: bananas, apples, oranges, pickles, Folgers coffee, Life cereal, Pepperidge Farm cookies, Breyer's ice cream, Cheerios, Kix cereal, Nestlé Quik, Apple Jacks, Minute Maid orange juice, Lipton tea, Ruffles potato chips, Hershey's cocoa, Bachman hard pretzels, A1 Steak Sauce, Thomas' English muffins, Häagen-Dazs ice cream, Tuscan milk, Tropicana orange juice, Poland Spring bottled water, Chock Full o'Nuts coffee, Minute Maid lemonade, Maxwell House coffee, Raisin Bran cereal, Banana Nut Crunch cereal, Mister Salty pretzels, Wonder Bread, Reese's Peanut Butter Puffs cereal, Wheaties, Honey Comb cereal, Campbell's soup, Fig Newtons, Sugar Crisp cereal, Yoo-hoo chocolate drink, Ritz crackers, Shredded Wheat, Cocoa Krispies, Heinz ketchup, Hellmann's mayonnaise, Breakstone whipped butter, Quaker Oats, Pop-Tarts, Chips Ahoy! cookies, Healthy Choice ice cream, Pringles potato chips, Rice Krispies, Bisquick, Diet Coke, Pepsi, Canada Dry Ginger Ale, Alpha-Bits cereal, Corn Flakes, Prego Italian sauce, Rold Gold pretzels, Froot Loops, Reddi-wip, Skippy peanut butter, Ragú pasta sauce, and Evian bottled water. Jerry obviously thinks highly of

Soft Scrub cleanser with bleach, because he's always got a bottle at the ready in the kitchen. After all, it kills 99.9 percent of germs, Jerry's mortal enemy. Another visible product in the cleaning family is Comet cleanser. When Kramer comes calling looking for Tums, Jerry points him to the top of the refrigerator, where the former is seen grabbing a packet of Alka-Seltzer.

Jerry plays popular board games, too, like backgammon, Scrabble, Clue, Yahtzee, and Battleship.

The Right Relationships Are Everything

How do others in Jerry's life circle perceive him? His girlfriends and ex-girlfriends furnish us with a wealth of insight into his character. When Elaine eavesdrops on a conversation in the sauna room of a local health spa (in "The Implant") that includes one of Jerry's former lady friends, Sidra, we glean a little more about the man and what makes him tick. Jerry had previously broken up with Sidra because he believed—incorrectly as things turned out—that she had breast implants. The reason he supplied her for calling it quits—that he was getting back together with his mentally ill girlfriend—was par for the course in Jerry's world. "He's one of those guys who is obsessed with neatness and order," Sidra says. "Everything has gotta be just so. He would have made a great Nazi."

It was, in fact, Elaine who assured Jerry that he was correct in surmising that Sidra's breasts were counterfeits. However, a chance meeting in the sauna turns everything on its head. When Elaine slips on the steamy floor therein and grabs hold of Sidra's breasts to keep from falling down, she uncovers the truth. Sidra's breasts are real indeed—the genuine articles.

Jerry's relationships with the opposite sex unmask a great deal about his character or, more often than not, his character shortcomings. He has many girlfriends throughout the series. In fact, Jerry goes through girlfriends faster than he does bags of potato chips and quarts of milk. He habitually comes up with excuses for the myriad breakups. Elaine classifies most of them as "stupid reasons." Jerry's absolute lack of commitment is the stuff of legend.

In the episode "The Ex-Girlfriend," Jerry finds himself dating George's most recent ex, Marlene, who doesn't think his standup act is the least bit funny. She believes this fact alone would preclude them from having a lasting relationship and informs Jerry that she "can't be with someone if [she doesn't] respect what they do." His pithy rejoinder to this rather snippy brush-off: "You're a *cashier!*"

In the episode "The Bubble Boy," Jerry's girlfriend du jour, Naomi, laughs—in George's words—like "Elmer Fudd sitting on a juicer." Reason enough for the relationship to be short-lived. In "The Masseuse," Jerry dates a professional masseuse named Jody, who refuses his repeated suggestions and entreaties to give him a massage. Like so many others, their massage-less relationship withers on the vine.

"The Cigar Store Indian" is yet another episode that is most revealing of Jerry's character. Here, he fancies a woman named Winona, a Native American. Initially, Jerry is unaware of her lineage. So, when he buys Elaine a cigar store Indian as a gift and mimics Indian war party chants and gyrations, Winona takes offense. Upon learning of her heritage shortly thereafter, Jerry attempts to make amends for his flippant behavior, but is hopelessly inept in doing so. He keeps tripping up while desperately endeavoring to avoid words like *scalper* and *reservation* in conversation. The fly in the ointment is that he is compelled to explain how he purchased New York Knicks basketball tickets from a scalper and how he managed to secure reservations at a popular, super-busy restaurant called the Gentle Harvest.

In the episode "The Pie," multiple facets of Jerry's personality are laid bare, including his obsessive nature. He becomes fixated on why his latest girlfriend, Audrey, wouldn't sample a piece of his apple pie at Monk's Café—a dessert specialty that he had touted as the best in town. He tells her that his curiosity has gotten the best of him concerning this blatant apple pie pass, particularly since she is a known pastry person: "Surely, you could see how such a thing would prey on my mind."

Further evidence of Jerry's nitpicking, vis-à-vis his lady friends, is gleaned in "The Engagement." In this episode, Jerry hears the news for the first time that George has asked his girlfriend, Susan, to marry him, and that she has accepted. It comes as a real shocker to the man who has always been leery of venturing that far into matters of the heart. When George asks him how things are going with his latest squeeze, Melanie, Jerry tells him the relationship is over and why. "She's got the strangest

Jerry's Not Necessarily Top Ten Girlfriends

10. Dolores, whose name was shrouded in mystery but nonetheless rhymed with a part of the female anatomy ("The Junior Mint").
9. Tia Van Camp, a fashion model, who cast off Jerry after witnessing him seemingly picking his nose ("The Airport" and "The Pick").
8. Gennice, Bette Midler's peculiarly emotional understudy in the Broadway musical *Rochelle, Rochelle* ("The Understudy").
7. Audrey, who rebuffed Jerry's entreaties to taste his apple pie, despite being a pastry aficionado ("The Pie").
6. Donna Chang, who Jerry initially believed was Chinese, but who on their date revealed her real name: Donna Changstein ("The Chinese Woman").
5. Tawni, who had a fungicide tube in her medicine cabinet ("The Conversion").
4. Winona, a Native American woman, who was very sensitive to racial stereotyping ("The Cigar Store Indian").
3. Sidra Holland, who Jerry erroneously surmised had breasts that weren't the genuine articles ("The Implant").
2. Naomi, who laughed, according to George, "like Elmer Fudd sitting on a juicer" ("The Bubble Boy").
1. Rachel Goldstein, whom Jerry passionately necked with during *Schindler's List*, and who also saw George nude and in a state of "shrinkage" ("The Raincoats," "The Hamptons," and "The Opposite").

habit," he reports. "She eats her peas one at a time. You've never seen anything like it. It takes her an hour to finish them. I mean . . . we've had dinner other times. I've seen her eat corn niblets, but she scooped them."

In the episode "The Seven," Jerry finds fault with yet another of his girl-friends, this one named Christie. He can't understand why she has worn the very same articles of clothing on three consecutive dates. Mentioning that Albert Einstein wore the same outfit day in and day out, George attempts to assure him that it's really no big deal. Jerry quips, "Well, if she splits the atom, I'll let it slide."

"The Slicer" is still another episode in which Jerry endures some rough sledding with the woman in his life. His date here is Dr. Sara Sitarides, a der-matologist, and Jerry finds serious fault with her describing the work she does as "lifesaving." With his resentment building to an unstoppable crescendo, he cannot help but blurt out in a fit of frustration: "You call yourself a lifesaver. I call you Pimple Popper MD!" Later, Jerry bears witness to a patient of Dr. Sitarides thanking her, in no uncertain terms, for saving his life. The man had a dangerous form of skin cancer. Despite Jerry being chagrined upon learning this, there is no turning back the clock in the relationship. The "Pimple Popper MD" remark saw to that.

The preponderance of the evidence suggests that Jerry doesn't actually respect too many people. Whether it is Marlene, the cashier, or Sara, the derma-tologist, Jerry is quick to find faults in what people do for a living and how they conduct themselves. He dumps a girlfriend because she has "man hands," and another because she likes a certain Dockers pants commercial that he detests. He even has problems with a woman who is very much like him. Her name was Jeannie Steinman, and Jerry actually proposes to her in the episode "The Invitations"—ring and all. Jeannie had saved Jerry from getting struck by a car, and he realized that they had so much in common, including the same initials. By the next episode, "The Foundation," we discover (to no one's surprise) that there will be no nuptials between Jeannie and Jerry. "I can't be with somebody like me," Jerry says. "I hate myself." When Elaine returns from a trip, the topic of Jerry and Jeannie's status is hashed out in Monk's Café. He recounts the fine points surrounding the breakup. Via a flashback scene, we see both Jeannie and Jerry simultaneously exclaiming "I hate you!" and then—free from the yoke of engagement—laughing at what just transpired.

Jerry: It was unprecedented. I mean . . . it was the first truly mutual breakup in relationship history.

(*The flashback ends; we return to the present.*)

Jerry: No rejection, no guilt, no remorse.

Elaine: You've never felt remorse.

Jerry: I know . . . I feel bad about that.

The Miracle Called Friendship

When all is said and done, Jerry is indeed a self-absorbed, callous, thirty-something yuppie. However, he is not without commendable character attributes. There are not too many men, after all, who value friendship quite the way Jerry does. In the episode "The Bizarro Jerry," he reveals how much spending time with his friends really means to him. Granted, he often takes sadistic pleasure at their misfortunes, but he cares deeply about his relationships with George, Elaine, and Kramer. When Kramer gets a job—quite by accident and not a paying one—Jerry sees his entire way of life at risk. Because he has job responsibilities now, Kramer is just not there for him like he used to be.

Suffice it to say with Kramer venturing off to work each morning, Jerry's reassuring apartment routine is cast asunder. He complains to Kramer that the duo rarely have time to kibitz anymore. Later, when Elaine informs him that she's been hanging out with her new friend, Kevin, and his friends, Jerry exclaims with palpable anguish in his voice how the "whole system" is crumbling around his feet. The collapsing system to which Jerry is referring is one of life's most precious relationships: friendship. Fortunately for him, though, fate intervenes. Kramer gets fired and Elaine's association with Kevin, who she notes is very, very different from Jerry, comes to an abrupt end. She had, in fact, said of Kevin: "He is reliable. He is considerate. He's like your exact opposite." Elaine's succinct character assassination prompted Jerry to brand Kevin the "Bizarro Jerry," a riff off of "Bizarro Superman," where up is down and down is up. Nevertheless, Elaine's depiction of Jerry as at once unreliable and inconsiderate says an awful lot about the man's character. She is, after all, one of his best friends.

Jerry Seinfeld: The Actor

The non-sitcom character, the Jerry Seinfeld with a Social Security number, was born Jerome Allen Seinfeld on April 29, 1954, in Brooklyn, the most populous borough in New York City. In the mid-1950s, Brooklyn still bled "Dodger Blue" and its denizens had a very colorful way of expressing themselves. Brooklyn had, by that point in time, earned a reputation for being simultaneously gritty and community-oriented, although the postwar flight to suburbia was already in full throttle. Not too long after the birth of their son, Kalman and Betty Seinfeld relocated the family to Massapequa in New York's Nassau County, which was a half-hour drive from Brooklyn and the hustle and bustle of the big city.

It is in this suburb on Long Island's south shore that "Jerry," as he was known, and his older sister, Carolyn, spent their formative years. Young Jerry attended Birch Lane Elementary School and Massapequa High School. But not in his wildest dreams could this quiet and unassuming grammar and high school student have envisioned the degree of fame he would one day achieve as a trailblazing comedian—one who left an indelible mark on both his chosen profession and the entertainment industry at large. It would also have been impossible to visualize the size of his future net worth. Did somebody say *billionaire*?

Even if it wasn't always apparent, Jerry Seinfeld had the "art of comedy" and an unquenchable desire to "make people laugh" on his radar. While growing up, he greatly admired radio and television personality Jean Shepherd, who was renowned for his unscripted, comedic monologues and fondness for spinning a good yarn. Shepherd's 1983 theatrical film, *A Christmas Story*, which was based on his childhood in Hammond, Indiana, was not a success when it first debuted, but it has since become a holiday classic with its frequent broadcasts on television. The future comedian appreciated the man's singular flair for

Funny man Jerry Seinfeld made quite a journey, from obscure standup comedian to television legend.

Paul Smith/ Featureflash/ Shutterstock.com

"taking something small and making it big." Sound familiar? He listened, too, to Bill Cosby's 1965 record album, *Why Is There Air?* and marveled at the man's comedic timing and unrivaled capacity to mimic everything from a bouncing ball to kids on a playground. But it was comedian Robert Klein whom the young Seinfeld christened his ultimate inspiration. "He was a New York middle-class kid, and through that I could see a path for myself," he recalled in an interview with the *New York Times*.

For many comedians the passions that drive them are unhealthy doses of emotional pain and unhappiness, typically beginning with a challenging and joyless childhood. From Charlie Chaplin to Richard Pryor to Darrell Hammond, it's an all too familiar story. But, by all accounts, Jerry Seinfeld was among the exceptions to this rule. He was raised in a stable middle-class household in a pleasant suburban village within earshot of the Atlantic Ocean. Seinfeld described his largely benignant upbringing as "pretty Jewish. We went to temple, kept kosher, two sets of dishes."

Break That Face

Kalman Seinfeld, the family patriarch, was a cutup in his own right, always endeavoring to "break that face," which was his personal expression for making people laugh. Dour businessmen's mugs were persona non grata as far as Mr. Seinfeld was concerned. Jerry Seinfeld recalled his father recounting what daily life was like while serving in the Pacific Theater during World War II. His dad would write down each and every joke he heard, store them in a box, and retrieve them when situations—and there were so very many of them—warranted a good laugh and tension buster. "In the army, that's kind of how you get through it," Seinfeld told the *New York Times*. "People would tell jokes by the score, because what else are you going to do to maintain sanity?"

Jerry Seinfeld affectionately described his father as "very funny, quick, and very sociable—the kind of guy you'd want at a party. He was always making people laugh. I watched the effect that he had on people and I thought, 'That's for me.' He also turned me on to the secret that it's fun to be funny. That's really why I do it." Kalman Seinfeld, a commercial sign maker, was a bona fide inspiration—a man who untiringly offered his son encouragement as he forged a career path that most parents would have summarily dismissed as a "pipe dream" unworthy of a serious adult. But that's just it: Jerry Seinfeld wasn't a serious adult in the traditional sense. He was a funny one, committed—above all else—to getting laughs, not ulcers, in earning a living and forging a career.

Higher and Higher Education

When Jerry Seinfeld enrolled in the State University of New York at Oswego in the autumn of 1972, he was—like most of his peers—trying to find his way and uncertain about what exactly he wanted to do in the immediate future, let alone with the rest of his life. To add insult to injury, Oswego was an extremely cold place in which to ruminate and chart one's life course. The city is situated on the windy shores of Lake Ontario in what is known as the "Blizzard Belt." Nevertheless, it was the only state school at the time that offered practical, hands-on courses in the radio and television mediums—precisely the kinds of academic avenues that the college-aged Seinfeld desired venturing down and exploring. Fellow Oswego classmate Al Roker—who would also achieve a fair share of fame down the road—does not recall a single instance where Jerry Seinfeld tested out even a modicum of standup material on the frozen grounds of Oswego. "It's so cold in Oswego that people don't laugh," Roker joked to the *New York Daily News*. "It's hard to laugh when your teeth are chattering."

While Jerry Seinfeld was a far cry from the campus clown and went about his business rather inconspicuously, his Scales Hall housemates at the university found him to be a very funny person indeed and genuinely enjoyed the pleasure of his company. During his sophomore year, though, he transferred to Queens College of the City University of New York. Located in Flushing, Queens, home of his favorite baseball team, the Mets, it was an institution of higher learning with—when contrasted with Oswego—decidedly more hospitable climes in the wintertime. A short trip on the Long Island Railroad or automobile adventure on the Long Island Expressway could get him to school and back. At Queens College he began writing and performing standup, getting a feel for what worked and what didn't work with audiences. Graduating in 1976, Seinfeld earned a bachelor of arts degree in communications and theater. He wrote a college thesis on standup comedy, which is what intrigued him above all else. Come what may, the business of standup is where Jerry Seinfeld intended to make his stand.

Standup Guy

Jerry Seinfeld has, on occasion, referred to "getting born" in 1976—America's bicentennial year—and not because it was the United States' two-hundredth birthday or, for that matter, because he hung a sheepskin on his bedroom wall that spring. From his perspective, 1976 was the year a star was born: Jerry Seinfeld. On the very day that he graduated, Seinfeld performed his standup routine at Catch a Rising Star in Manhattan. This was his first appearance in a comedy club. During 1976 he also won an audition and a prestigious spot on a Comic Strip lineup, a recently opened comedy club that was all the rage on Manhattan's Upper East Side. His standup routines quickly became popular with club regulars. He was known in the club as "Doctor Comedy," because "there wasn't a bit Jerry couldn't fix." He landed an emceeing gig there as well, which paid seventy dollars per week. In the grander picture, the Comic Strip served as a launching pad for Seinfeld and other young comedians, including Eddie Murphy, Paul Reiser, and Adam Sandler. It was his various standup appearances throughout New York City—the city that never sleeps—that got him noticed by big shots like Rodney Dangerfield, who included him in his *It's Not Easy Bein' Me* HBO comedy special in 1986. Jerry Seinfeld's comic star and distinctive brand of observational comedy landed him a spot on the May 7, 1981, edition of *The Tonight Show Starring Johnny Carson*. His performance was so well received that he was brought back time and again, frequently dropping in on *Late Night with David Letterman* as well.

Those early years on the comedy club circuit—before reaching national audiences on Carson and Letterman—were, nonetheless, a struggle. It's the nature of the business. Nothing comes easily there and one must pay his or her dues. There wasn't all that much money coming in. Seinfeld's initial salvation was that he lived at home with his parents, which enabled him to focus squarely on his comedy act, though he did briefly wait tables at a Brew Burger chain restaurant in Manhattan and peddle light bulbs via the telephone with pal Mike Costanza (whose last name Seinfeld would use for the character George). His college roommate at Oswego, Larry Watson, recalled that period on his website lawrencewatson.com: "In the early days, Jerry and I would go together to the comedy clubs when I visited New York. It was an ordeal. We'd wait all night for Jerry to go on. I really admired him for keeping his edge until he got up there."

While diligently working to perfect his craft, Jerry Seinfeld very definitely paid his dues. "I once opened for Vic Damone at a nooner on a basketball court in Brooklyn," he revealed to the *New York Times*. "They're going, 'Who is this kid?' Oh, god! They're sure you're not worth the trouble. But I'd win over some of those rooms." In 1980, Seinfeld moved to Los Angeles and the tinsel of Hollywood.

Jerry as Frankie

That same year, Jerry Seinfeld was asked to audition for a role on the popular ABC television sitcom *Benson* (1979–1986), starring James Noble as the governor of some unnamed state, and Robert Guillaume, the titular character, as his head of household affairs. Discovered, as it were, while performing his standup act at a New York City comedy club, Seinfeld would be playing—assuming he got the job—a young man named Frankie, who happened to be an aspiring standup comedian as well as the governor's personal joke writer. Was there a trend starting here—the standup comedian Seinfeld in the fictional role as a standup comedian?

Lo and behold, he got the job, which was a recurring part that paid four thousand dollars an episode. By today's standards—and taking into account what Jerry Seinfeld ultimately earned with *Seinfeld*, and what he was offered to come back for one more year and a tenth season (five million dollars an episode)—four thousand dollars doesn't sound like a great deal of money. But to a near-broke young comedian, it was a considerable sum and a most welcome paycheck. The twenty-six-year-old Seinfeld—who could have passed for a teenager back then—appeared in three consecutive episodes. At the next rehearsal, he was startled to learn that there was no script for him to read through with the rest of the cast. He had been unceremoniously fired. An assistant director gave him the bad news. "It happened so fast, it was like a car accident," Seinfeld remembered. The overall experience delivered the comedian a sucker punch that he's never forgotten.

In fact, Jerry Seinfeld subsequently regretted that he had taken the job in the first place. His stock and trade was standup comedy, not acting in a bit part on a weekly television show. He vowed then and there—from that day forward—to never, ever be involved in another TV program that didn't afford him creative input and control of his own destiny. He considered the entire *Benson* experience a total embarrassment—a humiliation that still rankles him all these years later.

By Seinfeld's own admission, he was never much of an actor. He's a comedian whose forte is telling jokes, not wowing audiences with his vast range of emotions. On *Seinfeld*, his performances were always self-aware. We all knew what his role was. Seinfeld was the show's very funny straight man and *Seinfeld* Land's comedic anchor. It had next to nothing to do with acting and everything to do with being funny.

In fact, Jerry Seinfeld followed in the lofty tradition of straight men and, too, straight women. Actress Margaret Dumont comes to mind as one of the all-time best, playing it straight—and the ideal foil in seven movies from 1929 to 1941—to the manic Marx Brothers. Bing Crosby appeared as Bob Hope's more straight-laced right-hand man in a series of popular movies—"Road to . . ." pictures—from 1940 to 1962. Bud Abbott was Lou Costello's very recognizable straight man and indispensable to the comedic duo's success. They, in fact, parlayed their talents in ever-changing venues—from vaudeville to radio in the 1930s and 1940s, and then both the big screen and the small screen in the 1950s. Following on Abbott and Costello's heels were the funny pair of Dean Martin and Jerry Lewis, with the former playing straight man to the frenetic latter in a series of movies—seventeen in total—from 1949 through 1956. Television sitcom pioneer Desi Arnaz certainly knew how to mine the most laughs by letting his wife, the wired Lucille Ball, do what she did best, while he played straight man to her in the hit show *I Love Lucy*. The success of both *The Andy Griffith Show* and *The Mary Tyler Moore Show* in the 1960s and 1970s, respectively, was rooted in their eponymous leads playing, in effect, the straight man and straight woman to an ensemble of more overtly comedic characters. Originally, *The Andy Griffith Show* was supposed to revolve around Andy as the comedy nucleus, but the show's star quickly realized that the sitcom would work better with him in the guise of straight man to his hyper deputy, played by Don Knotts. Decades later, Jerry Seinfeld found the winning formula in *Seinfeld* by establishing himself as—comparatively speaking—the most normal character among the show's ensemble as well as the center of the action. In other words, something of a straight man, which was vital to the show's success.

Life After *Benson*

It's fair to say that after the *Benson* debacle things turned decidedly rosier for Jerry Seinfeld. After appearing on Carson, Letterman, and Merv Griffin, too, and getting the imprimatur from standup legend Rodney Dangerfield, Jerry landed his first television special. It was called *Jerry Seinfeld: Stand-Up Confidential* and premiered on HBO in 1987. The show featured a mix of standup routines and sketches. Cast members included standup comedienne Carol Leifer, the inspiration for *Seinfeld*'s Elaine Benes character, and Larry Miller, who played the malevolent doorman in the *Seinfeld* episode "The Doorman." Miller is also one of Seinfeld's longtime friends. They met in 1978 on the New York City standup comedy scene. He's most recently served as a warm-up act for his old friend, who continues to do what he loves—standup comedy—on a consistent basis, despite owning a Porsche collection second to none. Recalling his salad days, Seinfeld ironically remarked to the *New York Times*: "I miss opening for Frankie Valli and Ben Vereen, walking out as an unknown and there's no applause."

Jerry Seinfeld: Stand-Up Confidential was one more feather in the comedian's cap. He wasn't just another standup comic anymore. When NBC approached him to develop a potential sitcom for the network primetime schedule, it was clear that his star was on the rise. Jerry Seinfeld was bankable material, the big-wigs reasoned, so they would give him a shot. Little did they know how bankable he really was, and how much money would pour into NBC's coffers throughout the 1990s because of the show that both he and Larry David originated while casually patronizing a Korean fruit market in Manhattan.

"The Seinfeld Chronicles," which originally aired in the summer of 1989, was *Seinfeld*'s opening salvo. NBC executives disparagingly called pilots shown during July and August the "Garbage Dump Theater." While the show took a little while to get its mojo, it very definitely changed the way all of us look at television, and considerably raised the sitcom bar. It changed the lives of the show's various stars, too, who will forevermore be associated with their iconic roles in the series.

Jerry Seinfeld, for one, would thereafter be seen as the impresario of a groundbreaking piece of art—something that had never before been seen on television. *Forbes* magazine estimates that the standup comedian is worth about eight hundred million dollars today—give or take several million. He's come a long way since playing Frankie, the wannabe (and not especially good) standup comedian on *Benson* to the Jerry Seinfeld of the new millennium, who can write his own ticket and name his own price.

Jerry's Lady Friends

One of the most fascinating aspects about Jerry Seinfeld is that he played a character named Jerry Seinfeld on a show called *Seinfeld*. The show had this remarkable capacity of blending the real with both the unreal and the surreal. The situations the characters found themselves in were authentic and so were they, more or less, even if they were saddled with a mother lode of neuroses and weren't exactly the nicest people on the planet.

So many of the *Seinfeld* scripts were based on actual occurrences in the writers' lives, although the stories were refashioned for comedic effect, of course, to neatly fit into the incomparable worlds of Jerry, George, Elaine, and Kramer. Some of the very best episodes showcased the rocky romantic relationships of television's fabulous four. Jerry's romances were, as previously noted, typically brief. His girlfriend counter for the series' run—of those either seen or mentioned—totals a whopping seventy-three.

One former girlfriend of Jerry's on the show, his good pal Elaine, summed up his problem in the episode "The Fix-Up":

Elaine: You know what your problem is? Your standards are too high.

Jerry: I went out with *you*.

Elaine: That's because *my* standards are too low.

How does a guy playing himself, sort of, distinguish himself from the television show in the Game of Love? Jerry Seinfeld's love life off the *Seinfeld* set was poles apart from the character Jerry's amorous adventures. Still, his relationships with the opposite sex have, on occasion, had a *Seinfeld* feel to them. When, for instance, he met Shoshanna Lonstein in New York City's Central Park in May 1993, Jerry Seinfeld was thirty-eight and she was only seventeen and a senior in high school. With *Seinfeld* at the height of its popularity, the show's lead star was, not surprisingly, prime paparazzi prey. His relationship with Lonstein was big news. Howard Stern dubbed it a "May–August" romance and said to Seinfeld, a guest on his radio show, "So, you sit in Central Park and have a candy bar on a string and pull it when the girls come."

Jerry Seinfeld and Shoshanna Lonstein threw in the towel in 1997. He claimed that the fishbowl environment in which they lived—with the insatiable, gossip-fueled press coverage—contributed to the difficulties of making the relationship work. Attending UCLA, and spending the preponderance of her time in Los Angeles to be near her boyfriend, Lonstein became homesick for New York City, her hometown, which was another reason furnished for the breakup. "I wanted to run around and play," Lonstein admitted many years later. Jerry Seinfeld was just too busy with *Seinfeld* to do much running and playing.

In a 1991 *People* magazine, Seinfeld described the difficulties inherent in a boy-girl relationship this way: "You can call a guy and say, 'Want to hang out from 11:15 p.m. to 11:45 p.m.?' and he'll go, 'Sure.' But call a woman and say that, and she hangs up on you."

Prior to his monumental *Seinfeld* fame, Jerry Seinfeld was briefly engaged to a hotel manager in 1984. However, his feet quickly turned cold and he broke it

For a short spell, the real Jerry Seinfeld lived at the real 129 West 81st Street address before moving on up to deluxe apartment in the sky.
Photo by Thomas Nigro

off. He wasn't ready for the commitment. "I realized I don't want to start a family. I want to be out on the road," Seinfeld explained to *People* magazine. Other flames in his life included comedienne Carol Leifer and Los Angeles public relations consultant Stacey Effron, whom the comedian sporadically dated from 1987 to 1992. Effron told the aforementioned *People* magazine: "In a lot of our conversations about marriage and kids, he'd say, 'Ugh, that's for normal people, and I'm not normal.'"

As the years pass and the wrinkles begin appearing, and the hair turns gray or falls out altogether, people's views of the world change. This obviously happened to Jerry Seinfeld when he met Jessica Sklar in the Reebok Sports Club, a fancy-schmancy fitness center within walking distance of the former's bachelor pad on Manhattan's Upper West Side. As with Shoshanna Lonstein, this matchup had *Seinfeld* episode written all over it—sans the humor. Seventeen years younger than Seinfeld, Sklar was married at the time to hot-tempered Eric Nederlander, a Broadway producer and "bad-boy theater scion," to use the *New York Post*'s colorful description of him. A little over a month after their honeymoon in Italy, she asked for a divorce.

Naturally, the tabloid press had another field day with another Jerry Seinfeld relationship. Was he or was he not a home wrecker? "I was manipulated, misled, and completely caught off guard by Jessica's infidelity," the bad-boy theater scion complained to the *New York Post*. "Jerry and Jessica have no respect for decent values. They deserve each other." Since his divorce from Sklar, Nederlander has remarried, divorced, and been involved in a contentious custody battle. The mother, Lindsey Kupferman, made it known that she wanted full custody of their young daughter. The fact that he's been in court on multiple occasions, fighting abuse and harassment charges from his latest gal pal, bolsters her case. And it certainly reveals something about the man to whom Jessica Sklar bid adieu after a marriage shorter than a baseball season.

When Jerry Seinfeld announced his wedding engagement in 1999, it caught a lot of people who knew him by surprise, including his ex-girlfriend Stacey Effron. She was the recipient of his Sherman-esque statement on the subject of marriage and family a decade earlier. What a difference a decade can make. Effron wondered how Sklar and Seinfeld would get along as husband and wife, sharing the same living quarters. She said: "Jerry is a total neat freak. Just the way his show depicted him—but even worse in real life. Everything has to be in the right place, right down to the television clicker and soap next to the kitchen sink."

Three kids later—Sascha, born in 2000; Julian Kal, in 2003; and Shepherd Kellen, in 2005—and the Seinfelds are still together. In fact, Seinfeld recently said that as a single man he considered married men "pathetic and depressing." Married at forty-five, he now perceives single men as "meaningless and trivial." It would appear, too, that Jessica Seinfeld has learned to tolerate her husband's über-neat and orderly ways of doing things. She's also found the time to write two best-selling cookbooks: *Deceptively Delicious: Simple Secrets to Get Your Kids Eating Good Food* and *Double Delicious! Good, Simple Food for Busy, Complicated Lives.* A plug from Oprah Winfrey, with her golden touch, helped *Deceptively Delicious* hit number one on the *New York Times* bestseller list.

6

George Costanza

Lord of the Idiots

G eorge Louis Costanza is the son of Frank and Estelle Costanza. He was born in Brooklyn and still lives in New York City—sometimes with his parents in Flushing, Queens, during uncertain financial times, which are not all that uncommon.

George Costanza: The Apple Doesn't Fall Far from the Tree

To say the least, George's relationship with his mother and father is dysfunctional. His best friend since high school, Jerry Seinfeld, has dubbed them "psychopaths" and believes that George "could have been normal" had the embittered, incessantly bickering Mr. and Mrs. Costanza divorced when he was a very, very young boy. They didn't, however, and the adult George is a neurotic basket case because of it—as insecure as they come, and with very low self-esteem. Despite being a grown man in his thirties, his equally neurotic parents maintain an unhealthy sway over him. Harboring doubts about just about everything in his life—and about every move he makes—is the norm. Upon receipt of a soothing massage from a masseur in the episode "The Note," George even questions his sexual identity.

Many of the character thorns that bedevil George revolve around his appearance. He is short, on the chunky side, and increasingly balding as the years pass. In "The Subway," he says, "I always get the feeling that when lesbians look at me, they're thinking, 'That's why I'm not a heterosexual.'" In addition to his less-than-macho demeanor and physique, he's notoriously slow-witted and has real difficulty concentrating. In fact, reading a brief, ninety-page book, like Truman Capote's novella *Breakfast at Tiffany's*, is too tall an order for him. George has referred to himself as "Lord of the Idiots." The truth, though, is that the man is no intellectual lightweight—that is, when one cuts through the thick layers of his angst-ridden and unsure façade. In the episode "The Abstinence," we discover the true measure of George's brainpower—a genius-level I.Q. But, alas, he is typically too preoccupied with sex to access his considerable mental prowess.

Adults are all products of their respective upbringings. The George Costanza of the present was largely ordained when he was an impressionable youth. "Divorce is always hard," he reflects in "The Shoes." "Especially on the kids.

George Costanza: a nonpareil loser in the Game of Life.

'Course, I am the result of my parents having stayed together, so ya never know!"
Being raised by two exceptionally off-kilter, quarrelsome, froward parents
obviously took its toll on young George. Couple this very trying home life with
George's non-athletic build and nerdish mien and it's no surprise that his
everyday life in the rough-and-tumble of the old neighborhood was littered with
potholes and disappointments. They were also harbingers of things to come.

In "The Outing," George recalls the first time he met Jerry—a memorable
encounter courtesy of his non-athleticism. He was climbing a rope in gym
class, slipped, and landed on top of him. George's high school gym teacher,
Mr. Heyman, purposely mispronounced his last name as "Can't Stand Ya"
and encouraged school jocks to give him painful wedgies, including the most
humiliating of them all: "atomic wedgies," in which the pair of underwear is
pulled completely over the victim's head. With teeth like "baked beans," Mr.
Heyman was exhibit A for the maxim "Those who can't do, teach. And those

who can't teach, teach gym class." In the episode "The Library," we see George's old high school gym teacher and tormentor living as a homeless person. It seems that the man never quite recovered from being fired after young George reported his bullying ways to higher authorities.

A further nagging childhood memory of George's involves a kid named Lloyd Braun, another nemesis from his youth. On more than one occasion, George has heard his mother exclaim, "Why can't you be more like Lloyd Braun?" He is absolutely convinced that his parents wish they had Lloyd for a son instead of him.

The Lying Game

"I lie every second of the day," George candidly admits in "The Apartment." "My whole life is a sham." But does being raised under the parental thumbs of Frank and Estelle Costanza really explain why George is so overtly dishonest, selfish, and stingy? Among his circle of friends, his duplicitous nature is the stuff of legend. George regularly concocts convoluted deceptions to gain an upper hand on the job, in relationships, and in the general game of life. He frequently attempts to circumvent financial and legal obligations via some elaborate scheme. He is typically unsuccessful in these endeavors but—rest assured—never, ever learns his lesson. It has been said of George that lying is so inbred in him—so much his second nature—that he could pass a lie-detector test at any given moment and under any circumstances.

"It's not a lie if you believe it," George informs Jerry in "The Beard." Indeed, his fabrications know no bounds and come in all shapes, sizes, and hues. While working for the New York Yankees, George leaves his car parked in the stadium garage overnight, assuming that his employer—"The Boss" George Steinbrenner—will infer that he has been burning the midnight oil and that he is, more importantly, a super-conscientious, completely dedicated company man. In "The Voice," George sees no moral dilemma in masquerading as a disabled person in order to obtain executive bathroom privileges at Play Now, a playground equipment company and his latest place of employment. His charade, however, is exposed when his boss, Mr. Thomassoulo, catches him in the act of lifting a "two-hundred-pound motorized cart with one hand." As he is wont to do in such circumstances, George tenaciously clings to his disability ruse, claiming that "during times of great stress, people are capable of superhuman strength," like the Incredible Hulk, for instance. In this same episode, we behold varied, competing aspects of George's complex, multi-layered personality. Play Now wants him to leave so badly that his boss is willing to do just about anything to make that a reality. Getting rid of George once and for all—keeping him from turning up every day to fulfill the basic obligations of his contract—is Mr. Thomassoulo's mission. But among George's myriad character traits is an admirable, bulldog-like tenacity that few of us possess. George calmly endures the hostility of his co-workers who hurl epithets instead of salutations at him in

> You are a local hero after getting your picture in the paper for removing a golf ball from the blowhole of a beached whale, saving its life.
>
> *Move ahead one space, and when you return the ball to Kramer, tell him to work on his slice.*

The incredibly interesting life of George Costanza knows no boundaries. Card from the *Seinfeld* Scene It game.

the hallways. Play Now eventually plays hardball and cranks the heat up in his office in an attempt to make sitting in it all day unbearable, but the steadfast George is unbowed. When he arrives at work one day and finds that his office is completely boarded up, things look pretty hopeless for him. Perhaps Mr. Thomassoulo and Play Now have at long last vanquished their least-favorite son. But the wily George is never to be underestimated. He manages to wiggle his way through the air vent that leads to his office. After making his way to his desk, George dials Play Now's secretary, Margery, and passes on—in no uncertain terms—the important message to Mr. Thomassoulo that he's in his office if needed.

In the episode "The Boyfriend," we observe George being George. Desperate not to lose his unemployment benefits, he goes to extraordinary lengths to win over his unemployment officer, Mrs. Sokol. First, he creates a fictitious company, Vandelay Industries, with whom he has a fictitious job interview. George then gives Mrs. Sokol Jerry's telephone number and importunes him to please answer the phone with the greeting "Vandelay Industries." As is invariably the case with George, this deception doesn't get him very far. When Kramer answers Jerry's phone and doesn't follow George's script, the cat is out of the bag.

But George isn't done yet in attempting to win over Mrs. Sokol. After dating her daughter doesn't cinch the deal, he discovers that Mrs. Sokol's a baseball fan, and a Mets fan to boot. The wheels begin to turn as George promises her that he will get 1986 Mets star Keith Hernandez to show up—live and in person—at her office. Mrs. Sokol gives him one hour to make good on his promise, or the unemployment benefits will end. Jerry had recently met Hernandez at the gym, and George is intent on taking advantage of their newfound friendship. Needless to say, he doesn't deliver the goods.

In the episode "The Outing," George is even willing to be presumed gay in order to break up with his girlfriend, Allison. Despite a newspaper account making the rounds that he and Jerry are lovers, Allison doesn't buy his lie. Jerry, on the other hand, can't convince—try as he might—the author of the piece that he is straight.

Ebenezer Costanza

George is an astonishingly cheap man. His extremely parsimonious nature habitually causes problems for both himself and those around him. In the episode "The Strike," we see the lengths to which George will go to save a buck. Inspired by a card that he received at Dr. Tim Whatley's Hanukkah party—which informed him that a gift donation had been made in his name to The Children's Alliance, a charity—George creates a bogus organization called "The Human Fund." Expected to buy Christmas gifts for his fellow employees at Kruger Industrial Smoothing—a holiday tradition of theirs—George gives each and every one of them a card, notifying recipients that a gift has been made in his or her name to The Human Fund. He explains to Jerry that he got the idea from Dr. Tim Whatley and the Christmas gifts that he bestowed upon his friends. Jerry is nonetheless perplexed.

> Jerry (*reading the card*): "The Human Fund. Money for people."
>
> George: What do you think?
>
> Jerry: It has a certain understated stupidity.

George's miserly subterfuge, though, is uncovered when his boss, Mr. Kruger—for tax write-off purposes—forks over a check for twenty thousand dollars, payable to The Human Fund. When the accounting department alerts Kruger that the charity does not exist, George has a lot of explaining to do. Here again, we witness his uncanny ability to think quickly on his feet. George informs his boss that he passed out the cards with the phony charity message because he was embarrassed that his family doesn't celebrate Christmas, but an alternative holiday called Festivus, which was created by his father, Frank Costanza, to counter the crass commercialism of the holiday season. George is compelled to invite Mr. Kruger to his father's annual Festivus dinner to prove that he is telling the truth, which, of course, he isn't.

George's tightfistedness and penchant for having bad things happen to him take him to many venues. He seeks compensation from a local hospital after a distraught patient of theirs leaps to his death and lands—where else?—smack-dab on the roof of his car. And, to add insult to injury, George had earlier been so elated that he had secured such a premium parking spot. Call it "George karma," but this is a recurring theme in the life and times of this star-crossed man. A conversation in the episode "The Bris" supplies abundant insight into George's character. Mrs. Sweedler, a hospital administrator, invites him into her office to discuss the day's tragic event. George promptly tells her that the patient's suicide impacted him in "a very, very personal way" and feels that "the hospital is somehow responsible for compensating the other, still living *victim* of this horrendous, horrendous tragedy." Mrs. Sweedler is taken aback. She cannot believe that George seeks to profit from this calamity and throws him—along with the estimate for the damages to his car—out of her office.

In "The Implant," death takes a holiday, as it were, with George accompanying his girlfriend, Betsy, to the Motor City to attend her aunt's wake. Exasperated that he has to make such an expensive trip—New York to Detroit—George discovers along the way that the airline gives grieving families a discount. All they have to do is supply a copy of the decedent's death certificate. Getting said copy thereafter becomes George's *raison d'être*.

The pièce de résistance vis-à-vis George's desire to save a buck occurred in "The Invitations." In this episode, George is with his fiancée, Susan Ross, and shopping around for wedding invitations in preparation of their impending nuptials. By this point in time, he is also desperately trying to avoid getting hitched, but the future Mrs. Costanza is making wriggling out of it extraordinarily difficult. Taking Kramer's advice as a possible exit strategy, George insists upon a pre-nuptial agreement, which he hopes will insult the bride-to-be and have her call off the marriage. Noting that she makes more money than George, Susan finds the notion of a prenup perfectly acceptable. It's back to the drawing board for George. Knowing that she can't stand cigarettes, he takes up smoking as another possible way out. This ploy, though, goes up in smoke when a single puff on a cigarette makes him very sick.

With the fateful day fast approaching, George ultimately bows to what he now sees as the unavoidable and purchases wedding invitations—the cheapest ones possible, of course. When Susan initiates the process of sending them out to the lengthy guest list of invitees, she detects a peculiar taste on the envelope sealants—really and truly peculiar. Continuing the licking and sealing, we see her getting increasingly bedraggled in the process until she is completely overwhelmed and passes out. George discovers her unconscious on the couch and gets her to the hospital. Jerry, Elaine, and Kramer join him there, where a doctor informs George that Susan has passed away. The glue on the cheap wedding invitations, it seems, was toxic and the probable cause of her death. Although not intentionally, George's penny-pinching ways augured this woman's death. Had Susan employed a sponge rather than her tongue to seal the wedding invitation envelopes, she would have lived to become Mrs. George Costanza—or maybe not, considering who her resolute husband-to-be was.

The Dating Game

While his best friend, Jerry, enjoys a well-earned reputation for briefer-than-brief romantic encounters, George's affairs of the heart are typically on the short side, too. With one notable exception: Susan Ross, to whom he became engaged, as noted above. Susan, in fact, endured innumerable indignities in her relationship with George, including the loss of her job at NBC. Kramer vomited on her during their introduction and—due to his carelessness with the Cuban cigars given to him by George—burned down her father's beloved country cabin. After originally breaking up with George, she entered into a lesbian

Susan (Heidi Swedberg) and George: the unhappy couple.   *NBC/Photofest*

Restrained jubilation. George reports the news that his fiancée has passed away.
NBC/Photofest

relationship, which intrigued George to no end. And, of course, Susan would pay the ultimate price for her association with George.

George's more traditional relationships with the opposite sex didn't lead to engagements and wedding bells. In fact, they repeatedly disintegrated because of his double-dealing nature and closet full of insecurities. Immediately upon learning of his fiancée's untimely passing in "The Invitations," George phones actress Marisa Tomei, who had punched him in the face in a previous episode, "The Cadillac," for simultaneously coming on to her and admitting that he was "sort of engaged." He tells her this go-round that he's free as a bird now—unattached. George reminds Marisa that he's that "short, funny, quirky bald man" that so charmed her—before, of course, she learned of his engagement. "I got a funeral tomorrow but . . . my weekend is pretty wide open," he says in attempting to make a date. George receives no answer but the dial tone speaks volumes.

George's self-doubting disposition haunts many of his relationships with women. In the episode "The Fix-Up," he prepares to go on a blind date while enunciating his standards for such encounters: very attractive girls who aren't very smart. In "The Lip Reader," George gets a dose of his own medicine when his girlfriend, Gwen, breaks up with him and employs his oft-used line "It's not you, it's me." He thereafter becomes obsessed with what the real reason is. George is convinced that Gwen saw him on television—captured as a spectator in an unfortunate

George's Not Necessarily Top Ten Girlfriends

10. Robin, who threw her son a birthday party, where George trampled women, children, and a clown to escape a small fire ("The Fire").

9. Noel, a gifted pianist, whose recital was ruined by Elaine's raucous and inappropriate laughter ("The Pez Dispenser").

8. Jane, who was informed by Jerry's girlfriend, Rachel, about having seen George naked ("The Hamptons").

7. Sylvia, who believed George owned the Costanza house, only to be disabused of that notion in scathing terms by Estelle ("The Cigar Store Indian").

6. Audrey, who had a rather large proboscis, which Kramer candidly pointed out ("The Nose Job").

5. Cheryl Fong, a lawyer and cousin of Ping, who was suing Elaine for knocking him off his bicycle ("The Visa").

4. Monica, who convinced George to take an IQ test as part of her college course ("The Café").

3. Cynthia, a friend of Elaine's, who agreed to both get fixed up with George and keep the latter fully apprised of the relationship ("The Fix-Up").

2. Marlene, who dated both Jerry and George, and who had a penchant for dragging out conversations and leaving lengthy phone messages ("The Ex-Girlfriend").

1. Susan Ross, George's fiancée, who met an untimely death courtesy of the latter's supreme tightfistedness ("The Pitch" to "The Invitations," and, in a flashback, "The Betrayal").

candid camera moment—messily eating an ice cream sundae at the U.S. Open tennis tournament in Flushing Meadows.

In "The Boyfriend," George dates Carrie—his unemployment officer's daughter—in the hopes of extending his unemployment benefits. After enjoying a Big Mac on her first date with him, she ends their relationship after their second one. "I been thinkin' about it," Carrie says. "You got no job. You got no prospects. You're like Biff Loman."

George gets bored rather easily in the relationship game. In the episode "The Stand-In," he informs Jerry that he's had his fill of girlfriend Daphne Bowers because of the ennui. However, before he can tell her that it's over between them, Daphne advises George that his friend Al Netche warned her to break it off with him. Al cautioned her that George would only break her heart because of his inability to commit to anything. Upon hearing Al's assessment of his character, George wants to prove the man wrong. He tells Jerry that, to spite Al, he would even go so far as to marry Daphne. In "The Conversion," George displays more of that bull-headed tenacity by converting to the Latvian Orthodox religion to win over Sasha. He even cheats on the conversion exam.

It's always been a bumpy ride for George along life's many highways and byways. In the episode "The Red Dot," he loses his job with Pendant Publishing after getting caught in the act with the cleaning woman—on his desk, no less. George cannot quite understand what is so off-putting about having sex in his office. He was not apprised that this kind of thing was against the rules when he took the job. And, besides, he's always had a thing for cleaning women. In "The Little Jerry," we learn that George likewise gets aroused by the prospect of dating a woman behind bars—in this instance, Celia Morgan, the prison librarian. He loathes the idea of her getting out on parole and ending a good thing. For his own personal benefit, George does what he can to torpedo the parole and keep her incarcerated.

High Anxiety and More

"I can't carry a pen," George admits in "The Parking Garage." "I'm afraid it'll puncture my scrotum." This is but one of his innumerable phobias, including the fear of contracting a serious illness. In the episode "The Pilot," George believes with all his heart that a discoloration on his lip must be cancer, and that he will not live to see the show that he and Jerry created—*Jerry*, the show about nothing—get picked up by the network. He is convinced that God will never allow him to achieve success, and that there's no chance in hell that he'll be around to reap the show's most certain monetary windfall. Jerry then expresses his wish that George would "at least die with a little dignity," to which his friend retorts: "I can't die with dignity. I have no dignity. I want to be the one person who doesn't die with dignity. I live my whole life in shame. Why should I die with dignity?"

George is very definitely a hypochondriac. He lives in fear of not only getting the Big C, but also being diagnosed with lupus, an autoimmune disease that can impact different parts of the body, including the skin, joints, brain, blood cells—the whole kit and caboodle.

George is a curious fellow, indeed, who often refers to himself in the third person. He says things like: "George is getting upset." The man has many unusual obsessions, too, including one involving bathrooms. While out and about, he loves nothing more than patronizing clean and appealing public restrooms. In the episode "The Busboy," we learn that George knows the locations of the finest bathrooms in town. He quit his real estate job in "The Revenge" because his boss, Mr. Levitan, wouldn't allow him to use his private bathroom. George feels that it is beneath him to patronize—when nature calls—the repellent men's room in the hallway, which is shared with employees from another company, Pace Electronics. George likewise has a fascination with toilet paper. In the episode "The Face Painter," he educates his date, Siena, on how the product has remained pretty much the same through the years: "It's just paper on a cardboard roll, that's it. And in ten thousand years it will be exactly the same because really, what else can they do?" His toilet paper fixation didn't end there. George and Jerry discuss toilet paper matters in the episode "The Script," with the former wondering what Civil War soldiers employed on the battlefields. Jerry mocks George's toilet paper enthrallment by suggesting that there ought to be a toilet paper museum that celebrates "toilet paper advancements down through the ages," such as the "development of the perforation" and "first six-pack."

While he has unlimited audacity in matters of lying and scamming, George is typically a coward in his actions. In the episode "The Fire," he tramples over young and old alike, including a clown, to escape a barely significant blaze at his girlfriend Robin's house during a birthday party for her son. He later attempts to justify his actions.

George: What looked like pushing . . . what looked like knocking down . . . was a safety precaution. In a fire, you stay close to the ground, am I right? And when I ran out that door, I was not leaving anyone behind! Oh, quite the contrary! I risked my life making sure that exit was clear. Any other questions?

Fireman: How do you live with yourself?

George: It's not easy.

Although it's the exception to the coward rule, George can, on occasion, exhibit an act of courage. In the episode "The Marine Biologist," we see him do just that. After Jerry tells Diane—a woman that both he and George knew from their college days—that George is a marine biologist, she is interested in seeing him. If he wants to date her, George is thus compelled to play along with the marine biologist deception. He nonetheless complains that Jerry should have told her that he was an architect instead, which is something he always wanted to be. A walk on the beach and an unforeseen crisis finds George, the marine biologist, getting called into action to rescue a whale in distress, which he does quite courageously. As things turn out, it was one of Kramer's golf balls—he had been on the beach attempting to hit golf balls into the surf—that landed in the noble creature's blowhole, which George dislodges at great risk to himself. George tells the gang of his heroics: "As I made my way past the breakers, a strange calm came over me. I don't know if it was divine intervention or the kinship of all living things, but I tell you, Jerry, at that moment, I was a marine biologist!"

In the episode "The Opposite," we see the essence of George revealed when he radically alters his behavior and modus operandi in life. "It all became very clear to me sitting out there today that every decision I've ever made in my entire life has been wrong," he laments. Jerry then gives his friend some useful advice: do the opposite of what his instincts are telling him to do. With nothing to lose, George decides to give it the old college try. Going against his normal grain works wonders. George gets both a date with an eye-catching blonde and a job with the New York Yankees. "This has been the dream of my life ever since I was a child," he says, "and it's all happening because I'm completely ignoring every urge towards common sense and good judgment I've ever had."

Jason Alexander: More Than George Costanza

The man who breathed life into the incomparable George Costanza just chronicled was Jason Alexander. While the neurotic character with less-than-Adonis good looks and rather low self-esteem was nothing new to television—and had long been the butt of laughs on sitcoms—it's fair to say that George Costanza took the archetype to a higher and funnier plateau. It is general knowledge that the George character is based on *Seinfeld* co-creator Larry David, who thought Alexander was ideal for the part.

Jason Alexander was born Jay Scott Greenspan on September 23, 1959, in

Jason Alexander, who moved from the Broadway stage to the *Seinfeld* set.
s_bukley/Shutterstock.com

Newark, New Jersey. His parents, Alexander and Ruth, soon relocated the Greenspan family to the town of Livingston, about eight miles away but worlds apart from Newark. The man who would subsequently achieve both fame and fortune playing a neurotic, duplicitous cheapskate on *Seinfeld* for nine seasons was raised and attended school in this leafy suburb of New York City. Growing up in the shadows of the Big Apple, he quickly became enraptured with the acting craft, fast forgetting about his serious case of the jitters, which caused him to toss his cookies all over the stage while playing a Norse explorer in a fourth-grade play.

Initially, young Jay Greenspan entertained the notion of becoming a professional "up-close" magician, but was quickly disabused of the idea when he discovered that his small hands and stubby fingers were not quite up to snuff in creating that all-important sleight of hand necessary for concealing cards, coins, and such. In both Livingston High School and community theater the actor-in-training appeared in myriad productions, including *The Sound of Music*, *Guys and Dolls*, *The Odd Couple*, and *Oliver*.

As evidence of just how serious he was about forging a career as an actor, the fifteen-year-old Jay Greenspan assumed the stage name of Jason Alexander. His selection of Jason was a play on his mother's frequent references to him as "Jay, my son"; Alexander paid homage to his father. Nevertheless, Alexander did admit to initially requesting Jason Scott—Scott being his middle name—but discovered that there was already a Jason Scott registered with the Screen Actors Guild. In the end, having a last name that began with the letter *A* worked out well in his chosen profession. Since callbacks for auditions are done alphabetically, the last name of Alexander ensured that he would learn straightaway whether or not he was still being considered for a part. And time is of the essence in the acting profession.

It came as no surprise to Jason Alexander's family and friends in Livingston, New Jersey, that he was awarded a full scholarship to attend Boston University's School of Fine Arts, where he came ever so close to earning a degree. However, the career wheels were already in motion during his college years in the late 1970s and early 1980s. While he had every intention of graduating from school, he began landing acting jobs, including a part in *The Burning* (1981), a not especially memorable horror film. *Yada, yada, yada*: A deranged killer is on the loose at Camp Blackfoot in upstate New York and the campers are in grave danger, including Dave, played by Jason Alexander. (Somewhat coincidentally, there was a *Seinfeld* episode called "The Burning" in the show's final season.) His next role was in a made-for-television movie called *Senior Trip* (1981), starring Scott Baio. As everyone in show business knows, one has to start somewhere.

On the heels of this less-than-auspicious debut on both the big and small screens, Jason Alexander secured a lead role in the Broadway musical *Merrily We Roll Along*—a Stephen Sondheim and George Furth collaboration. While the play bombed big time at the box office—it shut down after just two weeks— Alexander nonetheless considered it a critical career step. The visibility he achieved in that two-week window while on the Broadway stage got him noticed by the very people who could—and would—get him work in the future. In an InDepth interview on Broadwayworld.com, he recalled thinking that "maybe if I'm lucky, I'll make it to Broadway by the time I'm forty." He was in his early twenties when he arrived there. "And there I am standing in a room with Sondheim and Prince and George Furth and [choreographer] Ron Field and I feel like, 'What just happened here? I fell through the rabbit hole! This is amazing!'"

Stephen Sondheim subsequently wrote about the problems that portended *Merrily We Roll Along*'s swift demise, noting that there were young actors playing older characters and just not pulling it off, with "one notable exception, a very young Jason Alexander, who at age twenty played a middle-aged man better than anybody I know." This was high praise from the revered composer, lyricist, and giant of the theater world.

As to whether he prefers performing on stage versus the other performance mediums (television and movies), Alexander told a gathering of acting students at Utah Valley University: "At the end of the day, even though theater is the most grueling, the most taxing, the most frightening, it is also the most rewarding because you have to have consummate skills to do it well and you know that when the curtain goes up, it's you. It's you and the audience. And no matter what the director said, the writer said, no matter what you rehearsed, no matter what, what, what, what, what, it's you that is going to make or break the experience and that illusion for the audience. And that's a thrill."

Career Man

While the young actor considered returning to Boston University to finish his final year—he had dropped out after his junior year to pursue acting opportunities—a frank college advisor told him point-blank: "We're teaching you how to have a career. You have a career. Why would you come back?" Another factor that contributed to his not returning to Boston University was an artist named Daena E. Title, whom he met, fell in love with, and married on May 31, 1982. Still together decades later, Jason and Daena Alexander have two children: Gabriel, born in 1991, and Noah, born in 1996. (As a postscript to Alexander's higher education experience, Boston University, in the midst of the *Seinfeld* run in 1995, awarded him a well-deserved honorary degree.)

Jason Alexander's stage career did indeed blossom after the ill-fated *Merrily We Roll Along*. Throughout the 1980s, he appeared in numerous Broadway plays, including Kander and Ebb's *The Rink*, Neil Simon's *Broadway Bound*, and *Jerome Robbins' Broadway*. Alexander was awarded a coveted Tony Award in 1989 for his work in *Broadway*. Being recognized as having given the "Best Performance by a Leading Actor in a Musical" was a major accomplishment. (Ironically, he was nominated for an Emmy Award in the category of "Outstanding Supporting Actor in a Comedy Series" for seven consecutive years for his work on *Seinfeld* but never once won. He is the only cast member not to have won an Emmy. What's wrong with this picture?)

The pre-*Seinfeld* years were extremely busy ones for Jason Alexander—on all fronts. Away from the bright lights of Broadway, he landed a recurring role in the 1984–1985 season—the only season—of the television comedy *E/R*. In 1987, he starred in his very own sitcom on CBS, *Everything's Relative*. Alexander played a character named Julian Beeby, but the show never caught on and was canceled after just ten episodes. During this time, the man who would very soon assume the role of George Costanza on *Seinfeld* also appeared in TV commercials, including one for McDonald's McDLT in 1985. Alexander sang and danced throughout the ad that touted the scrumptiousness of McDonald's new sandwich: a burger festooned with mayonnaise, lettuce, and tomatoes. This was actually McDonald's attempt to compete with Burger King's popular Whopper. While the McDLT was cast asunder in the early 1990s, Jason Alexander's energetic and entertaining pitch for it remains a popular favorite on YouTube and elsewhere. With regard to doing commercials through the years, he has no regrets. "I did a spot for Western Union that ran on and off for eight years," he told *Mental Floss* magazine. "It will put my kid through college." His TV commercial credits include everything from Lipton Onion Soup Mix to Canada Dry Ginger Ale to Kentucky Fried Chicken.

A Doer and a Talker

Jason Alexander is a remarkably talented man. Courtesy of his iconic role as George Costanza, there are many fans who are unaware that he is more than just a funny guy. During the *Seinfeld* years he supplied voice-overs for animation, including Abis Mal in *The Return of Jafar* (1994) and Hugo in *The Hunchback of Notre Dame* (1996), two well-received Disney films. "The people who know him only as George don't understand what a wonderful singer-dancer-performer he is," said director Robert Iscove to *People* magazine. Iscove worked with Alexander in a Disney television remake of Rodgers and Hammerstein's *Cinderella*. "If you look at him and that body, you don't expect him to dance and move that very well, but he's very good at that, and he has a wonderful Broadway voice."

Jason Alexander stands just five feet five inches tall, which equals Al Pacino's height and surpasses Michael J. Fox's by an inch. While he's never been cast as a romantic leading man—his shortness, baldness, and chubby frame prohibit it—he's gotten a lot of mileage out of that body of his. "I started balding at age seventeen," Alexander once recalled, "and after first being sad, I really embraced it. I was always cast older than my actual age, which generally meant better roles."

In 2011, Jason Alexander surprised his legions of fans with a new look—hair atop his head. He tweeted, "The biggest image people have of me is from the reruns of *Seinfeld*, and I'm just trying to put my hair back to the way it was then." With his new 'do, he's certainly got more covering his head now than George

Say it ain't so: post-*Seinfeld* hair for Jason Alexander.
ChameleonsEye/Shutterstock.com

Costanza ever had. His hairline has more aptly returned to the Livingston High School days. "I'm waiting for Jerry to rag on me," he added. "When he sees me with this, I'm sure I'll get an e-mail saying, 'What the hell are you doing?'"

It's been said that Alexander was positively excited to assume the George Costanza role because it gave him a chance to play a "nice guy" for a change. Around the time of "The Seinfeld Chronicles," the pilot episode, he had taken on a series of not-especially-nice-guy roles, including the part of Philip Stuckey, the depraved lawyer who attempts to rape Julia Roberts's call-girl character in *Pretty Woman* (1990). Now, it would be well-nigh impossible to make the case that the character of George Costanza is *a nice guy*—not by any stretch of the imagination. However, in *Seinfeld* Land the manic George is perversely lovable, which is why fans always want to know how much of Jason Alexander—if anything—is in George Costanza.

"Larry [David] once told me he has the two worst traits a person could have—a vicious temper combined with no guts," Kenny Kramer told the *New York Observer*. George is certainly prone to irritable outbursts and is as pusillanimous as they come. But what about Jason Alexander versus George Costanza? Jerry Seinfeld remarked to *People* magazine at the end of the series run that it "wasn't a complete stretch for Jason" to play the character. "Jason always has allergies and ailments that are very Costanza-esque," he added. Even Alexander conceded that he had more than a few things in common with the hapless George. "I never had a good year," he told the *New York Times*. "I had nine years of orthodontia, and the day the braces came off, the hair started falling out."

While Jason Alexander may share a trait or two with George Costanza, he's definitely not his clone. He is, in fact, very generous with his time and money. Alexander is involved in numerous charities, including Autism Speaks, Aid for AIDS, and Feed the Children. He has also taken a very public role in OneVoice, an organization that seeks out moderate-minded Israelis and Palestinians to find solutions to the longstanding Middle East conflict.

On the lighter side, Alexander is a confirmed Trekkie—the term used to describe a zealous fan of the original *Star Trek* television series (1966–1969). He has an encyclopedic knowledge of the show and does a not-too-shabby impersonation of William Shatner's character, Captain Kirk. In fact, he realized a dream when he appeared in an episode of *Star Trek: Voyager* in 1999. He played a character called Kurros.

Reflecting on life after *Seinfeld*, Alexander told the *Harvard Crimson*: "If I could just be paid for every time somebody yells, 'George,' just 'George,' I'd be doing very, very, very well. 'Shrinkage' would come in second, by the way." With reports of Jason Alexander's net worth being seventy-five million dollars, he's doing very, very, very well—even without recompense for all those "George" calls.

7

Elaine Benes

Queen of the Castle

laine Marie Benes is the sole female presence in the perversely close-knit gang of friends that include Jerry Seinfeld, George Costanza, and Cosmo Kramer. In many ways, she is "one of the boys," but she's simultaneously very sexy and alluring to men. Elaine doesn't take guff from anyone—man, woman, or child. "Shut up!" and "Get out!" are familiar Elaine catchphrases that are typically accompanied with some pretty forceful shoves.

Elaine Benes: Whence She Came

Unlike her three best pals, Elaine is not a native New Yorker. She hails from the state of Maryland and was raised in Towson, a tony suburb of Baltimore. Elaine is a Baltimore Orioles fan. Her father, Alton Benes, is a cantankerous and intimidating writer—a Mickey Spillane type—who has published a string of successful novels. He likes to drink, too—what hard-boiled guy doesn't?—and Elaine says that he abandoned the Benes family when she was just nine years old. A Korean War veteran, the man is wont to hark back to his days in the service. When he initially addresses Jerry as the comedian among Elaine's entourage in "The Jacket," Mr. Benes tells him: "We had a funny guy with us in Korea . . . a tail gunner. They blew his brains out all over the Pacific. There's nothing funny about that!" Despite her father's obvious failings, Elaine is like him in many ways. She is highly intelligent, very assertive, and quick to anger.

Elaine was educated at a finishing school in Towson and attended Tufts University in Massachusetts, where she graduated with a degree in French literature. She has a very high I.Q., except when she abstains from sexual intercourse for an extended period of time, which causes her intelligence quotient to drop like a rock and her behavior to become conspicuously dumber. Fortunately for her, she's a serial dater, so dry spells are typically short in duration. Elaine worries sometimes that she will run out of men.

Elaine moved to New York City and met Jerry Seinfeld in 1986. The pair entered into a romantic relationship that lasted just over three years. Coincidentally, 1986 was also the year that Jerry moved into the building at 129 West 81st Street and bonded with his across-the-hall neighbor, Kramer. After ending their romantic entanglement, Jerry and Elaine remain close friends and each other's confidant.

Anger Mismanagement

Elaine has a well-earned reputation for being impulsive and hot-tempered. She unexpectedly flies off the handle, waging battles with a diverse array of people, ranging from Frank Costanza to Poppie the restaurateur to the proprietor of Monk's Café. She is unafraid to get physical—down and dirty—during her recurring fits of rage. Pity those poor individuals caught in the crossfire.

In "The Little Kicks," she very literally gets into a fistfight—with Frank Costanza, no less, a man old enough to be her father. We also discover in this episode what a dreadful dancer Elaine is and how she's the butt of endless jokes in her place of employment because of it. George describes her lack of dancing prowess as "a full-bodied dry heave set to music."

In fact, Elaine is surprisingly dense with regard to how the wider world sees her. In the episode "The Package," she is given—from her perspective at least—short shrift at the doctor's office. After combing over her medical chart while awaiting her doctor, Elaine thinks she knows the reason. The word "difficult" leaps off the chart. This negative patient review was the by-product of a past doctor's visit, when Elaine refused to wear a gown for an examination of a shoulder mole. So as not to have to put on said gown "made of paper," she had specifically worn a tank top to the office. Never one to let sleeping dogs lie, Elaine makes a case to her present doctor that the "difficult" brand is unwarranted. He tells her not to worry and that he'll erase the offending word from her chart. Elaine, though, sees through the ruse and accuses the doctor of faking an erasure. It was, after all, written in pen.

Elaine is never one to walk away from an argument and is often the instigator of them. She holds very strong opinions on many subjects, including a

She's intelligent, assertive, and superficial. Nobody messes with Elaine Benes.

pro-choice stance on abortion that is very dear to her heart. In the episode "The Couch," Elaine reveals that she does, on occasion, abide by principles—at least in certain areas of her life. In a scene set in Poppie's restaurant, we learn of one of these principles. Elaine will not patronize establishments whose owners support "fanatical anti-abortion groups," and this includes eschewing the pizza from Pacino's and the duck from Poppy's.

When Elaine doesn't like someone or something, she lets those around her know it in no uncertain terms. This character trait is at its most apparent in "The English Patient." In this episode, she makes her distaste for the multiple-Oscar-nominated film *The English Patient* well known immediately after seeing it. Outside of the theater, Elaine runs into friends, Carol and Lisa, who can't wait to hear her opinion of the movie, fully expecting that it will concur with theirs—because who, after all, could not possibly like this romantic masterpiece, starring Ralph Fiennes as Count Laszlo Almasy, and Kristin Scott Thomas as Katherine Clifton? Elaine couldn't, that's who.

Elaine may have destroyed the fictional "Soup Nazi," but not the real one. *Seinfeld* has been very, very good—despite his many protestations—to Ali "Al" Yeganeh.   *Photo by Thomas Nigro*

Elaine is a woman of incredible resolve, willing to take on people she feels have wronged her, be it Craig in the episode "The Wig Master," whose ponytail she sheers off while he's asleep, or Yev Kassem, the man unaffectionately known as the "Soup Nazi." Unlike her male counterparts, she refuses to knuckle under to the soup peddler's über-strict regimen in ordering his product. By venturing down this confrontational route, she is banned from ordering any soup at his shop for one whole year.

Later in the same episode, aptly named "The Soup Nazi," Elaine's recently purchased armoire is stolen. With her building's policy which prohibits the moving of any furniture on Sundays, Kramer has been entrusted to stand guard over it on the sidewalk. It is then that the theft occurs. When Kramer mentions in passing this ill-fated incident to his new pal, the Soup Nazi—who he feels is misunderstood—the man with the stringent soup-purchasing rules reveals a kinder, gentler side. He offers Kramer—free of charge—an antique armoire that has been collecting dust in his basement. The Soup Nazi, however, does not know that it is for Elaine, the woman who is persona non grata in his place of business.

This magnanimous act nonetheless inspires Elaine to call upon the Soup Nazi's stand and personally thank him. Rather ungraciously, the proprietor informs Elaine in no uncertain terms that he would have smashed the piece of furniture to bits with a hatchet before handing over anything to her. Elaine is understandably infuriated at this response.

When, thereafter, she discovers the recipes for the Soup Nazi's celebrated delicacies in one of the armoire's drawers, Elaine seizes the opportunity to get even with her nemesis. She tells Jerry that she could—if she had a mind to—employ the services of an airplane to drop fliers with the man's recipes on them all over the city. Despite Jerry pleading with her to leave the Soup Nazi be—he loves the soups and doesn't want to ruin a good thing—Elaine is determined to exact a measure of revenge. With the recipes in hand, she returns to the Soup Nazi's stand and gleefully threatens to cast his business asunder by revealing the recipes to the wider world. Feeling now that his business has been irreparably compromised, the Soup Nazi decides to close up shop for good and return to his native Argentina, but not before giving away the last vestiges of his famously tasty soups. Elaine not only pulls off the ultimate revenge, but she is absolutely euphoric in seeing it through. This is a recurring character trait of hers. She seeks to get even with people she feels have wronged her, but takes it to a higher level. Her modus operandi, metaphorically speaking, is: Take no prisoners. Kill the enemy.

Where the Boys Are

"I hate men, but I'm not a lesbian," Elaine says in "The Subway." For a person who purports to "hate" the opposite sex, she certainly has many men come in and out of her life. But then again, her relationships are typically short-lived and she sometimes breaks up for reasons that are as trifling as those of her best friend, Jerry.

One of her more extended romantic entanglements is with David Puddy, an auto mechanic and, later, a car salesman. The nature of their relationship is extraordinarily fickle. The couple splits up and gets back together with great frequency. In the episode "The Butter Shave," Elaine and Puddy reveal the tenuous nature of their relationship by breaking up, getting back together, and breaking up again on the airplane trip home from their European vacation.

Elaine, who usually prefers men of a higher pedigree, is willing to make exceptions with guys she finds very masculine. She likes the fact that Puddy works with his hands in a garage. However, when Elaine discovers that he is a man of faith in "The Burning," this bothers her because she wears her non-believer status on her sleeve. She wonders if he will be able to reconcile his religious beliefs with her in-your-face lack of faith. Puddy, however, is unfazed and matter-of-factly says, "I'm not the one going to Hell."

Elaine is also bothered by Puddy's transparent lack of commitment in their relationship and by some of his peculiar behaviors. Puddy, for example, paints his face and body when he attends the games of his favorite hockey team, the New Jersey Devils. As Elaine is being whisked away to serve her one-year prison sentence in "The Finale," she sees her on-again, off-again boyfriend and says rather plaintively, "Puddy, don't wait for me." His nonchalant response is sans any affection: "All right." This little give-and-take speaks volumes about the superficiality of their relationship as well as so many others in Elaine's life.

While Elaine has a very active sex life, she regularly finds fault with men in this carnal showground. "This whole sex thing is totally overrated," she says in "The Virgin," as she describes men's antsy post-deed behavior. Elaine complains that the male animal undergoes a complete metamorphosis moments after the sex act and desires exiting the premises with alacrity, almost as if they're wanted by the police. "It's always about being up early" the next morning. "They all turn into farmers suddenly," she says.

In the episode "The Stall," Elaine dates a very handsome but much younger man named Tony, who Jerry dubs a *mimbo*, his portmanteau word for a male bimbo. Elaine vehemently denies that Tony's good looks are the catalyst for their relationship, but Jerry and company are—not surprisingly—skeptical.

George even develops a man-crush on Tony. He is impressed with his coolness—the fact that he wears his baseball cap backwards and that he is into extreme sports. After turning down George's invitation to go bowling—entirely too staid—Tony insists that they go rock-climbing instead. Kramer is invited, too, which doesn't please George, who hoped to spend the day with just Tony. Things, though, don't go as planned when George and Kramer ignore the man's pleas to secure his rope as he dangerously dangles in mid-air. He ultimately plunges from the mountainside, sustaining serious injuries to his body, including his pretty face, which is now completely bandaged. Elaine's fealty to Tony is now put to the test. When she expresses concern about what the accident might have done to his appearance, Jerry reminds her what she had said in the past about their relationship not being rooted in a physical attraction. "Are you kidding, he's a mimbo, I know that," Elaine admits. "But he's my mimbo, you know, and even if he is a hideous freak, maybe . . . maybe I can learn to love him. Maybe in some final irony, I'll learn what love really is."

Elaine has captivated many a man, some to the point of obsession, like Russell Dalrymple, president of NBC and the man responsible for giving the green light to Jerry and George's sitcom pilot. While he enjoyed only a single date with Elaine, the event had serious ramifications on his future. In order to part company once and for all with Dalrymple—who keeps pestering her with phone calls and such—Elaine makes the excuse that she couldn't possibly forge a relationship with an executive in a dog-eat-dog profession. She tells him that she prefers more altruistic men, like those, for instance, who work for Greenpeace.

This little snippet of misinformation prompts the totally obsessed Russell Dalrymple to join Greenpeace in order to win back Elaine. Meanwhile, his replacement as the new president at the network is not in the least bit impressed with Jerry and George's sitcom pilot and, without even awaiting the ratings and reviews, scuttles the prospect of any future episodes. On the other side of the world, Russell Dalrymple and his Greenpeace cohorts—in a bungled effort to sink a whaling ship—get hopelessly lost at sea and that's the last anybody will ever hear of them. Elaine's kiss-off of him is final and life returns to normal.

Elaine briefly dated Jake Jarmel, a rising-star author affiliated with her employer, Pendant Publishing. Their topsy-turvy relationship yet again furnishes us with insight into Elaine's character, specifically her argumentative temperament. In "The Sniffing Accountant," we witness one of Elaine's innumerable pet peeves bubble to the surface. She finds fault with Jake in this episode for

Elaine's Not Necessarily Top Ten Boyfriends

10. Darryl Nelson, whose race was a matter of some speculation ("The Wizard").
9. "Crazy" Joe Davola, a psychotic individual, who intended on doing real harm to both Jerry and Elaine ("The Opera").
8. Tony, whom Jerry christened a "mimbo"—his descriptive term for "male bimbo" ("The Stall").
7. Joel Rifkin, who unhappily shared a name with a prolific serial killer in the news ("The Masseuse").
6. Aaron, a "close-talker," who took an unusual shine to Morty and Helen Seinfeld ("The Raincoats").
5. Ned Isakoff, a Communist, whom Elaine got blacklisted from his favorite Chinese restaurant ("The Race").
4. Hal Kitzmiller, who suffered from serious back problems and bought Elaine a special mattress to help ward off a similar affliction ("The Nap").
3. Phil Totola, Jerry's friend, who "took it out" during their date ("The Stand-In").
2. Jake Jarmel, best-selling author, who immensely disliked the use of exclamation points ("The Sniffing Accountant," "The Opposite," and "The Scofflaw").
1. David Puddy, mechanic and later car salesman, whom Elaine dated and broke up with on multiple occasions ("The Fusilli Jerry" to "The Finale").

not using exclamation points when she feels they are appropriate. Here, Elaine's penchant for never, ever letting sleeping dogs lie is laid bare. When she arrives home and finds her boyfriend preparing a romantic dinner for two in her apartment, the stage is seemingly set for a beautiful evening—good food, a bottle of wine, candlelight, the whole nine yards. But after Jake innocently informs Elaine that she got a few phone messages that he took down for her, the mood suddenly and inexplicably turns sour. As Elaine pores over the messages, she observes that Jake didn't employ a solitary exclamation point while transcribing them. She, very definitely, would have used one after "Myra had the baby" and grumbles to Jake about his apparent apathy. An argument over exclamation point use in sentences then ensues with Jake exiting the apartment with the parting shot, "Well, you can put one on this one: 'I'm leaving!'"

Back together again in the episode "The Opposite," Elaine is cast aside once more by Jake after he discovers that she purchased a box of Juicy Fruit candy before rushing to his bedside in the hospital after he had been involved in a serious accident. Courtesy of her over-stuffed mouth and cow-like chewing of the candy, he can't help but take notice. The mere thought that, after receiving the awful news, Elaine would have candy foremost on her mind disgusts him. Jake asks her to leave.

It seems that whomever Elaine dates, there is always some nagging peripheral issue that clouds the romantic picture. There is rarely any smooth sailing in Elaine's relationships. In the episode "The Masseuse," she dates a man named Joel Rifkin, who unfortunately shares the same name with a serial killer in the news. Arrested in 1993, Joel "the Ripper" Rifkin is believed to have murdered as many as seventeen—and possibly more—people. He also has the distinction of being New York City's most prolific serial killer. Kramer enlightens everybody that Rifkin became a serial killer because he was adopted, just like David Berkowitz, the "Son of Sam." As a parenthetical aside, we later learn that Elaine's Joel Rifkin was adopted, too.

Elaine does her utmost to convince her new beau to change his first name and avoid the embarrassment and the confusion of being linked with an unsavory mass murderer. While thumbing through a football magazine in Joel's apartment, she suggests that he change it to "O. J. Rifkin." Of course, the only famous O. J. in the football world is O. J. Simpson, who not too long after Elaine's suggestion was arrested for allegedly murdering his ex-wife and her friend in a very brutal fashion.

Initially, Joel is reluctant to change his name and rejects the "O. J." suggestion outright. A series of events at a New York Giants game at Giants Stadium, though, alters his hard line. When public address announcer Bob Sheppard requests—in his famous dulcet tones—Rifkin's presence at the stadium box office, it puts things in a new light. Elaine and Joel had left an extra ticket at the box office for Kramer to pick up, but in classic Kramer form, he had forgotten the requisite ID necessary to secure it—hence the call from on high.

Indeed, when the name Joel Rifkin reverberates throughout the stadium via its sound system, it sets off a mild panic. Elaine, in fact, feels compelled to inform the person seated in front of her that her Joel Rifkin is not *the* Joel Rifkin. After the Giants Stadium ordeal, Joel Rifkin, the non–serial killer, comes to the conclusion that maybe the name change isn't such a bad idea after all. Both he and Elaine compile their own lists of alternative first names.

Elaine rejects Joel's suggestion of Stuart. "I never met a normal guy named Stuart," she says. He then offers the names Todd and Alex, which are likewise shot down. Elaine's explanation for the latter veto: "In college I sat next to an Alex in Art History. And he was always drinking coffee . . . and after every sip he would go, 'Aaaah!'" Elaine rejects Ned in a heartbeat. "Ned's a guy who buys irregular underwear," she says. (She subsequently dates a guy named Ned Isakoff with irregular political affiliations, not underwear.) Elaine shoots down Ellis and Remy, too, leaving Joel in a state of great frustration, a not-uncommon place for Elaine's gentlemen friends to be.

Some further relationships that shed light on Elaine's character include one with Hal Kitzmiller, a man with a chronic back problem who purchases all his furniture at an ergonomic shop called the Lumber Yard. When he ships a mattress to Elaine's apartment after their first date in the episode "The Nap," she feels he is being entirely too presumptuous. Hal explains that the mattress was custom designed specifically for her height and weight and that his intentions were honorable. He merely wanted Elaine to avoid the sort of back problems in the future that plague him in the present.

Elaine dates an eclectic group of men. She goes out with baseball star Keith Hernandez, but can't abide his smoking habit. She embarks on a relationship with card-carrying Communist Ned Isakoff, whom she inadvertently gets blacklisted from his favorite Chinese takeout joint, Hop Sing's. Elaine had already been blacklisted by them and placed on their "no delivery list." She also dates Lloyd Braun, George's childhood nemesis, and in the episode "The Non-Fat Yogurt," gives him, as things turn out, a very bad idea to employ in his line of work. In fact, the idea ultimately costs him his job and his sanity. Lloyd worked for Mayor Dinkins, who was at that time in a nip-and-tuck re-election race against a challenger named Rudy Giuliani.

Elaine suggested that Lloyd pitch a policy idea to his boss: the wearing of name tags. She felt that if all city residents were required to wear them, the city would be a much friendlier place. It would be more akin to living in a small town, where everybody knows everybody else. Lloyd was won over by the notion and made the case to Mayor Dinkins, who promptly made the wearing of name tags part of his campaign platform. However, soon after this new policy is adopted, a news flash reports: "Mayor Dinkins has fired his top advisor, Lloyd Braun, who is believed to be responsible for the name tag fiasco."

Perhaps Elaine's most intriguing relationship is with Kevin, the personality flip side of Jerry. Kevin has friends, Gene and Feldman, who are strikingly similar physically to George and Kramer, but the polar opposites in terms of behavior. They are the Bizarro Jerry, George, and Kramer. Gene resembles George, yes, but he is gentle, considerate, and generous. Like Kramer, Feldman is something of a lanky doofus, but he always knocks on Kevin's door and is let in by him. Feldman comes bearing groceries, too, and never mooches off his friend. Even Kevin's apartment is akin to Jerry's, only everything is reversed—the mirror image. Kevin owns a PC and not a Mac, a unicycle instead of a bicycle, and a statue of Bizarro, rather than Superman, in his apartment.

Ultimately, Elaine proposes that she and Kevin "just be friends," as is the case with Jerry, her ex-boyfriend. He likes the idea and she begins hanging around with Kevin and his buddies. But Elaine contentedly kibitzing with caring and sensitive sorts just couldn't last. Kevin doesn't appreciate the fact that Elaine raids his refrigerator and starts eating olives out of the jar without first asking him. This behavior is perfectly acceptable and quite the norm at Jerry's place.

The friendship with the Bizarro Jerry, George, and Kramer comes to a crashing end when Kevin gleefully announces a big surprise: he has secured tickets to the Bolshoi at Lincoln Center. This exciting news prompts Elaine to give Kevin one of her patented "Get out!" shoves, which sends him to the ground. Kevin's pals, Gene and Feldman, rush to his aid and cast the blame on Elaine.

As is always the case with Elaine—as well as Jerry, George, and Kramer—friendships with individuals on decidedly different wavelengths don't last for very long. Kevin and company, the polar opposites of Jerry and friends, preordained that Elaine's congenially hanging out with them was destined to end with a bang and not a whimper. Elaine's closest relationships in the friend department are with Jerry, George, and Kramer. She has numerous girlfriends, but the intensity of these friendships appear tepid, fleeting, and less intimate.

Elaine's 1990s Fashion Sense

With her coif of curls, Elaine more often than not sports a blazer with padded shoulders and lengthy skirts with colorful floral designs. When it comes to footwear, practical and comfortable are more important than style to her. She wears saddle oxfords and Mary Janes—granny shoes, if you will—and socks to match. Elaine opts not to reveal much skin, choosing instead to be simultaneously eye-catching and a tough nut to crack.

Elaine's fashion sensibilities are very 1990s, with her sartorial tastes leaning toward blazers, denim jackets, and fleece zip-ups with Aztec prints, which she wears well with jeans. She has a thing for the aforementioned floral prints, too—smaller, compact designs to begin the decade and then bigger, more retro-1970s ones toward the new millennium. Elaine likes her mini backpacks, too, and often wears dark colors—notably black—that underscore her perky attractiveness.

Julia Louis-Dreyfus: Queen of Comedy

Elaine Benes was brought to life by Julia Louis-Dreyfus, who was born Julia Scarlett Elizabeth Louis-Dreyfus in New York City on January 13, 1961. Her French-born father, Gerard, and American-born mother, Judith, divorced when their daughter was just a toddler. They both remarried not long after, supplying Louis-Dreyfus with four half-sisters—two from her mother's marriage to surgeon L. Thompson Bowles, and two from her father's second marriage. She considers both her parents and stepparents as equally important in her life. Lauren Bowles, a half-sister nine years her junior, is also an actress and appeared as a Monk's Café waitress in nine episodes of *Seinfeld*.

Julia Louis-Dreyfus has a rather storied family history. Her paternal grandfather, Pierre Louis-Dreyfus, served with courage and distinction under General Charles de Gaulle in the Free French Air Force during World War II, flying eighty-eight missions for the French Resistance. She is also the great-great-granddaughter of Léopold Louis-Dreyfus, who founded the Louis Dreyfus Group, which traded in commodities and managed international shipping in the middle of the nineteenth century. This French-based multinational conglomerate is still in business all these years later, and more successful than ever.

Louis-Dreyfus spent the lion's share of her childhood in Washington, D.C., where her stepfather plied his trade as a doctor and as dean of the George Washington University Medical School. Dr. Bowles also worked with a philanthropic organization called Project Hope, which assisted medical personnel in the developing world, and lived for spells in Sri Lanka, Colombia, and

The ideal actress for the part of Elaine Benes. Julia Louis-Dreyfus with Jerry Seinfeld and their Screen Actors Guild Awards in 1997.

Paul Smith/ Featureflash/ Shutterstock.com

Tunisia with his family, including young Julia. "So, I had this out-of-America perspective, even a third world perspective, once I came home," she told the *Guardian.* "You do end up thinking differently."

Regarding growing up in the shadow of a divorce, Julia Louis-Dreyfus had this to say on the subject: "My parents got along with one another, so I wasn't playing referee. But it was still hard. It's made me desire a very stable family life." And that's just what she's achieved in her marriage to Brad Hall, whom she first met in college and then worked alongside in repertory theater and later on *Saturday Night Live.* They were married in 1987 and are still together more than a quarter of a century later. The couple has two children: Henry, born in 1992, and Charles, born in 1997. Both boys, by the way, were born during the *Seinfeld* run, with Louis Dreyfus's pregnancies concealed—as best as they possibly could be—from the viewing audience.

"Whenever I felt down, my mom would remind me that a sense of humor gets you through just about anything," Julia Louis-Dreyfus recalled. A sense of humor was something that she exhibited in spades while growing up. Her childhood idols and role models in comedy and show business were a diverse lot that included Lucille Ball, Mary Tyler Moore, Madeline Kahn, Teri Garr, and Diane Keaton. She particularly admired the works of screenwriter and director Preston Sturges, whose female leads were simultaneously sexy *and* funny. Sturges's Hollywood credits, which he amassed before Louis-Dreyfus was even born, included *Sullivan's Travels* (1941), starring Veronica Lake and Joel McCrea; *The Palm Beach Story* (1942), starring Claudette Colbert and Joel McCrea; and *The Beautiful Blonde from Bashful Bend* (1949), starring Betty Grable and Cesar Romero.

"Julia was always funny," said her half-sister Lauren Bowles to *People* magazine. "And she always liked the attention that came from it." Louis-Dreyfus began to express an interest in acting, too, in the all-girl Holton-Arms School in Bethesda, Maryland. "Any play that was ever put on at Holton, I was part of," she told *Capitol File* magazine. "There were things that I did in school that, had there been boys in the classroom," she added, "I would have been less motivated to do so. For instance, I was president of the honor society." Graduating from Holton-Arms School in 1979, Julia Louis-Dreyfus thereafter attended Northwestern University in Evanston, Illinois, where she studied theater. But like *Seinfeld* co-star Jason Alexander, she didn't quite make it to graduation day, preferring instead to answer the career door rather than remain a sorority girl when opportunities knocked. (Again, like Alexander, Louis-Dreyfus received an honorary degree from her alma mater—but a prestigious doctor of arts for her—when she delivered the 2007 commencement address at the school.)

Live from Chicago and New York

After dropping out of college in the early 1980s, Julia Louis-Dreyfus performed with Second City, a well-known improvisation theater troupe in Chicago. This improv group touts an impressive roster of alumni, including Stephen Colbert, Tina Fey, Alan Arkin, Shelley Long, and Steve Carell. She followed up her Second City work by performing with the Practical Theatre Company, which was the brainchild of Brad Hall, her future husband. Through her work in the ensemble's production of *The Golden 50th Anniversary Jubilee* in a small Chicago cabaret called Piper's Alley, Louis-Dreyfus got the attention of the powers-that-be at *Saturday Night Live*. Dick Ebersol, executive producer of *SNL* from 1981 to 1985—between Lorne Michaels's two stints—happened to be in the Windy City, checked out the show, and promptly signed her. At the age of just twenty-one, she became the youngest cast member in *SNL* history—a distinction that still stands. "I'm very nervous about it and terribly excited, and I think it'll be great fun," she said at the time. Brad Hall was also hired as a writer-performer, as were the two other members of the Practical Theatre Company, Gary Kroeger and Paul Barrosse. Hall spent two seasons with *SNL*—1982 through 1984—and is best remembered as the show's "Update" anchor during that time period. Looking back on how much *SNL* meant to her as a fledgling comedienne and how much it meant to her to land a job on the show, Louis-Dreyfus told *Capitol File* magazine: "When *SNL* first began, I was their demographic—a young teenager watching Gilda and Belushi and Bill Murray and all those guys—and I was just riveted. It was a huge Cinderella-getting-to-go-to-the-ball kind of experience."

Julia Louis-Dreyfus would toil on *Saturday Night Live* for three seasons: 1982 through 1985. However, her initial optimism and enthusiasm level quickly headed south because her mantra to "have fun at all costs" just wasn't possible, she discovered, in the *SNL* pressure cooker that existed in the early 1980s. "My cast included Eddie Murphy, Marty Short, Christopher Guest, Billy Crystal, and Joe Piscopo," she told the *Guardian*. "It was very intimidating and I really didn't know what I was doing. It wasn't a very happy time in my life. I went there thinking it'd be all for one, but it was a dog-eat-dog world and I did not understand the dynamics at all. I've been back to host a couple of times and it seems like a much happier cast. But back then there was a lot less camaraderie."

It's been said, though, that every cloud has a silver lining. In Julia Louis-Dreyfus's *SNL* cloud, the silver lining was Larry David, who also worked on the show during her time there. "He was on it one year and we were happy to be miserable together on the show," she recalled. "You know what? He never got a single sketch on the show—not a single one. And then so many years later, they made the *Seinfeld* pilot, which I've never seen. And they told Jerry and Larry, you need a woman regular—so here I am. *SNL* finally paid off handsomely, but in a delayed reaction sort of way." (Larry David claims to have gotten a total of one *SNL* sketch on the air.)

Hollywood, Here She Comes

After Julia Louis-Dreyfus's unhappy spell in the "political environment" of *SNL*, she made her big-screen debut in a movie called *The Troll*. Suffice it to say, this 1986 fantasy-horror film was not nominated for any Academy Awards. Louis-Dreyfus played a character named Jeanette Cooper; Brad Hall was also in the cast. Perhaps most noteworthy about this film is that it could honestly be called the very first Harry Potter movie—before J. K. Rowling could sue for a trademark infringement. *The Troll*'s lead characters were Harry Potter Jr., played by Noah Hathaway, and Harry Potter Sr., played by Michael Moriarty. Regarding her contribution to *The Troll*, Louis-Dreyfus remembered with a laugh, "Hey, it got me and my husband a vacation in Rome!" She also appeared in a made-for-TV movie that same year, *The Art of Being Nick*, starring Scott Valentine, who at that time was playing Nick Moore, Mallory Keaton's boyfriend, on the hit sitcom *Family Ties*. Still another movie that debuted in 1986 featured Julia Louis-Dreyfus in the cast—*Soul Man*, which starred C. Thomas Howell and Rae

Dawn Chong. Louis-Dreyfus played Lisa Stimson in this controversial flick that got mostly horrible reviews but was nonetheless a big success at the box office. The hullabaloo surrounding the movie involved its premise: a spoiled rich kid has his money supply cut off by his millionaire father, but he hopes still to attend Harvard Law School, and figures the only way he can gain admission is if he were somehow black and the beneficiary of affirmative action. It gets worse, but you get the picture.

On the heels of *The Troll*, *The Art of Being Nick*, and *Soul Man*, Julia Louis-Dreyfus landed a small part in Woody Allen's *Hannah and Her Sisters*. To say that her movie credits had taken a dramatic turn for the better would be an under-statement. She said of that experience: "I could hardly hold it together when Woody was around. I was so in awe."

In the years immediately prior to her winning the role of Elaine Benes on *Seinfeld*, Julia Louis-Dreyfus had a recurring role in a sitcom developed by Andy Borowitz and Gary David Goldberg. The latter wrote for, created, and produced hit shows like *Family Ties*, *Brooklyn Bridge*, and *Spin City*. *Day by Day*, however, was not one of his winners. It lasted only thirty-three episodes during 1988–1989, in which Louis-Dreyfus played a character named Eileen Swift. The show revolved around an at-home daycare center run by a husband-and-wife team, who had both left their monetarily rewarding but ulcer-inducing careers. Had *Day by Day* been a ratings-grabber, Louis-Dreyfus quite possibly would not have been available to audition for *Seinfeld*, or even interested for that matter, because— remember—the show's long-term prospects were anything but guaranteed.

The incredibly talented Julia Louis-Dreyfus gets her due in 2010—a star on the Hollywood Walk of Fame.   *RoidRanger/Shutterstock.com*

As things turned out, Julia Louis-Dreyfus beat off some stiff competition for the role of Elaine Benes, the sole female regular cast member. It wasn't just any role either. As the character was written and acted by the talented Louis-Dreyfus, Elaine was a trailblazing female character in the sitcom genre. She was not in any way, shape, or form constrained. Elaine's actions were on par with the males in her circle and she did what she wanted to do—no holds barred, no feelings of guilt. Elaine was never, ever consigned to a stereotypical female box and Louis-Dreyfus brought the character to bold new benchmarks week after week, whether she was debating which men in her life were "sponge-worthy," or throwing George's toupee out the window, or abstaining from sex when her life falls apart.

Gary Lee Goldberg, who passed away in 2013, had high praise for Julia Louis-Dreyfus. "You're looking at a real actress here," he told *People* magazine after *Seinfeld* exited the air in 1998 and most everyone wondered how the cast members would fare in its aftermath. Being so inextricably linked with the characters of Jerry, George, Elaine, and Kramer, it wasn't going to be easy. Goldberg, though, was confident that Louis-Dreyfus would have little problem moving on to other projects without being forever typecast as Elaine. "Just give the audience a little chance to get over it, and then they'll be ready to accept her in other roles." And he was quite prescient. She holds claim to being the only actress to have won Emmy Awards for roles in three distinct sitcoms: *Seinfeld*, *The New Adventures of Old Christine*, and *Veep*. She also holds the record for Emmy nominations by an actress. Julia Louis-Dreyfus has come a long way from *SNL* and has proved that talent and determination can overcome even the most tenacious brand of typecasting.

8

Cosmo Kramer

Hipster Doofus

Among his circle of friends, Cosmo Kramer is, without question, the most enigmatic. In fact, he's an enigma wrapped in too many riddles to count. Kramer's life in the here and now is completely unorthodox and his past is shrouded in some mystery. The big guy's mother is Barbara "Babs" Kramer and, by all accounts, he didn't have a warm and fuzzy relationship with her while growing up; apparently, she had an insatiable thirst for the grape. He has his father's wedding ring in his possession and, if we take him at his word (in "The Chinese Woman") that he is "the last male Kramer" extant, we can assume the Kramer patriarch is no longer among the living. "We're facing extinction," Cosmo notes with genuine concern and bona fide fear at the prospect of a world devoid of Kramers.

Cosmo Kramer: Oddball Next Door

In the episode "The Big Salad," Jerry is curious as to why Kramer is such a "stickler" for rules when playing a friendly game of golf among friends. "You know when I was growing up, I had to be in bed every night by nine o'clock," Kramer informs Jerry. "And if I wasn't . . . well . . . I don't need to tell you what happened!" He enlightens a couple of patrons of the arts over dinner that he ran away from home—far away, as a matter of fact, by boarding a steamship to Sweden when he was just seventeen years old. He never finished high school but earned his general education (GED) diploma at some later point in his life, perhaps during his short-lived and "classified" stint in the army.

The bits and pieces that we glean from his childhood and early adulthood paint an unfinished portrait of the man and how he evolved into the "hipster doofus" with the off-beat vertical 'do, his passion for fresh fruit, and a bushel load of eccentricities. His wardrobe, for example, is outdated, and his pants are a size too big and on the short side. While Kramer can be superficial and insensitive at times, he can also be insightful and, occasionally, even caring. If one had to select a member of the gang with something resembling a conscience, Kramer would be it, hands-down. By default, perhaps, considering the competition, but he nonetheless reveals a magnanimous side every now and

The ultimate hipster doofus: Cosmo Kramer is dressed to kill.

again that Jerry, George, and Elaine sorely lack. Kramer assists strangers in need and attempts to involve his friends in random acts of kindness on occasion—a Herculean task indeed.

"I'm not crazy," says Kramer in "The Trip." "I may look weird, but I'm just like you. I'm just a regular guy." Despite the man's categorically humble description of himself, one would be hard-pressed to classify Kramer as a "regular guy." He is an intriguing, multi-layered, irregular guy if ever there was one. Tall and gangly, he frequently makes outlandish noises to express how he's feeling and has a mother lode of pithy retorts at his disposal, including "Giddy-up," "Wo, wo, Gingga," "Yo-Yo Ma," "Yo, diggity dog," and "Wrong, Mujumbo." Kramer is the King of Onomatopoeia, too, with a dictionary all his own.

In the episode "The Little Kicks," we learn that an air conditioner had whacked Kramer on his head at some point in 1979. This unfortunate happenstance could explain some of the man's more unusual behaviors and flights of fancy. Always concerned for his friend Jerry's well-being, we witness Kramer advising him not to walk too close to the curbside—a fundamental lesson in street safety—because of the possibility of getting clipped by a "two-ton cab." He reasons that the lesser of two evils is getting hit on the head by a falling "eighty-pound air conditioner."

In the episode "The Letter," Kramer has his portrait painted by Nina, a talented artist and Jerry's then girlfriend. When a couple of senior citizen art collectors, Mr. and Mrs. Armstrong, lay eyes on the oil painting for the first time, they are mesmerized by it. Mr. Armstrong says, "He is a loathsome, offensive brute, and yet I can't look away." Mrs. Armstrong adds, "He transcends time and space." Kramer in oil colors mirrors Kramer in flesh and blood—simultaneously distasteful and captivating. Mr. and Mrs. Armstrong plunk down five thousand dollars for the painting and describe its subject as a "man-child crying out for love. An innocent orphan in the postmodern world."

Kramer's singular visage was everywhere in the 1990s, including this spare tire cover, which echoes his portrait by Jerry's girlfriend Nina in "The Letter."

Courtesy of Joseph Nigro

Law and Disorder

Among Kramer's assorted personality quirks is a palpable disregard for the basic rule of law. He frequently gets his friends in trouble by suggesting that they disobey rules in general. In the episode "The Handicap Spot," Kramer importunes George to park in a spot reserved for the handicapped with the requisite state-issued special license plates. With the gang on the hunt for a flat-screen TV at a shopping mall—an engagement gift for a friend—and pressed for time on the way to the engagement party, George doesn't need a whole lot of convincing. Kramer's explanation—that handicapped individuals don't want "special spots" because they want to be treated like everybody else—suffices.

Heeding Kramer's advice in such delicate matters invariably leads to minor problems that often snowball into major ones. That's precisely what occurs in this episode. An honest-to-goodness handicapped person arrives and finds the spot taken. Forced to park farther away from the stores, she gets into a serious accident while making her way there and lands in the hospital. And, here again, we see the conflicting aspects inherent in Kramer's character. While he was the one leading the charge to park in the handicap spot, he is the only one who would even consider—for a moment—visiting the injured party in the hospital. After calling on her at St. Elizabeth's Hospital, Kramer tells Jerry and Elaine that he's fallen madly in love with the wheelchair-bound woman. "She's got everything I've always wanted in another human being," he says. "Except for the walking."

Kramer's track record with women, though, portended that this relationship would not fully flower and—lo and behold—it didn't. He tells Jerry and George that he's not only been dumped, but—worse than that—he has been branded a "hipster doofus" with an appearance not up to her exacting standards.

In the episode "The Parking Garage," Kramer's forgetfulness finds the gang on a frenzied search for his car in a multi-level indoor shopping mall parking garage. Unfortunately for Jerry, nature's call couldn't have come at a more inopportune time. He desperately has to go to the bathroom, but there are none to be found in the parking garage.

Kramer's initial impulse in situations like Jerry's is to flout the rules of polite society. He implores him to urinate behind a parked car and not to worry about it. Jerry, though, is adamant about not urinating in the garage. He'll just wait it out—hold it in like a real man. Kramer finally convinces Jerry to go with the flow, as it were, by lecturing him on what "holding it in" does to the bladder. He's not one to give up easily. His stubborn streak is a mile long and gets a lot of people in trouble, including himself on many occasions. Kramer believes that his friend Jerry is overly cautious about abiding by society's picayune rules. He, on the other hand, is willing to circumvent these rules when he feels it's called for.

Taking Kramer's advice is invariably risky and, sometimes, dangerous to a person's health and well-being. After urinating behind a parked car, heaving a sigh of relief, and zipping up his fly, Jerry turns around and finds a security guard staring him in the face.

In the episode "The Package," Kramer takes his unique brand of independence from societal mores and laws one giant step further. He reveals his deceitful side, too, in a ham-fisted attempt to commit mail fraud against the United States Post Office. The whole scheme, however, is designed to benefit Jerry, his buddy, whose stereo has ceased working, and not himself. Without his friend's knowledge or consent, Kramer's plan involves sending the defunct stereo through the mail—insured for four hundred dollars—to Jerry's address. Before mailing the package, Kramer smashes it into assorted pieces. In such a wretched condition upon delivery, Jerry could then present the stereo as exhibit A to the post office—evidence of their gross mishandling of his package—and collect the insurance money. Kramer's endgame: Jerry buys a new stereo with the insurance windfall—neat, simple, and nobody gets hurt. Everybody comes out on top.

Kramer tells Jerry that there is absolutely nothing untoward about his scheme because the post office will just "write off" the expense of paying for Jerry's new stereo. Jerry is nonetheless skeptical and complains that Kramer hasn't even a clue what a write-off is. What's important, Kramer says, is not that he understands the accounting ABCs of write-offs, but that the post office and other big enterprises understand them.

In the best-laid plans of mice and Kramer, Jerry is the one under investigation for mail fraud, which is a federal offense that, if convicted, could lead to serious jail time. And if the investigation itself isn't bad enough, Newman, Jerry's number-one nemesis, is leading the charge against him. "How I've longed for this moment, Seinfeld," Newman says. "The day when I would have the proof I needed to haul you out of your cushy lair, and expose to the light of justice the monster that you are. A monster so vile . . ."

In the episode "The Baby Shower," Kramer yet again convinces Jerry to agree to something that his gut instinct tells him not to—something illegal. Kramer sells Jerry on the idea of an unlawful cable hookup installed by a Russian man named Tabachnik, and his unidentified assistant. Jerry ultimately reconsiders going through with it, but like so many Kramer-inspired situations, it doesn't end tidily.

Jerry informs Tabachnik that he doesn't want the cable hookup after all, but agrees to pay him for his time. However, when Tabachnik tells him the price for services—four hundred dollars—Jerry is taken aback. Kramer had quoted him one hundred and fifty. Jerry opts not to pay Tabachnik's exorbitant price—his extortion—for essentially doing nothing, and gets his television screen smashed in retaliation. Again, Kramer's persuasiveness and persistence gets his pal in another fine mess.

For a man with such an off-the-wall and unpredictable personality, he has a peculiar knack for convincing people to do things that they would not otherwise do. Kramer even persuades Elaine to hire an assassin to silence once and for all a neighborhood dog that has been keeping her up at night and making her life miserable. The hired gun, as it were, happens to be Newman, a postman with a legitimate axe to grind against the canine species, which doesn't exactly put out the welcome mat for the men and women who deliver the mail, rain or shine, come hell or high water.

Kramer Versus Kramer

It is patently obvious that Cosmo Kramer has a heaping helping of idiosyncrasies and phobias on his plate. One of his more prominent phobias is known as coulrophobia, which is a fear of clowns. Kramer admits that he's been scared of them since his childhood. We never learn if there was a particular incident that stirred this deep-seated fear, but then there doesn't always have to be. For impressionable youths, clowns can be a scary lot. Their painted smiles, scripted joviality, and penchant for doing outlandish things like riding around on tiny bicycles or walking around on stilts, understandably disconcert many youngsters. So it's no big surprise that the mere sight of one would unnerve the adult Kramer, who is so tightly wound.

Kramer likewise suffers from musophobia, a fear of mice, which he shares with both Frank Costanza and the world's elephant population. In the episode "The Raincoats," we witness firsthand Kramer's frenzied reaction at the mere mention of the word *mouse*. As people with this very real phobia are wont to do, he panics and runs from the room.

One of the more peculiar tics in Kramer's psyche is his reaction to Mary Hart, co-anchor of the syndicated TV program *Entertainment Tonight*. In the episode "The Good Samaritan," he suffers something akin to a seizure upon hearing the sound of her voice. But Kramer is not alone in being in the grip of what could very possibly be "The Mary Hart Syndrome." An unidentified woman is responsible for bringing to light this very real malady. She was known to suffer debilitating epileptic seizures whenever she heard Hart's voice. An expert on the medical condition known as epilepsy concluded it was very likely "the pitch and quality of the voice as a sound that caused the epileptic episodes." When the woman ceased watching *Entertainment Tonight*, her seizures ended. While Kramer has not been diagnosed with epilepsy, he is ultra sensitive to sounds.

Kramer is also an extremely irrational individual. Sometimes being told to "drop dead" strikes a very literal chord with him, and sometimes it doesn't. Lola, the handicapped woman, told him to "drop dead" and, while stung by the remark's cruel sentiment, he didn't take it literally. In the episode "The Betrayal," however, we see Kramer's superstitious side reveal itself when his friend Franklin Delano Romanowsky, a.k.a. "FDR," tells him to "drop dead" after a snowball-throwing incident. Kramer takes this jab to heart and fears that—barring some kind of ethereal intercession—he will, in fact, *drop dead.* Kramer insists that both he and FDR break a chicken wishbone. "All right, FDR, this wish is for all the marbles," he says. "You win . . . you get your wish. I drop dead. I win . . . I don't drop dead and get 100 percent anti-drop-dead protection . . . forever!"

When Kramer loses the wishbone contest, he frantically seeks out other possibilities for a stay of execution. He crashes Newman's birthday party, hoping to strike a deal with him. As he enters the celebratory scene, a group of the postman's co-workers are singing to him. Kramer initially complains about not being invited to the affair, prompting Newman to quip—to the delight of his postal peers—how it must have gotten "lost in the mail." He then gets down to the business at hand. "Well, Newman . . . I need your wish to protect me from FDR," Kramer says rather plaintively. After some intense back-and-forth bartering for the wish, he agrees to give Newman his next forty-nine birthday wishes—and the deal is done.

Kramer is also renowned for being completely candid. Sometimes his straightforwardness gets him—and, of course, others—into hot water. However, he is often lauded for his frankness—for telling it like it is. There is no artifice surrounding the big guy, no posturing airs, which is commonplace in the Manhattan neighborhood and city that he calls home. In the episode "The Nose Job," we see Kramer's notorious directness at work when he conveys to George's girlfriend, Audrey, something that nobody else would dare tell her. "Well, you're as pretty as any of them [attractive New York women]," he says. "You just need a nose job." While Kramer's no-inner-monologue candor unnerves Elaine, Audrey—the recipient—expresses appreciation of the man's forthrightness.

Kramer's one-of-a-kind personality also enables him to soothe the savage breast on occasion. He actually gets along with George's parents, Frank and Estelle Costanza, which is a remarkable accomplishment in itself. They even permit Kramer to crash at their Queens home when they're away and, if he so desires, entertain lady friends there. The Costanzas' very own son, George, has never been granted such privilege and it rankles him that Kramer has.

Jerry's parents, Morty and Helen Seinfeld, are fond of Kramer as well. He calls them once a week. Jerry wonders why he's calling the Seinfelds on a regular basis. "Well, maybe if you called more often, I wouldn't have to," Kramer bluntly replies. He even moves into the Seinfelds' retirement village in Florida and, with Morty Seinfeld's backing, runs for condo board president. In the episode "The Wizard," Kramer enters the Seinfelds' condo without knocking and makes a beeline for the refrigerator. He encounters his friend Jerry along the way.

Jerry is surprised to discover his old pal from across the hall living in a Florida retirement community with exclusively elderly neighbors. "This is where people come to die," Jerry says. Kramer nonetheless insists that the relaxing, slow-paced environment has done him a world of good. Jerry also warns his parents of the downside of feeding Kramer—how they run the serious and expensive risk of it becoming a regular occurrence.

Kramer's Likes and Dislikes

Cosmo Kramer loves an invigorating winter swim so much that he's joined a Polar Bear Club. The man relishes a good Cuban cigar and is fond of milkshakes, which he drinks all the time. There is perhaps nothing he likes better, however, than a fine piece of fruit. In fact, Kramer takes his enthusiasm for fruit to an almost mystical level and expects the produce peddlers in his path to sell him only the highest quality, freshest, and most delicious fruit available. He particularly loves mangos, avocados, and plums that are red inside. He even buys plantains, which, he says, are a "delicacy." Kramer considers supermarket fruit unfit for either man or beast. Sometimes, even his favorite local fruit merchant, Joe, lets him down. In "The Mango," Kramer bites into a peach that he considers beneath Joe's usually high standards. He decides to return the once-bitten piece of fruit to Joe, which Jerry finds quite peculiar.

Alas, the Kramer–Joe the Fruit Man confrontation has an unfortunate denouement. For starters, Kramer does not get restitution for the bad peach, which Joe calls "an act of God." But worse than that, he gets banned from shopping at the store altogether. Supplying him with a comprehensive list, Kramer asks Jerry to do his fruit shopping for him, but the cagey proprietor quickly catches on. Jerry is banned, too, creating a real dilemma for the fruit-loving Kramer.

Interestingly, Kramer purports to have a visceral distaste for public libraries and never got a library card because of their clientele. In "The Library," we learn that he considers library patrons a tightfisted lot. "People sitting around reading newspapers attached to huge wooden sticks trying to save a quarter . . . *oooh*," he says sarcastically. Yet Kramer is a notorious freeloader and moocher who raids Jerry's refrigerator and cupboards on a constant basis. He has no problem, either, with borrowing tools and appliances without asking permission. This behavior, though, is all part of the mystique that surrounds the man. If Kramer's uninvited comings and goings bothered Jerry, and they clearly don't, he could very easily lock his door and be done with the repeated intrusions.

Never let it be said that Kramer is satisfied with the status quo. In the episode "The Junior Mint," he is busily staining the wood floors in his apartment with the intention of putting up "fake wood" wallpaper. His game plan is to give the place the look and feel of a log cabin. In the episode "The Merv Griffin Show," Kramer discovers chairs and pieces of the set from the long-running talk show in a dumpster on the street. After engaging in some serious dumpster diving, he ultimately reconstructs the exact set of the show in his apartment and resurrects his singular version of the talk show there. Kramer's nonconformity and doggedness are unrivaled.

The Money Train

Exactly how can Kramer afford to live on Manhattan's fashionable Upper West Side? After all, his employment history is rather spotty, to say the least. He spends an awful lot of time in his apartment, too, and is hardly combing the job market for full-time work. Nevertheless, he's rarely behind the financial eight ball. We know for a fact that he has had some luck betting on the horses and that he once had a job with H&H Bagels, but went on strike when the employees demanded a certain minimum wage that wasn't attained until twelve years later. At that point in time, Kramer is called back to H&H Bagels for a second go-round as a bagel baker. We see him on the job—an unfamiliar sight—kneading the dough for the bagels. But when his chewing gum drops out of his mouth and into the doughy mélange, his exasperated manager fires him on the spot. Not surprisingly, this job termination doesn't exactly displease the man who seemingly prefers being on strike to working in the dark, sticky recesses of a bagel shop.

Whether the backbone of his bank account is some sort of past lawsuit settlement or inheritance, we never quite uncover. The mystery that shrouds Kramer's life and times is at once layered and thick. But despite his legendary employment gaps, Kramer actually does a whole host of interesting things to earn a dollar here and a dollar there. He appears in a guest role on the sitcom *Murphy Brown*, starring Candice Bergen. He works on the soap opera *All My Children* as a stand-in. He authors *The Coffee Table Book of Coffee Tables*, which is plugged on *Live with Regis and Kathie Lee* and ultimately optioned by Hollywood for a fair chunk of change.

Kramer, who has certainly led an adventurous life, sells some of his anecdotes from his storied past to J. Peterman, Elaine's boss, for use in the catalog man's autobiography. A wannabe screenwriter, Kramer writes a movie treatment called "The Keys," in which he hopes to cast actor Fred Savage. He is also an author and amateur historian and naturalist. With the gang gathered in Jerry's apartment discussing George's loss of his new apartment to an *Andrea Doria* survivor, Kramer reveals an authoritative knowledge of the ship's collision with the *Stockholm* on a foggy night in the environs of Nantucket Island. George is staggered by his friend's familiarity with the tragic accident:

> Kramer: It's in my book: *Astonishing Tales of the Sea*. Fifty-one people died.
>
> George: Fifty-one people? That's it? I thought it was, like, a thousand!
>
> Kramer: There were 1,650 survivors.
>
> George: That's no tragedy! How many people do you lose on a normal cruise? Thirty? Forty? Kramer, can I take a look at that book?
>
> Kramer: Oh, yeah. I also got *Astounding Bear Attacks*.

Kramer's résumé is very definitely a work in progress; it's what makes him such an incomparable persona. He is at once headstrong and extremely creative. He's tried his hand at an array of jobs and entrepreneurial endeavors that few among us can duplicate. He's modeled underwear for Calvin Klein, been a department store Santa Claus at Christmastime, and driven a hansom cab in New York City's Central Park. Kramer's invented a beach-scented cologne, peddled old records, and opened up a rickshaw business with the intention of employing the area's homeless people as "drivers."

What is always apparent is that the wheels are perpetually turning in Kramer's mind. He's a restless spirit who doesn't mind being a tennis ball boy one minute and a police lineup stand-in the next. But, in the bigger job picture, Kramer's creative juices reign supreme. He's a man of ideas, although they are not always practical, like opening a restaurant with only one item on the menu: peanut butter and jelly sandwiches. Win or lose, Kramer has chutzpah, exhibiting a willingness to boldly go where no entrepreneur has gone before—be it with an idea for a "bladder system" for oil tankers to prevent future oil spills or the invention of a combination ketchup-and-mustard condiment.

Love and Cosmo Kramer

In the game of love, it's fair to say that Kramer does remarkably well for a gawky eccentric leading an unconventional lifestyle with an uncertain and unsteady source of income. Granted, he has fewer romantic relationships with the opposite sex than Jerry, George, or Elaine, all of whom could be described as serial daters, but he makes more conquests than most men his age. Just like his friends, Kramer's relationships are short-lived and often end for seemingly inconsequential (but not for him) reasons. In the episode "The Maid," Kramer breaks up with his girlfriend, Madeline, after she moves downtown to the Lower East Side of Manhattan. He can't abide the fact that she lives so far away—downtown, while he lives uptown. A long-distance relationship is just unacceptable and logistically impossible. Kramer desperately misses his Upper West Side neighborhood when he ventures that far afield and gets stranded in lower Manhattan. In this foreign milieu, a panicked Kramer calls Jerry on a payphone at the corner of First and First, wondering how the same street can intersect with itself. "I must be at the nexus of the universe," he wails.

One of Kramer's more bizarre relationships occurs in the "The Friars Club." In this episode he finds himself in a sack in the Hudson River and accuses his girlfriend, Connie, of trying to kill him. With a couple of accomplices, she had, in fact, dumped Kramer's body in the river because she thought he was dead—not just in a sound sleep—and couldn't go to the police for fear that "Joey might find out." Kramer's peculiar karma inspires stranger-than-strange situations. We never do learn the fate of Connie, who calls her lawyer, Jackie Chiles, after the police arrive at her apartment to arrest her. Jackie declines to assist her when he learns whom she's accused of attempting to bump off: Cosmo Kramer. He

Kramer's Not Necessarily Top Ten Girlfriends

10. Pam, who was entangled in a capricious love triangle with Jerry and Kramer, who both vowed to get a vasectomy to prove their devotion to her ("The Soul Mate").
9. Noreen, a friend of Elaine's, who once dated Dan, a "high-talker," and contemplated suicide ("The Chinese Woman").
8. Tina, a friend and roommate of Elaine's, who drove the latter up the wall while involved with Kramer ("The Truth").
7. Olive, a cashier at Monk's Café, who had the ideal fingernails for scratching Kramer's perpetually itchy back and arousing him along the way ("The Pie").
6. Emily, who had "jimmy legs" that kept Kramer awake at night ("The Money").
5. Connie, with mafia ties, who believed Kramer was dead and had him unceremoniously dumped in the Hudson River ("The Friars Club").
4. Toby, who worked with Elaine at Pendant Publishing, heckled Jerry at a standup appearance, and lost her pinky toe in a freak accident ("The Fire").
3. Cheryl, a lab technician, whom Kramer endeavored to convince to falsify a yogurt analysis and spare his investment in a non-fat yogurt business ("The Non-Fat Yogurt").
2. Marion, a quiet librarian and part-time poet, who labored under the supervision of Mr. Bookman ("The Library").
1. Leslie, a "low-talker" and designer of the puffy shirt that Jerry wore on the *Today* show ("The Puffy Shirt").

had previously represented Kramer as a client and recognizes the potential perils of getting involved with the man.

Kramer dates a broad cross-section of women, including a "low-talker" and a lady friend who disturbs his sleep patterns with her "jimmy legs." He falls head over heels for a girlfriend of Jerry's named Pam and, when he learns that she doesn't want to start a family, goes so far as to get a vasectomy. Kramer's dating sometimes comes attached to more benefits than drama. In the episode "The Pie," he dates Olive, a waitress at Monk's Café, who sports some very long fingernails that can reach that seemingly unreachable itch on his back. "Ohhh . . . she's a maestro!" he informs Jerry and George. "The crisscross . . . the figure eight . . . strummin' the ol' banjo . . . and this wild, savage free-for-all where anything can happen." His roving eye in the episode "The Library" zeroes in on a librarian. "This is a lonely woman looking for companionship . . . spinster . . . maybe a virgin," Kramer says. "Maybe she got hurt a long time ago. She was a schoolgirl. There was a boy. It didn't work out. Now she needs a little tenderness. She needs a little understanding. She needs a little Kramer."

In "The Smelly Car," Kramer even manages to sweep a lesbian off her feet and steal her away from Susan, George's ex-girlfriend and future fiancée. Elaine cannot believe it. "I don't get this," she says. "This woman has never been with a man her entire life?" His reply says it all: "I'm Kramer." And indeed he is: the man with "kavorka," as noted by a Latvian Orthodox priest, possessing "the lure of the animal."

Michael Richards: Breathing Life into the Hipster Doofus

Writing in the December 1992 *Atlantic Monthly*, Francis Davis referred to Cosmo Kramer for the very first time as a "hipster doofus." Larry David appreciated the description so much that he incorporated it in the episode "The Handicap Spot." Nobody, but nobody, could have played the "hipster doofus" quite like the actor tapped to infuse life into this character based on Larry David's former next-door neighbor, Kenny Kramer. Like Kenny Kramer, Cosmo Kramer was a madcap eccentric who lived down the hall and danced to the beat of his own drummer.

The man who portrayed Cosmo Kramer with such enchanting élan was born on July 24, 1949, in Culver City, California, home of the MGM Studios. The city's proud municipal motto was "The Heart of Screenland." Michael Richards is the oldest of the *Seinfeld* cast members—Jerry is five years younger; Jason Alexander, ten years younger; and Julia Louis-Dreyfus, twelve years his junior. He is also the only one to have grown up on the West Coast, where, in fact, *Seinfeld* was filmed during its lengthy run, but three thousand miles away from the place Jerry, George, Elaine, and Kramer called home: New York City.

Michael Anthony Richards was the only child of Phyllis and William Richards. His father, an electrical engineer by trade, died an untimely death in an automobile accident. Michael was just two years old when he lost his dad. His mother, who worked as a medical records librarian, never remarried. She was a single parent in the sedate 1950s and early 1960s, when this parental arrangement wasn't nearly as commonplace as it is today. Michael credits his mom for passing on to him a wild and crazy sense of humor. "God, she was a crack-up," he recalled to *People* magazine.

Young Michael was an antsy kid. He loved exploring the Baldwin Hills range and the San Fernando Valley, which were home to him. There was nothing he liked better than investigating every nook and cranny of this sprawling and picturesque terrain while furiously peddling away on his bicycle. He also enjoyed going to the area's movie theaters and watching as many feature films as time and money would allow. "Those early treks of mine produced an extraordinary freedom as well as a soulful sense of my own individuality," he later mused.

Kramer in Training

As early as grade school, Michael Richards had comedy and acting in mind as a future career. He remembered being inspired by a junior high school drama class and feeling, for the very first time, that his life "suddenly had purpose." And he liked entertaining his peers, too. "I enjoyed making my friends laugh by clowning around in classes, and I did get in trouble for it," he told writer Michael M. Marsellos. "I didn't know that I was actually doing what my calling in life demanded."

The man who inspired the Cosmo Kramer character: Larry David's friend Kenny Kramer, addressing a crowd during his Seinfeld Reality Tour in 2008. *Paul McKinnon/Shutterstock.com*

Michael Richards attended Thousand Oaks High School in Ventura, California, and was, by all accounts, a Kramer-in-training, widely known for his broad physical humor and comedic antics. A classmate remembered Michael as the class clown: "He couldn't come to class unless he fell over two or three desks." The man who would one day stand on his head during his audition for the *Seinfeld* role was learning the trade. Appreciating the many opportunities available to him during his childhood, Richards once remarked, "I am grateful that the public schools introduced me to the performing arts."

After graduating from high school, Richards enrolled in classes in both Ventura College and Los Angeles Valley College, where he performed in theater and contemplated, at that juncture in his life, a possible career as a dramatic actor. However, his higher education and dreams of the future were put on hold in 1970, when, at the age of twenty-one, he was drafted into the army. At that snapshot in time, the war in Vietnam showed few signs of winding down. The heavy casualty rate added an uneasy heft to receiving a draft notice in the mail. Fortunately for Richards, he was shipped off to West Germany and not the jungles of Southeast Asia. His service included working with the V Corps Training Road Show. He directed a series of plays, including educational productions aimed at improving race relations in the military ranks, and others that offered up cautionary tales of the dangers of drug abuse. "This was a successful, educational operation, boosting the morale of our men and incorporating the arts into service," Richards recalled years later with genuine pride. After two years in the army, he was honorably discharged and returned to the States in 1972. He lived in a commune in the San Fernando Valley for a spell—a time when he was "finding himself."

Richards later enrolled in the California Institute of the Arts, where he met future wife Cathleen Lyons. He then attended Evergreen State College in Olympia, Washington, where he specialized in drama and theater and earned a bachelor of fine arts degree. Not too long after exiting the college scene, Richards realized that his strong suit was comedy—not drama—and that's the road he traveled down. He even partnered with Ed Begley Jr. in a short-lived improv act.

Michael Richards married his college sweetheart in 1974. They divorced in 1992—during the *Seinfeld* run—after eighteen years of marriage; the union produced one child, a girl named Sophia. But in the mid-1970s, the then-optimistic newlyweds moved south to San Diego. It was there that Richards developed his standup act and began assiduously working the comedy club circuit. The tall, gangly comic was frequently spotted at the San Diego Repertory Theater and in clubs in Los Angeles. "I would commute to Los Angeles from San Diego," he recollected, "and get in line at five o'clock and wait until one a.m. to do three minutes." That was the nature of the business, and he was prepared to soldier on until he was discovered. "I was very inspired," Richards said in the *Seinfeld* DVD commentary. "I did have the feeling that it was the route to go. I didn't question this course at all."

Through his zany standup performances for the San Diego Repertory Theater, the Mark Taper Forum in Los Angeles, and the Comedy Store in Hollywood, Michael Richards was indeed getting noticed. Standing six feet three inches tall, with that lanky frame of his, he was pretty hard to miss.

Thank God for *Fridays*

Michael Richards's big break was being cast in ABC's not-too-successful attempt at putting together a *Saturday Night Live* sketch show, which aired twenty-four hours earlier on the weekly TV schedule. Fittingly, it was called *Fridays* and debuted in the spring of 1980. The show was filmed live on the West Coast, which starkly contrasted with *SNL* and its "Live from New York" brand. Richards described the *Fridays* gig as his "first real paying job as a comic actor." Other cast members included Melanie Chartoff, Mark Blankfield, and Larry David. Reflecting to *LA Weekly*, Chartoff said of the show's casting: "They wanted relative unknowns. They didn't want names. They wanted all of us to get discovered together." Of course, some members of the cast of *Fridays* were discovered, including Richards and David, just not in the immediate aftermath of the show.

The producer of *Fridays*, John Moffit, recalled that after the show's cancellation in 1982, "Larry David said he was so worried that he'd be homeless that he looked around various side streets in New York where he could live. He found a place . . . on 46th Street where there was a big updraft of heat underneath a grate." This snippet of trivia is a testament to both how difficult the business can be and how perseverance can pay off. And it certainly did for Larry David and Michael Richards. Their careers at the tail end of the decade were on the cusp of skyrocketing.

Richards nonetheless did some stellar work on *Fridays*, portraying popular recurring characters Vinnie, Dick, and Battle Boy. As the show evolved through its three seasons and fifty-four episodes, he grew increasingly popular, too, with the live audiences who loudly applauded his initial appearances on the stage. "Some of the stuff I did on *Fridays* was a start for characters I developed later on," he said.

A footnote to the *Fridays* experience was Richards's role in the infamous Andy Kaufman incident in 1981, when the latter was a guest on the show and performing in a sketch. The premise of the piece found four friends in a restaurant, including Richards and Kaufman, who periodically retreated to the bathroom to smoke a joint. Midway through the bit, Kaufman went completely off script and refused to read the remainder of his lines. In response to this unacceptable and embarrassing behavior on live TV, Richards got up, disappeared from the camera's lens, and returned with the sketch's cue cards, which he angrily threw on the table in front of an equally peeved Andy Kaufman. In retaliation, Kaufman threw a glass of water in Richards's face, which ratcheted up the tension on the set. Things then turned really ugly when a fight broke out between the show's co-producer, Jack Burns, and Kaufman.

As both the in-studio and television audiences watched the spectacle in disbelief, one was left to wonder what was really going on. Although it certainly looked like a completely unrehearsed and unscripted event, it was, in fact, staged. Michael Richards, Jack Burns, and others were in on it. This "sketch gone awry" was recreated in the 1999 film *Man on the Moon*, which recounted the turbulent life and times of the late Andy Kaufman. It starred Jim Carrey as the unconventional and troubled comedian. Michael Richards declined to appear in the movie as himself. Looking back, Melanie Chartoff had this to say of the Kaufman appearance and ensuing mêlée: "In my opinion, it was kind of desperate. But it certainly got us on the map." Although it did get the show some much-needed publicity, it didn't help in the long run. *Fridays* was canceled in 1982 to make room for an expanded version of *Nightline* with Ted Koppel. This popular late-night news program had seen the ratings skyrocket with its coverage of the Iranian hostage-taking of diplomats and personnel from the American Embassy in Tehran—a 444-day affair, from November 4, 1979 to January 20, 1981.

A Real Character as Character Actor

After the cancellation of *Fridays*, Michael Richards began making guest appearances on various television shows throughout the 1980s. His credits include

Night Court, Cheers, Scarecrow and Mrs. King, Hill Street Blues, and *Miami Vice.* During this same time frame he landed a recurring role on *St. Elsewhere,* a highly rated medical drama, during its 1984–1985 season. And just before auditioning for the *Seinfeld* pilot, "The Seinfeld Chronicles," Richards was a regular in a sitcom called *Marblehead Manor* during its one season on the air (1987–1988). He also appeared in the films *Transylvania 6-5000* (1985), which starred Jeff Goldblum and Richards's former improv partner Ed Begley Jr., and *Problem Child* (1990), starring John Ritter. In 1996, during the *Seinfeld* run, he received top billing in the movie *Trial and Error,* which co-starred Jeff Daniels and Charlize Theron. "I'm brought in on projects where they need someone who's off-the-wall," Richards once said.

Funny man Michael Richards found himself the role of a lifetime: Cosmo Kramer on *Seinfeld.*
Paul Smith/ Featureflash/ Shutterstock.com

Worth noting in the pre-*Seinfeld* 1980s is that Michael Richards also auditioned for the role of Al Bundy in a FOX network show called *Married . . . with Children* (1987–1997). The casting director, Mark Hirschfeld, concluded that he just wasn't the right fit for the part, which ultimately went to Ed O'Neill. Hirschfeld, nevertheless, kept Richards in his Rolodex—that's where names and phone numbers were stored back in the day—and plucked out his name when he and others were putting together the cast for "The Seinfeld Chronicles" and searching for an actor to play Kessler—the Cosmo Kramer of the future—in this pilot. Had he won the part in *Married . . . with Children,* television history would have been altered because he would have never auditioned for *Seinfeld.* And it remains to be seen how both *Married . . . with Children* and *Seinfeld* would have fared with Michael Richards in the wrong show.

As to how Richards approached his comedy on sketch shows like *Fridays* and in television and movie appearances, he told *LA Weekly,* "Just commit to the material no matter how goofy it is and you're 75% there. Talent will give you another 10%, so 85% isn't bad."

Part III

Supporting Characters and Actors

9

Newman

Gone Postal

H is name is Newman—just plain Newman. He's got a first name—most everybody does—but nobody in his circle of friends and enemies seems to know it. His supervisor on the job refers to him as "Postal Employee Newman." On one occasion, in an embarrassing malaprop, a fleeting lady friend of his mistakenly cries out, "Goodbye, Norman" to him. Newman is short, rotund, and wears glasses. He dresses the part, too. It could be honestly said that he looks like a man who would go by the name of Newman, and Newman alone.

Newman's World

Newman resides in Jerry's apartment building and is his archenemy. Again, Newman's world is so inscrutable that we have no clue as to why he has such a pathological aversion to Jerry, whom he seems bent on taking down every chance he gets. Their standard greeting of "Hello, *Newman!*" "*Hello,* Jerry!" lays bare their mutual and utter disdain.

Even Jerry's mother, Helen Seinfeld, can't stand the sight of him and greets him in the same terse manner as her son. Newman is, however, on good terms with Kramer, who seems to see the best in people, even when the best is hard to find. They are friends who sometimes partner in get-rich schemes, like the rickshaw business they inaugurate in the episode "The Bookstore." After engaging in a contentious row over who will do the actual pulling of the rickshaw around the streets of Manhattan, Kramer advocates employing homeless people for the task. Newman sees real possibilities in going down this route, noting how the homeless have an "intimate knowledge of the street."

"Neither snow nor rain nor heat nor gloom of night stays these couriers from the swift completion of their appointed rounds." Yes, Newman works for the United States Post Office and is one of those couriers of whom Herodotus spoke so glowingly in 503 B.C. Those words are inscribed on the General Post Office building on 33rd Street and 8th Avenue in Manhattan, the very borough where Newman calls home, and not too far from the postal station where he plies his trade.

Newman takes his job very seriously and is, in one sense, a truly dedicated postman. But his hefty workload appears to be simultaneously driving him to distraction. He regularly blows his stack and launches into voluble broadsides against his employer. In the episode "The Old Man," George harmlessly asks Newman why postal workers sometimes *go postal*: "Because the mail never stops," he replies in earnest. "It just keeps coming and coming and coming. . . . But the more you get it out, the more it keeps coming in. And then the barcode reader breaks and it's Publisher's Clearing House day!"

Newman is exhibit A, offering us genuine insight into why so many postal employees have gone "postal" through the years. His vivid, often erudite, descriptions of his job duties unmask a person teetering on the edge; an individual under a tremendous amount of stress, day in and day out, with no relief in sight.

In the episode "The Diplomat's Club," Kramer needs an infusion of fast cash—$3,200—during a gambling bender with a guy named Earl at the airport—they are betting on arrival and departure times. Kramer phones Newman who, not surprisingly, tells his buddy that he doesn't have that kind of money. Kramer, however, knows otherwise and refers to a certain bag in Newman's possession that once belonged to someone famous—or infamous, in this instance: David Berkowitz, a.k.a. "Son of Sam," the serial killer who, before his arrest in August 1977, terrorized New York City's streets for two consecutive summers. According to Newman, he had worked alongside this troubled postal employee.

Convinced by the ever-persuasive Kramer, Newman shows up at the airport with the mysterious bag in hand. He explains to a skeptical Earl that what he has before him is not an ordinary United States Postal Service mailbag, but one that a mail carrier named David Berkowitz—yes, *that* David Berkowitz—once upon a time carried around.

Newman: "Son of Sam." The worst mass murderer the post office ever produced.

Earl: Where did you get this?

Newman: I took over his route. And, boy, were there a lot of dogs on that route.

To rush down to the airport with his prized possession to bail Kramer out shows, at the very least, that Newman values his friendships—perhaps because they are so rare. Newman, though, does have friends who work with him at the post office. Laboring within the confines of this mailing behemoth is akin to being in the armed services. The experience creates certain bonds that are inviolable—camaraderie that only postal employees can appreciate. And the fact that Newman once double-dated with David Berkowitz makes him kind of special while on the job.

Newman views his tasks within the post office as vital to society. "When you control the mail, you control *information*," he says with pride in "The Lip Reader." He takes genuine offense at any piece of mail being referred to as "junk mail" because it takes just as long to sort and deliver. Newman paints the goings-on at his workplace as somewhat sinister, with a lot of shenanigans occurring in the process of transporting letters and packages from point A to point B. "You don't know the half of what goes on here," he says conspiratorially in "The Junk Mail."

Newman is clearly a conflicted man—unhappy on so many levels. Living in the rat race that is New York City, with its eight million critics, is enough to drive any man over the edge. In the episode "The Andrea Doria," we come across Newman at perhaps his lowest ebb, depressed to the point that he's not delivering his daily mail load, but hoarding it instead in Jerry's storage space. For Newman to put so much on the line—it is, after all, a federal crime to tamper with the U.S. mail—and risk his otherwise secure position with the post office, is indicative that something is really eating at him and that his life is unfulfilled. It is Jerry, of all people, who discovers a depressed Newman lamenting his lot in life after not getting the transfer to the Aloha State that he was so desperately seeking. "The most sought-after postal route of them all," Newman says. "The air is so dewy sweet . . . you don't even have to lick the stamps. But it's not to be . . . so I'm hanging it up."

Before there was Newman, there was Neuman, who had a first name and a middle initial, too: Alfred E.

TM and © E.C. Publications, Inc. Visit www.madmagazine.com

Jerry is dumbfounded by Newman's dramatically changed attitude and complains of the illegality of storing undelivered mail in his space. "And yet," Newman defiantly replies, "it's perfectly legal to take a man's soul and crush it out like a stale Pall Mall."

Later in the same episode, Newman discovers that the job opening in Hawaii is available once again, because the fortunate postal employee who originally received the transfer had sticky fingers vis-à-vis certain Victoria's Secret catalogs passing through the mail. However, in order to still be a viable candidate for the Hawaii post, he's got to deliver all the mail that he has stored away—eight bags of it—without the powers-that-be at the post office discovering his egregious breach of trust. In a state of utter despair, Newman realizes that it's well-nigh impossible. He cannot possibly deliver eight bags, which amounts to eight days' worth of work. When Jerry sees Newman despairing at this missed opportunity of a lifetime and—the kicker—talking about staying put in the building they both call home, he offers words of encouragement. "You can't let this dream die," he says. "You moving away is my dream, too." By forging an unholy "alliance," as it were, Jerry agrees to assist Newman in delivering his backlog of mail.

Cyrano Newman

In the episode "The Soul Mate," multiple facets of Newman's personality are unmasked. Kramer has fallen head over heels in love with Jerry's girlfriend, Pam. Newman tells Jerry with unadulterated malevolence in his voice, "You really think you can manipulate that beautiful young woman like the half-soused nightclub rabble that lap up your inane observations!" This is hardly the first time that Newman has made it clear that he doesn't find Jerry or his standup act in the least bit amusing. Perhaps there is some jealousy on this front because Newman—despite being an overweight postal employee with an attitude problem—is no slouch in the intellect department. He has a way with words and is more than happy to help Kramer woo Pam—and woo her away from Jerry. Newman even takes a leaf out of Cyrano de Bergerac's book when he feeds Kramer some lines—while concealed behind a bookstore bookcase—that are sure to win over a beautiful woman. His words included such romantically charged verse as, "Her bouquet cleaved his hardened shell and fondled his muscled heart. He imbibed her glistening spell."

Evidence of Newman's erudition is seen on a recurrent basis, but perhaps no more so than in "The Finale." His enmity for Jerry reaches its apex when he learns that he is excluded from accompanying the gang to Paris on NBC's private jet for "one last hurrah"—one final adventurous fling before George and Jerry leave New York for California to work on their green-lighted sitcom, *Jerry*. "Hear me and hear me well!" Newman says dramatically. "The day will come—oh, yes—mark my words, Seinfeld! Your day of reckoning is coming, when an evil wind will blow through your little play world and wipe that smug smile off your face! And I'll be there, in all my glory, watching, watching as it all comes crumbling down!"

Newman the Man

As is the case with each and every one of us, there is more to Newman than meets the eye. He can sometimes be quite diabolical, and at other times he's the poster child for sniveling cowards. In the episode "The Reverse Peephole,"

Newman, the man, is seen in all his hues. We initially encounter him in a manic state, telling Kramer how Silvio, their building's super, has evicted him for being an "agitator" and performing work—the reverse peephole—without permission. "I'm *homeless*!" Newman wails. "I'm gonna be out on the street corner dancing for nickels. I'll be with the hobos in the train yard eating out of a bucket." Using his inexhaustible powers of persuasion, Kramer puts in a good word for Newman with Silvio, and the super relents. Newman can stay. But then Kramer discovers some hanky-panky going on between Newman and Silvio's wife that gives him pause. While he and Newman are taking an evening stroll, he brings up the sensitive subject, asking Newman if he's sleeping with the super's wife. "Well, there's very little *sleeping* going on," Newman boastfully replies.

Later in this same episode, Newman ascends a tree to retrieve what turns out to be a fur coat. His surprising athletic prowess is on display—climbing skills honed in the Pacific Northwest, we discover. Who would have guessed that this squat, portly fellow could "climb like a ring-tailed lemur," in Kramer's colorful description. Many overweight men and women are remarkably agile and startlingly graceful, and Newman, apparently, is one of them.

Newman's moral compass, too, is revealed as being a bit askew, with him conducting an affair with the super's wife—and right under the man's nose, so to speak. He appears perfectly willing to play a very dangerous game. If Silvio catches him in the act, he'll be kicked out of the building along with his friend Kramer, who had gone out on a limb for him.

So, clearly, Newman is not celibate. His charms are not lost on the ladies—some of them at least. He can win over women for the likes of Kramer, but can also enter into relationships of his very own. In the episode "The Big Salad," Jerry discovers something very surprising—even jarring—about his girlfriend, Margaret. It begins when Margaret is in his apartment, and Newman shows up at the door. They know each other from a past romantic relationship. Jerry is flummoxed at the notion of his girlfriend having once dated Newman and, worse than all that, learning that it was *Newman* who broke up with *her*.

Of course, it matters to Jerry a great deal that his girlfriend not only dated the man he calls "pure evil," but also liked him on top of that. Fixated on this rather unpleasant set of facts, Jerry confronts Newman and asks for an explanation as to why he broke up with Margaret. "You don't think she's attractive?" he asks. "No," Newman smugly responds. "I need a really pretty face. But, hey, that's me."

Again, we see Newman reveling in Jerry's discomfort and taking great pleasure in zinging his number-one adversary in the game of life.

Wayne Knight: A Knight to Remember

The man who would one day be immortalized as a cynical, disgruntled, corpulent mail carrier named Newman was born on August 7, 1955, in New York City. For employment reasons, his father soon after moved the family to the city of Cartersville, Georgia, in the Atlanta metropolitan area, which is where Wayne

Eliot Knight was both raised and educated. Upon reciting a poem in a school pageant, Knight caught the acting bug in kindergarten: "Fifty-one smiles is a lot of smiles, and they can go for miles and miles." He recalled to *The A.V. Club* that his kindergarten moment in the spotlight occurred at the tail end of the pageant. "Well, since that was the last thing on the show, everyone . . . applauded like crazy," Knight remembered. "And I'm thinking, 'I'm killin' 'em! I'm killin' 'em with this poem!'"

Knight was a very funny kid who made people laugh with an impersonation repertoire that included President John F. Kennedy and wry NBC newsman David Brinkley. His comedy idol was Groucho Marx. Knight opined, "Everyone else is like me: two arms and two legs." He joined his high school drama club but didn't let on that his professional ambition was to be a performer. "I kind of kept it quiet," he reflected, "because it's Cartersville, Georgia, and pretty much the last thing you want to say is that you want to be an actor."

In 1972, Wayne Knight attended the University of Georgia, where he studied theater. One of his professors in the performing arts informed the wannabe actor point-blank that he'd never make it in show business. Knight, however, was undeterred by this negativity and—like Jason Alexander and Julia Louis-Dreyfus—dropped out of college to pursue acting opportunities. Prior to becoming a full-fledged member of the ensemble, Knight interned for a spell with the Barter Theatre in Abingdon, Virginia, which first opened its doors in 1933 and touts an impressive alumni class, including Ned Beatty, Gregory Peck, Kevin Spacey, Ernest Borgnine, Patricia Neal, and Hume Cronyn. In 1979, Knight moved to New York City where he secured a part in the long-running Broadway comedy *Gemini*. He got the job by being quite audacious and directly contacting the show's producers. "I wrote them saying, 'I've seen your play and if you ever replace this role, if I don't get an audition for it, you are making a big mistake,'" he recounted to the *Los Angeles Times* in 1993. "They called me in. I auditioned for it and got the part."

As is so often the case with young actors, Knight initially struggled to make ends meet. In between acting jobs, he toiled as a salesman, a waiter, and even worked for a private investigation outfit. "I'd been waiting tables and a friend of mine had gotten this job at a detective agency," he recalled. "They said they didn't mind hiring actors because basically actors are better educated than guys off the street and they have a facility for lying."

Slowly but surely, Wayne Knight began to secure acting jobs in television and the movies, including a bit part in *The Wanderers* (1979). Prior to being cast as Newman—during the 1980s and early 1990s—he appeared in various television roles and in such big-name movies as *Dirty Dancing*, *Born on the Fourth of July*, *JFK*, *Basic Instinct*, and *Jurassic Park*. None other than Oliver Stone, who is known to be somewhat irascible, directed two of the films: *Born on the Fourth of July* and *JFK*.

Knight took his talents overseas in 1985 after winning a job on a British sketch comedy program called *Assaulted Nuts*. He starred alongside Emma

Thompson, among others, but unfortunately the show didn't catch on and lasted only seven episodes. In 1992–1993, Knight tried his hand with another sketch comedy ensemble, this one in the United States: *The Edge*, for the FOX network. The show lasted only one season—nineteen episodes—but it gave its cast members, which included both Wayne Knight and Jennifer Aniston, some all-important visibility.

Reflecting on getting the part on *Seinfeld* thereafter, Knight said: "That was just a straight audition. I came in, did the audition, got the job for the one-off of Newman."

Knight was remarkably fortunate in that he landed a recurring role—simultaneous to playing Newman on *Seinfeld*—in another popular sitcom, *3rd Rock from the Sun* (1996–2001). He portrayed Officer Don Leslie Orville, whose love interest was alien Sally Solomon, played by Kristen Johnson. Knight's Newman character is among

Hello, Newman! The inimitable Wayne Knight.
Helga Esteb/Shutterstock.com

television's favorite sitcom villains—in fact, as far as many people are concerned, he's the number-one nemesis of all time. Jerry Seinfeld has said that nobody ever questioned why his character hated Newman so much. It was an organically poisonous relationship that simply worked. As testament to his enduring popularity, Wayne Knight was the subject of an Internet death hoax in 2014.

10

The Costanza Family

They Really Are a Scream

T he Costanzas, Frank and Estelle, are George's dysfunctional parents. They reside in the New York City borough of Queens in a private home on 1344 Queens Boulevard. And since the apple doesn't ordinarily fall far from the tree, it's no surprise that George is a thirty-something basket case who faults his parents for making him the man that he is—*the poor excuse for the man that he is*. Frank and Estelle squabble round the clock, with recurrent displays of screaming and yelling. Their son says that's the way it's always been in the Costanza household. In the company of the Costanza patriarch and matriarch—one or both of them—there is never a dull moment. Frank Costanza's red-hot temper, abrasive personality, and trailer-truckload of phobias and off-the-wall idiosyncrasies ensure verbal fireworks. As for Estelle Costanza, her insufferable and overbearing personality makes her radioactive wherever she happens to be.

Frank Talk

Frank Costanza was born in Tuscany, Italy, which precludes him from ever being elected president of the United States. Article II of the Constitution unequivocally states, "No person except a natural born citizen, or a citizen of the United States, at the time of the adoption of this Constitution, shall be eligible to the office of President." Surprisingly, this constitutional prohibition greatly rankles Frank and is a contributing factor—one among many—to his unfathomable reservoir of bitterness. He has no interest in politics because of this slight. "They don't want me! I don't want them!" Frank says with characteristic fury in "The Doll."

A Korean War veteran, Frank proudly served with the "Fighting 103rd." He was his outfit's cook and, according to him, quite proficient in his culinary endeavors. However, despite the fact that he considers his wife's cooking positively awful, he never once put on an apron and prepared a meal after he returned home to the States. "Your meatloaf is mushy, your salmon croquettes are oily, and your eggplant Parmesan is a disgrace to this house," he informs his wife in "The Fatigues." As it just so happens, Kramer is at the Costanzas' house attempting to convince the obstinate Frank to pick up a spoon and spatula again. He needs his help in preparing foods for a "Jewish Singles Night" that he has organized at the Knights of Columbus, of which Frank is a member.

Frank, though, remains traumatized by what happened during the Korean War. One day as cook for his frontline comrades, he over-seasoned six hundred pounds of beef that was, to put it mildly, past its prime. Men dropped like flies after consuming the meat—no vacancy signs hung on the latrines—and Frank could never get over this harrowing spectacle of war.

Frank speaks fluent Korean, the language of that faraway land, because of his past business dealings there. He sold religious statues. In his travels as a salesman, Frank encountered South Korean billionaire Sun Myung Moon, founder of the Unification Church, a.k.a. the Moonies. In "The Understudy," he recollects, "He bought two Jesus statues from me. He's a hell of a nice

Comedian Jerry Stiller gave us Frank Costanza and Festivus—enough said.

Everett Collection/ Shutterstock.com

guy!" Frank also had an affair with a Korean woman named Kim, whom he deeply loved. But the clash of cultures made a long-term relationship impossible. Kim's family could not abide Frank Costanza who, in violating local custom, wouldn't remove his shoes upon entering their home. He cited possible foot odor as the sole reason for him opting to keep on his shoes. In the same episode, Frank stumbles upon Kim—for the first time in almost a half-century—working in a Manhattan nail salon. Old memories and notions of "What might have been?" are resurrected. Kim laments, "Oh, Frank . . . so many years. If only you had taken your shoes off."

Decades have passed and Frank still has a thing about removing his shoes in other people's homes. A simple request for shoe removal touches a nerve—a psychological third rail—that ushers the man into a fit of apoplexy.

Frank's hobbies, which he takes very seriously, include playing old "Latin American" vinyl records and collecting issues of *TV Guide*. In the episode "The Cigar Store Indian," Frank and Estelle return home after an extended absence and are met by George, who is living there, and Jerry, who is visiting. Thumbing through the mail that has piled up, Frank senses something is not quite right.

One of his *TV Guide*s is missing. Since it was a past issue, Jerry wonders what all the fuss is about. He learns then and there that Frank collects them and has to break the bad news to him that Elaine had taken the *TV Guide* in question with her as subway reading material. "The nerve of that woman," Frank says. "Walking into my house, stealing my collectible!"

Frank's neuroses span a wide gamut. His innumerable fears and eccentricities define who he is. They dominate his every waking hour. Frank is deathly afraid of mice and rats. In fact, the mere mention of these pests is enough to initiate a panic attack. Paradoxically, he has a genuine affinity for squirrels, with their furry tails, even though they are members of the rodent family. They are warm and fuzzy looking when they are shucking peanuts and walking along electrical and telephone wires, but rat-like nonetheless.

In the episode "The Conversion," we discover just how much Frank cares for New York's squirrel population when George informs the folks that he is converting to the Latvian Orthodox religion. Naturally, Frank and Estelle aren't too happy about this development. Without knowing anything about the religion, they nonetheless believe their son is involved with a dangerous cult and, of course, brainwashed. "Is this the group that goes around mutilating squirrels?" Frank asks with genuine concern in his voice, while pleading with George to stay away from these noble creatures.

Although it sometimes seems otherwise, there is more to Frank Costanza than loud blustering and continuous wrangling. Yes, he's got a soft spot in his heart for squirrels, but he's also the man who inaugurated an alternative holiday to Christmas: Festivus. It is celebrated on December 23 as a counterpoint to the mad rush that accompanies the holiday season. "Many Christmases ago, I went to buy a doll for my son," Frank recounts in "The Strike." "I reached for the last one they had, but so did another man. As I rained blows upon him, I realized there had to be another way." And that way was Festivus, with traditions all its own.

Rather than a Christmas tree, the Costanzas have a bare, undecorated aluminum pole in the living room. Prior to the holiday meal there is an "airing of grievances." Frank describes how this works: "At the Festivus dinner, you gather your family around and tell them all the ways they have disappointed you over the past year." In stark contrast to Christmas, with its merrily benign traditions like singing carols, opening presents, and sipping eggnog, post dinner at the Festivus celebration involves "feats of strength." It is said, "Festivus is not over until the head of the household is wrestled to the floor or pinned."

The Costanzas, Frank and Estelle, are indeed an odd couple. In "The Caddy," when their son's boss, George Steinbrenner, comes to their house bearing heartbreaking tidings, we see the family dynamics at work. From the other side of the front door, "The Boss" reveals that their only son, George, is presumed dead. Estelle gasps and sheds tears at the news, but Frank's got something that can't wait for Mr. Steinbrenner—criticism. He vociferously complains about the recent trade of outfielder Jay Buhner and blasts Steinbrenner for being clueless.

George's Earth Mother

Unlike her Italian-born husband, Estelle Costanza's ethnicity and religious background are shrouded in some mystery. Once upon a time—pre-Festivus—the Costanza family celebrated Christmas. In "The Money," however, Estelle informs her son, "Your father wanted a Mercedes, but I won't ride in a German car." This heartfelt sentiment is perhaps a clue that she is Jewish.

Estelle Costanza clearly loves her only son. She's got his baby picture on display in the house. And how many mothers out there would attempt to seduce a judge, as she did in "The Finale," to help their son avoid a jail sentence? While Estelle was unsuccessful in her efforts to sway the judge's verdict with her feminine charms, one can't fault her for trying.

Estelle's relationship with her husband, Frank, is a never-ending storm. George says that he never once saw his mother laugh, although she has been known to smirk and giggle on occasion, including in "The Fusilli Jerry" when driving with Kramer, who is receiving periodic catcalls for his "Assman" vanity license plates. She doesn't respect Frank, and he doesn't respect her. They are perpetually at odds. Frank and Estelle stay together, nonetheless, as many unhappy couples are wont to do, out of habit.

The Costanzas do, however, briefly separate and contemplate joining the dating game, much to their son's disgust; George simply can't bear the notion of his parents being "out there" and playing the field alongside him. Also, with his parents separated, George would have to pay two holiday visits instead of one, which he finds unacceptable. "There is no way that this is gonna happen," George rants upon hearing the news of the breakup in "The Chinese Woman." "You hear me? *No way*! Because if you think I'm going to two Thanksgivings, you're out of your mind!"

Motherly love notwithstanding, Estelle has utter contempt for her son and makes it known every chance she gets. In "The Engagement," when George's fiancée, Susan, tells Mrs. Costanza that she loves her son very much, Estelle replies incredulously, "You *do*?" and then inquires, "May I ask *why*?" She is constantly interfering in George's life, including his romantic liaisons. In "The Cigar Store Indian," Estelle has no problem spilling the beans on George's ruse with a girlfriend named Sylvia—that their home in Queens is also *his* home—by telling her: "George doesn't work. He's a bum. That's why he lives at home with us."

In "The Contest," Estelle injures her back and is hospitalized after accidentally catching George boxing the trouser mouse. "I come home and find my son treating his body like it was an amusement park!" she cries. In light of this indiscretion, she wants George to see a psychiatrist. In "The Conversion," Estelle

Jerry Stiller and Estelle Harris, who breathed incredible life into the perpetually bickering Frank and Estelle Costanza.   *s_bukley/Shutterstock.com*

is visibly upset at George's decision to convert to the Latvian Orthodox religion—to win the heart of Sasha, who is only permitted to date members of her own faith—and matter-of-factly queries her son, "Why can't you do anything like a normal person?" and—again—suggests he seek psychiatric counsel.

Estelle is definitely hard to please. She considers George's best friend's parents, Morty and Helen Seinfeld, a pair of snobs who think they are too good for the Costanzas. When the Seinfelds cite previous plans, which they do not have, as a convenient subterfuge to circumvent a Costanza dinner invitation in "The Raincoats," her negative opinion of the couple is reinforced. The moment Estelle discovers the truth—that Morty and Helen deliberately blew off the Costanzas' gathering—she characteristically expresses her disdain in no uncertain terms: "I never liked those Seinfelds anyway. He's an idiot altogether!"

While Estelle is renowned for finding fault with both her husband and son—and just about everybody else—she displays genuine fondness for Kramer, so much so that it riles her jealous husband. In "The Fusilli Jerry," Estelle accepts Kramer's invitation to chauffeur her home after cosmetic eye surgery and is convinced that the latter employed the same come-on—"stopping short"—that her husband Frank originated. Kramer, though, had merely struck a pothole and, as an instinctive and protective action, stuck out his arm in front of Estelle. Despite the Costanzas being separated at the time, Frank angrily confronts Kramer about utilizing his old move on Estelle.

While cohabitating, Frank and Estelle sleep in separate beds. In "The Money," the former explains that it's because of his wife's "jimmy arms." That is, Estelle's elbows are in constant motion while she's asleep. Resting alongside her is thus dangerous duty. In "The Junk Mail," Frank and Estelle get it on in Jerry's van—the one given to him by "Fragile" Frankie Merman.

Jerry Stiller: A Stiller Performer

Gerald Isaac Stiller is the actor who will be forever immortalized as Frank Costanza. He was born on June 8, 1927, in New York City to Austrian-Jewish and Russian-Jewish immigrants, William and Bella Stiller. The former drove a bus for a living, whereas the latter, a homemaker, raised "Jerry," as he was known in the family, and his three siblings: Arnold, Dorine, and Maxine.

Hardscrabble times were definitely the norm during Jerry Stiller's boyhood, particularly after the stock market crash in October 1929. "During the Depression, my father took me to vaudeville," Stiller recalled to *Esquire* magazine. "When we came home, we had no money. I remember my mother turning her pocketbook upside down. Not a penny. 'Go out and hack!' she screamed at my father. 'Nobody wants a cab,' he said. 'They can't afford it.' My mother kept at him. . . . As he headed for the door, he said to her, 'You hate vaudeville.' And she said, 'Maybe if I wasn't with you, I'd like it.' I remembered that all my life, and I would use it onstage with Anne [Meara, his wife and comedy partner]. The difference is our audience would laugh at it."

Jerry Stiller attended Seward Park High School on Manhattan's Lower East Side and was accepted into the University of Syracuse. He graduated in 1950 with a bachelor of science degree in speech and drama. "When I told my father I wanted to be an actor, he said, 'Why not a stagehand? You'll work every night,'" he recollected. Security above all else was a common mindset of the generation that survived the Great Depression.

While Stiller is primarily known as a comedian—and to younger generations will always be remembered as the man who played the perpetually petulant Frank Costanza on *Seinfeld* and the constantly conniving Arthur Spooner on *The King of Queens*—he has a rather extensive and diverse résumé.

His performance debut was not in a New York or Los Angeles comedy club like the Jerry named Seinfeld, but on stage alongside Burgess Meredith in the children's play *The Silver Whistle*, a fairy tale about a whistle with magical powers that has been lost by a princess. In the fledgling moments of his career, he also appeared in Kern and Hammerstein's *Show Boat* on the Chicago stage. His stage credits through the years include *Hurlyburly*, *The Ritz*, *Three Men on a Horse*, *The Three Sisters*, and *Much Ado About Nothing*.

Jerry Stiller, however, quickly realized that comedy was what he did best, what he most loved doing, and where he could actually earn a fair living. When he was accepted into the improvisational troupe known as the Compass Players, which subsequently became the well-known Second City ensemble, Stiller's career balloon took flight. He also met a fellow member of the Compass Players, Anne Meara, in 1953. They tied the knot a year later and Stiller and Meara were born—a husband-and-wife comedy team.

It didn't take very long for Stiller and Meara, the act, to be a familiar quantity in comedy clubs and in living rooms all across the country. Their long-running routine underscored the couple's differences, particularly in physical appearance and manner. Stiller was short—five four—while his wife is a couple of inches taller. He is Jewish and she is Irish-Catholic, which furnished endless fodder for their comedic interplay. Stiller and Meara performed on *The Ed Sullivan Show* thirty-six times through the years. This immensely popular variety show was a Sunday night institution that aired from 1948 to 1971, almost a quarter of a century, and got many relatively unknown guests welcome recognition that often propelled them to bigger and better things. Virtually everyone, it seemed, appeared on *The Ed Sullivan Show*, including Elvis Presley, the Beatles, and Barbra Streisand; Mickey Mantle, Willie Mays, and Wilt Chamberlain; George Carlin, Richard Pryor, and Rodney Dangerfield.

During the 1960s and early 1970s, television variety shows were in vogue and talented comedians, like Stiller and Meara, had no shortage of invitations to appear on the small screen. But by the late 1970s, the variety show was no longer a ratings grabber and was fast vanishing from the primetime landscape. The Stiller and Meara comedy act lost its most important venue and their career waned as a result.

Nevertheless, Jerry Stiller had little problem finding work and appeared in numerous television shows and movies. His pre-*Seinfeld* television credits include *Archie Bunker's Place* (on which Anne Meara was a regular cast member), *The Paul Lynde Show, Joe and Sons, Touched by an Angel,* and *The Stiller and Meara Show,* a pilot for a sitcom that aired in 1986 with Stiller playing a New York City deputy mayor married to a television commercial actress. Unfortunately, it never got beyond the pilot stage. Stiller's movie credits include *The Taking of Pelham One Two Three* (1974), *Airport 1975* (1974), *Hairspray* (1988), *Little Vegas* (1990), and *Highway to Hell* (1992).

His ticket to television immortality, though, was punched in 1993 when he was asked to audition for the role of Frank Costanza on *Seinfeld.* Veteran character actor John Randolph had originally played the part, but the *Seinfeld* brain trust were looking for someone more adept in the art of comedy. In an interview with *Esquire* magazine, Stiller remembered being out of work at the time and closing in on seventy years of age. The part asked him to play Frank Costanza as meek and the "Thurberesque husband" of Estelle. He had something else in mind, gave it a shot, and it worked like a charm. Stiller breathed life into the Frank Costanza character that fans will long remember and appreciate.

Jerry Stiller and Anne Meara have two children: actors Ben Stiller and Amy Stiller. In 2000, Simon & Schuster published the comedian's well-received memoir, *Married to Laughter: A Love Story Featuring Anne Meara.*

Estelle Harris: Non-Dulcet Tones

Estelle Nussbaum was born in New York City on April 4, 1928, to Polish-Jewish immigrants Isaac and Anna Nussbaum. While growing up on the gritty streets of old New York, Harris's parents owned and operated a candy store. The family subsequently moved to Tarentum, Pennsylvania, just northeast of Pittsburgh. Young Estelle attended Tarentum High School and recalls getting every part she auditioned for in school plays. She took on the comedic roles because she had an instinctual knack for making people laugh. Harris's motto—then as well as now—is that audiences remember you when you make them happy, and not when you make them miserable. In 1953, she married Sy Harris, whom she met at a dance, and promptly put thoughts of an acting career on ice.

Sy and Estelle Harris's marriage has endured more than a half-century and produced three children—Eric, Glen, and daughter Taryn, who is a retired police officer—plus three grandkids. While her children were growing up, Harris acted in mostly amateur theater and was content with that. Eventually, she worked in dinner theater and landed a few spots in television commercials. This visibility—with her one-of-a-kind high-pitched and raspy voice—inevitably led to bigger and better things.

In 1977, at the age of forty-nine, Estelle Harris received her first movie credit: Irma in the movie *Looking Up*, starring Marilyn Chris and Dick Shawn. During the 1985–1986 season of the television sitcom *Night Court*, she appeared as a character called Easy Mary in three episodes. With encouragement from her son, Glen, a freelance publicist in Hollywood at the time, Harris auditioned for the role of George Costanza's mother on *Seinfeld*. The actress admits to being initially perplexed at the script of "The Contest," not realizing its premise and defining storyline. When she finally found out the nature of the episode's subject matter—masturbation—she was floored, not believing for a moment that the scrupulous television censors would green-light the show. As for the role of Estelle Costanza, which has brought her everlasting fame, Harris says that she appreciated the humor inherent in the character, but didn't relate to her on a human level. After all, with a husband like Frank and an only son who is the world's biggest loser, Estelle Costanza has it pretty bad. Suffice it to say, Jerry Stiller and Estelle Harris set the standard for "impossible parents" in the annals of the television sitcom. They also behaved as the orthodox television version of an elderly, bickering Jewish couple, despite the fact that Frank and Estelle Costanza's ethnicities were never specifically addressed. However, Larry David referred to George Costanza in an interview as half-Jewish, and Jason Alexander said that when Estelle Harris was cast as his mother, one mystery was cleared up. George had a Jewish mother.

Since *Seinfeld*, Estelle Harris has parlayed her fame into a winning formula. After showing what she's capable of as Estelle Costanza, she has landed numerous acting jobs. Estelle Harris's golden years have been golden indeed. Her singular voice has been in demand time and again on television and in the movies. For instance, she provided the memorable voice for Mrs. Potato Head in *Toy Story 2* (1999). Other notable voice work by Estelle includes Death's mother on *Family Guy*, Thelma on the animated Disney sitcom *The Proud Family* (2001–2005), and Old Lady Bear in the Disney animated film *Brother Bear* (2003). In 2015, Harris appeared as "Granny Smith" in an ad for Redd's Green Apple Ale.

The diminutive Harris—at five three—has also served as a spokesperson for Iams Senior Plus cat and dog foods. She's an inveterate canine aficionado and is wont to talk about her four-legged friends, including a beloved Maltese who bears a striking resemblance to Zsa Zsa Gabor.

In 2013, Harris announced that she had skin cancer successfully removed from her nose; she wanted her fans to know that it wasn't a nose job. And don't be surprised if you run into her at garage sales, for the actress is always on the prowl for antiques. Estelle Harris admits to this one addiction.

Morty and Helen Seinfeld

Meet the Parents

D espite being their contemporaries and, on the surface, having a great deal in common with Frank and Estelle Costanza, Morty and Helen Seinfeld are quite unlike them. Both as parents and human beings, Morty and Helen shine brightly when contrasted with the always-squabbling Costanzas from Queens. They are argumentative on occasion, set in their ways, and eccentric in their own right (especially Morty), but the Seinfelds are, by and large, agreeable sorts.

Not surprisingly, the Costanzas' behavior—with the relentless vitriol—turns their stomachs, so much so that they resort to making excuses to avoid them. Although they don't always achieve this in the Florida condo communities they call home, they prefer the serene life in their golden years. In the episode "The Raincoats," the Seinfelds avoid having dinner with the Costanzas—despite Estelle having prepared a big pot of paella—by telling George that they have other plans. They also reveal to Jerry for the very first time how they really feel about his best friend's folks. Plain and simply, they can't stand the sight of the Costanzas. As far as the Seinfelds are concerned, their incessant fighting makes being in their presence—even for a moment—very uncomfortable. Jerry is shocked to learn that they never, ever liked Frank and Estelle Costanza. He didn't think people of their age bracket could "detect abnormal behavior" among their own kind, as it were. Morty and Helen set him straight that they can indeed do so, especially where the Costanzas are concerned.

On the other hand, the Seinfelds think very highly of Jerry, their beloved only son, even if they aren't exactly sold on the merits of his profession and prospects of earning a decent living. While Morty is prone to flights of fancy, Helen is, typically, a voice of reason. She looks out for both her husband and her son and valiantly endeavors to keep them on the straight and narrow.

Raincoat Man

Jerry's dad, Morty Seinfeld, made a pretty fair living as a salesman, peddling raincoats for thirty-eight years. He takes particular pride in having invented the beltless trench coat, which he considers his grandest achievement in life. In "The Raincoats," we are clued in on the origins of this sartorial innovation. Morty, the story goes, went to work for a man named Harry Fleming in 1946. While in Fleming's employ, he invented a popular fashion in a roundabout way. After tripping over a toy of young Jerry's one night, and removing the belt on his trench coat to threaten his son with a whipping, Morty caught a glimpse of himself in the mirror. He liked what he saw: the beltless trench coat.

Morty Seinfeld is not one to rest on his laurels and lounge around, day in and day out, in his retirement. He is always thinking about ways to earn money—including resurrecting his beltless trench coat—the "Executive," as it was called—and constantly frets over dollars and cents. Saving a buck is job-one with him. In the episode "The Cadillac," during one of Jerry's visits to his parents' condo, Morty Seinfeld, the cost saver, struts his stuff, preparing to go out to dinner at 4:30 in the afternoon to catch the early-bird special: "a tenderloin, a salad, and a baked potato for $4.95."

Morty is civic-minded, too, and active in condo politics. He serves as the president of the tenant board. His term, unjustly, comes to an abrupt end after his son buys him a new Cadillac. Seeing Morty driving around in such an impressive set of wheels sets tongues wagging and the rumors flying in the condo complex. On the gossip grapevine, word spreads like wildfire that the Seinfelds are living well beyond their means. Worse than all that, a chorus of whispering voices say that Morty has sticky fingers and is pilfering from the tenant board's till to pay for his extravagant lifestyle.

In something of an ironic twist, Morty is impeached from his position as tenant board president when Mrs. Choate, a woman on the tenant committee that he was counting on to support him, unexpectedly changes her vote. In the episode "The Rye," none other than Jerry mugged this very lady on the streets of Manhattan, taking from her person by force a loaf of marble rye bread and calling her an "old bag" for good measure. Now, when Morty insists his son is not a thief, the newly empowered Mrs. Choate declares, "Like father, like son. I vote to impeach!"

Mother Knows Best

Helen Seinfeld is very protective of her family. "How could anyone not like him?" she's been heard to say in reference to her son. This maternal love for him goes a long way in explaining why Helen has utter disdain for Jerry's neighbor Newman. She despises the man and exhibits the same contempt toward him as Jerry does.

Helen worries about Jerry all the time. In "The Pen," even his plans to go scuba diving concern her. "What do you have to go underwater for? What's down there that's so special?" Her son's pithy response: "What's so special up here?"

Helen's mother, Nana, is still among the living and so is her loquacious brother, Leo. In the episode "The Pony Remark," Jerry inadvertently insults an elderly relation named Manya at a dinner at the latter's residence. Unbeknown to him, Manya had ponies when she was a young girl in Poland. She thus takes great umbrage when he recalls, while growing up, that he couldn't stand kids who owned ponies. In fact, Manya storms away from the dinner table, plunging the room into silence, and dies of a heart attack that evening.

The immediate aftermath of her passing unmasks a great deal about the Seinfeld family dynamics, including Helen's saintly patience with her son and Morty's profound tightfistedness. For starters, sticking around for Manya's funeral means that the Seinfelds lose their non-refundable "supersaver" airplane tickets for their return trip home. This pecuniary fact of life is foremost on Morty's mind. Meanwhile, Jerry is concerned that family and friends will blame him for the old woman's sudden passing. After all, she had just had a checkup and been given a clean bill of health from her doctor. Did stress in the wake of Jerry's pony remark augur the heart attack that killed her? Initially, Jerry is on the defensive, but not for very long. It's the conflict of interest that bothers him most of all. He's got a championship softball game on the very afternoon of the Manya's funeral service.

To underscore the Seinfeld family's mindset, which is in stark contrast with the Costanzas', Helen Seinfeld makes it clear that Jerry is under no obligation to attend the funeral service and, if he wants to participate in the softball game, that's what he should do—and she means it. She wouldn't hold his not showing up for the funeral against her son, and neither would Morty. In the big picture, Jerry can do no wrong in his parents' eyes, whereas George Costanza can do no right when it comes to his own.

Barney Martin: The Funny Cop

Barney Martin led a long, interesting, and diverse life. Landing the role of Jerry Seinfeld's father on *Seinfeld* was the proverbial icing on the cake—recognition, finally, for making us laugh for so many years in so many character roles. At the show's wrap party in 1998, Martin said, "Playing Jerry's dad was like having whipped cream on top of a mountain of ice cream."

In many respects, Barney Martin was the quintessential New Yorker—from a simpler but more rough-hewn snapshot in time. He was born in the New York City borough of Queens on March 3, 1923. Al Smith was New York's governor, and Warren G. Harding the president of the United States in the so-called "Roaring Twenties." Like many men of his generation, Martin fought overseas in World War II. He was a navigator for the U.S. Air Force. After the war he returned home to the States, entered the police academy, and was accepted into the New York City police force. His street savvy enabled him to rise through the ranks from beat cop to detective. Always known as a very funny and equally clever man while on the job, he wrote material for deputy police commissioners, spicing up their otherwise dour briefings with flashes of wit and humor. Martin put in twenty years as a cop while simultaneously freelancing as a television

Jerry with his folks, Morty and Helen Seinfeld (Barney Martin and Liz Sheridan).
NBC/Photofest

writer for the likes of *Name That Tune*, a game show, and *The Steve Allen Show*. In 1956, he even appeared as one of the impostors, Jack Bothwell #2, on the popular *To Tell the Truth*: "Will the real Jack Bothwell please stand up!"

Throughout the 1960s, Martin secured various roles on television, turning up in everything from *The Patty Duke Show* to *The Soupy Sales Hour* to *Car 54, Where Are You?* His TV parts in the early days of his acting career were typically small. He often played characters credited as the "deli owner," "bartender," and "handy man." Martin got his big break in show business when Mel Brooks cast him in *The Producers* in 1968. He played Goering in this classic comedy with its lead characters—blustering theatrical producer Max Bialystock and timorous accountant Leo Bloom—out to make a fortune by producing an absolute flop of a play called *Springtime for Hitler*. After his performance in this exceedingly funny and well-received movie, Martin began getting more substantial work. He frequently found roles on the Broadway stage, appearing in such plays as *South Pacific*, *The Fantasticks*, *How Now Dow Jones*, and *All American*. He is recognized for having breathed life into the role of Amos Hart, the ambitious and selfish Roxie's timid and vulnerable husband, in the Bob Fosse musical *Chicago*. He introduced the song "Mr. Cellophane."

Barney Martin's multiple television credits in the 1970s and 1980s included *The Odd Couple* (1970–1975), *Happy Days* (1974–1984), *The Tony Randall Show* (1976–1978), *Barney Miller* (1974–1982), *Benson* (1979–1986), and *Hill Street Blues* (1981–1987). He also played Ralph Marolla—Liza Minnelli's father—in the 1981 movie *Arthur*, starring Dudley Moore.

Interestingly, Martin came from an Irish-Catholic background, yet played with such honesty and humor Jerry's very Jewish dad. Countless Jewish *Seinfeld* fans, he once said, lauded him for the authenticity in his performance. They told him, too, how much he reminded them of their own fathers. Barney Martin's old New York upbringing—accent included—had an awful lot to do with his playing Morty Seinfeld so convincingly.

Sadly, Martin died of lung cancer on March 21, 2005, at the age of eighty-two. At the time of his death, he and his wife, Catherine, had been married for sixty-two years. The couple had two children—a son and a daughter. Passing away from cancer in 2002, Martin's daughter predeceased him by three years.

Liz Sheridan: Actress with a Cause

Liz Sheridan, who played Jerry's overprotective, unsmiling, but nonetheless doting mother, appeared in every season of *Seinfeld*. No other actor in a recurring role on the series could make such a claim. Sheridan was born on April 10, 1929, in the village of Rye, New York, on the shores of the Long Island Sound. She grew up in Larchmont, a leafy Westchester County town not far from the action of New York City.

Sheridan's parents were Frank Sheridan, a classical pianist, and Elizabeth Poole-James, a concert singer. Not surprisingly, she had the performing bug in her genes and began a career as a dancer and actress in the 1950s. While plying her trade in the big town's nightclubs and musicals, Sheridan, nicknamed "Dizzy," met a fellow aspiring thespian—then a total unknown in the business—by the name of James Dean. In 1952, after a brief romance, the pair got engaged but never quite made it to the altar.

In 2000, Liz Sheridan penned a memoir about her yearlong affair with the "rebel without a cause," entitled *Dizzy & Jimmy*. Its subtitle said it all: *My Life with James Dean . . . A Love Story*. Since its publication the book has garnered many favorable reviews. *Publishers Weekly* described *Dizzy & Jimmy* as follows:

> The effervescent Sheridan, known as Dizzy, was a dancer living in a theater district residence hall for aspiring actresses when she met the twenty-one-year-old Dean, an Indiana farm boy who had come to New York via Hollywood. Their instant attraction was soon consummated. Sheridan portrays Dean as a sometimes-corny romantic, who immediately began talking about being "together forever" and "who needed always to touch and be touched." While Dizzy managed to work, dancing in nightclubs all over New York or in summer stock musicals, Jimmy was either more unlucky or more choosy, and brooded over his disappointments.

While their love affair was short-lived, Sheridan remembered it as "just kind of magical." She said, "It was the first love for both of us." At one point the couple shared an apartment on Manhattan's Upper West Side—Jerry Seinfeld country—but couldn't keep up with the rent at the time because the pickings were pretty slim in their line of work. Sheridan recalled that Dean "looked kind of lost" when she first met him. "But Jimmy wasn't a rebel, and he had no cause," she said. "I think he was just shy."

Sheridan's relationship with the iconic James Dean piqued the interest of Jerry Seinfeld on the set of the show. She told *People* magazine that he approached her and asked, "So, you were a friend of James Dean, huh?" and occasionally queried, "Got any good Dean stories?" She has long hoped to see her memoir made into a movie. Appearing on BlogTalk Radio, she was asked, "If you had the ability to have dinner tonight with anyone in history, who would it be and why?" Her unexpected response: "Jerry Seinfeld. Why? I'd ask him to help me raise the money for my movie." Sheridan, however, was not holding out much hope for a get-together, noting how difficult it is to break through the Praetorian Guard protecting Seinfeld from everybody and anybody. "I don't even know how to get in touch with him," she said. "He's got so many people in front of him; you can't get to him. And I don't have his phone number."

A year later, Seinfeld finally touched base with Sheridan, but he gently turned her down. She recounted how their brief chat went: "I asked him if he was a good father. He said, 'I try.'" She then broached the subject about her movie idea. "I asked him if he would possibly be interested in the movie . . . about the book I wrote, *Dizzy & Jimmy*. And he said, 'It sounds terribly interesting' . . . like a project he would love to do, but he's so caught up in busy, busy, busy."

Liz Sheridan's many television credits through the years include *Kojak* (1973–1978); *Remington Steele* (1982–1987); *Family Ties*, *Murder, She Wrote*, *Blossom*; and *Alf*, in which she had a recurring role as neighbor Raquel Ochmonek. In 2008, she co-starred with Andy Griffith and Doris Roberts in the independent film *Play the Game*. A bit racy and even controversial to some, we find Grandpa Joe, played by Griffith, discovering the benefits of Viagra and getting back in the game with Edna Gordon, played by none other than Liz Sheridan. An octogenarian sex scene between Sheriff Andy Taylor and Helen Seinfeld?—well, it sounds like material for a *Seinfeld* episode.

It should also be noted that Sheridan, like Barney Martin, was not Jewish. Yet the acting duo made a very believable New York–born Jewish couple.

Liz Sheridan was married to jazz trumpeter and writer William Dale Wales from 1985 until his death in 2003. They had been together since 1960. The couple's union produced a daughter. At the time of her husband's passing, it was reported that he had left his wife on the hook for close to $80,000 in credit card debt, forcing her into personal bankruptcy and a "fresh start." Sheridan, nonetheless, took it all in stride, not looking for any sympathy. She says the three most important people in her life have been James Dean, her husband, and Jerry Seinfeld.

12

More Inhabitants of *Seinfeld* Land

Susan Ross, J. Peterman, and Uncle Leo

Susan Biddle Ross: Unlucky in Love

Susan Biddle Ross is an executive with NBC until she gets unceremoniously axed when her boss, Russell Dalrymple, spies George Costanza planting a wet one on her. Her parents are very well-to-do and saddled with ample baggage that she'd just assume the whole world didn't know about. We learn in the episode "The Cheever Letters" that her father once had a homosexual liaison with writer John Cheever, and that her mother has a penchant for hitting the bottle. She has a more or less normal brother named Rickey and a disabled aunt. Mr. Ross, his daughter says, "never laughs," and there's no evidence to the contrary. That's about the only thing he has in common with Estelle Costanza.

Susan meets Jerry and George for the first time in the episode "The Pitch." She is on hand at the executive meeting where the boys pitch their sitcom idea to the NBC brass. Right off the bat, Susan expresses her support for Jerry's observational brand of humor and believes that crafting a pilot about the so-called "show about nothing" is worth a try. George, meanwhile, is absolutely convinced that Susan took a shine to him during the meeting. The pair hook up afterward and, a short while later, turn up at Jerry's apartment. The beginning of a turbulent, unpredictable relationship is at hand. There, too, she's introduced to Kramer, setting in motion a series of unfortunate events.

After taking a healthy swig of Jerry's milk—without checking its expiration date—Kramer upchucks on the star-crossed woman. From that moment on, Susan exhibits a real disdain for him, not in the least appreciating the man's uniqueness and colorful personality. In fact, the Susan–Kramer karma is downright combustible. In the episode "The Bubble Boy," Kramer accidentally sets fire to her father's country cabin—one that had been in the family for generations—with a Cuban cigar given to him by George, who, in turn, had gotten it from none other than Mr. Ross. Kramer ultimately comes between Susan and Mona, her lesbian lover, in "The Smelly Car." Susan had taken up with Mona after her initial breakup with George, which led him to wonder whether he was responsible for her *switching sides*. Susan tells him in no uncertain terms that the notion is preposterous, but George wants answers to the big relationship questions: "If you and Mona were ever to dance, how do you decide who leads? I mean . . . do you take turns? Do you discuss it beforehand? How does that work?" Susan dismisses George's queries as idiotic, which sums up the nature of their on-again, off-again relationship.

In their first go-round as a couple, George quickly tires of Susan as his girlfriend. In the episode "The Virgin," he feels that his independence is at stake and starts brainstorming ways to break up. Jerry reminds George that Susan is a big supporter of their potential show with NBC, and that if he dumps her, the chances of a pilot ever being filmed would be slim to none. George's idea is to get Susan to dump him. He tells Jerry that she's got a major crush on David Letterman, and that if he could get the comedian to meet with Susan, his troubles would be solved. That is, Susan would fall head over heels for Letterman, leaving George the odd man out. Jerry doesn't think much of this plan.

In the episode "The Pick," George and Susan's boyfriend-girlfriend status goes back and forth like a ping-pong ball. George, after begging for reconciliation, realizes that he made a mistake and that he was better off unfettered. He comes up with a foolproof plan to end their relationship once and for all. George will have her catch him in the act of picking his nose. At Monk's Café, George informs Jerry and Elaine that the pick worked like a charm. The look on Susan's face upon catching him in the act spoke volumes, he gleefully reported. Susan and George would get together yet again—after her lesbian encounter— and forge what would be a more lasting relationship. George, in fact, proposes to Susan and they set the wedding date. Susan has a lot of relatives, so there will be close to two hundred guests at their reception. As the blissful day approaches, however, George feels like a trapped animal and is desperately searching for some kind of graceful, or even non-graceful, exit from his predicament. But Susan isn't going to let something so mundane as a nose pick, or even a pre-nuptial agreement, preclude her from walking down the aisle. Her untimely death after ingesting toxic glue from her wedding invitation envelopes is the one thing that could derail her big day, *and it did.*

Heidi Swedberg: Death Becomes Her

Heidi Swedberg, who played George Costanza's girlfriend and then fiancée, will always be remembered for her role as Susan Ross, particularly her totally unexpected and entirely unsentimental death scene. In the *Seinfeld* universe, her character's sudden passing was shocking and hilariously funny to many viewers, and not so hilarious to others, who felt that the show had somehow breached the line of good taste. But that's what *Seinfeld* did all the time by ignoring traditional sitcom rules and crossing all kinds of lines.

Heidi was born on March 3, 1966, in Honolulu, Hawaii, to parents Kay and Jim Swedberg. Her father, a laser physicist, later moved the family to New Mexico, where Heidi attended high school. After graduating in 1984, she ventured to Kentucky to try her hand in the acting business, at the Actor's Theatre of Louisville. Soon

The Not Necessarily Top Ten *Seinfeld* Fictional Movie References

10. *Prognosis Negative* ("The Dog")
9. *Blimp: The Hindenburg Story* ("The Puerto Rican Day")
8. *The Other Side of Darkness* ("The Comeback")
7. *Ponce de Leon* ("The Dog" and "The Movie")
6. *Death Blow* ("The Little Kicks")
5. *Checkmate* ("The Movie")
4. *Chunnel* ("The Pool Guy")
3. *Chow Fun* ("The Pool Guy")
2. *Rochelle, Rochelle* ("The Movie")
1. *Sack Lunch* ("The English Patient")

after getting her feet wet, Heidi Swedberg won roles in both television and the movies, beginning with a part in the hit series *Matlock*, starring Andy Griffith. The year was 1989 and she played Sister Katherine, a nun. A year later, she was cast as Sister Agnes in the movie *Too Much Sun*, a comedy starring Alan Arbus and Robert Downey Jr. Swedberg also won parts in *Kindergarten Cop* (1990), starring Arnold Schwarzenegger, and *Hot Shots!* (1991), a parody of *Top Gun* starring Charlie Sheen. Her television credits in the 1990s include *Northern Exposure* (1990–1995); *Brooklyn Bridge* (1991–1993); *Murder, She Wrote*; *Star Trek: Deep Space Nine*; and *Touched by an Angel* (1994–2003).

Heidi Swedberg appeared in twenty-eight episodes of *Seinfeld*. For a little perspective, the characters of Frank Costanza and Estelle Costanza appeared in twenty-seven episodes, Morty Seinfeld in twenty episodes, and Helen Seinfeld in twenty-one episodes.

Swedberg is married to Philip Holahan and has two daughters. Neither one is named "Seven," in honor of Mickey Mantle's number. While still acting, she is devoting a great deal of her time to teaching music to children. She's an accomplished ukulele player who travels extensively and hosts various clinics.

"I grew up with music in my life," Heidi Swedberg told *Dadnabbit*. "Everyone in my family was musical, and I have one sister who is a musician. We all sang together all the time—in the car, everywhere. I think that's part of how you keep four girls busy without spending any money." Swedberg described her work and why it's essential to stay with music and not, as so many people do, jettison it in adulthood: "When we reach adulthood, we tend to leave music behind. You're in band or choir when you're younger, but then you go out into the 'real world,' and you leave performing to the professionals. You don't make your own anymore."

The J Man

Jacopo Peterman, a.k.a. J. Peterman, is Elaine's eccentric and impulsive boss at J. Peterman Catalog, a company specializing in distinctive clothing and accessories. The J. Peterman Catalog descriptions of their myriad attire are typically flowery and verbose. The company's owner sounds equally flowery and verbose in his everyday conversation at the office and out and about on the town.

J. Peterman, the man, is unconventional to say the least. He collects unusual things, like a piece of cake from the 1937 wedding of the former King Edward VIII and Wallis Simpson, which he purchased for the not-inconsiderable sum of $29,000. In the episode "The Frogger," we gain further insight into Peterman's unusual personality when Elaine—not knowing at first that it's an invaluable piece of pastry—eats the slice of cake and then replaces it with an Entenmann's brand cake from the supermarket. When Peterman has the cake appraised by a man named Lubeck, a vintage pastry authority, both he and his employee are in for a rude awakening. The scene takes place in Peterman's office.

> Peterman: All right, Lubeck. How much is she worth?
>
> Lubeck: I'd say about two-nineteen.
>
> Peterman: Ha, ha, ha, ha, ha! $219,000! Lubeck, you glorious titwillow. You just made me a profit of $190,000.
>
> Lubeck: No, $2.19. It's an Entenmann's.
>
> Peterman: Do they have a castle at Windsor?
>
> Lubeck: No, they have a display case at the end of the aisle.

To ensnare the guilty party, Peterman investigates the Entenmann's cake switcheroo by examining surveillance camera footage from his office. Of course, the guilty party is Elaine. But rather than get angry and fire her on the spot, Peterman gently tells her what her punishment will be. "Do you know what happens to a butter-based frosting after six decades in a poorly ventilated English basement?" he asks Elaine, who doesn't have a clue. "Well, I have a feeling that what you are about to go through is punishment enough. Dismissed."

Peterman is very tolerant of his employees and gives them a lot of latitude. He didn't fire Elaine for the wedding cake debacle and loss of his twenty-nine-thousand-dollar investment. He didn't send her packing for abusing the company credit card. Peterman kept Elaine on the job despite her testing positive for opium. (This was due to the poppy seeds in her muffins.) And he didn't say sayonara after he left her in charge of the catalog and she put the "Urban Sombrero" on its cover—an absolute fiasco. However, he did give Elaine her walking papers for not liking *The English Patient*, but then threw her a lifeline when she agreed to visit and live for a spell in the Tunisian desert, where the movie was filmed.

J. Peterman is a peripatetic kind of guy. He routinely jet-sets around the world. When Elaine is handed the reins of the catalog (in "The Foundation"), Peterman is already in Burma. "Elaine, I'll be blunt," he says. "I'm burnt out. I'm fried. My mind is as barren as the surface of the moon. I can run that catalog no longer."

John O'Hurley: Renaissance Man

Fans frequently recognize John George O'Hurley as Elaine's impulsive and avant-garde boss, J. Peterman. Over a period of three years, he appeared as the eccentric Peterman in twenty episodes of *Seinfeld*. O'Hurley remarked in a Forbes.com video that he fashioned Peterman's rather unique speaking voice and delivery by combining "'40s radio drama" with "a bit of a bad Charles Kuralt." His general inspiration for the part was the real J. Peterman catalog. The actor, in fact, was asked to pore over the catalog before breathing life into the character. O'Hurley had never before

In "The Secret Code," George and Elaine pay their respects to J. Peterman (John O'Hurley) after the passing of his mother, whose last word—"Bosco" (George's ATM code)—left Peterman baffled.

NBC/Photofest

heard of the mail-order company, but admits to being bemused with what he described as the catalog's "long Hemingway-style adventure stories about an Oxford button-down." Thus was born J. Peterman, the verbose adventurer, of *Seinfeld*.

There is a lot that fans don't know about the actor who infused so much life into this memorable character. O'Hurley was born on October 9, 1954, in Kittery, Maine. His father, John O'Hurley, Sr., was an ear, nose, and throat surgeon. Young John attended the prestigious Kingswood Oxford School in West Hartford, Connecticut, a secular private high school with rigid standards. Accepted into Providence College in Rhode Island, O'Hurley graduated with a bachelor of arts degree in theatre in 1976.

A career in acting beckoned as John O'Hurley found work in daytime soap operas: *The Edge of Night*, *As the World Turns*, *General Hospital*, and *The Young and the Restless*. His eclectic résumé includes numerous television credits, the hosting of the popular game show *Family Feud*, and voice work that utilizes one of his greatest assets. He's partnered with professional ballroom dancer Charlotte Jorgensen on *Dancing with the Stars*, hosted an infomercial for an air purifier, and played King Arthur in the St. Louis, Las Vegas, and Los Angeles productions of Monty Python's *Spamalot*. O'Hurley has voiced King Neptune on *SpongeBob SquarePants*, hosted Purina's *National Dog Show* for more than a decade, and narrated Coors Light beer commercials.

Presently, John O'Hurley is a large investor in the real J. Peterman Company, from which the *Seinfeld* character was drawn. After a bankruptcy in 1999, the business resurrected its brand in 2001. Its founder, John Peterman, started the company in 1987 with five hundred dollars and an unsecured loan of twenty thousand dollars. Originally, Peterman—who was briefly a minor league baseball player in the Pittsburgh Pirates farm system—peddled a solitary item: a cowboy coat that was described as a "horseman's duster." By 1999, the company was a $75 million concern, but a too-aggressive expansion portended its demise. "When you strike out or make an error, if you think about it, you're gonna do the exact same thing again," Peterman told NBC. "So I learned to forget about my mistakes." His company—in its second incarnation—is credited with coining the marketing term "Red Wednesday Sale," or "Black Friday's Impetuous Cousin," on the day before Thanksgiving.

As if that hasn't been enough to keep him busy, John O'Hurley is an accomplished pianist who, with cellist Marston Smith, has produced two well-received CDs: *Peace of Our Minds* and *Secrets from the Lake*. The man has even authored three books: *It's Okay to Miss the Bed on the First Jump: And Other Life Lessons Learned from Dogs*; *Before Your Dog Can Eat Your Homework, First You Have to Do It*, which became a *New York Times* bestseller; and *The Perfect Dog*, a children's book.

Say Uncle

Uncle Leo is Jerry's mother's brother. He has a son named Jeffrey, who works for the New York City Parks Department. Uncle Leo is very proud of him and constantly sings his praises to his nephew Jerry, much to the latter's annoyance. In the episode "The Pen," Uncle Leo is married to Stella, but subsequently goes out on dates and moves in with a woman named Lydia.

Uncle Leo is extremely demonstrative with greetings and takes offense when others don't reciprocate. With arms outstretched, his catchphrase upon encountering his nephew is "Jerry! Hello!" A terrible nightmare revolves around Uncle Leo's effusive greeting and plagues Jerry in "The Bookstore." Uncle Leo is in prison and doing pull-ups. The word "Jerry" is spelled out on his left hand, and the word "Hello" is spelled out on his right hand. The dream is inspired by Jerry's guilt for ratting out his shoplifting uncle in Brentano's, a local bookstore.

Uncle Leo's words "If anyone betrays me, I never forget" rattle around his brain while in the Land of Nod. In this episode we also discover that Uncle Leo has a criminal record—a mysterious conviction for a "crime of passion." When Jerry confronts his uncle about what he saw in the bookstore, a surfeit of insight into Uncle Leo's character is gleaned:

> Jerry: Leo, I saw you in Brentano's yesterday.
>
> Leo: Why didn't ya say hello?
>
> Jerry: Because you were too busy stealing a book.
>
> Leo: You still say hello!

After Jerry warns him that he could get arrested for his thieving ways, Uncle Leo explains why that would never happen. He is, after all, an old man, and he'd play the part to the hilt. He'd appear addle-brained and get a pass for his transgression. Uncle Leo is also paranoid with regard to anti-Semitism. In "The Shower Head," when he gets a medium-cooked hamburger that he ordered medium rare, he shoots from the lip, "I bet that cook is an anti-Semite." When Jerry replies, "He has no idea who you are," Leo is unconvinced: "They don't just overcook a hamburger, Jerry."

After his lunch with Uncle Leo at Monk's Café, Jerry is a guest on *The Tonight Show with Jay Leno*, which is in New York. The host takes note that Jerry has brought an unusual entourage to the taping, and the latter singles out his Uncle Leo. Jerry then riffs on his uncle's habit of blaming every mishap on anti-Semitism: "The spaghetti's not al dente? Cook's an anti-Semite. Loses a bet on a horse. Secretariat? Anti-Semitic. Doesn't get a good seat at the temple. Rabbi? Anti-Semite."

Len Lesser: Lesser Is Better

For decades, Len Lesser appeared in a wide range of plays, television shows, and movies. While his large, piercing eyes, hawk-like nose, and tough-looking visage were a recognizable quantity, very few people could match the face with a name. As a man pushing seventy, Lesser would, at long last, achieve much-deserved recognition for being both a fine actor and bona fide funnyman. His role as Uncle Leo on *Seinfeld* put him on the map for all time, even though he'd been around seemingly forever, turning up on such television shows as *The Munsters* (1964–1966), *The Wild Wild West* (1965–1969), *Get Smart*, *The Monkees* (1966–1968), *Bonanza*, *Kojak*, and *The Love Boat*. His movie credits included *Kelly's Heroes* (1970) and *The Outlaw Josey Wales* (1976), both starring Clint Eastwood, and *Papillon* (1973) with Steve McQueen and Dustin Hoffman. Lesser's Uncle Leo took the popular sitcom character—that of the oddball relative—to an especially amusing stratosphere. Employing a testily bristling demeanor in the role, he also added a demonstrable New York Jewish touch to the ensemble.

Len Lesser as the incomparable Uncle Leo, enjoying a bite to eat with his
favorite nephew in "The Shower Head."   *NBC/Photofest*

"Uncle Leo became a whole new thing for me," Lesser told the *National Post*,
a Canadian newspaper. "After sweating out every job, my God. Now it's everywhere I go. I was at the Wailing Wall in Jerusalem, watching people put notes
in the wall, it's an esoteric day, very silent, very nice. All of a sudden: 'Uncle Leo,
where's the watch?'"

He was born Leonard King Lesser on December 3, 1922, in the New York
City borough of the Bronx. His father, a Polish émigré, ran a mom-and-pop gro-
cery store. At the tender age of fifteen, Lesser entered the City College of New
York and graduated four years later with a bachelor's degree. He enlisted in the
United States Army in the aftermath of the Pearl Harbor attack on December
7, 1941, and saw action in the Pacific Theater. Upon his return home from his
World War II service, Lesser studied the acting craft and soon began appearing
on stage. He married actress Janice Burrell in 1954; the union produced two
children, a boy and a girl. The couple divorced in 1982.

Len Lesser passed away on February 16, 2011, at the age of eighty-eight.
Upon learning of his death, Jason Alexander tweeted a tribute to the man who
will long be remembered as Jerry's Uncle Leo: "Len was a tremendous guy. He
was a smart actor-comedian who knew exactly what he was doing in the creation
of Uncle Leo. I enjoyed many wonderful conversations with Len, who was so
openly grateful to be part of our show and so humble about his stunning contribution to it. . . . 'Hellooo, Uncle Leo.' And goodbye. Sleep well. Much love."

13

And the Rest

Friends, Enemies, and More

Jerry, George, Elaine, and Kramer regularly interact with a cast of characters that includes both old and new friends, myriad acquaintances, steadfast nemeses, romantic pursuits, hard-nosed bosses, assorted businesspersons, and unconventional professional types, too. Their intermingling with all of the above adds further color to their life and times, and supplies even greater insight into their peculiar personalities and unending flights of fancy.

Good Friends Are for Keeps

Friends come in all ages, hues, and sizes. As for the last, there is temperamental little person Mickey Abbott, a good pal of Kramer's. In the episode "The Stand-In," the pair meet for the first time when they are both employed as stand-ins on the soap opera *All My Children*. Both Mickey and Kramer have acting ambitions and sometimes pursue unusual thespian opportunities, including showcasing their theatrical talents as hospital patients diagnosed with specified diseases in "The Burning." For the benefit of medical students in training, Mickey suffers from bacterial meningitis, and Kramer from gonorrhea. Mickey also works as a department store elf alongside Kramer's Santa Claus at Christmastime in "The Race." He marries Karen in "The Yada Yada," but has been married more than once. Mickey's also got children from prior relationships. His father—a dentist who accused Jerry of being an "anti-Dentite"—and mother are both normal-sized.

Little person actor Danny Woodburn played Mickey Abbott on *Seinfeld* with feisty flamboyance and more than a degree of lovability. Born on July 26, 1964, in Philadelphia, Pennsylvania, Woodburn is a graduate of his hometown's Temple University School of Film and Theater. The pint-sized actor is an untiring advocate for little people issues and serves on the Screen Actors Guild Performers with Disabilities Committee.

In stark contrast with the spirited and usually well-meaning Mickey Abbott, there is Jack Klompus, Morty Seinfeld's *friend*—for lack of a better description—and neighbor down in the Florida condo community they both call home. Klompus is ill tempered and oily, and has got some real issues with his sometime chum Morty. He is married to the equally obnoxious Dorothy and is the proud

Actor Danny Woodburn, who infused the character of Kramer's little friend, Mickey Abbott, with big heart.   *Helga Esteb/Shutterstock.com*

owner of a space pen—the kind that the astronauts use. At one point in the episode "The Pen," he insists on giving said pen to Jerry, which augurs a touchy to-do between the Seinfeld and Klompus families.

When Jerry bestows upon his father an expensive Cadillac Fleetwood in the episode "The Cadillac," Klompus absolutely believes that Morty Seinfeld came by the car in a more nefarious way. He spreads rumors that the Seinfeld patriarch, while serving as president of the condo's board of directors, has been dipping into the communal till. Due to raging gossip that the Seinfelds are mysteriously living beyond their means, Morty is impeached from the board. Humiliated, Morty and Helen Seinfeld are compelled to leave their Florida residence under a cloud of suspicion.

A Jack Klompus footnote worth noting here is that in the episode "The Money," it is revealed that he purchased Morty Seinfeld's Cadillac from him for six thousand dollars— it was worth at least five times that amount—because Jerry's folks felt their son needed the money. Jerry promptly buys it back from Klompus—who insists on fourteen thousand dollars and a tidy profit of eight thousand dollars—to seal the deal. Prior to delivery, the latter accidentally drives it into a swamp in Florida's "Alligator Alley," but—in keeping with his less-than-exemplary character—refuses to pay for the car's repairs.

Comedian Sandy Baron breathed life—as only he could—into the unctuous Jack Klompus role. He was born Sanford Beresofsky on May 5, 1937 in Brooklyn, New York. Baron got his start in the Catskill Mountain resort venues, which were very popular in the 1950s and 1960s, particularly for up-and-coming Jewish comedians. His success there led to roles on Broadway and in both television and the movies. In 1964, at the height of the Civil Rights movement, the comedian released an album entitled *The Race! Race!* Its jacket described the contents as a "rollicking comedy album about hate, prejudice, bigotry and other such nonsense." Baron passed away from complications of emphysema on January 21, 2001, at the age of sixty-four.

Bryan Cranston, *Seinfeld's* Dr. Tim Whatley and *Breaking Bad's* Walter White, receives his star on the Hollywood Walk of Fame in 2013.   *Jaguar PS/ Shutterstock.com*

After the rumpled, hoarse-voiced Jack Klompus comes Dr. Tim Whatley, the "Dentist to the Stars," who periodically works on Jerry's smile and is considered a friend as well. Whatley dates Elaine in "The Label Maker," but that doesn't turn out well. She accuses him of being a "re-gifter" for giving to Jerry the label maker that she had previously given to him. Whatley converts to Judaism in "The Yada Yada," which especially irks Jerry, who feels the conversion has been done for all the wrong reasons. That is, Jerry believes his dentist and friend did so solely to make Jewish jokes with impunity.

Dr. Tim Whatley is, too, the man who inadvertently gives George a gift-giving inspiration in the episode "The Strike." He had given to George, and the others in attendance at his Hanukkah party, cards stating that a donation had been made to a charity, The Children's Alliance, in their honor. After being informed that he had to give Christmas gifts to his co-workers at the office—a holiday tradition at his then place of employment, Kruger Industrial Smoothing—George "pulled a Whatley," only in his case he decided to *invent* a charity. The so-called Human Fund, in effect, was George's attempt to avoid spending money on his co-workers.

Finally, while under the effects of anesthesia in "The Jimmy," Jerry frets that his libidinous doctor-friend may have violated him during a tooth-filling procedure. Prior to that alleged violation of his person, he had noticed that Whatley had *Penthouse* magazines in the office waiting room.

Bryan Cranston played Dr. Tim Whatley. He was born on March 7, 1956, and achieved his stardom in the post-*Seinfeld* universe. Cranston starred in the FOX network's popular sitcom *Malcolm in the Middle* as the hapless father, Hal, appearing in all 151 episodes during the series run (2000–2006). His supreme claim to fame came a couple of years later in the AMC network crime-drama *Breaking Bad* (2008–2013), in which he had the leading role of Walter White. For his efforts, Cranston won an Emmy award for "Outstanding Lead Actor in a Drama Series" four times. He says he based the bedraggled, harried character on his own father, who had abandoned the family when Bryan was just eleven years old. Living on their California poultry farm, Cranston was raised, in part, by his grandparents.

Romance With and Without Exclamation Points

Outside of Susan Ross, who gets the relationship gold medal for longevity, there is David Puddy, the winner of the silver. While Puddy's relationship with Elaine endures over time, it takes the meaning of "on-again, off-again" to absurd heights, as the couple break up and get back together on a regular basis. Puddy is Jerry's auto mechanic. In "The Fusilli Jerry," he learns a sexual technique, "The Move," from his client, too, which he promptly tries on Elaine—who, in turn, recognizes it as Jerry's handiwork. (She had, after all, dated him in the past.)

Puddy is tall, as handy as they come, and speaks in a deep monotone. In other words, he is very masculine from Elaine's vantage point, which goes a long way in excusing some of his more irritating idiosyncrasies. And indeed, Puddy does things that exasperate her to no end, including painting his face and body to show his support for his favorite hockey team, the New Jersey Devils. He is also a germophobe and believes in God. Elaine, on the other hand, is a devout atheist. Her lack of faith doesn't concern Puddy in the least; after all, as he puts it, *he's* not the one going to Hell. Puddy may not be an intellectual, but he gets a job as a car salesman, which Elaine feels is a major step up—from auto mechanic—on the career ladder. The role of David Puddy was ideal for actor Patrick Warburton, whose square jaw and deadpan delivery made his recurring character one of the more popular on *Seinfeld*. Born on November 14, 1964, in Paterson, New Jersey, Warburton's overly serious demeanor found him in big demand, particularly as a voice-over talent. He supplies the voice of Joe Swanson on *Family Guy* and can be heard on video games and television commercials. After playing *Seinfeld*'s Puddy, he was one of the stars of the NBC sitcom *Rules of Engagement* (2007–2013). In his patented straight-faced style, Warburton played Jeff in this popular romantic-comedy series.

Elaine also dates Jake Jarmel, her employer Pendant Publishing's star author, multiple times. In "The Sniffing Accountant," we learn that Jake doesn't care much for exclamation points, which leads to a serious row and breakup with his lady friend, who feels they have an important place in the writing game. Jake doesn't appreciate Elaine's seeming lack of commitment in their second relationship go-round. In "The Opposite," he can't understand how she could have possibly purchased Juicy Fruit candy after receiving the awful news that he had been hospitalized as a result of a serious accident. On the fashion side, Jarmel sports a pair of unique eyeglasses that he purposely purchased in Malaysia so that they would be one-of-a-kind in the States. Marty Rackham played Jake Jarmel in three episodes. He first appeared on *Seinfeld* as an LAPD officer in the episode "The Trip," inviting both Jerry and George to get into his police cruiser.

Enemy Territory

Aside from the enemy to top all enemies, Newman, there are plenty of other dissenters in the *Seinfeld* universe. Kenny Bania, a hack comedian, actually thinks very highly of Jerry. Jerry, however, feels that Bania is a "timeslot hit" in that he typically follows him onstage. Also irritating to Jerry is Bania's childlike enthusiasm, bad material, and gushing catchphrases like "It's the best, Jerry! The best!" Busy character actor Steve Hytner unquestionably left his mark as Kenny Bania. His post-*Seinfeld* television credits are also considerable, including recurring roles in such series as *Working, Roswell,* and *The Bill Engvall Show.*

"Crazy" Joe Davola is hands down the most dangerous of nemeses in *Seinfeld* Land. Suffering from major psychological problems, the man has a penchant for violence. Davola is a writer who worked for NBC and came to believe that Jerry was responsible for a script of his getting rejected by the powers-that-be. He thereafter became a stalker, endeavoring at all costs to make Jerry pay for his presumed crime. While an emotional basket case, Davola is, contrarily, a fine physical specimen. He lifts weights and practices the martial arts. While venturing through Central Park on one of his stalking missions in the episode "The Opera," Davola is confronted by young, would-be muggers, who are effortlessly dispatched. In the episode "The Pitch," he even kicks Kramer in the head.

Davola also dates Elaine, who doesn't realize that he is the same guy who is so intent on doing Jerry harm. When she learns that her Joe and Jerry's Joe are one and the same, she discovers that she, too, is in danger. In a frighteningly close call, Elaine escapes from the psychotic Davola's apartment by blasting him in the face with Binaca, a flavored breath spray. He subsequently attempts a full-scale attack on Jerry, but—fortunately for all concerned—breaks his own leg in the process. Peter Crombie portrayed the unhinged "Crazy" Joe Davola. Prior to his appearances on *Seinfeld*, he played "Subway Vigilante" Bernhard Goetz in the *American Playhouse* production of "The Trial of Bernhard Goetz."

Lloyd Braun has the dual distinction of being both nemesis and boyfriend. That is, he's George's adversary from childhood and Elaine's boyfriend for a short spell in the present. Foremost, George deeply resents Braun because he believes—with ample evidence—that his parents would have preferred Lloyd as their son over him.

Elaine, though, has no such past history with Lloyd Braun to cloud the present. She is impressed that he works as a close advisor to Mayor Dinkins, who is running for reelection. In "The Non-Fat Yogurt," Elaine even offers him a potential policy position—making New Yorkers wear name tags—that she hopes will become part of the mayor's platform. Lloyd, in fact, passes it on to the mayor and it is formally adopted. The name tag plan, however, is widely ridiculed by the public, and Lloyd becomes the fall guy. He loses both his prestigious position and his sanity, spending time in a mental institution. Lloyd becomes very paranoid after his mental breakdown. In "The Serenity Now," he takes a job with Frank Costanza's newest business venture—selling computers via the telephone—and finds himself again in competition with George. While believed to be doing a bang-up job as a salesman working out of Frank's garage, it turns out that Lloyd Braun never even plugged in his telephone, nor had he sold a single computer.

Two actors assayed the role of Lloyd Braun: Peter Keleghan (the character's first appearance, in "The Non-Fat Yogurt") and Matt McCoy ("The Gum" and "The Serenity Now").

In and Out of the Workplace

Next to J. Peterman, George Steinbrenner ranks as the most colorful boss in *Seinfeld* Land. He is George Costanza's ultimate superior while George is employed with the New York Yankees as assistant to the traveling secretary. Steinbrenner is blustery and impulsive—very much so in decision-making, including firing managers on a whim and, yes, hiring employees as well. In the episode "The Opposite," George first meets the man aptly nicknamed "The Boss." Frustrated and prone to outbursts while under stress, which he is during the job interview, George recounts Steinbrenner's many bad decisions through the years, prompting the always impetuous bossman to cry out in no uncertain terms: "Hire him!"

Seinfeld co-creator Larry David furnished the loud and garrulous voice of George Steinbrenner, who was only seen from the back in all his appearances on the show. With the exception of "The Opposite" and "The Jimmy," a six-foot-four-inch man by the name of Lee Bear supplied the back-of-the-head acting shots of Steinbrenner. "I got the job through central casting," he told Long Island *Newsday*. "They were looking for someone who looked like Steinbrenner and I didn't know what he looked like." Bear further recounted: "They didn't tell me anything. I was supposed to react to what Larry was doing and saying. I was in seven episodes. There were a total of nine. They had another guy in the first two but he had to get out of town, then they had another cast call and got me." The flesh-and-blood George Steinbrenner later lauded Bear for capturing the essence of his body language.

Mr. Wilhelm is George's immediate supervisor at the stadium office. He suffers from memory lapses on occasion and, on one particular occasion, gets abducted by an office carpet–sweeping cult. In "The Millennium," he gets the more influential job after which George had been lusting: head scouting director for the cross-town rival team, the New York Mets. All that was standing in the way of George securing this new position was getting terminated from his job with the Yankees, which he valiantly endeavored to do by, among other things, dragging the team's most recent World Series trophy through the parking lot with his car and wearing, and spilling his lunch on, the legendary Babe Ruth's old uniform. When, however, the axe is about to fall on him, Mr. Wilhelm assumes responsibility for the egregious acts of his underling and gets the job that George so coveted. Familiar character actor Richard Herd played Mr. Wilhelm. Born on September 26, 1932, Herd's television credits date back into the 1970s, with appearances on such shows as *Kojak*, *The Rockford Files*, and *The Streets of San Francisco*.

After toiling in the employ of the New York Yankees, George lands a job at Kruger Industrial Smoothing. His boss, Mr. Kruger, contributes money to his bogus charity, The Human Fund, and subsequently attends the Festivus celebration at the Costanza house in the episode "The Strike." George had concocted an explanation for concocting the phony charity: His family didn't celebrate Christmas—nor did they buy presents—and he was too embarrassed to admit this to co-workers. Kruger, in the big picture, appreciates George's sense of humor, particularly when the latter opts to exit office meetings on a "high note" in "The Burning." Because of the man's capacity to entertain him in the workplace setting, Kruger ultimately fires everybody in the company except George, which leaves the sole employee with a surfeit of work. Whereas George preferred the on-the-job nickname of "T-Bone," Kruger nicknames him "Koko" and later "Gammy." Daniel von Bargen played Mr. Kruger. After an extended battle with diabetes, von Bargen passed away on March 1, 2015, at the age of sixty-four.

In addition to J. Peterman, Elaine had other bosses in her life, including Mr. Lippman at Pendant Publishing, where she worked for many years. Elaine, in "The Red Dot," convinces her boss there to give a down-and-out friend of hers, George Costanza, a job, which he does. Soon after the hiring came a firing when Mr. Lippman learns that his new employee had sex—on his office desk—with the cleaning woman.

Mr. Lippman is not always pleased with Elaine's work, including the time she edited Jake Jarmel's work and added, from his perspective, entirely too many exclamation points. Pendant Publishing, on the financial precipice, ultimately intends on merging with a Japanese company in the episode "The Opposite." But Mr. Lippman refuses to shake his potential Japanese partners' hands—a grave insult in their culture—and the deal falls apart. He had a bad cold at the time and didn't want to spread his germs. After Pendant Publishing's demise in "The Muffin Tops," Mr. Lippman runs with an idea of Elaine's and opens up a bakery that sells only tops of muffins—because that's what consumers like best—called Top of the Muffin to You! In "The Serenity Now," courtesy of Mr. Lippman and the male members of his family, young and old, Elaine discovers that she has "Shiks-appeal"—that is, a non-Jewish woman's attractiveness to Jewish males.

Two actors portrayed Mr. Lippman: Harris Shore in the "The Library," and Richard Fancy in ten subsequent episodes, including "The Finale." Born on August 2, 1943, in Evanston, Illinois, Fancy touts an extensive list of television and movie credits, including a long-running role on the soap opera *General Hospital.* He also appeared in such films as *Being John Malkovich* (1999) and *The Girl Next Door* (2004).

After Pendant Publishing's passing, Elaine assumed the position as assistant to Justin Pitt at Doubleday. Mr. Pitt is both a very eccentric and very wealthy man who was once a close friend of the late Jacqueline Kennedy Onassis. Elaine, in fact, reminds him of the former first lady. The British-born Mr. Pitt has Elaine performing mostly trifling tasks while in his employ, including de-salting his pretzel rods, locating the ideal pair of socks, and sharpening his pencils. He eats Snickers candy bars with a knife and fork and doesn't like fountain pens. Ink, in fact, is prohibited in the office. In "The Mom and Pop Store," Mr. Pitt experiences his dream-come-true when Elaine wins him the opportunity to hold one of the Woody Woodpecker balloon's ropes in the annual Macy's Thanksgiving Day Parade.

When Elaine discovers that she is being included in Mr. Pitt's will in the episode "The Diplomat's Club," she remains at the job despite being unhappy in her role. She loses her position, however, when her boss becomes convinced that she—with Jerry as an accomplice—is trying to kill him to collect the inheritance. Mr. Pitt testifies to their poor character while the gang is on trial in "The Finale."

Ian Abercrombie played Mr. Pitt throughout season six. He was born on September 11, 1934, in England. The highly respected British actor passed away January 16, 2012, of a heart attack at the age of seventy-seven. Abercrombie left as his legacy a lengthy roster of stage, film, and television credits.

While Jackie Chiles isn't a boss in the workplace, he's Kramer's lawyer and, later, the whole gang's defense counsel in "The Finale." Chiles is an African-American, mustachioed, bespectacled attorney who dresses to the nines. He also flaunts a flamboyant vocabulary, which he liberally employs in the courtroom.

After an overly hot caffe latte seriously burns Kramer in the episode "The Maestro," Chiles takes on his client's case against the coffee maker, Java World. He again works on Kramer's behalf in "The Caddy," after the latter is injured in automobile accident indirectly caused by Oh Henry! candy bar heiress Sue Ellen Mischke, who, by wearing only a bra on the streets, distracted drivers. Once more, Chiles believes Kramer has a winning case in "The Abstinence"—against the tobacco company this time—when his client's face prematurely ages from an excess of cigar smoke in his apartment smoking lounge. "Your face is my case," he confidently tells Kramer.

Finally, Jackie Chiles defends Jerry, George, Elaine, and Kramer for violating a small town's Good Samaritan Law. In the end, though, he comes up empty in all these cases. Chiles was particularly victimized by Kramer's impulsively bad decisions in settling cases without consulting his legal counsel. That is, he settles for a lifetime's worth of free coffee from Java World as opposed to a considerable monetary settlement, and agrees to become the Marlboro Man on a Times Square billboard rather than continue fighting Big Tobacco with the big pockets.

Comedian Phil Morris portrayed Jackie Chiles, a parody of real-life attorney Johnnie Cochran, who had become highly recognized in the 1990s in his staunch defense of O. J. Simpson. Morris was born on April 4, 1959, in Iowa City, Iowa, the son of actor Greg Morris, who starred in the popular series *Mission: Impossible* (1966–1973). Phil Morris's television credits are lengthy, notably for his prolific voice work in animated series, such as *Justice League*, *The PJs*, and *Legion of Super Heroes*.

Part IV
A World of Its Own

14

The *Seinfeld* Team Effort

Poetry in Motion

With the help of catchy musical transitions, *Seinfeld* flawlessly bounced from one rapid-fire scene to the next. It seemed so effortless at times that it was easy to forget all the hard work—and the many long hours—that went into producing each and every episode. It was a creative effort that included the show's two creators, a troupe of talented writers, and the musical genius of composer Jonathan Wolff.

The Impresario

During *Seinfeld*'s initial run, it was Jerry Seinfeld who got the lion's share of press attention when the subject of "show creator" came up. After all, the show was not only called *Seinfeld*, it starred Jerry Seinfeld as Jerry Seinfeld. That's a lot of Seinfeld. Larry David, the co-creator, was a more obscure figure. With the notable exception of supplying the voice behind the bombast of George Steinbrenner, his appearances on the show were infrequent and brief. It was the way he wanted it. He was a behind-the-scenes guy—and the most important one at that.

It was only after *Seinfeld* that Larry David became a recognizable quantity in his own right, with the success of HBO's *Curb Your Enthusiasm*. That said, he was nonetheless integral to *Seinfeld*—a man who respected comedy and the process of developing ideas with a free-flowing give-and-take. He challenged ideas, which either made them better or killed them outright. The show's creators hired some of the best comedy writers in the business and put them to work originating story ideas that could be fleshed out into full-length shows. Ultimately, their ideas had to pass comedic muster with Larry David.

Jerry Seinfeld has more than once told the story of how the idea for *Seinfeld* came to pass. Initially, he was having a difficult time coming up with a concept for a show. This writer's block on his part was the inspiration for the *Seinfeld* episode "The Pitch," wherein Jerry and George try their darndest to conjure up a sitcom idea to pitch to NBC executives. In real life, Jerry Seinfeld and his standup comedian friend Larry David—whom he had enlisted to brainstorm potential sitcom ideas—had stopped in a Korean fruit market one night on the streets of Manhattan. As they were walking around the store, they quipped to one another about some of the more unusual products for sale. Their original concept of the show was born. It revolved around the question: "Where do comedians get their ideas?" Sometimes, apparently, in a Korean fruit market.

When Larry David appeared with Jerry Seinfeld on *Comedians in Cars Having Coffee*, he remarked that his ex-wife believed that one of the reasons their marriage ended was because he gave up coffee for tea. While David mused that he had merely traded one hot liquid for another, his friend thought otherwise. Seinfeld spoke of ruining "the mood" with the switch, and compared David's action to ordering a salad in an ice cream parlor. This banter between them was the hallmark of the *Seinfeld* creative process. It married ideas, energy, and respect for comedy. It's no surprise that many members of the *Seinfeld* creative team subsequently worked on Larry David's *Curb Your Enthusiasm*.

The Word on *Seinfeld* Writers

In addition to the show's two creators, *Seinfeld*'s lengthy roster of writers and creative influences through its long and successful run features an impressive lot of men and women who tirelessly labored to develop and refine storylines. With each episode containing multiple, interwoven plot threads that engaged the show's four main characters, it was no small order. *Seinfeld* unfolded like a play—theatrical rather than cinematic. Writers thus came up with ideas—slice-of-life Seinfeldian vignettes, of course—with this in mind. They pitched them first to Larry David. His comedic sense of what was funny, and what would work for a *Seinfeld* episode, were virtually always on the mark. When an idea was given the imprimatur from on high, a script was quickly written and handed over to the show's myriad story editors, who would sometimes tinker with it a little, or—if they deemed it necessary—perform a radical makeover.

Outside of Jerry Seinfeld and Larry David, Peter Mehlman has the most across-the-board *Seinfeld* creative credits (1991–1998) on his résumé. Among these are as writer and co-writer on "The Nose Job," "The Visa," "The Implant," "The Sponge," "The Hamptons," and "The Yada Yada." Mehlman, too, is recognized as the father of some of the show's most popular catchphrases, including "sponge-worthy," "shrinkage," and "yada, yada." The man donned various hats in the *Seinfeld* creative process—notably assuming key roles as the show's co-executive producer and producer.

Standup comedienne Carol Leifer, who once dated Jerry Seinfeld and who is often cited as the basis for the Elaine Benes character, worked as both writer and story editor for the show. She was the sole writer of "The Rye," a *Seinfeld* classic, and co-writer of "The Hamptons" with Peter Mehlman. Alec Berg, who later took on the co-producer job of *Curb Your Enthusiasm*, was a strong creative influence in the latter years of the series (1994–1998). His *Seinfeld* writing credits include co-authorship of such episodes as "The Doodle," "The Summer of

George," and the controversial "The Puerto Rican Day." Jeff Schaffer, who, like so many other *Seinfeld* alumni, worked with Larry David on *Curb Your Enthusiasm*, also had a hand in writing the aforementioned episodes. David Mandel, who went on to direct several episodes of *Curb Your Enthusiasm*, received writing credits for "The Bizarro Jerry," "The Susie," "The Butter Shave," "The Voice," "The Betrayal," and "The Puerto Rican Day," the penultimate regular episode of *Seinfeld*. In fact, "The Puerto Rican Day" touts as its writers a rather extensive group: Berg, Schaffer, Mandel, Jennifer Crittenden, Spike Feresten, Bruce Eric Kaplan, Gregg Kavet, Steve Koren, Dan O'Keefe, and Andy Robin. This creative group hug, as it were, as the series drew to a close, duly recognized many of the show's prolific writers and creative talents.

In *Seinfeld*'s first few seasons, the always-busy Jerry Seinfeld and Larry David penned the majority of the scripts. During the early years of the show (1991–1994), Larry Charles was brought in to contribute his talents as a writer to the series as well as take some of the burden off of its two creators. He was renowned for supplying scripts with a somewhat dark edge, notably "The Baby Shower," in which Jerry experiences a nightmare replete with FBI agents gunning him down in a hail of bullets, and "The Limo," wherein Jerry and George inadvertently get entangled with neo-Nazis. Charles also wrote "The Bet," an episode that was never filmed because its content—Elaine acquiring an illegal handgun to protect herself—was considered too provocative, even for a *Seinfeld* episode, and, the worst sin of all, not especially funny.

Seinfeld writers often wrote from their own experiences. Larry David based "The Revenge" on his unhappy stint on *Saturday Night Live*, which led him to abruptly quit, then entertain second thoughts, and return to the show as if it had never happened. In "The Strike," writer Dan O'Keefe introduced an alternative holiday to Christmas, Festivus, which was something his own father had contrived. Peter Mehlman's authorship of "The Smelly Car" was inspired by a lawyer friend of his who couldn't—no matter how hard he tried—eliminate a bad odor from his vehicle. And "The Serenity Now," written by Steve Koren, is grounded in something his own father blurted out when he was younger. While driving in the car with the family, Koren remembered his dad once exclaiming, "Serenity now!" as a temper-controlling exercise. Of course, that was Frank Costanza's line in the show. "The Mom and Pop Store," written by tag team Tom Gammill and Max Pross, featured a plotline in which George believes he has purchased actor Jon Voight's old car. This was based on a real-life experience of Gammill. An auto dealer told him that the car he was interested in—and the one he eventually bought—previously belonged to Jon Voight. That very car was used in the series.

In the Director's Chair

In *Seinfeld*'s nine years on the air, two directors helmed the lion's share of episodes: Tom Cherones on the show's front side, and Andy Ackerman on the backside. Born in 1939, Cherones—who directed the pilot episode, "The Seinfeld Chronicles"—earned a master's degree in broadcast and film communication from the University of Alabama and served in the United States Navy, rising in rank to lieutenant, from 1961 to 1965. Cherones's directing credits include *Ellen* (1994–1995), *Caroline in the City* (1995–1996), and *NewsRadio* (1996–1999).

From both a different generation and geographical slice of the country, Andy Ackerman was born in Los Angeles, California, in 1956. Aside from directing over eighty episodes of *Seinfeld* from 1994 to 1998, Ackerman directed every episode of the Julia Louis-Dreyfus hit show *The New Adventures of Old Christine* (2006–2010), and also reunited with Larry David on *Curb Your Enthusiasm*. Among Ackerman's other directorial credits are *Cheers*, *Frasier* (1993–2004), *Everybody Loves Raymond*, and *Two and a Half Men* (2003–2015).

It's worth noting that in the *Seinfeld* DVD commentary, the show's cast members repeatedly praise the work of Ackerman. Cherones, on the other hand, is rarely mentioned. Silence sometimes speaks volumes.

A Wolff in *Seinfeld*'s Clothing

The *Seinfeld* sound is an integral part of the show and one of the many distinguishing factors that set it apart from prior and competing sitcoms in the early 1990s. For the first several years of *Seinfeld*, the show commenced with Jerry performing a standup bit. The credits rolled simultaneously while musical accompaniment complemented his act and neatly segued into the opening scene. Musical interludes were also employed during the show's frequent fast-paced scene changes, which were highly effective in bridging the multiple storylines that wended their way through each episode.

The man behind the *Seinfeld* sound is composer Jonathan Wolff, who was born in Louisville, Kentucky, on October 23, 1958. "I always played music as a kid," he recalled to Taxi.com.

Wolff moved to Los Angeles in the 1970s to attend the University of Southern California as a math major, but quickly saw that music was his calling and an artistic venue where he could, in fact, forge a bankable career. "I realized there was a substantial living to be made playing on TV and film scores," Wolff said. "That's where I familiarized myself with the corridors of the business and learned how composers work. It was a breeding ground for studio musicians."

In the fledgling days of Wolff's musical career, he hit the road with the likes of Tom Jones, Andy Gibb, Diana Ross, and John Davidson. His labors as a peripatetic musical director soon got him noticed and he began working with both television and movie composers. A big break came his way when he replaced composer Paul Shaffer on the sitcom *Square Pegs* (1982–1983). Subsequent television jobs included *Who's the Boss?* (1984–1992), *Saved by the Bell: The College Years* (1993–1994), and *Dave's World* (1993–1997). Wolff thrived on taking on an assortment of work that called for vastly different musical arrangements.

"I love the variety," Wolff said. "In one day, we might record a children's song, thrash-metal rock, and a Prokofiev piano concerto. It's fun to do that kind of wide range of things."

Jonathan Wolff remembered well his first interaction with Jerry Seinfeld. The meeting of minds came about courtesy of a mutual friend, comedian George Wallace, who introduced the pair to one another. Wallace informed Wolff that Seinfeld was having problems finding the right music for his new show.

The pilot, "The Seinfeld Chronicles," employed a very traditional TV theme that Jerry Seinfeld and Larry David felt neither captured the essence of the show, nor did it work with the interwoven standup material. The show had been

Seinfeld director extraordinaire Andy Ackerman, Jason Alexander, and Larry David pay tribute to Julia Louis-Dreyfus at the Hollywood Walk of Fame, May 4, 2010.   *Joe Seer/Shutterstock.com*

picked up by NBC—albeit with little confidence, as reflected in the network's minuscule order of four episodes. The early years of *Seinfeld* not only opened each episode with Jerry doing standup, but cut to it again in the middle of the episodes. What the show's creators wanted was music that would both underscore and enhance Jerry's standup bits, but not in any way, shape, or form get in their way.

Wolff received a call from Seinfeld, who showed him what other composers had come up with. He promptly zeroed in on the problem, which was that the theme needed a "signature melody"—one that accentuated its quirkiness.

Jonathan Wolff welcomed the challenge of inventing the *Seinfeld* sound and set to work on composing music that he thought would do the innovative show justice. Doing his homework, he sat down and watched hours and hours of Seinfeld performing standup. What Wolff came up with was a very unusual television theme for a very unusual sitcom—one that contained an ear-catching mix of finger snapping, lip popping, and shakers that would quickly become recognizable as the *Seinfeld* sound. Actually, Wolff exceeded everyone's expectations, creating something that worked perfectly with the fast pacing and originality of the show.

"The melody is Jerry's voice," Wolff said. In fact, he employed sounds that complemented but never, ever interfered with the voice—the bass comes to mind.

The Operatic *Seinfeld*

Jonathan Wolff can take justifiable pride for his work on *Seinfeld* and how the theme music became so identifiable with the show. It was his hope to somehow encapsulate the show's mood in the music, and by all accounts he did—and did it very well. Reflecting on his post-*Seinfeld* work, Wolff spoke of the show's "twangy bass" and how some of his composer friends have complained to him that they can't use anything resembling it—to this day—because it's so associated with *Seinfeld*.

Despite being in the industry for years, Jonathan Wolff finally received some genuine acclaim due to his contribution to the show. The composer looked upon the opening theme as operatic in scope.

Wolff is renowned today for being a prolific composer of TV theme music and an artist who utilizes the very latest in technology and computerized recording apparatuses. Aside from being a gifted musician, Wolff is a high-tech whiz. This knowledge of electronics and computers to aid and abet his music making enabled him to score entire episodes of *Seinfeld* in just four hours. He'd receive a videotape of the Thursday night show on Wednesday night and have it back—with the music in place—by Thursday morning. *Seinfeld* was unusual in the annals of television in that the opening musical score, depending on Jerry's specific standup routine and the storyline, was never the same twice. Every week's opening was unique and based on Jerry's monologue. This kind of thing was unheard of in television.

Jonathan Wolff never complained, though, about the new *Seinfeld* openings coming down the pike week after week. He thrived on the pressure and welcomed the recurring weekly challenges.

Life After *Seinfeld*

Typecasting is often the bane of actors who created popular characters on very successful shows. When the series ended, the *Seinfeld* actors left wearing their Jerry, George, Elaine, and Kramer masks. A show that became a phenomenon is a tough act to follow for any actor. But the question has been posed to Jonathan Wolff, too, whether he felt that working with *Seinfeld* and creating its music had helped or hindered his career in the post-*Seinfeld* universe.

"It hasn't hurt me," Wolff said. He further noted that being affiliated with a winner is always a big net plus in the dog-eat-dog world of Hollywood. Suffice it to say, *Seinfeld* has gotten Jonathan Wolff a lot of work.

15

The World of *Seinfeld*

Offbeat, Idiosyncratic, and Pathos-Free

A ccording to the Free Dictionary, one among several definitions of the word *idiosyncrasy* is "a physiological or temperamental peculiarity." In the incomparable World of *Seinfeld*, idiosyncratic behaviors run amok. Kramer, for one, is an idiosyncratic live wire. George's idiosyncrasies include taking off his shirt before using the bathroom facilities. So much of the show's popularity is, in fact, rooted in its characters' unusual traits, phobias, personality disorders, and bizarre flights of fancy. The World of *Seinfeld* is at once offbeat and pathos-free.

The writers of *Seinfeld* masterfully infused the show's characters with qualities that we can identify in ourselves and in those around us. Naturally, they are embellished in many instances for comedic maximization. But the longer we live, and the more human beings we encounter in the daily grind otherwise known as life, the more we come to appreciate that Jerry, George, Elaine, and Kramer are a great deal more than celluloid exaggerations of humanity at large. There are married couples who behave like Frank and Estelle Costanza. The smarmy Newman doesn't only live down the hall from Jerry; he is ubiquitous on every family tree, in every neighborhood, and in every workplace. Since many of the *Seinfeld* characters and storylines are based on actual people and real events, it stands to reason that the World of *Seinfeld*, idiosyncrasies and all, is a fascinating place to visit.

A World of Their Own

For starters, the World of *Seinfeld* is chock-full of neurotic characters who have rightly been dubbed "narcissists." Psychiatrists and therapists have penned scholarly articles about them—articles that themselves read like something from a *Seinfeld* script. Above all else, Jerry, George, Elaine, and Kramer seek personal gratification and self-preservation, and are not typically concerned about how they achieve these ends. While narcissistic behavior is not in the least bit admirable, it is nonetheless hilarious in the hands of inspired comedy writers like Larry David, Jerry Seinfeld, and company.

In the episode "The Pony Remark," George exhibits a whiff of narcissism simultaneous with making a keen observation about both the nature of funeral services and human nature. He educates Jerry on why dead people aren't likely concerned about who turns up at their funeral services. The odds are that they are not scouring the solemn rooms in funeral parlors and taking attendance. When Elaine interjects that maybe, just maybe, they are there in spirit, George sees the absurdity of that notion, too. He points out that if the recently deceased now resided in another dimension—an infinite realm with unlimited possibilities—would their specter loom at a pedestrian wake on this humdrum earthly plane? The answer is no.

When word leaked out that *Seinfeld*'s ninth season would be its last one, Jerry Seinfeld told *Newsweek* magazine: "We didn't change the culture. We just reflected it a little more intimately." Wacky and unpredictable as it typically is on the surface, the World of *Seinfeld* is supremely recognizable once its surreal veneer is stripped away. For viewers, it hardly matters that Jerry, George, Elaine,

This collector's edition of the epic Parker Brothers game turned the Monopoly board into the *Seinfeld* universe.

and Kramer's world is a world of their own. It is one that so captivates us because it doesn't quite exist in reality. For instance, the foursome call home sweet home New York City in the 1990s. While this decade coincided with Mayor Rudy Giuliani's aggressive war on crime—when, in fact, major crime statistics took a nosedive—New Yorkers certainly weren't leaving their doors unlocked, like Jerry and friends. Considering, too, the extremely high cost of living in the Big Apple in the 1990s—it's doubly so today—money is never really an overriding issue, even when George finds himself in the unemployment lines, or when the latest Kramer get-rich scheme implodes. It's implied that any and all money issues will somehow be resolved.

Jerry, George, Elaine, and Kramer do a lot of hanging around, too. They love nothing more than chewing the fat in Jerry's apartment, which functions as an all-purpose meeting place. Likewise, the foursome can regularly be found in their preferred eatery—the always bright and cheery-looking Monk's Café—having breakfast or lunch and shooting the breeze some more. In the fast-paced New York City where they collect their mail, the gang appears to have a surplus of free time on their hands. The icing on the proverbial cake is that they frequently date and regularly have casual sex.

An awful lot, too, has been written about the *Seinfeld* characters and their mental health issues. George, for one, is a hypochondriac who, in the episode "The Heart Attack," fears he is having just that while exhibiting the classic symptoms like shortness of breath and tightness in the chest.

Deliberating in a smoke-filled room, a.k.a. Jerry's living room.   *NBC/Photofest*

Jerry: I know what this is. You saw that show on PBS last night, *Coronary Country*. (*Jerry turns to Elaine.*) I saw it in the *TV Guide*. I called him and told him to make sure and not watch it.

George: There was nothing else on. Oh, the left arm . . . the left arm.

Jerry: He saw that show on anorexia last year and ate like an animal for two weeks.

George: Why can't I have a heart attack? I'm allowed.

Aside from the fact that he wasn't having a heart attack, there is one fundamental thing that George got wrong here. He posed the question, "Why can't I have a heart attack?" and answered it with: "I'm allowed." But, no, not in the World of *Seinfeld* are you *allowed* to have a heart attack. Others may have heart attacks and die in their world, but not Jerry, George, Elaine, or Kramer. Their health and wellness, at least physically, is assured.

Really, the World of *Seinfeld* is a community all its own. Residents within this world enjoy lifestyles that are uniquely theirs, but snippets of all they do are mirror images of what the human species is capable of when unleashed. That is, with a surfeit of leisure time, no all-consuming financial worries, and an assembly line of romantic partners there for the picking. And, of course, no longstanding health issues. George, after all, completely recovers from the debilitating effects of "The Summer of George," where doctors weren't certain he'd ever walk again.

Pathos-Free Zone

As *Seinfeld* took flight, it became apparent that the show's complete and utter lack of pathos had widespread and untapped appeal. And this was hardly how sitcoms through the years worked the crowd. The connection between the viewing audiences and Lucy Ricardo, Mary Richards, Fred Sanford, "Hot Lips" Houlihan, and Alex P. Keaton involved more than just laughs. We cared about these characters and rooted for them. We wanted Ralph Kramden to achieve success as the "Chef of the Future" and for that suitcase full of money to really be his. There was no such dynamic at work on *Seinfeld*. It somehow just wasn't necessary. We could appreciate the *Seinfeld* characters as one-of-a-kind oddballs while not ever feeling sorry for them when they screwed up, or screwed up the lives of others, which they did as a matter of course. We could observe their small-mindedness and moral failings with a certain detachment, and not bat an eye that they weren't becoming better human beings, absorbing invaluable life lessons, and accruing wisdom with the passage of time.

The Best Medicine

It has been said that "laughter is the best medicine." Who, really, could argue with that sentiment? And *Seinfeld* makes us laugh—period. It makes us laugh at things that—on paper and in reality—are not necessarily funny and sometimes even the antithesis of funny. *Seinfeld* put virtually every aspect of life in play for a joke and an amusing storyline, including physical and mental illness, chemical addiction, murder and suicide, disability, and the great equalizer—death itself. We get an interesting sample of *Seinfeld* coming at us from all angles without, of course, employing pathos, or even good taste, in the episode "The Butter Shave." Here George excitedly tells Jerry about his new job and how his employer—because he's using a cane in the wake of "The Summer of George"— believes he is handicapped.

> George: Jerry, let's face it. I've always been handicapped. I'm just now getting the recognition for it. Name one thing I have that puts me in a position of advantage. Huh? There was a guy that worked at the Yankees—no arms! He got more work done than I did. Made more money. Had a wife, a family. Drove a better car than I did.
>
> Jerry: He drove a car with no arms?
>
> George: All right. I made up the part about the car, but the rest is true. And he hated me anyway!
>
> Jerry: Do you know how hard it's getting just to tell people I know you?

George is perfectly willing to masquerade as a handicapped person to secure a job and more perks at the office. But we don't hold him accountable for his total lack of principles and questionable moral underpinning, nor do we root for him to lose his job and get what he deserves, even though we suspect that this will be the eventual outcome. It's the Pathos-Free Zone that we are in.

In this same episode, we encounter Kramer shaving his face with butter and then fully bathing in its yellow velvetiness. His butter bath has Newman fantasizing about cannibalism. That is, eating the heavily buttered, juice-laden Kramer, seasoned with oregano and Parmesan cheese.

In the episode "The Voice," we witness what we knew was on the horizon: George's handicap ruse blowing up in his face when it is discovered that he is, in fact, able-bodied. However, we relish watching him connive ways to stick around on the job—he had signed a yearlong contract—even though he has been asked to leave in no uncertain terms. "Siege mentality, Jerry," George says. "They really want me out of there. They've downgraded me to some sort of bunker. I'm like Hitler's last days here." We don't feel bad that George is in such a predicament, nor do we feel bad that Play Now, his employer, is really putting the screws on him. And we don't feel bad that, sooner or later, he will be in the unemployment lines again.

In this same episode, we see Kramerica, Kramer's business—the oil tank bladder system—go kaput after an unsuccessful trial run involving the dropping of a big ball of oil out a window. We hear police sirens en route to the scene, perhaps to arrest Kramer, which we are not all that worried about. In the final scene, however, we discover that Kramer came away unscathed. Jerry, though, inquires about Darren, Kramer's intern assistant from NYU, who believed in Kramerica's mission and helped him conduct the experiment. "Darren is going away for a long, long time," Kramer says sans any concern or pangs of conscience. Kramer, it seems, is perfectly willing to permit a college kid to take the rap for him. Now that's not very nice, but we don't sympathize with Darren either in the Pathos-Free Zone that is *Seinfeld*.

In the episode "The Visa," *Seinfeld* takes its Pathos-Free Zone abroad to Pakistan, where Babu Bhatt gets deported due to a series of blunders and some indifference on the part of

Seinfeld co-creator Larry David, who insisted from the get-go that the show be pathos-free.
RoidRanger/Shutterstock.com

Jerry, George, and Elaine. While away on business, Jerry recruited Elaine to pick up his mail for him. Apparently, he didn't think his neighbor Kramer up to the task. When he returned home, Elaine took her sweet time in bringing the mail over to him. And, lo and behold, in Jerry's pile of mail was Babu's visa renewal application. Babu, whom Jerry had helped secure an apartment in the building, had an adjoining mailbox, and the mailman had mistakenly placed Babu's very important piece of mail in Jerry's. This series of unfortunate events—with Babu not renewing his visa on time—set the wheels in motion for his deportation back to Pakistan.

After his deportation, Babu is back in his native land, where he doesn't want to be, seething with resentment and rage. The mere thought of Jerry, whom he once held in high esteem for helping him out, makes him spitting mad. "I'm going to save up every rupee," Babu says. "Someday, I will get back to America, and when I do, I will exact vengeance on this man. I cannot forget him. He haunts me. He is a very bad man. He is a very, very bad man."

Without question, "The Invitations" is the episode that took *Seinfeld*'s pathos-free mantra to new heights. Here we find George getting the word from a

The Not Necessarily Top Ten *Seinfeld* Real Movie References

10. *Home Alone* ("The Junior Mint")
9. *Beaches* ("The Understudy")
8. *Weekend at Bernie's II* ("The Comeback")
7. *JFK* ("The Boyfriend")
6. *The Godfather* ("The Bris")
5. *Citizen Kane* ("The Voice")
4. *Thelma & Louise* ("The Dealership")
3. *Star Trek II: The Wrath of Khan* ("The Foundation")
2. *Last Tango in Paris* ("The Junk Mail")
1. *The English Patient* ("The English Patient")

doctor that his fiancée, Susan Ross, has just died, seemingly as a direct result of his astonishing miserliness. When the doctor breaks the news of Susan's untimely passing, he asks George if Susan had been in contact with a cheap glue product recently, one typically found in inexpensive envelope sealants. George mentions the wedding invitations as a possibility and how they were "expecting about two hundred people."

In the World of *Seinfeld* with its Pathos-Free Zone, life goes on, come what may—death included. George fancies a cup of joe and a swift return to business as usual. He'll even try to hook up with actress Marisa Tomei, who previously jettisoned him when she learned that he was engaged, on the day after the funeral for his fiancée. Why not? His weekend's free. Meanwhile, Jerry's chief concern is that he got engaged in something of a pact with George, and now feels trapped. Poor Susan Ross is dead. George doesn't even bother to call her parents and break the bad news.

Seinfeld is not a documentary, not real life, but a TV sitcom like no other. We can tune in next time and not hate Jerry—like Babu does—for what he did or didn't do. And Babu doesn't elicit any sympathy from us for the straits he's in, courtesy of Jerry and company, either. He'll get his chance at exacting revenge, like so many others, in "The Finale."

Laugh and the World Laughs with You

Seinfeld's lack of pathos and moral compass is what has riled its many critics—both when the show was on in primetime and now in reruns. Certain disapproving voices feel that what can be presented as funny should be confined within certain boundaries of good taste and inoffensive political correctness. Even though *Seinfeld* is not depicted as reality, these critics believe with all their hearts that what Jerry, George, Elaine, and Kramer do on a sitcom matters in the bigger picture, beyond all the laughs. Even if they are not representative of the average Dick and Jane, they believe that these characters' words and actions have the capacity to make meaner the hearts of Americans. But the *Seinfeld* characters are, in the end, amusing caricatures with individual personalities that embody all that we are and so much of what we are not. Laughing at their antics and unscrupulousness doesn't make us on par with Jerry, George, Elaine, and Kramer. So what if their pettiness often borders on the pathological? That is the joke. So what if they say and do mean things to one another all the time? That is the joke.

If extraterrestrials invaded Mother Earth and examined what makes human-kind tick by watching *Seinfeld*, perhaps there would be cause for concern if they viewed the show's cast as representative of humanity. It would be something akin to the dignitaries from the Soviet Union who called on Gomez, Morticia, Uncle Fester, and Lurch in the *Addams Family* episode "The Addams Family Meet the VIPs." The Russians had selected one family that was supposed to personify the typical American household and, what do you know, came up with the Addams family. Of course, after spending some time with the Addamses and observing Gomez relaxing on a bed of nails, a disembodied hand named "Thing" go about its business, and Uncle Fester generating electricity via his mouth, the Russians decide that it's best to maintain good relations with America and its advanced breed of people.

But in the meantime, we can look upon *Seinfeld* as representative only of groundbreaking comedy written by talented writers who were willing to push the envelope more than most, and get laughs from terrain that has become heavily guarded by politically correct folly.

16

Seinfeld Controversies

No-Holds-Barred Comedy

I t's not surprising that *Seinfeld* generated its share of controversy through the years. After all, a primetime show with an entire episode, "The Contest," tiptoeing around the subject of masturbation was not typical television fare. Kramer accidentally setting fire to a Puerto Rican flag in the episode "The Puerto Rican Day" drew a lot of flak. And so did many other episodes with themes that were not appreciated, actions that were deemed immoral, and character portrayals that were considered ethnic and racial stereotypes.

In the episode "The Bookstore," J. Peterman refers to opium as "the Chinaman's nightcap," which prompted Media Action Network for Asian Americans (MANAA) to demand an apology, claming that "Chinaman" was an appalling racial slur on par with the N-word. The term was excised in subsequent reruns of the show. Some Jewish groups even criticized *Seinfeld* for stereotypically portraying Jews and ridiculing their religious traditions.

Foremost, *Seinfeld* is a show that thumbs its nose at political correctness, not accepting the premise that there are protected classes and groups immune from being humorous prey. *Seinfeld* played the homeless population for laughs, which didn't sit well with some viewers. In the episode "The Bubble Boy," a young man with an immunodeficiency disease living in a plastic bubble is the butt of jokes. George's fiancée dying with very little remorse expressed by the show's main characters, believe it or not, even riled some devoted fans who thought the show had finally gone too far. But this is what *Seinfeld* did time and again, and what made it so funny for so many years. *Seinfeld* went places that other sitcoms dared not go. With few exceptions, it didn't play within the traditional primetime boundaries.

From a devoted *Seinfeld* fan's perspective, it's hard to fathom that there are people who don't find the show funny. It's even more difficult to swallow that when the show ended there were some critical voices who cried, "Good riddance," because they believed that *Seinfeld* actually polluted the culture by celebrating everything that was wrong about the materialistic, self-absorbed 1990s that gave birth to the ambitious and insatiable yuppie and the dot-com boom and subsequent bust. From these individuals' perspectives, Jerry, George,

Elaine, and Kramer represented the worst of humanity. They sincerely held that the show's immense popularity was because the audience wished to be like them, to live like them, and to think like them. Essentially, they felt that *Seinfeld* had a perverse agenda to encourage its viewers to throw their fellow man and woman under the bus in pursuit of their own self-interests. What these critics failed to see is that the show was about making people laugh and making them laugh harder than they ever had before. And, yes, it made some folks angry for failing to be politically correct and not playing by the new rules of polite society, but that's what bold satire has always done.

All Bets Are Off

Strange as it may seem, controversy concerning episode content actually infiltrated the *Seinfeld* set during its second season. The hullabaloo involved an episode called "The Bet," which is sometimes referred to as "The Gun." It was slated to be the fourth episode of the show's sophomore year. In the end, though, "The Bet" was never produced because the actors thought the script was too dark—overly incendiary without being funny, which is the sitcom kiss of death.

As written, the controversial nature of the plot revolved around a bet made between Jerry and Elaine. Jerry just didn't believe that Elaine would purchase an illegal handgun, which she claimed she needed for protection on the mean streets of Manhattan. Commenting on this aborted episode in the DVD commentary, Julia Louis-Dreyfus said, "I read the script and I remember thinking, 'We're not going to do this.'"

The hottest potato in the script found Elaine pressing a gun to her head and crying out: "Where do you want it, Jerry? The Kennedy?" And then switching gears, pointing the gun to her stomach, and exclaiming, "The McKinley?" Elaine was referencing the last two American presidents who were assassinated: John F. Kennedy, who was shot in the head by Lee Harvey Oswald, and William McKinley, who was shot in the stomach by an anarchist named Leon F. Czolgosz.

Larry Charles, who worked on the show for its first five seasons, wrote the teleplay for "The Bet." He is credited with adding dark touches and absurdities to *Seinfeld* scripts. Charles penned the famous dream sequence in the episode "The Baby Shower," wherein Jerry gets gunned down in a hail of bullets. Other episodes with his special signature include "The Opera," with deranged stalker "Crazy" Joe Davola on the loose; "The Bris," with a suicide played for laughs; and "The Limo," where Jerry and George get entwined with neo-Nazis.

However, "The Bet" just didn't fly. During rehearsal for the show, Julia Louis-Dreyfus had had enough and turned to Jason Alexander. "I'm not doing this," she said, and he concurred that the gun content was a bit over the top, even for an episode of *Seinfeld*. With the cast in something of a revolt, it was agreed that "The Bet" wouldn't be shot. Involved in the decision was NBC executive

Glenn Padnick, who was actually happy that the cast objected and that the show would never air.

"You know, it would have been an interesting show," Larry Charles said in hindsight on the DVD commentary. "But we couldn't solve the 'funny' problem of it. It never seemed to quite be as funny as it should be and, because of that, the balance was off and the darkness kind of enveloped it, and it could never really emerge from that darkness and become what it should have been. So, it was disappointing but also understandable." Larry David and Jerry Seinfeld promptly penned the episode "The Phone Message" as its replacement.

Flag This Show

As previously noted, there were countless controversial *Seinfeld* moments and entire episodes that raised the hackles of various special-interest groups. "The Puerto Rican Day," in the show's ninth and final season, was one such episode. When it originally aired, on May 7, 1998, it attracted 38.8 million viewers, the most ever for a *Seinfeld* episode up to that point. "The Puerto Rican Day" was the episode that preceded the "The Chronicle"—the retrospective "Clip Show"—and "The Finale."

In "The Puerto Rican Day," Jerry, George, Elaine, and Kramer are on their way home after attending a Mets game at Shea Stadium. They had left early to beat the inevitable stadium parking-lot snarl at game's end, but encountered one in Manhattan instead—on Fifth Avenue—the result of the annual Puerto Rican Day parade. To make a long story short—with all kinds of Seinfeldian plot twists and turns—Kramer sets fire to the Puerto Rican Day flag by mistake, stomps on it to put out the blaze, and is set upon by an angry mob. Parade revelers trash Jerry's car in this episode, too, which prompts Kramer to say, "It's like this every day in Puerto Rico."

NBC was immediately swamped with irate phone calls and letters. (There were no e-mail, texts, and tweets back then.) Protestors, without delay, showed up outside the network's headquarters at Rockefeller Center. The brass issued an apology: "We do not feel that the show lends itself to damaging ethnic stereotypes, because the audience for *Seinfeld* knows the humor is derived from watching the core group of characters get themselves into difficult situations." The president of NBC even added his two cents: "Our appreciation of the broad comedy of *Seinfeld* does not in any way take away from the respect we have for the Puerto Rican flag."

The apology didn't exactly quell the anger. "It is unacceptable that the Puerto Rican flag be used by *Seinfeld* as a stage prop under any circumstances," said Manuel Mirabal, president of the National Puerto Rican Coalition. He deemed the episode "an unconscionable insult" and complained not only about the flag burning but how Hispanic parade spectators were portrayed as "insensitive" and "dressing in clothing that has not been worn in forty years."

Bronx Borough president Fernando Ferrer also weighed in on "The Puerto Rican Day." He told the Associated Press that the show "crossed the line between bigotry and humor" and complained of both the episode's depiction of Puerto Rican men and the implication that rioting and vandalizing property are everyday occurrences in Puerto Rico. NBC chose not to rerun "The Puerto Rican Day," despite it being the highest-rated *Seinfeld* episode ever (it would be surpassed only by "The Finale" a couple of weeks later). In the original *Seinfeld* syndication package, "The Puerto Rican Day" was not included as well. However, slowly but surely—with the passage of time—it has begun to appear. Still, some local stations opt not to run the episode because of all the past controversy surrounding it. Happily, for *Seinfeld* fans, the DVD box set includes the episode, flag burning intact, and all other controversial shows and moments, uncensored and in their entirety.

Getting in Hoch

There have, in fact, been a host of vocal critics through the years of *Seinfeld*—many of whom accused the show of reinforcing ethnic and racial stereotypes time and again. African Americans, for one, have been among some of the biggest detractors, noting that very few blacks were cast in parts, and when they were, they were often stereotypical, like Jackie Chiles, played by Phil Morris, who did an amusing parody of O. J. Simpson lawyer Johnnie "If the Glove Does Not Fit, You Must Acquit" Cochran.

One especially harsh critic was actor Danny Hoch, who went so far as to incorporate Jerry Seinfeld into his act in a very negative light. In a monologue at Off-Broadway's Performance Space 122 in New York, he branded the comedian "the enemy." His disdain for *Seinfeld* and its creators, he says, is grounded in an invitation that he received to appear on the show—and one that he initially accepted. The part he was being asked to play, in "The Pool Guy," was that of a not-quite-right-in-the-head Latin pool boy at a health club—a character who spoke in an exaggerated, comical Spanish accent. Courtesy of the inept tag team of Jerry and Newman, who are chiefly responsible for his precarious predicament, the pool boy nearly dies toward the end of the episode. Jerry had inadvertently pulled him into the pool and, upon diving into the chlorinated drink, Newman landed atop him, knocking him out cold. Jerry and Newman then get involved in a contentious back-and-forth, debating as to who is more responsible for the pool boy's sticky situation, and who should give him the mouth-to-mouth resuscitation necessary to save his life. In the final analysis, they cannot come to an agreement.

"I normally don't do sitcoms because they really have no substance and are about passivity rather than activity," Hoch explained to the *New York Observer*. "When I read the script, I saw what the part could possibly be, and so I called up and said, 'This isn't your stereotypical Spanish-speaking pool guy, is it?' Because, otherwise, I wasn't getting on the plane. And they said, 'Not at all—it can be whoever you want to be.' But when I got there, I found out it was the stupid, one-dimensional role that I didn't want to do."

Hoch claims that during a run-through of the script of "The Pool Guy," he read the part in a "higher-strung" version of himself, and that everybody on the scene laughed. He felt that the laughter he generated—by delivering the lines *his way*—embarrassed Jerry Seinfeld, who still wanted him to do it in a ridiculous, over-the-top accent.

When he decided not to do the show, Hoch remembered that Jason Alexander and Julia Louis-Dreyfus supported his decision to follow his instincts, if indeed he had such a problem with what he was being asked to do. He said, however, that Michael Richards told him to just suck it up and play the part, or else it would be given to another actor, which it was: Carlos Jacott, who played Ramon the pool guy in a very funny episode.

The Kosher Debate

At the end of *Seinfeld*'s nine-year run, *Washington Post* television critic Tom Shales wrote that the show was not "too Jewish," as NBC executive Brandon Tartikoff complained in its pilot stage, but "too self-hatingly Jewish." Shales, it should be noted, was not a big fan of the show in general. He regularly complained in his columns about *Seinfeld*'s nasty streak and its cast of coldhearted characters.

The Jewish issue stirred in the *Seinfeld* ether from the get-go, particularly after the show became a sensation. There were competing sides on the question of whether or not *Seinfeld* was perpetuating a negative Jewish stereotype or shattering that very same stereotype by portraying everybody as equals—on an even keel. No one on *Seinfeld* was spared from looking foolish. Engaging in off-the-wall and neurotic behaviors was for Jew and Gentile alike.

"You write about what you know," Larry David, who is Jewish, told *Laugh Factory* magazine. Jerry Seinfeld is also Jewish. Therefore, it's not surprising that they would include in their show Jewish characters and plot lines unique to their experiences of growing up in Jewish families. So, the character Jerry Seinfeld is Jewish. George has a Jewish mother but an Italian father, even though Jewish actors Estelle Harris and Jerry Stiller played them like—what some critics claimed—a stereotypical, squabbling Jewish couple. Jerry's parents, Morty and Helen, were likewise cited by some critical voices for living a stereotypical life in a Florida retirement village, with the former carefully guarding every penny. And, of course, there was Uncle Leo, who encountered anti-Semites under every rock.

In fact, when *Seinfeld* episodes specifically dealt with Jewish subject matter—like a girlfriend keeping kosher—the Anti-Defamation League would be inundated with phone calls about the show and its perpetuation of negative stereotypes. Throughout the show's run there was a fierce debate as to whether it was doing more harm than good in the area of perceptions.

So what about Tom Shales and his contention that *Seinfeld* was "too self-hatingly Jewish"? Was it the case? Some of the controversial Jewish moments in the show include:

- Elaine, a non-Jewish character, seeking out a rabbi's counsel in the episode "The Postponement." He then reveals one of her big secrets to a national television audience.
- In the episode "The Bris," Elaine locates a *mohel* to perform a circumcision at a *brit milah* for her friend's child. He hates children and is so inept that he misses his target and slices the finger of Jerry, the child's godfather.
- Jerry is caught—by Newman, of all people—making out with his girlfriend during a screening of *Schindler's List* in the episode "The Raincoats." Newman then gleefully tells Jerry's parent what he witnessed.
- In the episode "The Serenity Now," Elaine is concerned about her "Shiks-appeal"—that Jewish men find her attractive when they learn that she is not Jewish. She seeks a rabbi's help, but he comes on to her rather than solving her dilemma.
- And, finally, there was the episode "The Soup Nazi," and other references to Nazis throughout the series, which were always controversial.

Rabbi Jonathan Pearl and his wife, Judith Pearl, concurred with critic Tom Shales's assessment of *Seinfeld*. Their organization, the Jewish Televimages Resource Center, pays close attention to how Jewish men, women, and traditions are portrayed on television. "*Seinfeld* became unfunny," Rabbi Pearl told JWeekly.com, when the show "dealt with Jewish issues." He added, "I think when someone pokes fun out of love and affection, it comes through no matter how stereotypical or offensive it might seem." But he did not see *Seinfeld* as having much love and affection in its character portrayals. In fact, he believed that

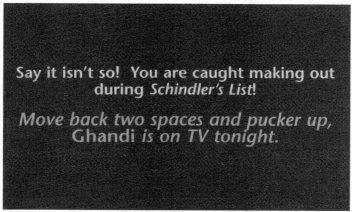

Say it isn't so! You are caught making out during *Schindler's List*!

Move back two spaces and pucker up, Ghandi *is on TV tonight.*

Jerry's got his priorities in order (even if *Seinfeld* Scene It experienced a "Moops" Trivial Pursuit moment by misspelling *Gandhi*).

the show was unashamedly unsympathetic toward Judaism, with regrettable stereotypes that depicted Jews and Judaism in a negative light.

The national director of the Anti-Defamation League, Abe Foxman, disagreed with Rabbi Pearl. As a big *Seinfeld* fan, he believed that both Shales and Pearl were reading more into the show than they need be. "Getting more positive messages out about Judaism is not what *Seinfeld* is about," Foxman told JWeekly.com. "It's comedy." Foxman did, however, take *Seinfeld* to task for a few moments in the show, including "The Soup Nazi" because—as he sees it—the episode trivialized the Holocaust.

In the big picture, though, Foxman lauded the show for its portrayal of Jews. "The Jewishness of the *Seinfeld* characters was worn comfortably and naturally on their sleeves. There were no bizarre or eccentric Jews. *Seinfeld* is human, universal."

"The Jews have arrived," added Encino Rabbi Harold Schulweis, who praised the show for depicting its Jewish characters as average Americans along with everybody else. "*Seinfeld* accurately reflects a lack of purpose and spirituality in the life of most American Jews today," Schulweis said.

The overall consensus is that *Seinfeld* did employ exaggerated stereotypes—but for comedic effect. Regardless of race, ethnicity, religion, sexual orientation, physical disability—no one was spared from taking a hit.

Critical Critics

As this chapter illustrates, *Seinfeld* was not universally loved. What television show ever is? Yet, despite its fair share of critics attacking it from all angles, the extent of its popularity was remarkable. "The revolutionary concept here consists of cutting a couple of times per episode to Jerry performing his act at a comedy club where, naturally, everybody laughs at all his jokes," wrote Rick Marin of the *Washington Times*. "Theoretically there's some sort of—I hesitate to use the word—'counterpoint' between the standup material and what loosely passes for the plot. Now, Jerry Seinfeld is funny—in sort of an upscale, Jewish George Carlin kind of a way—but he's not that funny. The standup situations obviously aren't real, so it sounds like he's working a room of laugh-track machines."

Believe it or not, there were more than a few *Seinfeld* critics with political axes to grind, feeling that the show represented the erosion of a culture and reflected all that was wrong with our grasping, survival-of-the-fittest, looking-out-for-number-one society. "Call me a hopeless Puritan," Elayne Rapping wrote in the *Progressive*, "but I see, in this airwave invasion of sitcoms about young Manhattanites with no real family or work responsibilities and nothing to do but hang out and talk about it, an insidious message about the future of Western civilization."

Seinfeld actually got under a lot of people's skin. "Why do I find myself becoming uneasy about the show?" asked John J. O'Connor of the *New York*

Times. "Increasingly, it seems, *Seinfeld* wants to be about something, and that something is either painfully obvious or awkwardly jarring. The show has never been terribly concerned with political correctness. Its depictions of minorities, from Babu the Pakistani who was eventually deported because of Jerry's carelessness to the Greek diner owner with an apparent yen for amply endowed waitresses, can be patronizing. And its attitudes toward women can become downright hostile."

When *Seinfeld* bade farewell to the weekly primetime lineup, John Leonard of *New York Magazine* was not unhappy about the forthcoming change in Thursday night television programming. "The passing of *Seinfeld*," he wrote, "that Cheez Doodle of urban fecklessness, into cryogenic syndication inspires no tear in this cave. Jerry, George, Kramer, and Elaine never spoke for my New York, not on a Southern California soundstage, lean and mean in their terrarium, wearing prophylactic smirks to every penis joke."

17

Seinfeld Land

The Uncanny New York Experience

A mong the many things that concerned skittish NBC executives about the long-term survivability of *Seinfeld* was its strong New York flavor and cast of characters. They believed these fictional individuals enjoyed lifestyles too far removed from the preponderance of primetime viewers. Despite the fact that the show was filmed almost entirely on sets three thousand miles away from the City That Never Sleeps—Stages 9 and 19 at the CBS Studio Center on 4024 Radford Avenue in Studio City, California—*Seinfeld* was New York to its marrow. References to things New York were made all the time. New York City addresses were bandied about with regularity, even if they weren't always geographically accurate. Real New York businesses and hotspots were mentioned constantly, like Papaya King at 179 East 86th Street, the place that serves a hot dog second to none—superior even to filet mignon—at least as far as Kramer is concerned.

Other New York locales were thinly veiled homages to genuine establishments, such as Schnitzer's Bakery, maker of the must-have marble rye bread that Jerry—after offering fifty dollars for the loaf—snatches from an "old bag" named Mabel Choate. In actual New York, Schnitzer's is the since-shuttered Royale Pastry Shop at 237 West 72nd Street. The Soup Nazi, located at 259A West 55th Street, between Broadway and Eighth Avenue—the Hell's Kitchen neighborhood—is actually the address of the Original Soup Man, a chain of soup specialty restaurants begun by Ali "Al" Yeganeh. It was known as the Soup Kitchen International and even closed its doors for a spell. Happily, it's now back with its original name. Yeganeh, it's worth mentioning, was *not* happy at being linked with *Seinfeld* in the manner that he was. However, it obviously didn't hurt his business over the long haul—quite the contrary. After all, *Seinfeld* fans are a ubiquitous lot. And while the Soup Nazi himself wasn't portrayed as a particularly nice guy, his soups were considered out of this world. Reportedly, Yeganeh has banned or, at the very least, strongly urged his franchisees from utilizing any *Seinfeld* or "Soup Nazi" references in their promotional efforts. Nevertheless, the website Originalsoupman.com certainly plays up the *Seinfeld* connection, including the reprising of Al's Original Soup Man rules: "For the most efficient and fastest service, the line *must* be kept moving. Pick the soup you want! Have your money ready! Move to the *extreme* left after ordering!"

Kenny Kramer's *Seinfeld* Reality Tour calls on 255 West 55th Street—just off Eighth Avenue—to both sample the soups and abide by the rules that inspired the "Soup Nazi."

Photo by Thomas Nigro

Exterior shots of genuine New York City locales were also used extensively throughout the show's run. The most recognizable of them is Tom's Restaurant, a bona fide Greek diner on 2880 Broadway near Columbia University, whose outside façade—with its large "Restaurant" light-up sign—is now inextricably linked with the fictional Monk's Café, Jerry and company's favorite place to grab a bite to eat. Tom's Restaurant is a culinary haven for Columbia University students. Barack Obama frequented the eatery while he was attending the university.

The exterior of Jerry's apartment building on 129 West 81st Street is also an unforgettable Upper West Side Manhattan image, even if the shot is of a Los Angeles apartment building complex at 757 South New Hampshire Avenue. Jerry and Kramer's actual New York address does correspond with a real building, though, called The Shelby, which a younger, not-nearly-as-famous Jerry Seinfeld once called home. Monk's Café, for the record, is just across the street from the West 81st Street building, but Tom's Restaurant is located on 112th Street and Broadway in the Morningside Heights section of Manhattan, more than a mile away from the apartment.

Elaine has called home 16 West 75th Street, then 78 West 86th Street, and suffered from Chinese takeout delivery problems. According to Menupages. com, there are more than a thousand Chinese restaurants in New York City alone. The Costanzas, Frank and Estelle—and sometimes their son, George, too—reside at 1344 Queens Boulevard in Flushing, Queens, which is also the home of the New York Mets. The exterior shot of their house is actually a domicile in Astoria, Queens, which is not too far from Flushing on a city map. The authentic address of 1344 Queens Boulevard, however, would put the Costanzas in Forest Hills, a more upscale sliver of this sprawling New York City outer borough. The Costanzas live approximately six miles due east of Manhattan's Upper West Side.

The Underground Railroad

The New York City subway scene has always made for good TV. *All in the Family* (1971–1979), starring Carroll O'Connor, Jean Stapleton, Sally Struthers, and Rob Reiner, set an episode almost entirely in a New York City subway. It is called "Mike the Pacifist" and Archie Bunker is on a train with his daughter, Gloria, and son-in-law, Mike Stivic, a.k.a. "Meathead." Just like the Costanzas, the Bunkers and Stivics live in Queens.

Mike: You've moved us through three cars already.

Archie: There was a gang war in the first car.

Mike: What gang? It was three kids fighting over a strap to hold on to.

Archie: I'll bet if you went back now the little one would be hanging from the strap.

When this episode of *All in the Family* was shot in 1977, New York City subway cars no longer had leather straps to grab hold of while standing, but metal ones instead that rocked back and forth with every twist and turn, start and stop. Subway riders were, nonetheless, still referred to as "straphangers" in local news reporting. But in the world of television—particularly in sitcom land—historical accuracy isn't really a necessity.

Fifteen years later, *Seinfeld* took the New York subway experience to another level in an episode aptly called "The Subway." We find the gang—having descended into the belly of the beast—on their way to Times Square. At Times Square, they will individually transfer to a unique subway line to reach their respective destinations. New York City's subway system covers a lot of ground, with its 842 miles of track wending to and fro and far and wide.

In the busy hub that is Times Square, Jerry, George, Elaine, and Kramer go their separate ways. Kramer has got to pay off some vehicular tickets that he's accumulated. We see him riding the Number 1 train, the Seventh Avenue or Broadway local as it's sometimes known, which takes riders from South Ferry on the southern tip of Manhattan to West 242nd Street and a neighborhood called Kingsbridge in the Northwest Bronx. Kramer's played golf in Van Cortlandt Park at this subway line's last stop, or its first one, depending on which way you're headed. George has got a job interview. Elaine is on her way to a wedding, where she is slated to be the "best man" in a same-sex marriage, which was not yet legally recognized in New York State—or anywhere else for that matter—in 1992. Jerry is venturing farther than them all, to the more distant Coney Island to pick up his formerly stolen car, which is in a police impound lot there.

On Jerry's subway jaunt, he wakes up from an extended catnap replete with lots of writhing—a time-honored tradition while hurtling through the subterranean recesses of New York City—and finds a nude man with a serious weight issue seated directly across from him. Jerry gives this fellow subway rider a little sarcastic lip about his choice of clothing—none—and body, which is the antithesis of eye-candy. "I'm not ashamed of my body," the nude guy responds, to which Jerry retorts, "That's your problem, you *should* be."

The gang went their separate ways in the belly of the beast at Times Square in "The Subway."

Photo by Thomas Nigro

Jerry then engages the man in a less confrontational back-and-forth. He soon finds himself engrossed in a thoughtful discussion about the New York Mets' chances in the upcoming 1992 season, with the subject of nudity and obesity all but forgotten. Jerry and the nude guy strike a deal that the twosome will sit naked together at the World Series should their favorite team win the pennant.

The postscript to this quintessential New York subway car experience is that Jerry did not have to sit in his birthday suit alongside the nude guy at the 1992 World Series. The Mets were 72–90 for the season, finishing in fifth place just a couple of games ahead of the last-place Philadelphia Phillies. The 1992 New York Mets were so lackluster that they inspired the book *The Worst Team Money Could Buy*, by sportswriter Bob Klapisch. It's worth noting, too, that Jerry arrived at the impound lot late—it was already closed for the day—because he had lost track of time while having a grand old time with the nude guy at Coney Island. The pair enjoyed Nathan's Famous hot dogs and rode the equally famous roller coaster, the Cyclone, together. People meet all the time in the New York City subway system. It's the beginning of many beautiful friendships.

Meanwhile, Elaine's subway train runs into a snafu—a not-unusual state of affairs in the labyrinthine transit network—and experiences a delay. We hear that familiar voice in Elaine's head—her inner monologue—venting: "Okay, take it easy. . . . I'm sure it's nothing. Probably rats on the track. We're stopping for rats. God, it's so crowded. How can there be so many people? This guy really smells. Doesn't anyone use deodorant in the city? What is so hard? You take the cap off. You roll it on."

George, too, gets sidetracked on his subway expedition and opts not to go to his job interview. Instead, he accompanies a stranger to the historic Hotel Edison at 228 West 47th Street. He ends up getting handcuffed to a bed while his companion steals his money—the grand sum of eight dollars—and his clothes, the only suit he owns: a $350 Moe Ginsburg. To put it mildly, she is disgusted at the paltry sum of her pillage because George had informed her that he played the market, implying that he was extremely well heeled. After being in the same location for over thirty years, Moe Ginsburg, the men's clothier at 162 Fifth Avenue in Manhattan's Flatiron neighborhood, closed up shop in 2002. A main reason cited for the closing was the 9/11 terrorist attacks on the World Trade Center, which negatively impacted sales. Famous clientele, aside from George Costanza, included Rudy Giuliani, Ed Koch, Johnnie Cochran, and Robert De Niro.

A can't-miss horseracing tip that he overhears on his subway ride alters Kramer's plans as well. He ventures over to the nearest Off Track Betting (OTB) parlor to lay down some money—six hundred dollars—on Papa Nick, a 30:1 long shot. Kramer wins eighteen thousand dollars, which helps him pay off all his vehicular debts and pick up the tab later in the day at Monk's. In December 2010, the last OTB parlor in New York City shut its doors, citing poor revenue. OTB was at long last permitted to open up shop in the city during the 1970s and their various parlors promptly became happening places with the gambler set. By the 1980s there were approximately two hundred OTB locations in town.

Cosmo Kramer: Big Man About the Big Town

Kramer covers an awful lot of ground in New York City. He takes advantage of so much of what the big city has to offer. And he's not a Manhattan snob either. Kramer's not averse to venturing to the city's outer boroughs, which is in stark contrast with some of his more hoity-toity neighbors who don't know they exist. He does, however, get hopelessly lost in lower Manhattan—on the corner of First and First, the "nexus of the universe"—in the episode "The Maid." To clarify Kramer's whereabouts, Jerry asks him whether he is near Famous Ray's Pizza, Original Ray's Pizza, or Famous Original Ray's Pizza. A 2011 pizza parlor census tallied up forty-nine variations of Ray's Pizza in New York City alone. One shop very cleverly called itself "Not Ray's Pizza."

We know that Kramer enjoys knocking back a few at the historic Pete's Tavern at 129 East 18th Street in Manhattan's Gramercy Park neighborhood. The renowned watering hole first opened for business in 1864. The writer O. Henry lived close to Pete's Tavern and was a regular patron. Legend has it that he penned *The Gift of the Magi* in the saloon. And *Seinfeld* is not the only television show whose characters frequent Pete's Tavern. Men and women of *Spin City*, *Law and Order*, and *Sex in the City* have also dropped by. Nowadays, because of New York City's strict laws prohibiting smoking in bars, restaurants, and just about everywhere else, Kramer would be compelled to take his love of a good cigar outdoors. Smoking is prohibited in New York City's parks, too.

Truth be told, Kramer is quite the gadabout on the New York City scene. In the episode "The Visa," he gets booted—quite literally—from Mickey Mantle's Restaurant at 42 Central Park South for attempting to apologize to the baseball legend for what had occurred at an earlier Yankees fantasy camp in Florida. Kramer explains to Jerry and Elaine that the camp was aborted prematurely after he plunked former Yankee Joe Pepitone, initiating a bench-clearing brawl with the likes of Moose Skowron, Hank Bauer, and Mickey Mantle. During the scuffle, Kramer accidentally knocked out Mickey Mantle with a punch.

Not only is Yankees legend Mickey Mantle involved in Kramer's singular world, but so is Joe Pepitone, a former Yankee who had a mother lode of potential, but never quite became the superstar that he was forecast to be. He was known more for his sizeable hairpieces, his eccentric behavior, and bringing a hair dryer into the conservative baseball clubhouses of the 1960s. Pepitone later authored an appropriately titled memoir: *Joe, You Coulda Made Us Proud*. Well, if nothing else, he is forever immortalized as the man who charged the pitcher's mound to get at Cosmo Kramer, who had purposely thrown a beanball at him in a baseball fantasy camp. *Seinfeld* frequently played inside baseball, if you will, with references to historical events and personages like Joe Pepitone, who older baseball fans—particularly New Yorkers—would remember.

The great Mickey Mantle passed away in 1995, only two years after the Kramer incident, of liver cancer, not

JOE PEPITONE • 1B-OF

Former New York Yankees ballplayer and convicted felon Joe Pepitone is perhaps more famous for being on the receiving end of a Cosmo Kramer knockdown pitch at a baseball fantasy camp. *Courtesy of Bill Hlubik*

Although he didn't physically appear on the show, baseball legend Mickey Mantle, seen here on a 1965 trading card, plays a key role in "The Visa." Kramer knocks him out cold during a fight at a Yankees fantasy camp and later calls on the Hall of Famer at his New York City restaurant to apologize.   *Courtesy of Mark Keating*

complications from getting socked in the face. Hank Bauer and Moose Skowron are gone, too. In 2012, Mickey Mantle's Restaurant closed its doors for good after twenty-four years in business. Christopher Villano, the restaurant's owner since 2002, cited "increasing food prices, shifting city regulations, and land-lord interference" for the closure. But the restaurant and several Yankee names from the past are not just part of baseball lore, but the *Seinfeld* legacy as well.

Yes, it's fair to say that Kramer goes places that very few New Yorkers go. In the episode "The Summer of George," Kramer and his Tony Award dine at Sardi's in the theater district. He swims in the not-especially-clean East River in the episode "The Nap." After complaining that the pool where he regularly performs his laps has a certain undesirable element, he tells Jerry: "Well, I had been swimming for three hours . . . and I was in a real groove . . . so I decided to keep going. But at ten they start the 'Aquasonics.' Thirty-five geriatrics throwing elbows! It was like I was swimming through a flabby-armed spanking machine."

Returning home after his East River swimming adventure, Jerry wonders what is the source of the horrible odor coming from Kramer. When he learns that it's the East River's calling card, Jerry questions his friend's sanity. Undaunted, Kramer reports that he witnessed two others in the East River with him, only they were "floating" and not "moving much."

In the episode "The Marine Biologist," Kramer is again by the sea, out on the Rockaway Peninsula in Queens, on this go-round, attempting to hit golf balls into the Atlantic Ocean surf. Non–New Yorkers don't often realize that there is an extensive area of ocean coastline in the New York City boroughs of Brooklyn, Queens, and Staten Island. It is here, too, where George rescues a whale in distress because of a stray golf ball hit by Kramer that landed smack-dab in its blowhole. A trip to the Rockaways from the Upper West Side of Manhattan is approximately a twenty-mile car ride. It can be accessed via the subway, too. The gang could be enjoying an ocean breeze in an hour and fifteen minutes by hopping on the A or C train.

In the episode "The Lip Reader," Kramer is in Queens once more, having taken a job as a ball boy at the USTA National Tennis Center, home of the U.S. Open Grand Slam tennis tournament, in Flushing Meadows. Jerry and George also attend a tennis match there, and the latter is captured by the television cameras at the concession stand with egg—well, actually hot fudge sundae—on his face.

In the episode "The Burning," Kramer calls on Mount Sinai Medical Center at 101st Street and Fifth Avenue in the guise of an actor, not a patient. He is there to *pretend* he has a disease for the benefit of medical students. "See, they hire actors to help the students practice diagnosing," he tells an incredulous Jerry. When Kramer is given gonorrhea as his pretend disease, he is visibly disappointed. He'd rather pretend to have the disease of his little friend and fellow actor, Mickey Abbott: bacterial meningitis. In addition to this bit of acting work, Kramer and the diminutive Mickey get jobs as stand-in actors on the soap opera *All My Children*, which was filmed at the time at an ABC studio at 320 West 66th Street. While on the subject of Kramer and ABC, he appears on *Live with Regis and Kathie Lee*, filmed in a studio at 7 Lincoln Square, to promote his coffee table book about coffee tables.

In the episode "The Strike," Kramer returns to work at H&H Bagels after a twelve-year walkout in quest of better wages. Actually, the federal minimum wage finally caught up with what he and his striking co-workers were demanding twelve years earlier. The location of his employer—2239 Broadway near West 80th Street—is, in fact, very close to his apartment. Kramer can walk to work without breaking a sweat or hailing a taxicab.

To leave no stone unturned in the historical record of Kramer's employer, there were two additional H&H Bagel retailers: one across town on the Upper East Side—Second Avenue between East 80th Street and East 81st Street—and another in the Hell's Kitchen section of Manhattan, on West 46th Street. When Kramer was on the payroll, H&H Bagels was an extremely popular Manhattan-based bagel producer—the largest in New York City during its heyday in the 1980s and 1990s, and one of the largest in the world, when it was estimated that the company churned out as many as eighty thousand bagels per day. "Like no other bagel in the world" was its slogan. The H&H Bagel location where Kramer toiled was open twenty-four hours a day, too. Alas, on June 29, 2011, New York City marshals shuttered Kramer's erstwhile employer, H&H Bagels on the Upper West Side, after its owner, Helmer Toro, was indicted for pilfering his employees' withholding taxes to the tune of five hundred thousand dollars. He ultimately was found guilty and sentenced to fifty weekends in jail. It's little wonder Kramer and company went on strike against this less-than-transparent bagel business.

On another fast-food front, Kramer encounters a bedeviling problem with a new Kenny Rogers Roasters restaurant that opens up in the neighborhood at 71st Street and Broadway. In the episode "The Chicken Roaster," the eatery's bright red neon chicken sign floods Kramer's apartment with light—so much light that his Venetian blinds can't keep it at bay. "It's killing me," he tells Jerry. "I can't eat. I can't sleep. All I see is that giant red sun in the shape of a chicken." Kramer, though, does not hold singer Kenny Rogers—co-founder of the chain of the eponymously named restaurants—responsible. "I don't think that Kenny Rogers has any idea what's going on down there," he says.

Interestingly, Kramer wasn't the only one who had issues with this particular Kenny Rogers Roasters. A real-life lawyer named Aaron Chess Lichtman, who leased an office on the second floor above the chicken joint, placed a hand-lettered sign outside his window that read: "Bad Food." Lichtman reasoned, "They have cheesy music played loud enough to hear in the hallway of the second floor. In my opinion, salt, grease, and rubbery corn do not make for good food. But if you are going to buy it, there is a place next door for half the price." Like Kramer, Lichtman also found fault with the eatery's "high voltage" neon sign, which had been placed above his office windows. "It makes it appear as though my office is in their dining room," he said. The owners of this particular Kenny Rogers Roasters filed a two-million-dollar lawsuit against Lichtman, claiming that his sign was a "malicious falsehood," with the sole purpose of putting the chicken roasters out of business. New York Supreme Court Justice Charles Ramos tossed out the lawsuit, decreeing that Lichtman's actions represented freedom of speech, which is protected by the First Amendment. Ramos said Lichtman's words expressed an opinion, not a statement of fact.

In Kramer's New York City (in "The Wig Master"), he gets arrested as a pimp in the Jiffy Park parking lot on 11th Avenue and 44th Street, where both he and George park their cars for the bargain-basement price of seventy-five dollars per month. The charge against him: operating a brothel from his automobile. When Kramer goes to pick up the car in the lot, he encounters a little action inside the vehicle, which explains the good deal on the parking. He is also dressed like a stereotypical pimp, courtesy of a walking stick given to him by Elaine, a white hat that blew off a woman's head, and a jacket from a production of Andrew Lloyd Webber's *Joseph and the Amazing Technicolor Dreamcoat* at the Majestic Theatre at 245 West 44th Street. Mistaken for a pimp, Kramer is arrested by the vice squad and interrogated at a nearby police station.

East Side, West Side, All Around the Town

Elaine is in Sotheby's at 1334 York Avenue. She's bidding on the late President John F. Kennedy's golf clubs for her boss, J. Peterman. It is also the same elite auction house where Peterman wins a slice of wedding cake from the 1937 marriage of the former King Edward VIII to Wallis Simpson. He pays twenty-nine thousand dollars for the privilege, only to discover, a short time later, that Elaine mistakenly ate it.

Elaine and her date, former New York Mets star Keith Hernandez, kiss and cuddle at Fitzpatrick's Bar and Grill at 1641 Second Avenue. The place then became Molly Pitcher's Ale House, which closed in 2015. Previously,

Jerry and Kramer had met Hernandez at the West Side YMCA at 5 West 63rd Street. Kramer performs chauffeur duties for Hernandez when he drives the ex-ballplayer to LaGuardia Airport in Flushing, Queens, approximately seven-and-a-half miles due east from the west side of Manhattan. LaGuardia Airport, named after New York City's ninety-ninth mayor, Fiorello LaGuardia, the "Little Flower," is also where Jerry and George commandeer a neo-Nazi's limousine. John F. Kennedy International Airport, or JFK as it's informally known, in Jamaica, Queens, is where George and Kramer go to pick up Jerry and Elaine in the episode "The Airport." George is on cloud nine as he appears on the verge of pulling off the "perfect airport pickup." Kramer, though, who is behind the wheel, takes an unwanted detour—from George's perspective, at least—on the Long Island Expressway. George bemoans the fact that what he had timed to the minute—via the Grand Central and Van Wyck—has been cast asunder by Kramer's impulsive decision.

As circumstances unfold, Jerry and Elaine's flight is re-routed to LaGuardia Airport and then rerouted back to JFK, creating all kinds of mayhem and miscommunication. The topper to their New York City airport misadventures finds George on the receiving end of a beating from a shackled serial killer in a bathroom on a plane sitting on a JFK runway.

Champagne, anyone? Jerry, George, Elaine, and Kramer frequently patronize Champagne Video at 213 West 79th Street, between Broadway and Amsterdam Avenue. It's a shop where one can rent VHS movies, including adult films, in the age before DVDs, Netflix, and streaming. A great deal goes down at this independent video rental store in the neighborhood, including Elaine becoming smitten with the mysterious and unseen Vincent, who recommends movies. In the episode "The Couch," George, who had recently joined a book club, attempts to procure a VHS copy of the 1961 film *Breakfast at Tiffany's* at Champagne Video. He hopes to circumvent the actual reading of the ninety-page book. The movie, though, is out—and George is out of luck. Or so it seems. When the situation allows, George sneaks a peek at the computer and locates the name and address of the individual who has rented *Breakfast at Tiffany's*. Shortly thereafter, George turns up at the home of a man named Joe Temple, and ultimately watches the film with Joe and his daughter, Remy. George gripes that Joe doesn't have any popcorn in the house, and that there is entirely too much talking during the movie. When he gets up for a grape juice refill, young Remy takes his spot on the couch and refuses to relinquish it upon his return. A skirmish ensues and George spills the grape juice on the Temples' living room couch.

In the episode "The Smelly Car," George bumps into his ex-girlfriend, Susan Ross, and her new love interest, Mona, in Champagne Video. He simultaneously discovers that he forgot to rewind the movie, *Rochelle, Rochelle*, which he is return-ing a day late, and that it's going to cost him an additional fee of two dollars. When George objects that there is no sign in the store indicating the charge, Kramer advises him to take the movie back home, rewind it, and return it the next day. He would then be charged only a late fee of $1.49, which is considerably less than the two-dollar rewinding fee.

George takes Kramer's sage advice, but, unfortunately, the movie gets stolen from Jerry's car. He is thus compelled to pay not a two-dollar fee, but the replacement cost of the video: ninety-eight dollars. To compound his misery, George has to borrow thirty-five dollars from Susan to pay for it.

Sadly, Champagne Video has since shut its doors, one more victim of advancing technologies. If Blockbuster couldn't make it, the mom-and-pops certainly weren't going to be able to buck the tidal wave of streaming videos.

New York City Roundup

A further roundup of the *Seinfeld* gang on the mean streets of Manhattan finds Jerry visiting the New York Pubic Library at 42nd Street and Fifth Avenue to discuss Henry Miller's *Tropic of Cancer*, a long-overdue book that he says he returned. He didn't. After attempting to interfere with the U.S. mail, Kramer gets cross-examined by the postmaster general at the U.S. Post Office Cooper Station at 11th Street and Fourth Avenue, which is also Newman's workplace. He also calls on the Permanent Mission of Cuba to the United Nations at 315 Lexington Avenue to swap his jacket for some fine Cuban cigars. Owned by the Republic of Cuba, this prime New York City property is valued at $18 million.

George diligently toils at Yankee Stadium in the Bronx under the watchful eyes of George Steinbrenner. Presumed to be neo-Nazis, George and Jerry encounter trouble at Madison Square Garden, located at 2 Penn Plaza—the same sports arena where a face-painted David Puddy, Elaine's boyfriend, roots, roots, roots for his favorite hockey team, the New Jersey Devils, against the New York Rangers, the home team.

George and Jerry pitch a sitcom idea to NBC big shots at 30 Rockefeller Plaza. Jerry is also ridiculed there as a guest on the *Today* show hosted by Bryant Gumbel, who finds one of his articles of clothing—a puffy pirate-looking shirt—highly amusing. Inadvertently, Jerry had agreed to wear it because Kramer's girlfriend, Leslie, the designer of the shirt, is a "low-talker." The misunderstanding occurred at the Saloon, a Broadway restaurant located across the street from Lincoln Center. Speaking of Lincoln Center, Elaine acts as a "beard" in the episode (appropriately titled) "The Beard," by accompanying a gay man to see *Swan Lake* at the Metropolitan Opera there, and thus fool the latter's possibly homophobic boss with overt displays of affection.

In the episode "The Pick," Kramer drops in on Calvin Klein at the Trump Tower on Fifth Avenue to protest that the company poached his idea for a beach-scented perfume that they are now marketing as "The Ocean." After registering his complaint with Calvin Klein himself, Kramer is thrown off his game by a healthy dose of flattery. Klein describes him as "graceful" and "very lean, but muscular." In sum, "spectacular."

Then, of course, there's Uncle Leo shoplifting in Brentano's, an independent bookstore at 597 Fifth Avenue. Brentano's independence didn't serve it well when the bookstore giants, Barnes & Noble and, later, Borders, came to town. But time and technology does a number on big guys and small guys alike, as Borders is now out of business and Barnes & Noble is closing stores and not opening them in Manhattan.

Jerry and George visit the lobby of the Westbury Hotel at 15 East 69th Street to meet Elaine's hard-nosed, hard-drinking father. The Westbury Hotel is yet another casualty of time. In 1999, it was converted into condominium apartments. One can get a three-bedroom apartment with four-and-a-half baths for eight million dollars there. (God only knows what the monthly maintenance fees are.) The cast of *Seinfeld* could afford to live at what once was the Westbury Hotel, but not too many *Seinfeld* fans.

In the episode "The Doodle," Elaine gets a suite in the Plaza Hotel on Fifth Avenue and Central Park South when she lies to a prospective employer, Viking Press, by claiming that she's from out of town. She supplies the publisher with Jerry's parents' Florida address as her own. When the elder Seinfelds come to town, Jerry implores Elaine to let them stay in the Plaza Hotel suite while his apartment is being fumigated for a flea infestation. Morty, Helen, Uncle Leo, and Nana, too, take full advantage of the luxurious accommodations, room service, pay-per-view movies, and other perks. They run up a huge tab that does not go unnoticed by Mr. Mandel at Viking Press, with offices at 375 Hudson Street. Elaine's attempts at explaining the numerous charges that include hours of massage, a dozen in-room movies, shoe shines, and all kinds of snacks gets her nowhere. She doesn't get the job.

In "The Cartoon," while duly employed with J. Peterman Catalog, Elaine drops in on the cartoon editor named Mr. Elinoff at *The New Yorker*, located at 20 West 43rd Street. She wishes to ascertain the meaning of their latest cartoon, featuring a cat and a dog in an office milieu. The feline is telling a canine co-worker, "I've enjoyed reading your e-mail."

Elinoff: Ha! It's merely a commentary on contemporary mores.

Elaine: But *what* is the comment?

Elinoff: It's a slice of life.

Elaine: No, it isn't.

Elinoff: Pun?

Elaine: I don't think so.

Elinoff: Vorshtein?

Elaine: That's not a word. You have no idea what this means, do you?

Elinoff: No.

Elaine: Then *why* did you print it?

Elinoff: I liked the kitty.

This little chat nonetheless furnishes Elaine with an opening and she gets a cartoon of hers published in the magazine: a pig at a complaint department window saying, "I wish I was taller." Later it is revealed that she subconsciously ripped off a *Ziggy* cartoon. In July 2012, *The New Yorker* published Elaine's cartoon in the magazine and asked its readers to caption it. It was almost fifteen years after "The Cartoon" aired, an episode that satirized the magazine's peculiar choices of cartoons and other pretensions. One final footnote on this subject is that Mr. Elinoff's "Vorshtein" response to Elaine's query has made it into the Urban Dictionary at Urbandictionary.com, as so many other *Seinfeld* words and expressions have. It is defined thusly: "A word used tersely to answer a fundamental question that cannot be explained by means of logically reasoning."

Jerry, George, Elaine, and Kramer frequently went to the movies. The Regency Theater at 1987 Broadway is where Jerry and his girlfriend neck while not watching *Schindler's List*, and where Elaine purchases Juicy Fruit at the concession counter before heading over to see her hospitalized boyfriend, Jake Jarmel. It, too, has since closed its doors. Nearby, SONY Lincoln Square, a mega-multiplex, no doubt contributed to its demise. Elaine both saw and loathed *The English Patient* at the Guild 50th at 33 West 50th Street. This 450-seat theater, which opened in 1938 at Rockefeller Center, has, as of 1999, been consigned to the trash heap of history as well. The place's original lease established a minimum ticket price of twenty-five cents "to keep things high-toned" and the riffraff out.

St. Luke's–Roosevelt Hospital Center at 425 West 59th Street hosted Jerry, George, Elaine, and Kramer on a few occasions. It is the hospital where Jerry and Kramer observe an operation in real time and drop, by accident, a Junior Mint candy into the patient's—a former boyfriend of Elaine's—open body. This very same healing institution is where a suicidal patient leaps to his death and lands on George's car, causing substantial damage that he tries to recoup from the hospital. George's fiancée, Susan, also breathes her last at this place after ingesting toxins from the glue on the envelopes of her cheap wedding invitations. A year later and George, after slipping on party invitations, is learning to walk all over again there.

Elaine toils for multiple years at Pendant Publishing at 600 Madison Avenue. On her diverse résumé is a job as personal assistant to an executive for Doubleday, the eccentric Justin Pitt, who originally hires her because she reminds him of a young Jacqueline Kennedy Onassis, who was an old friend. Mr. Pitt lives on 641 West End Avenue at 91st Street. He loves Snickers candy bars and eats them with a knife and fork. He feels privileged, too, to have won an opportunity—thanks to Elaine—to be one of the line handlers of the Woody Woodpecker balloon in the Macy's Thanksgiving Day Parade.

The New York Health & Racquet Club, located at 24 East 13th Street, is where George urinates in the shower; Elaine exercises and drools alongside John F. Kennedy Jr.; and the boys play basketball with Jimmy, who is new in town and who always refers to himself in the third person. When Elaine meets Jimmy in the episode "The Jimmy," she thinks he's referring to the man she's had her eye on, a blond Adonis named Hank. Jimmy, though, is referring to Jimmy when he says, "You know, Jimmy is pretty sweet on you" and "Jimmy's been watching you. You're just Jimmy's type."

Kramer is the guest of honor at 1535 Broadway, the New York Marriott Marquis. It's a benefit dinner for "Able Mentally Challenged Adults." Courtesy of the lingering effects of Novocain, he is mistaken for one. But it turns out well for him in the end because singer Mel Tormé, the "Velvet Fog," is also on hand and dedicates the song "When You're Smiling" to a smiling-from-ear-to-ear Kramer.

Elaine shops at Barneys New York (the apostrophe was jettisoned in 1981), an upscale clothing and accessories department store at 106 Seventh Avenue. She accuses the place of employing "skinny mirrors" that make clothing items look good while you're trying them on in the store, but not so good when you get home. This particular Barneys is no more.

In the episode "The Voice," Kramer takes on an intern from New York University (NYU) at 566 LaGuardia Place. A student named Darren is shown the finer points of what it takes to run a company—in this case Kramerica, a business whose *raison d'être* is to end, once and for all, maritime oil spills. Dean Jones, of NYU, cancels the internship when he discovers what Kramer has been having Darren do for him, including laundry and mending chicken wire. Later, Darren shows up at Kramer's apartment, claiming that—internship or no internship—he's devoted to Kramerica and its ideals. With very little coaxing needed, Kramer announces that "Kramerica Industries lives."

In the episode "The Outing," a college-aged reporter named Sharon from NYU publishes a piece in the university newspaper that brands Jerry and George a gay couple. While vehemently denying that he is gay, Jerry nonetheless makes it clear that he believes there is nothing wrong with being so. George uses the excuse that he is gay to break up with his girlfriend, Allison. (Jason Alexander holds that the phrase "Not that there's anything wrong with that," vis-à-vis being gay, is the single most popular utterance of the entire series.)

On the food front, George plucks an éclair out of the garbage from the Little Pie Company at 424 West 43rd Street. Jerry buys fellow standup comedian Kenny Bania a cup of soup at Mendy's kosher restaurant and delicatessen at 61 East 34th Street.

In the episode "The Friars Club," Jerry tells George that he's considering joining the club, and that fellow comedian Pat Cooper is willing to sponsor him. Founded in 1904, the Friars Club at 57 East 55th Street, between Madison Avenue and Park Avenue, is a private organization. Its membership consists mostly of entertainers and the club is renowned for hosting no-holds-barred, racy celebrity roasts. In 1999, with Jason Alexander acting as the roast master,

Insufferable comedian Kenny Bania's preferred restaurant for a bowl of soup.
Photo by Thomas Nigro

Jerry Stiller was roasted. Everyone from Jack Benny to Drew Carey to Donald Trump has been on the Friars Club rotisserie.

New York Central

Jerry, George, Elaine, and Kramer are frequently spotted in New York City's Central Park, with its 1,317 square miles and 840 acres running from 59th Street to 110th Street, south to north, and Fifth Avenue to Central Park West, east to west. Kramer once swiped Anthony Quinn's T-shirt in the park while the latter was doing sit-ups. Also in the park, he meets a dog named Smuckers, who coughs a lot like him. Kramer and Newman relax in this sprawling expanse of green, smoking stogies and enjoying a stimulating conversation about the Bermuda Triangle. George gleefully runs through the park after getting a job as a hand model, and he wastes pigeons there on another occasion. Jerry procures tickets to a Paul Simon concert in the park. Elaine, her close-talker boyfriend, Aaron, along with Morty and Helen Seinfeld, ride a hansom cab through it. Uncle Leo reports that his son, Jeffrey, is being commended by the New York City Parks Department for his stellar performances in conducting Central Park walking tours.

In the episode "The Understudy," George barrels over Bette Midler during a Central Park softball game between the cast of the musical adaptation of *Rochelle, Rochelle* and members of the Improv. "The show will go on, but not Bette Midler," a TV newsman later announces. "While playing softball in the park,

Ms. Midler was injured when another player thoughtlessly rammed her at home plate, all captured on amateur videotape." Jerry is dating Midler's understudy in this hilarious spoof of the to-do surrounding 1994 Winter Olympics skaters Nancy Kerrigan and Tonya Harding.

In the episode "The Face Painter," Kramer gets into a row with Barry, the monkey at the Central Park Zoo. In "The Soup," George and his girlfriend, Kelly, stroll through the park while he discourses on his love of the word "manure." In "The Sponge," Kramer refuses to wear a ribbon during an AIDS Walk New York fundraiser through the place, saying: "This is America. I don't have to wear anything I don't want to wear." He is attacked by an angry mob. In "The Rye," Kramer is a hansom cab driver for one brief shining moment and gives Japanese tourists a singular history lesson of the park: "This was designed in 1850 by Joe Pepitone. Ummm . . . built during the Civil War so the northern armies could practice fighting on . . . on grass."

In the episode "The Opera," "Crazy" Joe Davola, dressed like a clown, pummels a pack of punks who accost him in the park, and then ventures over to Town Hall, a non-profit theater and National Historic site, at 123 West 43rd Street, where he stalks a frightened Jerry at a performance of the Italian opera *I Pagliacci.*

In the episode "The Susie," George Steinbrenner and his Yankees hold a pinstriped ball at Tavern on the Green at 67 Central Park West, which operated from 1934 to 2009, when it closed up shop after filing for bankruptcy. It reopened in 2014.

Despite the show being filmed largely on a sound stage three thousand miles away from the hustle and bustle of the Big Apple, *Seinfeld* was New York City to the core. The characters' attitudes, job experiences, and misadventures were quintessential New York, even if it was their own distinctive version of life in the Big Town.

18

The Mornings After

The *Seinfeld* Phenomenon and Its Cultural Impact

T he *Seinfeld* phenomenon, as it were, didn't occur overnight. While the show initially received a fair share of critical praise for being an incomparable, clever sitcom, the ratings didn't exactly go through the roof of 30 Rockefeller Plaza. In fact, that distinctive *Seinfeld* buzz didn't permeate the cultural ether until the fourth season and thereafter.

Thursday's Child

At first, NBC couldn't settle on the right spot for the show in its primetime schedule. Finally, in 1993, the network permanently moved the show to Thursday night to replace the long-running series *Cheers*, which was exiting the television stage after a successful eleven-year run. During its first few seasons, *Seinfeld* had been bouncing between Wednesday nights and Thursday nights. A considerable audience first noticed the show when it followed *Cheers* at 9:30 p.m. After moving into that show's coveted Thursday night 9:00 p.m. slot, where it would remain, *Seinfeld* became not only a ratings-grabber but a veritable phenomenon. The Friday mornings after episodes aired inevitably found people of all ages, and from all walks of life, with *Seinfeld* on their brains. The show supplied a surfeit of breakfast-table banter, office water-cooler chitchat, and coffee shop repartee. *Seinfeld* rivaled sports talk in saloons and neighborhood gossip in salons. Seemingly overnight, the characters Jerry, George, Elaine, and Kramer had become sensations, and the actors who played them big stars who suddenly had the paparazzi nipping at their heels.

"They just wanted to do something fun," Jonathan Wolff, *Seinfeld* composer, remarked to *People* magazine about the show's two creators. Wolff remembered, though, that Jerry Seinfeld, Larry David, and the actors in the series really didn't think the show was going to last more than several episodes.

Apprehensive NBC executive Warren Littlefield once asked, "Shouldn't there be, like, any stories?" But what would make *Seinfeld* the huge hit that it eventually became—the aforementioned phenomenon—was exactly that. There weren't any stories per se, at least of the traditional sitcom variety. Not a single *Seinfeld* character was ever going to get married and host a chaotic wedding where the best man forgets the ring or some such sitcom cliché. No babies were going to be delivered by Jerry or Kramer in their building's malfunctioning elevator. Jerry wasn't going to be asked to play a comedic Cyrano de Bergerac to help George win over a girl, although Newman did it for Kramer. No, not on *Seinfeld*—never! Describing *Seinfeld*'s plotlines—the show's version of "stories"—is a whole lot more involved than recounting episodes of *I Love Lucy*, *All in the Family*, or *Frasier*.

The *Seinfeld* Alternate Universe

Jerry Seinfeld described to *People* magazine what the show was really about: "Imagine if all you do is hang out with your friends and have frequent romantic encounters, which don't really hurt, and work is only sporadically dealt with—you don't have to spend time at work except when it's interesting and exciting—and basically you're having a lot of coffee, a lot of lunches and dinners, a lot of swinging and a lot of hanging."

The *Seinfeld* phenomenon was grounded in the show's characters having a full twenty-two minutes each week to interact with one another and others in their exclusive universe. Questions concerning life's mundane trivialities and oddities were regularly posed by Jerry, George, Elaine, and Kramer and hashed out by one and all. There were, in fact, many life lessons that we learned on *Seinfeld*, like the rules that apply to double-dipping a chip, appropriate times and places to urinate, and other such matters of etiquette. In the episode "The Pick," Jerry's girlfriend casts him aside because she catches him in the act of picking his nose. He defends himself by claiming that he was merely scratching his nose, not picking it, because there was "no nostril penetration." This brand of multi-layered humor—dealing with the ordinary—was the essence of *Seinfeld*, and why so many people couldn't stop talking about the show, quoting its dialogue and repeating its catchphrases.

Sein Language

Key to the *Seinfeld* phenomenon was the show's contribution to the vernacular— i.e., its original catchphrases to describe particular behaviors, people, and events. *Seinfeld* has quite literally added to the English language—enhanced it with turns of phrases that will forever be remembered.

In the late 1970s, the ABC sitcom *Happy Days*, starring Ron Howard and Henry Winkler, was the rage. The character of Arthur Fonzarelli, "The Fonz," was the Cosmo Kramer of his day on the popularity front. The show's catchphrases, like "Aaaaaay!" "Sit on it!" and "Correctamundo," were heard all over the schoolyards and on the streets. But it's fair to say that the content of *Seinfeld*'s phraseology is somewhat more adult-oriented and has greater staying power.

What follows is a random sampling of the show's Shakespearean contributions to the English language.

"Serenity now!"

While Ralph Kramden had his "Pins and needles, needles and pins, it's a happy man that grins" mantra to repeat whenever he was feeling overly angry and upset, Frank Costanza, George's father, had a mantra of his very own to help keep his blood pressure under control, in the episode "The Serenity Now."

> Frank: Doctor gave me a relaxation cassette. When my blood pressure gets too high, the man on the tape tells me to say, "Serenity now!"
>
> George: Are you supposed to yell it?
>
> Frank: The man on the tape wasn't specific.

"Master of your domain"

This phrase originated from one of the all-time great *Seinfeld* episodes, "The Contest," and refers to complete and utter abstinence vis-à-vis gratifying oneself. Engaged in a contest to see who can go the longest without masturbating, Jerry wonders how his friends are getting along in this taxing act of self-restraint. He poses the immortal question, "Are you still master of your domain?"

"These pretzels are making me thirsty"

This famous line, from "The Alternate Side," specifically refers to Kramer's speaking role—his one sentence of dialogue as an extra—in a Woody Allen film. He receives ample advice from his three friends on how best to deliver the line and maximize his moment on the Big Screen, which—alas—doesn't come to pass.

Urinator

A *Seinfeld*-born term (from "The Wife") that describes a person in a health club who urinates in the shower rather than take the time to walk to the bathroom. Reasoning that they're all pipes leading to the same place, George has no problem being a "urinator."

Shrinkage

This invaluable *Seinfeld* contribution to the English lexicon, from the episode "The Hamptons," refers to what happens to a male's private parts when he goes swimming or showers in cold water. When Elaine asks in astonishment, "It shrinks?" Jerry promptly replies, "Like a frightened turtle."

Chucker

A *Seinfeld* gift to the patois, from "The Boyfriend," and a descriptive word that all of us who attended high school and played basketball in gym class can appreciate. The word refers to someone who shoots the ball every time he gets his hands on it, and never, for one moment, considers passing it to a teammate. Although the preponderance of evidence says otherwise, George vehemently denies being a "chucker."

Sponge-worthy

This is Elaine's evocative phrase (from "The Sponge") to describe the men she feels are deserving of her employing a finite contraceptive sponge during sexual intercourse. She cannot "afford to waste any of 'em."

George and Jerry in a scene from "The Smelly Car," the source of the term "de-smellify." *NBC/Photofest*

De-smellify

Jerry's catchy turn of phrase in "The Smelly Car" for his high hopes that a valet parking guy's nasty body odor would dissipate with the passage of time. Unfortunately for him—and many others—the "odor molecules" failed to "de-smellify" his vehicle this time around. In fact, the ghastly stench actually "gained strength throughout the night."

Ma-newer

Courtesy of George, in the episode "The Soup," we can now look at the word "manure" in a vastly different light. He says, "If you think about it, manure is not really that bad a word. I mean, it's 'newer,' which is good, and a 'ma' in front of it, which is also good. Ma-newer, right?"

Baldist

Only on *Seinfeld* (in the episode "The Tape") is there a special word for a woman who refuses to go out on a date with a man because he is follicly challenged. Jerry accuses Elaine of being a "baldist" because she's never dated a bald man.

Yada yada yada

In "The Yada Yada," George's girlfriend reveals a penchant for leaving out the most important details in her stories and recollections with the expression "Yada yada yada." The vernacular has never been the same since the episode aired.

Re-gifter

When Elaine dubs Dr. Tim Whatley a "re-gifter" in "The Label Maker," the phrase took on a life of its own. Countless men and women admitted to being "re-gifters," and just as many being the recipients of them.

Kavorka

Courtesy of the *Seinfeld* episode "The Conversion," the "Latvian" word *kavorka* is in the Urban Dictionary. Kramer was said to possess *kavorka*, which translates as "the lure of the animal." That is, a physical specimen completely irresistible to the opposite sex.

Shiks-appeal

Elaine Benes has done it again, supplying the world with a word, "Shiks-appeal," to describe the attraction of Jewish men to non-Jewish women. In "The Serenity

Now," Elaine reveals the extent of her "Shiks-appeal," receiving a mother lode of attention from Jewish males, including her former boss, Mr. Lippman, his young son, and Rabbi Glickman.

"No soup for you!"

After "The Soup Nazi" aired, the expression "No soup for you!" took the world by storm. A cantankerous soup peddler, who was a stickler for rules, uttered these now-immortal words.

Double-dipping

George's bad habit of "double-dipping" his potato chips popularized this term. Inspired by his actions in "The Implant," the Discovery Channel's *MythBusters* examined whether or not "double-dipping" adds unwanted bacteria to dips. Their conclusion: It's not a big deal because the dips—store bought and homemade—already contain traces of bacteria.

"Festivus for the rest of us"

Inspired by writer Dan O'Keefe's father, who created Festivus—an alternative holiday to what he considered the overly commercialized Christmas holiday—this expression first appeared in "The Strike." Frank Costanza is the television father of "Festivus," which is celebrated on December 23, and he's got his reasons for no longer celebrating Christmas. Since the episode first aired, increasing numbers of people very literally celebrate the holiday with its traditions of "airing of grievances" and "feats of strength." An atheist group garnered press attention when they erected a Festivus pole—the holiday's alternative to the Christmas

The Not Necessarily Top Ten Underrated *Seinfeld* Episodes

10. "The Doodle," where George agonized over whether a woman's sketch of him was a good or bad sign vis-à-vis a relationship.
9. "The Cheever Letters," where Susan Ross's father's big secret—a longtime, passionate affair with writer John Cheever—was unmasked.
8. "The Pen," which found Jerry and Elaine in Florida visiting the Seinfelds and learning entirely too much about Jack Klompus's "astronaut pen."
7. "The Pony Remark," frequently considered the episode that first established the *Seinfeld* benchmark in humor.
6. "The Dinner Party," where the gang's determined mission was to procure a chocolate babka and a bottle of wine for a party they were all attending.
5. "The Parking Space," which considered the urban conundrum of who has the right to street parking space, someone backing in—like George—or someone pulling in nose first.
4. "The Apology," where George testily bristled over not having received—from his vantage point—a well-deserved "Step Nine" apology from a recovering alcoholic.
3. "The Junior Mint," where a piece of Kramer's candy fell into the open body cavity of Elaine's former boyfriend during a major operation.
2. "The Pilot," where Jerry and George's sitcom pilot was at long last cast and shot.
1. "The Abstinence," where George transformed into a genius, and Elaine a blithering idiot, while they were both abstaining from sex.

tree—festooned with beer cans alongside a nativity scene and menorah in the Florida State Capitol building.

According to Jerry, George broke his glasses while playing basketball, because he was running from what?

When speaking about poultry, who informs George's father that "They're all chickens. The rooster has sex with all of them"?

In "The Money," what comedienne played Kramer's girlfriend, Emily, a woman afflicted with "jimmy-legs"?

No show in the annals of television is more steeped in trivia than *Seinfeld*. Its characters, plotlines, and dialogue are the stuff of legend. Fans never tire of hashing out the show's finer points. Card from the *Seinfeld* Scene It game.

Seinfeld: The Human Comedy

Regarding the whole *Seinfeld* phenomenon that took the mid-1990s by storm, Wayne Knight, who played Newman, made the following insightful comment to *People* magazine: "*Seinfeld* is proof you can do a funny show about a group of people, none of whom has any decency, and strike a chord with the public deeper than any warm-and-fuzzy show."

This singular group of friends—the likes of whom had never before been seen on television—with their capacity to screw up one another's lives, drew people to them. We just couldn't get enough of these hilariously self-centered people. Week after week, we tuned in to see what Jerry, George, Elaine, and Kramer would do next. We talked about their antics with our family, friends, and co-workers:

- "Did you catch what George said last night about being a quitter?"
- "How about Jerry's observation about the toxic combo of drinking and keeping secrets?"
- "Did you like the latest Kramer addition to the English language: 'Wrong, Majumbo'?"

Actor and comedian Don Knotts once told talk-show host Phil Donahue that *The Andy Griffith Show* was the very first sitcom in which the show's characters frequently veered off and spoke about things unrelated to the main storyline. Memorable scenes, for instance, involve Andy and Barney lazily sitting around on the front porch and reminiscing, even on one occasion lurching into their old high school theme song. Decades later, *Seinfeld* took this device to the next level. Life's humdrum grind endlessly sidetracks Jerry, George, Elaine, and Kramer. They can't help but observe the world they live in and offer their opinions and commentaries on the ordinary as well as the absurd happenings in life, like George expressing his disdain for having to ask a shopkeeper for change. He compared the unenviable task to asking someone to donate an organ.

In the overall picture, *Seinfeld*'s appeal was rooted in its singular ability to address the width and breadth of human relationships: friendship, sexual, parent-child, and employee-employer. Fans appreciated the show's unique take on these relationships, and found many with which they could readily identify. Jerry breaking up with girlfriends for reasons ranging from George having seen her naked to her being liked by his parents were the kinds of things that fueled the show's popularity. Fans tuned in week after week wanting more of the same. The off-the-wall antics and peculiar hang-ups of Jerry, George, Elaine, and Kramer amassed a bigger and bigger audience as the series progressed. There really had never been any sitcom characters quite like them.

The *Seinfeld* phenomenon was the genuine article. Ask anyone who was alive, alert, awake, and aware in the 1990s, and they'll tell you how real it was. Even people who didn't watch the show couldn't help but end up in the crosshairs of *Seinfeld* chatter. And the fact that the show went out on top in its last season proves that the phenomenon had legs. It was also a testament to how groundbreaking and how funny the show was—and still is all these years later in syndication.

Part V
The Episodes

19

Season One

Taking Flight

The first season of *Seinfeld* was a truncated one, consisting of only the four episodes that NBC ordered. They aired in May and June 1990. It was these make-or-break four episodes that garnered decent enough ratings. The network thus committed to a second season of twelve episodes, which would commence airing in January 1991. The pilot, "The Seinfeld Chronicles," was also rerun in 1990 and is now, in syndication, considered part and parcel of the show's first season.

Episode 1: "The Seinfeld Chronicles" (original air date: July 5, 1989)

Creators Jerry Seinfeld and Larry David wrote the pilot episode with Art Wolff in the director's chair and Castle Rock Entertainment producing the show, which it would do for the entire series run on NBC.

The pilot's overriding storyline involves a woman Jerry had met in Lansing, Michigan, named Laura, played by Pamela Brull. She is coming to town on business and asks Jerry if she can stay in his apartment while in New York. Naturally, he wonders whether or not she has romance on her mind. Animated back-and-forth exchanges between Jerry and

The show's first two truncated seasons are a must-watch for *Seinfeld* fans. They supply great insight into the subsequent character development of Jerry, George, Elaine, and Kramer.

A positively youthful-looking George, Jerry, Kramer, and Elaine getting the *Seinfeld* ball
rolling.   *NBC/Photofest*

George occur in the former's apartment and in Pete's Luncheonette over
breakfast, not Monk's Café, with a waitress named Claire, played by Lee
Garlington, adding her two cents.

Jerry's oddball neighbor named Kessler—the Kramer of the future—
appears for the first time, and his dog, Ralph, for the first and last time. As
things turn out, Laura has a fiancé and offers a disheartened Jerry this piece of
advice: "Never get engaged."

Episode 2: "The Stakeout" (original air date: May 31, 1990)

Jerry Seinfeld and Larry David also wrote the second episode of *Seinfeld*—the first official episode as a show in the NBC primetime lineup. Tom Cherones, who would direct the remaining shows of season one, made his *Seinfeld* directorial debut with "The Stakeout." This is also the debut of Julia Louis-Dreyfus as Elaine Benes, and Kessler is forevermore known as Kramer.

The storyline finds Jerry and Elaine at a party. He is flirting with a very attractive woman named Vanessa (played by Lynn Clark), whom Elaine knows personally. After the event, Jerry is hesitant to ask Elaine for Vanessa's phone number, or any other pertinent information that she might have. It's his policy not to discuss women with a former romantic partner, which Elaine is. The only worthwhile particular that he gleaned from Vanessa was the location of her employer. Morty Seinfeld thus offers his son some savvy fatherly advice: Go to her workplace and *accidentally* bump into her. Jerry follows through with this ingenious plan, which includes George, and snares a date with Vanessa.

Character actor Phil Bruns played Morty Seinfeld, for the first and only time, in this episode. Liz Sheridan also appears as Helen Seinfeld, a role that she would reprise in every season of *Seinfeld*. (She is the only actor among the supporting cast to appear at least once in all nine seasons.) The entire first season ran in late spring and early summer of 1990, not exactly a vote of confidence from the powers-that-be at NBC. Nevertheless, "The Stakeout" garnered good reviews and received a Writer's Guild Award nomination.

Episode 3: "The Robbery" (original air date: June 7, 1990)

Matt Goldman wrote the third episode of season one in which, courtesy of Kramer's forgetfulness in locking the door, Jerry's apartment is burglarized. This crime inspires George, who toils as a real estate broker, to find a new, safer place for his friend to call home. However, when he unearths the ideal living quarters for Jerry, he discovers that he'd like to move into it himself.

Elaine, meanwhile, anticipates moving into either Jerry or George's vacated apartment. In the final analysis, they all stay put and someone else gets the perfect apartment. George, though, desperately regrets letting it slip away, particularly when he sees how happy the new tenants are.

Episode 4: "Male Unbonding" (original air date: June 14, 1990)

Jerry Seinfeld and Larry David collaborated again as writers for this teleplay, which involves Jerry's desire to avoid seeing childhood friend Joel Horneck (played by Kevin Dunn), who insists on remaining pals and regularly getting together. Jerry informs George that if Horneck were a woman, he would have broken off the relationship a long time ago. George's advice to Jerry is to tackle the Horneck dilemma as if he were, in fact, a woman.

Jerry gives the plan a try, but the highly sensitive Horneck cries like a baby at the mere notion. With things patched up, the childhood friends attend a New York Knicks game together. Meanwhile, Kramer is developing his new business idea: a restaurant where the clientele can customize and prepare their very own pizzas. Worth noting, too, is Jerry's comment on George's new fanny pack: "It looks like your butt is digesting a small animal."

Episode 5: "The Stock Tip" (original air date: June 21, 1990)

Written once more by the show's busy creators, Jerry Seinfeld and Larry David, this episode finds George, upon receipt of a hot tip from his broker, investing five thousand dollars in a stock. He convinces Jerry to likewise invest, which he does to the tune of twenty-five hundred dollars. Subsequently, the source of the stock tip ends up comatose in a hospital while the stock precipitously plummets. A panicked Jerry sells his shares at a loss, but George holds on to his and the stock price eventually recovers and then soars.

Jerry also dates Vanessa, whom he met in "The Stakeout," for the very first time. However, their weekend trip to Vermont doesn't bode well for a long-term relationship. In "The Stock Tip," Jerry and George have the first of many conversations about Superman, the revered "Man of Steel."

20

Season Two

Rough Waters

After passing the ratings tests with season one's episodic trial balloon, a second season of twelve episodes was shot at the CBS Studio Center in Studio City, California, a new locale and somewhat different look for the show, too. The pilot and first season were filmed at the Ren-Mar studios in Hollywood.

Season two debuted on January 23, 1991. It was delayed a week because of news coverage of the Gulf War, "Operation Desert Storm," which began on January 17. Less-than-stellar ratings for the first four shows, though, prompted NBC to pull *Seinfeld* out of its primetime lineup for two months while the network bigwigs deliberated on its fate. "The Phone Message" aired on February 13, 1991, to a rather dismal Nielsen rating of 9.7, which tallies up the percentage of households tuned into the show, and a 15 share, which reflects the percentage of television sets in use tuned to the program. The next episode, "The Apartment," aired on the heels of the popular sitcom *Cheers*, on April 4, 1991, and nearly doubled the audience numbers—scoring a 16.9 Nielsen rating and 28 share, respectively. Better tidings for *Seinfeld* were in the offing.

Tom Cherones returned as director for the entire second season and received an Emmy nomination for "Outstanding Directing for a Comedy Series" to honor his work in the "The Pony Remark." *New York Times* critic David Kehr cited this particular episode as the moment *Seinfeld* became *Seinfeld* with its singular "sarcastic contempt" brand that it would take to greater heights in the ensuing years.

Episode 6: "The Ex-Girlfriend" (original air date: January 23, 1991)

In season two's opening volley, written by the prolific Jerry Seinfeld and Larry David tag team, George is in an unhappy relationship with Marlene, played by Tracy Kolis. His best buddy, Jerry, advises him to call it quits, which he does expeditiously.

George, however, insists that Jerry call on Marlene's apartment to pick up some books that he had left there. Reluctant at first, Jerry does as his friend asks and gets romantically entwined with his ex-girlfriend. George, though, gives his blessing, but the relationship is short-lived because Marlene doesn't find Jerry's standup act the least bit funny, nor does she respect his profession. Jerry finds this odd because she is a cashier.

Episode 7: "The Pony Remark" (original air date: January 30, 1991)

Written once again by the show's two creators, this episode received critical praise, but not especially good ratings. The plot's focal point finds Jerry at a dinner party where he inadvertently offends an elderly relative named Manya with an offhand remark about hating people who owned ponies when they were young. Highly insulted, old Manya, who had a pony as a girl, storms away from the table and dies of a heart attack later that night.

Jerry worries that he will be blamed for causing the fatal coronary. When he learns that Manya's funeral is on the same afternoon as his championship softball game, he faces a moral dilemma, too—play ball or attend the funeral. Jerry also places a bet with Kramer that he will not, as he purports, convert his apartment into multiple levels. Despite the conversion not coming to pass, Kramer does not ante up, claiming that since he never started the project, the bet is null and void.

This is the first episode featuring Barney Martin as Morty Seinfeld and Len Lesser as Uncle Leo. Romanian actress Rozsika Halmos played Manya. She passed away in 1999, at the age of eighty-seven.

Episode 8: "The Jacket" (original air date: February 6, 1991)

Still another Jerry Seinfeld and Larry David collaboration, this episode introduces Elaine's father for the first and only time in the series. Alton Benes is a hard-boiled, crusty writer, who is described by Elaine as a tough guy and difficult to get along with. The actor who portrayed him, Lawrence Tierney, was likewise a tough guy (he died in 2002 at the age of eighty-two) and—by all accounts—extremely difficult to get along with in real life.

The main plot of "The Jacket" involves Elaine getting together with her father and wanting both Jerry and George to be with her as "buffers" when she does. They agree, and Jerry wears his new suede jacket to the hotel, where both he and George—without Elaine, who is running late—await Alton Benes. This unplanned set of circumstances finds the pair in a very awkward conversation with the man. When Elaine at long last arrives—not soon enough—the foursome head out to dinner, with snowflakes in the air. Elaine and George suggest that Jerry turn his suede jacket inside out to protect it from the inclement weather. He, however, doesn't want to seem like a wuss in front of Elaine's macho father and ruins the jacket in the process. Kramer, though, happily takes it off his hands.

Uncle Leo (Len Lesser) makes his first appearance at Manya's
funeral in "The Pony Remark."   *NBC/Photofest*

Tierney was not asked to reprise his role as Alton Benes in subsequent
episodes. Jason Alexander said of the one-time experience of working with the
unstable actor: "Lawrence Tierney scared the living crap out of all of us."

Episode 9: "The Phone Message" (original air date: February 13, 1991)

Again, Jerry Seinfeld and Larry David teamed up to pen this teleplay, in which
George is freaking out because his girlfriend, Carol (played by Tory Polone), is
not returning his phone calls. At wit's end, he explodes and unleashes a series
of angry messages on her telephone answering machine.

Subsequently, George learns that Carol is out of town, which explains why
she had been ignoring his phone messages. On her scheduled return date,
George concocts a scheme with Jerry to catch Carol in front of her apartment
building and somehow confiscate the tape in her answering machine before she

plays the messages. Working in tandem, they accomplish the switcheroo, but discover that Carol has already heard the messages and thought that George's various rants were highly amusing and meant to be a joke.

Episode 10: "The Apartment" (original air date: April 4, 1991)

Peter Mehlman wrote the teleplay for "The Apartment." It was, in fact, the first time he had ever written dialogue. Courtesy of a humorous essay that appeared in the *New York Times Magazine*, Jerry Seinfeld discovered Mehlman's latent talents. Mehlman assumed many roles through the years for *Seinfeld*—writer, program consultant, and, ultimately, co-executive producer, replacing Larry David after season seven. He once noted, "The fact that *Seinfeld* never had touching moments made the network apoplectic."

In this episode, Elaine wants out of her apartment, which she feels is not up to snuff. When Jerry hears that one is available in his building, he clues her in on it. However, after thinking it over, he realizes that it would be a colossal mistake to have her living in the same building. Elaine's meddlesome nature would no doubt impact his privacy, freedom, and—yes—love life. George, meanwhile, starts wearing a wedding ring, believing that women are more attracted to married men. His plan goes awry, though, when he loses out on potential dates because women believe he is spoken for.

This was the first episode that aired in *Seinfeld*'s new timeslot, after *Cheers*, and garnered very good ratings—a sign of better things to come.

Episode 11: "The Statue" (original air date: April 11, 1991)

Another talented writer brought into the *Seinfeld* stable, Larry Charles, wrote this teleplay. Charles would remain on the writing frontbench through season five and pen some very memorable episodes.

His first contribution to the series revolves around a statue that once belonged to Jerry's grandfather and one that George covets in the here and now. It is the very same statue, he says, that his parents once owned and adored—the very same statue that he had accidentally broken a long time ago. George is convinced that he's never been forgiven for the mishap. He would love nothing more than to give it to them as a gift and get back in their good graces.

However, when Jerry has his apartment cleaned by a man named Ray (played by Michael D. Conway), the boyfriend of Elaine's client, Rava, the statue goes missing. Jerry and Elaine later spot the statue at Ray's place and naturally assume he made off with it, but he denies doing any such thing. In the guise of an old-school plainclothes detective, Kramer goes over to Ray's apartment, interrogates him, and gets the statue back for a grateful George, who—alas—ends up dropping it. It's "déjà vu all over again" for George as he watches it smash into a zillion pieces.

Episode 12: "The Revenge" (original air date: April 18, 1991)

Written solely by Larry David, this episode is largely based on the *Seinfeld* co-creator's personal experiences. George quits his real estate broker job with Rick Barr Properties because his boss, Mr. Levitan (played by Fred Applegate), has sent a memo around telling employees that they should not use the executive bathroom. George finds this directive extraordinarily petty and considers it the straw that broke the camel's back, as it were. He realizes, soon after, that he may have been too hasty in leaving and shows up for work as if nothing had happened. Apparently, Larry David had done something similar in the past while working for *Saturday Night Live.*

Levitan will have none of it, though, and George is officially out of work again. He then plots his revenge and, with Elaine's help, slips his former boss a Mickey at an office affair in a local restaurant. After completing the odious business at hand, George encounters Levitan and is told that he can have his old job back. The Mickey would soon say otherwise.

In another plot thread, Jerry believes that Vic, owner of the laundromat where he brings his dirty clothes, made off with a considerable sum of money, fifteen hundred dollars, that he had forgotten was in his laundry bag. He, too, decides to get even. With Kramer's help, the pair pour a bag of cement into one of Vic's washers. The cash is ultimately found, but after the vengeful deed of destroying the washer is a *fait accompli.* Vic didn't take the money after all and Jerry is compelled to pay for a new washing machine. There goes his fifteen hundred dollars. Burly, tough-looking John Capodice played Vic.

Although we never see him, this episode also introduces the character of Newman, who unsuccessfully attempts to commit suicide by jumping out of his apartment's second-floor window. Larry David originally supplied an off-camera voice for Newman, but it has been dubbed over by Wayne Knight for syndication.

Episode 13: "The Heart Attack" (original air date: April 25, 1991)

Written by Larry Charles, this episode revolves around George and his absolute conviction that he is having a heart attack. The medical diagnosis, however, is that he needs a tonsillectomy.

Rather than have his tonsils removed by doctors at the hospital, George takes Kramer's advice to visit a holistic healer named Tor Eckman, played by Stephen Tobolowsky. But a certain herbal tea concoction prepared by Eckman makes George deathly sick, and an ambulance is called to rush him to the hospital. The paramedics quarrel en route and crash the ambulance. In the end, George has his tonsils removed in the hospital and is also fitted with a neck brace—along with Jerry who had accompanied him—because of the ambulance accident.

Episode 14: "The Deal" (original air date: May 2, 1991)

Larry David returns as the sole writer of this episode, which involves old flames Jerry and Elaine inadvertently re-igniting the flame after viewing soft-core pornography on television in Jerry's apartment. They consent to have sexual relations again, but with certain rules in place that will make it informal and maintain the state of their friendship, such as "spending the night is optional." George is highly skeptical that the arrangement will work.

Later, Jerry gives Elaine $182 in cash as a birthday gift and she is offended, even though they established that they were *not* in a relationship. On the other hand, Kramer gives Elaine the birthday present—a little bench—that she really wanted. She thinks his gift is quite thoughtful, particularly in contrast with Jerry's cold cash. Jerry and Elaine begin officially dating after this disagreement, rendering all their informal rules null and void.

Episode 15: "The Baby Shower" (original air date: May 16, 1991)

Another Larry Charles contribution to the series—with the writer's patented edge on display—finds Elaine hosting a baby shower in Jerry's apartment while he is off performing in Buffalo. However, Jerry's trip is cut short and he experiences a dreadful nightmare while flying home. In a dream sequence, FBI agents confront a guilt-ridden Jerry immediately upon his return. At Kramer's urging, he had previously consented to have illegal cable television hooked up in his apartment. In the dream, the Russian cable installer is really an undercover agent. Jerry attempts a getaway but is gunned down in a fusillade of bullets.

This nightmare at twenty thousand feet so unnerves Jerry that he is more leery than ever of going through with the illegal cable upgrade. George, meanwhile, wants to confront Leslie, the guest of honor at the baby shower and a former girlfriend of his who humiliated him years ago while doing performance art. Specifically, she squirt Bosco chocolate syrup all over him. He is wearing the still-Bosco-stained red shirt as exhibit A.

Back at Jerry's apartment, Elaine is presiding over the baby shower while two Russians hook up illegal cable TV. George and Jerry crash the event, but the former, when all is said and done, chickens out and doesn't confront Leslie. In fact, he ends up being her toady. Jerry also takes the opportunity to say that he no longer wants the illegal cable TV installed, but is charged an exorbitant amount for the Russians' time. When he refuses to pay, they smash the screen of his television set.

Bronx-born actress Christine Dunford played George's ex, Leslie, and Vic Polizos was Tabachnik, the Russian illegal cable installer.

Episode 16: "The Chinese Restaurant" (original air date: May 23, 1991)

Written by Jerry Seinfeld and Larry David, "The Chinese Restaurant" is frequently cited as one of the show's "about nothing" episodes, with Jerry, George, and Elaine waiting impatiently and hungrily for a table at a Chinese restaurant.

After Elaine complains of being so famished that she feels like snatching something off of a diner's plate, Jerry offers her fifty dollars if she goes through with it and makes off with someone's egg roll. Elaine rails at the notion that restaurant policies are based on first come, first served. "It should be based on who's hungriest," she says.

George, meanwhile, desperately needs to call his girlfriend, but the payphone in the restaurant is perpetually occupied. Eventually, they get fed up and leave, which is when the maître d', played by veteran character actor James Hong, finally has a table for the Seinfeld party. (Hong's copious television credits span more than half a century and include *Bonanza* [1959–1973], *The Man from U.N.C.L.E.* [1964–1968], *Kung Fu* [1972–1975], *Dynasty* [1981–1989], and *MacGyver* [1985–1992].) Michael Richards as Kramer does not appear in this episode.

Episode 17: "The Busboy" (original air date: June 26, 1991)

Written again by the show's co-creators, the final episode of the second season involves a restaurant busboy named Antonio (played by David Labiosa), who inadvertently ignites a fire by leaving a menu too close to a candle. Fast-acting George extinguishes the small blaze and explains to the restaurant manager what happened. Antonio gets fired for his negligence and George feels guilty about being the cause of the termination.

With Kramer along for moral support, George visits the busboy's dilapidated apartment to offer an apology. Unintentionally, he sets free the man's cat. Days later, Antonio calls on George with fabulous news: there was a gas explosion at the restaurant where he formerly worked, which killed both his old boss and the individual hired to replace him. More good news: while searching for his missing cat, he landed a better job. Antonio thanks George for turning his life around.

Elaine, meanwhile, is valiantly attempting to get her boyfriend, Eddie (played by Doug Ballard), on a plane to Seattle and out of her hair. But when Eddie gets into an argument with Antonio during a chance meeting in Jerry's building's hallway, fists fly, with both men sustaining serious injuries. While he recuperates, taking care of the cat of the again-unemployed Antonio is George's obligation, and Elaine must tend to Eddie in her apartment during his convalescence.

21

Season Three

The Turning Point

Seinfeld's third season was also the show's first full season, in which twenty-two episodes were shot. Season three commenced airing on September 18, 1991. The characters were noticeably finding their voices and their personalities—the ones they would showcase for the remainder of the series. George's prior guilt trip and troubled conscience over getting the busboy fired in season two were less apt to occur in season three and beyond—as was his profiting on a stock tip. His penchant for lying would also conspicuously come to the fore in season three. And having gotten a taste of Kramer's off-the-wall physical antics in the episode "The Revenge"—as he was attempting to pour cement into a washing machine—season three would offer a whole lot more of that brand of zaniness. Elaine's unpredictable and unusual qualities would be more prominent, too. Storylines were less linear with multiple interwoven plots that, although not the sitcom norm, became a *Seinfeld* hallmark. The show's myriad players were nominated for eight Emmy Awards during season three.

Episode 18: "The Note" (original air date: September 18, 1991)

The new season premiered with a new twist to its theme music. At Jerry Seinfeld's urging, composer Jonathan Wolff added female backup vocals to harmonize over the familiar *Seinfeld* theme. Both Seinfeld and Larry David were impressed with the end-result and shot the first three episodes with this vocal complement. However, they did all of this without notifying NBC and the show's producer, Castle Rock Entertainment, which weren't nearly as impressed with the new sound. In the final analysis, only "The Note" aired with this altered theme music. The following two episodes' musical arrangements were redone sans any human accompaniment.

Written by Larry David and directed by Tom Cherones, season three's opening volley finds Jerry, George, and Elaine securing "doctor's notes" from Roy, Jerry's dentist, which enable them to get insurance-paid massage therapy. George, though, is upset that his masseuse is a man—a masseur, actually—and feels that he is, quite possibly, getting aroused while in his company. Jerry, on the other hand, totally unnerves his massage therapist by making an offhanded remark about a kidnapped boy in the news, and she fears that he has designs on kidnapping her young son.

Meanwhile, Kramer claims to have spotted baseball legend Joe DiMaggio in Dinky Donuts. Skeptical at first, Jerry, George, and Elaine are convinced that Kramer wasn't imagining things when the Yankee Clipper turns up at Monk's Café and actually dunks his donut in a cup of coffee.

Joe DiMaggio did not make a guest appearance on the show and is never seen. While *Seinfeld* frequently had honest-to-goodness celebrities appear as themselves, they sometimes merely made reference to an unseen famous individual and left the rest to our imaginations. Ralph Bruneau played Roy, Jerry's dentist. Other guest stars included Jeff Lester as Raymond, George's masseur; and Terri Hanauer as Julianna, Jerry's masseuse.

Episode 19: "The Truth" (original air date: September 25, 1991)

David Steinberg, a Canadian comedian who appeared on *The Tonight Show Starring Johnny Carson* more times than anybody else except Bob Hope, directed the second episode of the third season. Elaine Pope, who worked with both Larry David and Michael Richards on *Fridays*, wrote the teleplay for "The Truth," her first *Seinfeld* episode.

George's girlfriend, Patrice (played by Valerie Mahaffey), is at the epicenter of this story when she lands in a mental institution after their breakup. Jerry, who is in serious tax trouble, was counting on Patrice, an accountant who has all his vital papers, to help him wade through an IRS audit. When Jerry and George visit her at the institution, they discover that she heaved out, in a fit of rage, all of his important tax documents.

Kramer, meanwhile, is dating Elaine's roommate, Tina, played by redheaded character actress Siobhan Fallon. She is not too happy about this set of circumstances and complains about everything, from the couple's messiness to the overly loud tribal music they incessantly play. Elaine is not the least bit amused, either, when Kramer mistakenly walks in on her while she's buck-naked.

Episode 20: "The Pen" (original air date: October 2, 1991)

Written by Larry David and directed by Tom Cherones, this episode finds Jerry and Elaine in Florida visiting the former's parents, Morty and Helen, and planning on doing a bit of scuba diving while in the Sunshine State.

When neighbor Jack Klompus drops over to write Morty a check for monies owed from a prior dinner, Jerry can't help but admire the pen he is using. Klompus proudly informs him that the astronauts use the same kind of writing instrument in outer space because it can write upside down. He insists on giving the pen to Jerry, who, after some prodding, reluctantly accepts it. When Morty and Helen learn what their son did, they are mortified, because they know that word will spread throughout the retirement village that Jerry coveted the pen and made Jack Klompus give it to him. He eventually gives it back.

Meanwhile, courtesy of an awful night's sleep on the Seinfelds' uncomfortable sofa bed, Elaine gets a backache and takes one too many muscle relaxants, which make her behave quite loopy at a dinner honoring Morty Seinfeld. Jack Klompus, in his role as master of ceremonies, further adds to the affair's undoing by getting into a shouting match with the guest of honor. Morty chides him for taking the pen back from Jerry. A chiropractor then delivers Elaine even more bad news: She should not travel for at least five days in order to allow her back to heal.

Neither Jason Alexander as George nor Michael Richards as Kramer appears in "The Pen." It was the only episode in which Alexander did not appear, and the second, and last, episode that didn't feature Richards. This was the first of six episodes that featured Jack Klompus, Helen and Morty Seinfeld's insufferable neighbor. Comedian Sandy Baron portrayed him.

Episode 21: "The Dog" (original air date: October 9, 1991)

Written again by Larry David and directed by Tom Cherones, this episode finds Jerry on a plane bound for home and seated next to an inebriated passenger by the name of Gavin Polone (played by Joseph Maher), who has a dog named Farfel in the baggage compartment. (Gavin Polone is also the name of Larry David's agent, and the canine's curious moniker is an homage to Jimmy Nelson's hound dog ventriloquist dummy and the commercial "spokesperson" for Nestlé in the 1950s and 1960s.)

When Polone suddenly falls ill on the flight, Jerry is asked to assume guardianship of his dog after the plane makes an emergency landing in Chicago and the former is whisked away to the hospital. Feeling that he has little choice under the circumstances, Jerry agrees and is saddled for an indefinite period of time with a misbehaving, extremely raucous animal. Farfel is only heard barking and is never actually seen in the episode.

Back home, Jerry, George, and Elaine have plans to go to see *Prognosis: Negative* together, but Jerry is concerned, with good reason, about leaving Farfel alone in his apartment. George and Elaine go to the movies without him and discover that, sans Jerry on the scene, their conversation is exceptionally awkward. The only time they experience any kind of rapport is when they make fun of Jerry and his fussy idiosyncrasies.

Simultaneous with all of this, Kramer is having girlfriend issues with Ellen, who, like Farfel, is never seen by the viewer. He has real issues, too, with certain things that Jerry and Elaine have said about her. Elaine compared her personality to an Elephant Man exhibit "where they pull off the sheet and everyone gasps."

After not hearing from Polone for days, Jerry, at wit's end, intends on taking Farfel to the dog pound. Polone, though, calls in the nick of time and explains that his medical condition prohibited him from getting in touch sooner. Without Farfel as a roommate, Jerry's life returns to normal. Tom

Williams, who worked as a production assistant on the Jack Webb–produced shows *Dragnet* (1967–1970) and *Adam-12* (1968–1975), supplied the uncredited bark of Farfel the dog.

Episode 22: "The Library" (original air date: October 16, 1991)

Larry Charles wrote and Joshua White directed this episode wherein Jerry is accused of being delinquent in returning a book, *Tropic of Cancer*, to the New York Public Library—twenty years late, as a matter of fact. He pleads not guilty to a headstrong library investigator named Joe Bookman, but the facts remain muddled. Jerry ultimately concludes that he gave George the book while they were in high school and, as things turned out, it was never returned. It was, in fact, stolen from George's locker in the aftermath of a terrible experience in gym class.

Meanwhile, George spots a man who, he is reasonably sure, is his former physical education teacher and tormentor, Mr. Heyman, homeless and sleeping on the steps of the library. It both greatly disturbs him and inspires a high school gym class flashback scene where he is on the receiving end of a painful wedgie from his peers while Mr. Heyman stands idly by and mocks him by purposely mispronouncing his last name as "Can't Stand Ya."

George at last acquires conclusive but agonizing proof—in the form of an atomic wedgie—that Mr. Heyman is indeed a certifiable homeless person. He

Former physical education teacher Mr. Heyman resides in a refrigerator box in the shadows of a New York City Public Library stone lion in "The Library." *Photo by Thomas Nigro*

feels partially responsible for Heyman's straits because he had reported the locker-room bullying incident that led to his termination. On the other hand, Kramer's library experience involves an interest in Marion, a librarian (played by Ashley Gardner), who writes poetry that brings tears to his eyes.

The episode's final scene shows a tattered copy of *Tropic of Cancer* beside the former gym teacher, who is raving over and over to himself: "Can't stand ya . . . Can't stand ya." Veteran movie and television character actor Philip Baker Hall played the hard-nosed library detective, Joe Bookman. He returned for the show's finale, "The Finale," to testify against Jerry, his old nemesis. Although his scenes were brief, Biff Yeager played the very memorable, baked bean–toothed Mr. Heyman.

Episode 23: "The Parking Garage" (original air date: October 30, 1991)

Larry David wrote and Tom Cherones directed this episode that is considered classic *Seinfeld* material because of its outwardly simple story setup, which occurs from beginning to end in a shopping mall's parking garage.

Jerry, George, Elaine, and Kramer have forgotten where their ride home is parked. To complicate matters, Kramer is lugging around a very heavy air conditioner, which he has just purchased. With the intention of picking it up after the car is located, he decides to hide it. Jerry has to urinate badly, but there are no bathrooms in sight. Elaine is worried sick that her pet goldfish will die if they don't find the car soon and get home. And George is deathly afraid that he won't be on time for an engagement with his parents.

Ultimately, Jerry takes Kramer's advice to answer nature's call in some secluded and dark corner of the parking garage, but he is promptly arrested by mall security. Individually, George, Elaine, and Kramer go off in search of him. But when George replicates Jerry's act, he, too, gets arrested. When Jerry and George return to the parking garage scene, they encounter Elaine, but now Kramer is nowhere to be found. They ask assorted people for a lift around the garage to search for the car, but get rebuffed time and again until a woman, without hesitation, agrees to lend a helping hand. However, she quickly boots them out of the car—based on something George said—but they end up, very auspiciously, in front of their vehicle. Kramer, at long last, appears, claiming that he got sidetracked searching for his air conditioner, which he finally located. He puts the key in the ignition and the car won't start. (This was not part of the script.) Alas, Elaine's goldfish has already passed away and George doesn't make that engagement with his folks.

Episode 24: "The Café" (original air date: November 6, 1991)

Directed by Tom Cherones and written by Tom Leopold in his *Seinfeld* writing debut, this episode introduces Babu Bhatt, the owner of the Dream Café, a place that's not doing much, if any, business by the looks of things. Jerry can see Babu's eatery from a window in his apartment and he becomes fixated on the restaurant's dearth of customers. He eventually eats there and offers the owner some unsolicited advice on how to lure patrons to his door. Jerry tells Babu to make the restaurant menu solely Pakistani, instead of its current culinary mishmash that includes hot dogs as a dinner option. Babu agrees to make the changes but gains no new clientele and goes out of business. He blames Jerry for his entrepreneurial failings and brands him a "very, very bad man!"

Meanwhile, George is concerned that if he consents to be a guinea pig and take an I.Q. test for his girlfriend Monica's school course, she will discover that he's not the brightest bulb in the chandelier and promptly break up with him. He asks Elaine to help him out and take the test for him. While at Monica's apartment, George concocts a plan that involves passing the test out a first-floor window to Elaine and having it returned through the very same window in the allotted time. Repeatedly distracted by Kramer, Elaine scores a paltry 85 on the test. George gets Monica to give him a second whack at it, but Elaine fails to get it back in time this go-round. Monica discovers George's deception and ends the relationship. Elaine, however, scores a not-inconsiderable 151 on her second try.

Brian George played the excitable Babu Bhatt. The actor was born in Jerusalem, Israel, on July 1, 1952, to Jewish parents who had emigrated from India. The family soon after settled in London. Although he speaks with a distinct British accent while not in front of the cameras, George is renowned for his exaggerated and amusing Pakistani accents. Dawn Arnemann played Monica.

Episode 25: "The Tape" (original air date: November 13, 1991)

Three writers are credited with crafting the various plot twists and dialogue of this particular episode: Larry David, Bob Shaw, and Don McEnery. David Steinberg assumed directorial duties for the second time this season. The main storyline is grounded in a sexually charged but anonymous message left on a tape recorder employed by Jerry to record his standup act. When he plays the message for George and Kramer, the three of them become preoccupied with the mystery woman behind the voice. Jerry deduces who was seated nearest the tape recorder—the best possible message candidate in his opinion—and makes a date with her. He comes up completely empty, however, in the sexual chemistry department.

Elaine, meanwhile, informs George that *she* is the voice on the tape recorder, but asks him not to reveal her secret to Jerry or Kramer. George being George nonetheless becomes totally obsessed with this sliver of information and finds himself attracted to Elaine as never before. Unable to contain his feelings—and never much of a secret keeper to begin with—he blurts out her secret for all to hear. This inspires more than a little leering and salivating on the parts of Jerry, George, and Kramer. Elaine is unnerved by their behavior and quickly escapes their company.

Sidebar stories include George ordering a salve from China, which, when applied to the scalp, is guaranteed to grow hair. It doesn't. And Kramer takes on a new hobby: making home movies with his video camera. He conducts a mock interview with Elaine in the guise of a porn star.

Episode 26: "The Nose Job" (original air date: November 20, 1991)

Peter Mehlman wrote and Tom Cherones directed this episode that focuses on George and his girlfriend, Audrey (played by Susan Diol), who he claims is everything he ever wanted in a woman—with one notable exception: she's got a considerable proboscis. While at Jerry's apartment, Audrey casually mentions that she feels intimidated by all the beautiful women in New York. Kramer tells her that she needn't worry because she's beautiful, too; she just needs a nose job. This blunt remark startles everyone on the scene with the exception of Audrey, who appreciates Kramer's candor. Secretly, George hopes that she will take Kramer's advice.

Jerry, meanwhile, finds himself in a relationship with a very attractive actress named Isabel, played by Tawny Kitaen. Unfortunately, they have few common interests. And Kramer enlists Elaine's help in getting back an old jacket of his that he says makes women swoon.

Episode 27: "The Stranded" (original air date: November 27, 1991)

Three writers are again credited with writing an episode for the third season. This go-round they were Jerry Seinfeld, Larry David, and Matt Goldman. Tom Cherones directed "The Stranded," which was actually shot during the second season but shelved because Larry David was unhappy with the end result. And because it was filmed earlier, George is still employed as a real estate broker.

The episode opens with Jerry and George shopping in a local drugstore. While paying for his merchandise, the latter accuses the cashier of shortchanging him to the tune of ten dollars. She denies his accusation, and a security guard ushers him out of the place.

Later, George—the real estate man—invites Jerry and Elaine to a party being held on Long Island. While George is getting chummy with a female co-worker, Jerry and Elaine are bored silly. George ultimately leaves the party with his new squeeze, taking Jerry and Elaine's transportation with him. Kramer is summoned to pick them up. Having been hopelessly lost for hours—in the age before GPS—he arrives very, very late. In the interim, Jerry and Elaine keep the party hosts, Steve and Ava (played by Michael Chiklis and Teri Austin, respectively), up long past their usual bedtime. Ava is on the verge of throwing them out of the house when Kramer, at long last, turns up.

Feeling guilty, Jerry invites the couple to drop by his place anytime they're in New York City. Steve takes him up on the offer, showing up unexpectedly at Jerry's door. Jerry, who is on his way out at the time, nonetheless permits him to stay in the apartment until he returns. Kramer drops in and has a few drinks with Steve, who later brings in a lady of the evening. When Jerry returns, he is startled to find Steve cavorting with a prostitute in his apartment. Worse still, he is compelled to pick up the call girl's tab after Steve makes a quick getaway. And the sour icing on the cake is that the cops turn up and arrest Jerry.

Prior to this unfortunate turn of events for Jerry, George decides to get even with the drugstore, which he believes shortchanged him ten dollars, by stealing something valued at that amount. However, his plan backfires when a security guard catches him in the act. Jerry and George reminisce about their jail experiences in the episode's final moments.

Episode 28: "The Alternate Side" (original air date: December 4, 1991)

Written by Larry David and Bill Masters, and directed by Tom Cherones, this episode finds Jerry the victim of a carjacking and speaking with the carjacker via his car phone. In need of work, George temporarily takes over neighbor Sid's job while the latter is visiting a sick relative. The job entails moving locals' cars from one side of the street to another to comply with the city's Byzantine alternate-side parking rules.

Elaine, meanwhile, is dating a sixty-six-year-old man, who suffers a stroke on the eve of her breaking up with him. To add even more misery to the man's medical woes, George's sheer incompetence in moving cars in a timely fashion creates a traffic logjam that precludes an ambulance from getting to him as fast as it otherwise would. This delay compounds his neurological damage. Sid, who had entrusted the job with George, loses many of his customers after the debacle, which, in turn, does not allow him to monetarily assist his nephew with an operation to save his foot. He must have it amputated instead.

Simultaneous with all of this action, Kramer gets a bit part in a Woody Allen film—one line, in fact: "These pretzels are making me thirsty." However, he gets fired before his big screen moment after injuring Woody in a freak accident. Jay Brooks, who would return in the episode "The Parking Space," played Sid.

Episode 29: "The Red Dot" (original air date: December 11, 1991)

Written by Larry David and directed by Tom Cherones, this episode sees a giddy George duly employed once more thanks to Elaine, who got him a job at her place of employment, Pendant Publishing. To show his appreciation for what she did for him, George buys her a gift: a cashmere sweater. But true to form, he purchases an irregular, as it were, with—on close inspection—a small red dot visible within the fabric. When Elaine receives the sweater she is ecstatic and surprised, too, at George's uncharacteristic generosity. When, however, she discovers the red dot, the sweater is returned to George, along with a few choice words.

Meanwhile, George finds Evie, the cleaning lady at his new place of employment, quite alluring. He shares some scotch and later engages in sexual intercourse with her. The cleaning lady, though, is not a happy camper on the morning after and threatens to tell George's boss, Mr. Lippman, all about their escapades. Hoping to soothe the savage breast, George gives her the cashmere sweater as a present. This act temporarily assuages the cleaning lady until, of course, the red dot is spotted. She spills the beans on George and he is out of work once more.

In another plot thread, Jerry unintentionally involves himself with Elaine's boyfriend, a recovering alcoholic named Dick. Quite by accident, Jerry hands Dick the wrong drink at a party—one that contains alcohol—that causes the latter to both go on a bender and lose his job at Pendant Publishing. Dick parades through Pendant Publishing's halls drunk as a skunk in search of Jerry, whom he blames for his sorry predicament.

Helping George clean out his office, Jerry and Elaine hear Dick on the prowl in the hallway and the three of them cower in fear under a desk. Later, an inebriated Dick heckles Jerry at a comedy club. However, the episode's final scene shows a sober and smiling Dick laughing at the comedian's jokes.

Actor David Naughton played Dick. He is perhaps best known as the lead singer and dancer—the minstrel, if you will—in the Dr. Pepper advertising campaign of the late 1970s and early 1980s. He famously sang and danced to the lyrics "I'm a pepper, he's a pepper, she's a pepper." Bridget Sienna played Evie, the cleaning lady. Richard Fancy, who would reprise his role multiple times, played Pendant Publishing boss Mr. Lippman. Harris Shore had originally played the part of Mr. Lippman in "The Library."

Episode 30: "The Subway" (original air date: January 8, 1992)

Larry Charles wrote and Tom Cherones directed this unusual episode in that Jerry, George, Elaine, and Kramer pretty much go their separate ways, with the help of the New York City subway system. After getting off as a group at Times Square, they individually transfer to different subway lines to venture to unique destinations.

Jerry is on his way to Coney Island in Brooklyn, which is a pretty long trip as far as subway rides go from Manhattan. He's headed to an impound lot, there to pick up his stolen car that has been recovered. (It was stolen in the episode "The Alternate Side.") Due to the length of the subway ride, it's not surprising that Jerry dozes off en route. What is surprising is that he wakes up and finds a rather obese and completely nude man, played by Ernie Sabella, sitting across from him. After making some wry quips about the man's girth and lack of clothing,

Jerry chats with the naked straphanger about the New York Mets' prospects in the coming season, and they later enjoy Coney Island attractions together, including a ride on its famous roller coaster. They eat Nathan's Famous hot dogs, too. Courtesy of the grand time he had with the naked guy, Jerry arrives at the impound lot too late: it's closed for the day.

George, meanwhile, is heading to a job interview where he thinks his chances of securing employment are pretty good. However, on the train he encounters a woman, played by Barbara Stock, who strikes up a conversation with him. George's typical braggadocio leads her to believe that he is a man of means. The pair lands in a hotel, where George gets handcuffed to a bed and robbed of both his money—a whopping eight dollars—and his clothing. He misses his job interview, too.

Simultaneous with George's misadventures, Elaine is on her way to a lesbian wedding where she will assume the role of "best man." Her subway ride, though, encounters an unspecified snafu that engenders a lengthy delay. Elaine panics at the prospect of missing the wedding—she's got the ring—and, worse than that, being stuffed like a sardine in a subway car for an extended period of time with the huddled masses of New York City.

Kramer is definitely the luckiest of the foursome on this day. Paying off an assortment of vehicular-related fines is on his itinerary. But when he overhears two guys talking about a can't-miss horse at the track, he promptly takes a detour from his original plans and ventures to the nearest OTB parlor, where he lays down the money he intended on using to pay off his numerous tickets: six hundred dollars on a 30–1 long shot. His horse wins the race and he is eighteen thousand dollars richer.

Episode 31: "The Pez Dispenser" (original air date: January 15, 1992)

Larry David and Tom Cherones return once more as a writer-director team in this episode that largely revolves around a Tweety Bird Pez dispenser given to Jerry by Kramer.

After Jerry takes possession of the Pez dispenser, he thoroughly enjoys popping the Pez candies into his mouth. He and Elaine then accompany George to a piano recital featuring his girlfriend, Noel, played by Elizabeth Morehead. However, during the performance, Jerry places that same Tweety Bird Pez dispenser on Elaine's knee, which prompts her to laugh uncontrollably in the otherwise solemn setting. The boisterous guffawing greatly upsets Noel, who tells them all backstage how she will long remember its earsplitting pitch. She's blissfully unaware that Elaine is the culprit, and mum's the word on that.

Meanwhile, Kramer joins the Polar Bear Club, a group of hearty souls who swim in the ocean in the cold climes of the wintertime. He also reveals that he has invented a cologne with the unique scent of the beach and, despite being laughed at by a Calvin Klein flunky, firmly believes in its potential.

On the home front, Jerry is planning an intervention for an old friend and fellow comedian Richie Appel (played by Chris Barnes), who has a serious drug problem that began after he followed Kramer's advice and dumped a barrel full of Gatorade over the head of their softball coach, Marty Benson. Sadly, the man developed pneumonia as a result and later died from its complications. Richie never forgave himself and turned to drugs to ease his conscience.

At the intervention, Noel hears Elaine laughing, which she immediately recognizes as the laughter that torpedoed her recital. Angrily, she storms away and leaves George in the process. On a happier note, the Tweety Bird Pez dispenser returns to the vanguard once more. To make amends for the piano recital debacle, this time it conjures up a welcome childhood memory that helps Richie see the light and consent to treatment. In the final moments of the episode, Jerry reveals that Richie's only addiction now is to Pez candies.

Episode 32: "The Suicide" (original air date: January 29, 1992)

This is the second of two episodes written by Tom Leopold, a prolific sitcom writer who made a name for himself in the world of comedy through his work in *National Lampoon* magazine. Tom Cherones directed "The Suicide," which finds Elaine on a total fast for an upcoming ulcer test, George prepping to vacation in the Cayman Islands, and Jerry's neighbor, Martin, rushed to the hospital after an attempted suicide. Martin's girlfriend, Gina, adds a further wrinkle to the saga when she makes a play for Jerry in the company of her comatose boyfriend.

George and Elaine, meanwhile, call on a psychic, played by Mimi Lieber. George is told in no uncertain terms to cancel his trip to the Cayman Islands. However, before she can tell him the specific reason, Elaine chides her for smoking while pregnant, which she very obviously is. The expectant mother and psychic kicks them out, with George desperately pleading to know why he shouldn't go to the Cayman Islands. Ultimately, he gives his plane ticket to Kramer, who ends up having a grand old time in the company of model Elle Macpherson and others who are on hand for a shooting of the legendary *Sports Illustrated* swimsuit issue. Kramer gleefully reports that he played nude backgammon with Macpherson, which doesn't exactly make George happy.

Back at the hospital, Newman says that he's going to spill the beans to Martin—just as soon as the man regains consciousness—about Jerry's unseemly behavior with the comatose patient's lady friend. Jerry temporarily buys Newman's silence with a Drake's coffee cake, but a hunger-crazed Elaine, who has been fasting, snatches it from him before he can take one bite. Newman subsequently tells Martin the whole sordid story, which lands Jerry in a chokehold.

Australian model, actress, and entrepreneur Elle Macpherson, who holds the record for appearing on the most *Sports Illustrated* swimsuit issue covers—five—did not physically appear in this episode. Her romping in the sun and sand with Kramer is left to our imaginations. Gina Gallego played Gina, and C.

E. Grimes was Martin. This episode also marked the first physical appearance of Wayne Knight as Newman.

Episode 33: "The Fix-Up" (original air date: February 5, 1992)

Tom Cherones continues doing the lion's share of the directing by helming this episode, written by Larry Charles and Elaine Pope. The storyline revolves around George's reluctance to be "fixed up" with Cynthia, Elaine's friend, played by Maggie Wheeler. He ultimately gives in because she meets his criteria: not especially bright but very attractive.

George and Cynthia hit it off and have sexual intercourse in George's kitchen. Cynthia, though, isn't exactly enthralled with these kitchen encounters and tells Elaine all the details. She mentions, too, that she missed her period. When George learns that the condoms given to him by Kramer are defective, he prepares for the possibility of fatherhood.

Meanwhile, Elaine and Jerry feud over the pact that they had made to tell one another all the gossipy details of the George–Cynthia relationship. That is, what she learned from Cynthia and he got from the horse's (George's) mouth. Whereas he has been a man of his word, Jerry feels that Elaine has been keeping juicy tidbits of information from him. When all is said and done, George doesn't become a father.

Episode 34: "The Boyfriend" (original air date: February 12, 1992)

Written by Larry David and Larry Levin, and directed by Tom Cherones, this was a rare one-hour show when it first aired, although in syndication it is shown as two distinct half-hour episodes. Former New York Mets star first baseman Keith Hernandez guest stars as himself.

"The Boyfriend" gets rolling with Jerry agog at having met Hernandez at the YMCA. Hernandez, in fact, tells Jerry that he is a big fan of his standup, and a friendship is born. George, meanwhile, is frantically endeavoring to secure a thirteen-week extension on his unemployment benefits, but is making little headway in convincing the officer in charge of his case, Mrs. Sokol, that he merits it. Ultimately, he informs her that he interviewed with the fictitious Vandelay Industries for a position as a latex salesman. He supplies Jerry's home phone number as the office phone number, but the ruse implodes when Kramer doesn't answer with the salutation, "Vandelay Industries." George even dates Mrs. Sokol's daughter in hopes of getting the extension, but she promptly dumps him and brands him a loser. His last volley involves getting Keith Hernandez to appear at the unemployment office to meet one of his biggest fans—Mrs. Sokol—but this doesn't come to pass. Rae Allen, who had a recurring role on *The Sopranos* in 2004 as Aunt Quintina Blundetto, played George's skeptical unemployment officer.

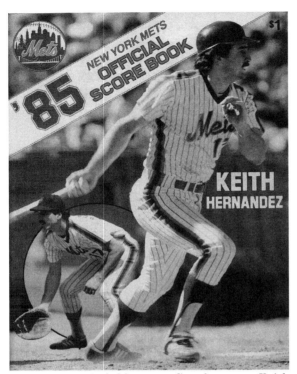

Former New York Mets star first baseman Keith Hernandez plays himself and gets to first base with Elaine, too, in "The Boyfriend."

In another plot twist, Hernandez breaks a date with Jerry in favor of Elaine. Hernandez and Elaine hit it off for a spell until she discovers that the ex-jock smokes, which is totally unacceptable to her. Kramer and Newman also make it clear how much they revile Hernandez and recount a tale of having gotten spat on by him after a Mets game several years earlier. Jerry is dubious from the start of their story and refers to it as the "Magic Loogie Theory," a play on the often-derided "Magic Bullet Theory" that the Warren Commission, which investigated the John F. Kennedy assassination, published.

In fact, the recounting of the spitting incident satirizes the famous Zapruder 8mm color film, which was taken by a private citizen, Abraham Zapruder, in Dealey Plaza on the afternoon that the president was killed. Jerry's detailed analysis of the Hernandez spitting affair pulls apart, thread by thread, Kramer and Newman's story. Eventually, Keith Hernandez himself sheds light on Kramer and Newman's long-held belief that he was the spitting perpetrator. It was relief pitcher Roger McDowell who actually spat on the pair. McDowell appears as himself in a flashback scene. Chagrined, Kramer and Newman remember having ragged on McDowell that very day. They agree now to help Hernandez move, which a fed-up Jerry had declined to do.

Episode 35: "The Limo" (original air date: February 26, 1992)

Directed by Tom Cherones and written with the edgy pen of Larry Charles—with the story by Marc Jaffe—this episode finds Jerry and George as passengers in a limousine that is meant to be chauffeuring a man by the name of Donald O'Brien—a Hitler-loving white supremacist.

The plot unfurls with George arriving at LaGuardia Airport to pick up Jerry, who has flown in from Chicago. However, the bad news is that his car broke down en route and they will have to find an alternate mode of transportation to get home. When Jerry and George spy a limousine driver holding up a sign that reads "O'Brien," the former remembers somebody by that name in Chicago complaining about an overbooked flight, and how he had to be at Madison Square Garden that night. Jerry concludes that O'Brien won't be in New York City anytime soon, so George suggests impersonating him and getting a limousine ride home. Jerry agrees with the plan and they assume aliases. George is "Colin O'Brien" and Jerry, "Dylan Murphy."

When the pair learn that the limo is on its way to Madison Square Garden, George assumes they're going to the Knicks–Bulls game. The chauffeur mentions that he has four passes, too, which Jerry and George reason are for the game. Excited, Jerry calls up Elaine via the limo telephone and tells her to meet him and George, with Kramer of course, at Madison Square Garden.

The chauffeur, though, stops to pick up two more passengers, Tim and Eva. Jerry and George are nervous now that they'll be exposed as impostors but, fortunately, Tim and Eva have never met O'Brien. Eva, nonetheless, expresses great admiration for O'Brien's writings and world view. Curious, George soon discovers what all the hero worship is about. O'Brien is a neo-Nazi and the head of the regional chapter of the Aryan Union.

In a state of panic now that they are headed to Madison Square Garden, where O'Brien is scheduled to deliver an address, Jerry and George quietly consider how to extricate themselves from this mess. They become especially concerned after taking notice of the number of firearms on Tim's person.

With anti-O'Brien demonstrators all around them in the environs of Madison Square Garden, Elaine and Kramer put two and two together and attempt to rescue Jerry and George from the developing mob scene. But when Kramer impulsively cries out, "O'Brien," to Jerry and George's passing limo, the angry mob descends upon it. Exiting the limo, George, who everyone there believes is neo-Nazi Donald O'Brien, is compelled to explain himself to a growing crowd of reporters and extremely angry demonstrators. Fearing for his life, he is last seen crying out, "Jerry!"

Peter Krause played Tim, and Suzanne Snyder, Eva. Krause has had recurring roles on multiple series, including *Sports Night* (1998–2000), as Casey McCall; *Six Feet Under* (2001–2005), as Nate Fisher; *Dirty Sexy Money* (2007–2009), as Nick George; and *Parenthood* (2010–2015), as Adam Braverman.

Episode 36: "The Good Samaritan" (original air date: March 4, 1992)

Jason Alexander makes his *Seinfeld* director's debut in this episode, written by Peter Mehlman. The multi-layered story kicks off with Jerry witnessing a hit-and-run accident involving a parked car. On his car phone speaking with Elaine, he informs her that he is in pursuit of the driver. When he sees that it is a beautiful woman behind the wheel, he neglects to confront her about the accident but instead makes a date with her. Her name is Angela, played by Melinda McGraw.

Kramer, meanwhile, experiences epileptic seizures when, apparently, hearing the dulcet tones of *Entertainment Tonight*'s Mary Hart on television. George and Elaine join a married couple, Michael and Robin, for dinner. However, all does not go well when George says, "God bless you" to Robin after a sneeze. Robin fumes that her husband didn't say it first and an argument ensues. Later, George and Robin get it on, but husband Michael is on to the affair.

Back to Jerry and his relationship with Angela. It becomes even more complicated when he discovers that she's been involved in yet another hit-and-run accident, this time damaging a car owned by a woman named Becky. It seems that Jerry has always had his eye on her, so he offers to pay for all the damages. This outward act of generosity on his part doesn't get him an *in* with her—quite the contrary. She accuses him of being the one who smashed into her set of wheels in the first place.

Ultimately, Jerry confronts Angela about her erratic driving and leaving the scene of two accidents. Kramer, not Jerry, secures a date with Becky but becomes unglued as he enters her apartment and hears Mary Hart's voice on the television. Accompanying Jerry, who's got an engagement outside of New York City, George gets out of town in the nick of time.

Ann Talman played Robin, and Joseph Malone was her husband, Michael.

Episode 37: "The Letter" (original air date: March 25, 1992)

This episode is one more collaboration of Larry David as writer and Tom Cherones as director. Jerry's got a new girlfriend named Nina—an artist who is painting a portrait of Kramer. For five thousand dollars, she sells the piece of artwork to an elderly couple who are completely mesmerized by it. Kramer subsequently dines with these geriatric art collectors, who are absolutely fascinated by the man and his life story.

Meanwhile, Jerry and George visit Nina in her studio. After Nina gives him prime tickets to a Yankees game—her father's seats in the owner's box—George feels compelled to purchase a painting of hers. (He picks out one that he later learns—much to his chagrin—costs five hundred dollars. He offers it to Jerry for ten dollars.)

An excited George brings Elaine and Kramer with him to Yankee Stadium. A Baltimore Orioles fan, Elaine wears her favorite team's cap while sitting in the owner's box. This doesn't sit too well with Yankee fans and the powers-that-be. She is asked to remove the offensive cap, but refuses. George, Elaine, and Kramer are then unceremoniously ushered away by security people. During their hasty departure from the ballpark, Kramer gets knocked in the head with a batted baseball.

After Jerry and Nina break up following an argument over the cap, the former receives a surprisingly moving letter from the latter. This prompts Jerry to reconsider the relationship until he discovers that the missive was entirely lifted from *Chapter Two*, a Neil Simon play.

When Elaine's picture—wearing her Baltimore Orioles cap—appears in the *New York Times* sports section the next day, she worries that her boss, Mr. Lippman, will see it and realize that she had lied to him. Elaine had been invited to Lippman's son's bris, but demurred with the excuse that she had to take care of her sick father.

Lippman, fortunately, appears none the wiser and invites Elaine once again to sit in the owner's box at Yankee Stadium. He had just secured free tickets from his accountant, who, coincidentally, is Nina's father. With her Baltimore Orioles cap on her head for another go-round, Elaine generates still more mayhem in the House That Ruth Built. Legendary broadcaster and Hall of Famer Phil Rizzuto is heard describing all the action to television viewers, including Jerry and George.

Catherine Keener played Jerry's artist-girlfriend, Nina. Elliott Reid and Justine Johnston portrayed the elderly patrons of the arts who were so captivated by the Kramer mystique. Reid began his career in the Golden Age of radio, appearing on such shows as Orson Welles's *The Mercury Theatre on the Air* (1938). He passed away at the age of ninety-three in 2013.

Episode 38: "The Parking Space" (original air date: April 22, 1992)

Directed by Tom Cherones and written by the tag team of Larry David and Greg Daniels—whose television writing credits include *King of the Hill* (1997–2010), *The Office* (2005–2013), *Saturday Night Live*, and *The Simpsons* (1989–present)— this episode is a shining example of the so-called "show about nothing" at its best. The prevailing storyline involves George backing into a parking space— taking his sweet time in doing so—and being challenged for the very same spot by Kramer's friend Mike, who is simultaneously pulling directly into it. George and Mike argue vociferously—for hours on end, as a matter of fact—over who has the right to that parking space. Their stalemate engenders a huge traffic jam on the street, with lots of angry and inconvenienced New Yorkers taking sides and voicing their displeasure.

Prior to this extended street row, George and Elaine had patronized a flea market outside of the city with Jerry's car, which they had borrowed, as their means of transportation. On the return trip, George is sporting an Indiana Jones–style hat that he picked up at the flea market. He also hears a peculiar noise emanating from the car's engine, which inspires Elaine to concoct a fairy tale to tell Jerry that could explain the vehicle's knocking sounds: They were set upon by a group of teenagers hankering for trouble and George had to perform vehicular feats of magic to break away from the wild throng.

Also part of the storyline is that everybody, including Mike, is expected at Jerry's place to watch a big fight on TV. Kramer, though, informs his pal that

Mike, who always behaves as if he really likes Jerry, actually thinks he's a phony. Out on the street with Kramer, Jerry unsuccessfully attempts to referee the parking dispute. He also confronts Mike about the "phony" remark. Rather unconvincingly, Mike says that it was meant as a term of endearment and not a put-down.

Ultimately, even the cops on the scene can't decide who's got the right to the parking spot, with one taking George's side and another Mike's. As darkness sets in, it appears that everyone has missed the big fight. Jerry arrives back in his apartment, only to hear the final countdown of a knockout that he didn't see.

Lee Arenberg played Mike. Years later, in season eight, he would reprise this role in the episode "The Susie."

Episode 39: "The Keys" (original air date: May 6, 1992)

The final episode in the third season was written by Larry Charles and directed by Tom Cherones. The main storyline revolves around Jerry taking away his spare set of keys from Kramer, who he feels has grossly abused the privilege by using his apartment as a personal playground while he is out of town. This decision on Jerry's part upsets Kramer and negatively impacts their friendship, but it also inspires the latter to fly to Hollywood, where he hopes to realize his dream and become an actor.

Meanwhile, Jerry, who has given Elaine his spare keys after taking them away from Kramer, is in desperate need of them but can't get in touch with her. He calls upon George, who has her spare set of keys, to let him into *her* apartment to locate his spare set. Reluctantly, George agrees, and the two enter Elaine's place. While there, they discover an unsolicited script that she has been writing for an episode of CBS's *Murphy Brown*. Both Jerry and George laugh heartily at the material therein, which they find ridiculously lame. When Elaine walks in on them she is disgusted, claims they have violated her privacy, and asks them to leave.

Much to everyone's surprise, Kramer is subsequently spotted on TV as the leading character's secretary—a man named Steven Snell—on an episode of the aforementioned *Murphy Brown*. Candice Bergen guest stars as herself. When this episode aired in the spring of 1992, *Murphy Brown* was a very popular show. Then Vice President Dan Quayle famously took the character, as played by Bergen, to task. On the campaign trail he said, "It doesn't help matters when primetime TV has Murphy Brown, a character who supposedly epitomizes today's intelligent, highly paid professional woman, mocking the importance of fathers by bearing a child alone and calling it another lifestyle choice." The vice president's remark didn't help the Bush–Quayle re-election effort much, but it certainly got *Murphy Brown* some welcome publicity.

22

Season Four

Notice and Accolades

It is fair to say that season four is when everything came together for *Seinfeld*. Although the show did not reach the top of the charts—or even the top ten—vis-à-vis the viewing audience, it was making serious inroads as increasing numbers of people watched the show and, more importantly, talked incessantly about its characters, the dialogue, and the episodes' innumerable plot twists and turns.

Seinfeld was nominated for eleven Emmy Awards for season four and came away the winner of three, including one for "Outstanding Comedy Series," which was the only time in its nine-year run that the show snared the top honor. For his work on season four, Michael Richards took home an Emmy for "Outstanding Supporting Actor in a Comedy Series"—the first of three that he would win for his role as Kramer. And Larry David was recognized as "Outstanding Writer in a Comedy Series" for the episode "The Contest," a *Seinfeld* classic.

Tom Cherones directed all twenty-three episodes of season four, which *TV Guide* recently ranked the greatest single season of any sitcom, before or after. In its parcel of memorable episodes are multiple story arcs, too, which wend their way through them, including the trials and tribulations of Jerry and George developing a sitcom idea and writing a pilot episode for NBC. The season culminates with "The Pilot," an hour-long episode with a storyline revolving around the pilot show in its filming stage. Additional story arcs in season four include George in his on-again, off-again relationship with NBC executive Susan Ross and "Crazy" Joe Davola intent on doing Jerry physical harm or something a little more final.

Episodes 40/41: "The Trip" (original air dates: August 12/ August 19, 1992)

The first episodes of season four—aired in two parts and written by Larry Charles—follow in linear progression season three's finale, "The Keys," which placed Kramer in Hollywood pursuing his dual dreams of forging a successful acting career and seeing his movie script treatment made into a blockbuster film.

Season four gets rolling with Jerry accepting a request to appear on *The Tonight Show with Jay Leno*. He is furnished two round-trip plane tickets to Los Angeles, and George accompanies him on the flight to the West Coast. Both Jerry and George reason, too, that they can hook up with Kramer while there and get the lowdown on how things are going with him.

When they touch down in the City of Angels, the headline news story reports that a serial killer, known as the "Smog Strangler," is on the loose. Puzzlingly, Kramer's movie script is found at the scene of the most recent "Smog Strangler" murder and the police figure they've got their man. They pick Kramer up for questioning and he does not take to being accused of multiple homicides very well. In fact, he becomes hysterical during an interrogation.

Meanwhile, in another room—the green room of *The Tonight Show*—George casually chats with guests Corbin Bernsen and George Wendt, who subsequently impart to Jay Leno their experiences in meeting some wacky guy backstage. George, a member of the studio audience, is visibly embarrassed upon hearing their unflattering descriptions of him, because he thought he had made a good impression on them. After the show, Jerry and George see a newscast with a picture of the suspected serial killer, Kramer, in custody. They promptly contact the police in hopes of saving their old friend from a serious miscarriage of justice.

A police vehicle arrives soon after to escort them down to the station with whatever information they have. En route, they encounter a man breaking into a car, and the police arrest him. Jerry and George are thus compelled to ride in the backseat with an unsavory character. Clint Howard, Ron Howard's younger brother and an actor who has a penchant for playing deranged-looking and objectionable sorts, is the lawbreaker. Later, when the police officers chauffeuring Jerry, George, and the car thief hear that the killer—not Kramer—may be in the very area through which they are passing, they leave their vehicle unattended to have a look around. Jerry and George take the opportunity to go to the police station unescorted, but inadvertently leave the back door open, which enables the handcuffed car thief to escape.

Kramer is exonerated when word comes down that another "Smog Strangler" murder has been committed—one that he couldn't have possibly done while he was in police custody. Jerry and George fly back home, but Kramer stays put in L.A. However, he soon turns up in New York with no explanation as to why he returned. A postscript to this story is that the car thief Jerry and George unintentionally let slip away was actually the "Smog Strangler." Their negligence in permitting him to escape enabled him to kill once more before being apprehended.

Episode 42: "The Pitch" (original air date: September 16, 1992)

Written by Larry David, this episode establishes the story arc for season four, wherein Jerry is asked to develop a sitcom concept for NBC. He takes on George as his collaborator and the fledgling comedy writing pair ultimately pitch an idea about a "show about nothing" to the NBC brass, who are not quite won over.

Interestingly, the mere notion of launching and then developing a storyline based on the experiences of Jerry Seinfeld and Larry David pitching their sitcom pilot to NBC did not go over well with a lot of people, including Jason Alexander, who thought it was "insane." Certain critics felt that a show that was not yet a big audience grabber—it finished number twenty-five in the Nielsen ratings for season three—had no business being that self-indulgent.

Nevertheless, *Seinfeld* being *Seinfeld* defied the conventional wisdom once again and allowed the storyline to unfurl throughout the season. Jerry Seinfeld and Larry David were right to believe in this plotline, too. The "show about nothing" pitch in this very episode is considered a memorable moment in the series. With him vowing not to compromise his artistic integrity or alter the show's concept one iota, George almost blows the deal with the NBC executives. Two recurring characters also debuted in this episode: Susan Ross, an NBC executive, and "Crazy" Joe Davola, a writer with considerable psychological baggage. Susan would become romantically involved with George—on and off—as well as enter into a lesbian relationship in season four, and then come back in season seven to both get engaged to George and die. In "The Pitch," Susan gets introduced to and vomited on by Kramer at Jerry's apartment—an inauspicious first encounter, to say the least. "Crazy" Joe Davola initiates his vendetta here against Jerry as well as Kramer, because of a verbal faux pas. Jerry had casually mentioned that he would see "Crazy" Joe at a party being thrown by Kramer—one for which he had received no invitation.

This episode introduces Heidi Swedberg as Susan Ross, Peter Crombie as "Crazy" Joe Davola, and Bob Balaban as Russell Dalrymple.

The following episode, "The Ticket," originally aired as part of a one-hour episode with "The Pitch" as its first half. In syndication, however, the hour show was separated into individual half-hour episodes, with two separate titles. Hence, for the purposes of episode counting, it is counted as two distinct shows.

Episode 43: "The Ticket" (original air date: September 16, 1992)

This continuation of "The Pitch" finds Jerry and George with a second chance to win over unconvinced NBC executives with their sitcom pilot idea. They accomplish their mission by promising to add a little something to the "show about nothing" concept, but are offered a meager thirteen thousand dollars up front to develop the show, which particularly displeases George, who was expecting a great deal more.

Meanwhile, "Crazy" Joe Davola is on the warpath and kicks Kramer in the head, which adds another layer to his already eccentric behavior and causes him to spew nonsensical sentences. On the other side of the world, Elaine is on holiday in Europe with her psychiatrist-boyfriend, Dr. Reston, who also happens to be Davola's shrink. Dr. Reston, played by Stephen McHattie, realizes from across the ocean that he neglected to supply his unstable patient with a needed prescription before he left town, which would explain the man's psychotic actions.

Intertwined storylines in this episode include Jerry tossing a watch given to him by his parents into a garbage can—because it never kept the right time— only to have it plucked out of the trash by his Uncle Leo, who believed that he got short shrift from Jerry when they encountered one another on the street.

Newman is simultaneously fighting a speeding ticket and enlists Kramer as his alibi. The story concocted by him has Newman in a mad dash to the suicidal Kramer's side, which would explain the excessive speeding. In defense of Newman, Kramer is coached to say on the witness stand that he wanted to take his own life because his lifelong dream of becoming a banker was unrealized. However, a short-term memory loss from the earlier blow to his head torpedoes Newman's entire defense.

"Crazy" Joe Davola is a recurring character in season four. The name is an homage to producer Joe Davola, Larry David's longtime friend in the industry. The real-life Davola's television credits include *Smallville* (2001–2011), *One Tree Hill* (2003–2012), *What I Like About You* (2002–2006), and *The Bronx Is Burning* (2007).

Episode 44: "The Wallet" (original air date: September 23, 1992)

Larry David wrote this episode that finds Jerry's parents coming to town for a visit; George tying to negotiate a better deal with NBC for their sitcom pilot; and Elaine plotting to break up with Dr. Reston, her psychiatrist boyfriend.

Predictably, George's negotiating tactics backfire and the sitcom deal is lost. He does, though, receive a box of Cuban cigars from Susan's father, which he passes on to Kramer. Meanwhile, Jerry's folks wonder how he likes the watch they had given him. Later, while being examined in a doctor's office, Morty Seinfeld believes that his wallet has been purloined.

Julia Louis-Dreyfus is back in the saddle in this episode and appears in a considerable role for the very first time since season three. A pregnancy necessitated her entirely missing the two episodes of "The Trip" that inaugurated the fourth season, and she appeared only in cameo roles in "The Pitch" and "The Ticket."

Episode 45: "The Watch" (original air date: September 30, 1992)

Larry David again wrote this teleplay, a sequel to "The Wallet," in which Jerry attempts to get the watch his parents gave him back from Uncle Leo, who had found it in a trashcan. In a separate plot turn, Kramer agrees to help Elaine end her romantic relationship with Dr. Reston by assuming the role of her new boyfriend

Meanwhile, George attempts to resuscitate the previous deal with NBC by tracking down the president of the network, Russell Dalrymple, at his home. He proves successful in getting the green light once more, but is compelled to accept eighty-eight hundred dollars instead of the original thirteen thousand dollars to make it a reality. By the episode's end, Elaine's got a new boyfriend, "Crazy" Joe Davola, whom she bumps into outside of Dr. Reston's office. She is unaware, though, that he is the same man with a vendetta against Jerry.

Episode 46: "The Bubble Boy" (original air date: October 7, 1992)

The "Larry" team of David and Charles collaborated in writing this episode, which revolves around a young man named Donald Sanger who lives in a germ-free plastic tent—a bubble, as it were—due to a life-threatening immune deficiency.

The episode opens with Jerry and Elaine agreeing to join George and Susan Ross at her family's lakeside cabin in upstate New York. Before making the trip, a man named Mel (played by Brian Doyle-Murray) drops by Jerry and Elaine's table at Monk's Café and tells them about his son, who both calls home a plastic bubble and is a big fan of Jerry Seinfeld. He politely asks if Jerry would visit him in person because it would be a real morale booster. As the Sanger family lives in the same direction of the Ross family cabin, Elaine convinces a reluctant Jerry to grant this heartfelt request. Following behind George and Susan, who have the directions to the Sangers' house, Jerry and Elaine get hopelessly lost due to George's aggressive driving maneuvers: speeding, with perpetual lane changes.

George and Susan thus arrive at the Sanger residence first and impatiently wait for Jerry and Elaine to turn up. In the interim, George engages Donald, who is a very unpleasant and difficult person to be around notwithstanding his condition, in a game of Trivial Pursuit. A dispute over an answer to a question—"Who invaded Spain in the eighth century?"—quickly turns the game on its head. Donald correctly replies, "The Moors," but the card, with an obvious misprint, reads "The Moops." George refuses to accept Donald's answer as the right one and the latter becomes unglued. He reaches out from within his bubble and physically attacks George. In the mêlée, Susan unintentionally punctures the tent's plastic, which necessitates a call to the paramedics.

Meanwhile, Jerry and Elaine are eating in a nearby diner when angry locals enter the place and relay the story of Donald, the "bubble boy," being attacked. Jerry and Elaine put two and two together and reach George and Susan before the rabble does. They drive off to the Ross family cabin and find it in flames. Kramer and Naomi (Jerry's girlfriend), who were not expected, had arrived earlier. The former had carelessly left a lit Cuban cigar unattended, which caused the blaze. The cabin that had been in the Ross family for generations is now a charred memory courtesy of Cuban cigars given to George by Mr. Ross, who in turn gave them to Kramer. It is the irony of ironies.

Jon Hayman supplied the voice of Donald Sanger, who is never fully seen. Jessica Lundy played Jerry's girlfriend, Naomi, who George says laughs like "Elmer Fudd sitting on a juicer."

Episode 47: "The Cheever Letters" (original air date: October 28, 1992)

With story help from Elaine Pope and Tom Leopold, the prolific Larry David penned the teleplay of this episode in the grand tradition of the fourth season, which further develops the story arcs. For starters, George is fretting about how to inform Susan's father that his beloved family cabin has burned to the ground. Both Jerry and George are attempting, too—without much success—to write their sitcom script for NBC.

Meanwhile, Jerry tells Elaine that her secretary, Sandra, talks to him too much before putting him through to her. When Elaine reports what Jerry said, Sandra quits her job and storms out of the office. In hopes that she will return to work, Elaine wants Jerry to patch things up with her. He agrees and makes a date with her, which is going very well until he crosses some invisible line during their "dirty talk" with the strangest of queries, "You mean the panties your mother laid out for you?"

In Kramer's world, he is apparently unmoved that his negligence caused the fire that turned the Ross family cabin into a heap of ashes. He asks George for more Cuban cigars because they make for very potent bribes in getting him into a prestigious golf course. When George breaks the bad news that he has no more, Kramer visits the Cuban Diplomatic Mission near the United Nations and swaps his jacket for some premium cigars.

Later, Jerry and George are at the Ross apartment when the only item that didn't get burned in the fire is delivered—a box that contains love letters exchanged between novelist John Cheever and Susan's father, who proclaims his undying love for his past lover.

Warren Frost and Grace Zabriskie are introduced here for the first time as Mr. and Mrs. Ross. They would return in future seasons' episodes: "The Rye," "The Foundation," "The Wizard," and "The Finale." The Ross family cabin is rebuilt, we learn, in season seven.

Episode 48: "The Opera" (original air date: November 4, 1992)

Larry Charles wrote this episode in his inimitable style, with "Crazy" Joe Davola up to his old tricks—first leaving a threatening message on Jerry's answering machine and then trapping Elaine in his apartment after she discovers a wall full of photographs of her taken with a telephoto lens.

Fortuitously, Elaine escapes from Davola's clutches with the help of cherry-scented breath spray. He has accused her of unfaithfulness now and she, too, must worry about the man's next move. Although, at this juncture, she still does not realize that her "Crazy" Joe is *the* "Crazy" Joe Davola.

Kramer, meanwhile, gets six tickets to *I Pagliacci*, an opera at Town Hall. He attends with Jerry, George, and Elaine. George says that Susan can't make it—she's picking up a friend at the airport—and Elaine's Joe obviously isn't coming either, so this leaves two extra tickets. Kramer and George scalp them.

Back at his apartment, "Crazy" Joe Davola dresses up like Canio from *I Pagliacci*, in full clown regalia. On his way to the theater, hoodlums accost him in Central Park but he turns the tables on the would-be muggers with fluent karate moves.

Comparing notes at the theater, Jerry and Elaine realize now that their "Crazy" Joe person and problems are one and the same. They justifiably fear that he'll be out to get both of them now. When Susan turns up unexpectedly, George is compelled to give her his ticket. She ends up sitting beside a heavyset Asian man who paid George's asking price for the scalped ticket. Kramer informs the gang that he sold his extra ticket to "some nut in a clown suit"—none other than "Crazy" Joe Davola.

Episode 49: "The Virgin" (original air date: November 11, 1992)

With story assistance from brothers Peter Farrelly and Bob Farrelly, Peter Mehlman wrote this episode, wherein Jerry discovers that his girlfriend, Marla (played by Jane Leeves), is a virgin, and George initiates a relationship that he knows is doomed from the start because he already has a girlfriend, Susan.

George is positively giddy, though, that he can now tell women—with some pride—his occupation: television writer. Nevertheless, he realizes that he's caught between a rock and a hard place with regards to Susan. Her support as an NBC executive is crucial to the success of the pilot that he and Jerry are developing. Breaking up with her could very well sound the death knell for the entire project.

Both Jerry and George continue to brainstorm but are finding it exceptionally difficult with all the interruptions from Kramer. With a meeting on the horizon with the NBC big shots, Jerry is concerned that they won't have anything to show them. George comes up with an idea for the sitcom that involves a man guilty of insurance fraud being sentenced by the court to serve as Jerry's butler. Surprisingly, the NBC honchos like it. Overly excited when they are given the thumbs up, George leaps to his feet and plants a wet one on Susan, which both leads to her getting axed from her job and the end of her relationship with the co-creator of *Jerry*.

Meanwhile, Elaine speaks very intimately in front of Jerry's girlfriend—before learning that Marla is a virgin—about how she always has a diaphragm on her person. Upon discovering the virgin truth, as it were, a chagrined Elaine races after her to apologize for her inappropriate words. In such a big hurry, she crosses the street against the light and is responsible for Chinese food delivery boy Ping (played by Ping Wu), crashing his bicycle.

Episode 50: "The Contest" (original air date: November 18, 1992)

In 2009, *TV Guide* ranked this episode number one in its "Top 100 Episodes of All Time" list, which included all sitcoms pre- and post-*Seinfeld*. Larry David, who wrote the script for "The Contest," won both a primetime Emmy Award and Writers Guild of America Award for his efforts. Tom Cherones was recognized with a Directors Guild of America Award for this episode.

"The Contest" gets rolling with George informing the gang at Monk's Café that his mother caught him in the act of masturbating, although that M-word is never uttered. In fact, it so shocked her that she ended up in the hospital. George thusly proclaims that he will never, ever do *it* again. Jerry, Elaine, and Kramer don't believe him for a second and the foursome enter into a contest as to who can go the longest without self-pleasuring. The boys pony up one hundred dollars each, but Elaine is required to cough up one-hundred-fifty dollars because it is so much a part of a man's lifestyle that they will have a much harder road to travel down, vis-à-vis the contest.

After spying a very nubile naked woman in a nearby apartment visible from Jerry's window, Kramer is the first to admit defeat. ("I'm out!" he yells, slapping a hundred-dollar bill on Jerry's table.) Meanwhile, Jerry is sorely tempted by

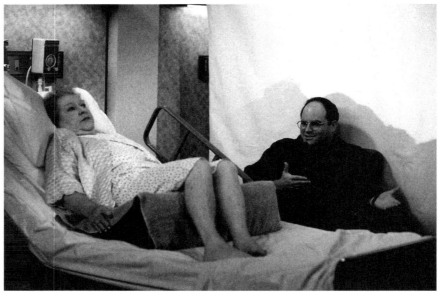

Seeing is believing: Estelle Costanza (Estelle Harris) hospitalized from shock in "The Contest."   *Wren Maloney/NBC/Photofest*

watching the very same woman and further bedeviled in his relationship with Marla, a virgin hesitant about having sex with him. George is turned on, too, watching silhouettes, through a curtain in his mother's hospital room, of a nurse giving a shapely young woman a sponge bath. After encountering him at the health club, Elaine now has a major crush on John F. Kennedy Jr. With the exception of Kramer, who is now free from the contest constrictions and sleeping like a baby, Jerry, George, and Elaine experience fitful nights.

Courtesy of JFK Jr.'s intoxicating sex appeal, Elaine is the second person to cash in her chips. She also discovers that he is interested in her and planning to stop by Jerry's apartment to pick her up for a date. Things go awry for Jerry, however, when he tells Marla about the contest, which she finds quite repellent and leaves before they can consummate their relationship. Elaine then wonders why John F. Kennedy Jr. didn't turn up as promised, but George tells her that he did indeed. He drove off with Marla, the virgin, whom we see in the show's waning moments in bed with him. Like JFK Jr., Kramer is also a happy camper and in bed with the naked woman from across the way. It is not settled here who won the contest—Jerry or George—although the latter admits in "The Finale" that he cheated. He had taken credit in a subsequent episode ("The Puffy Shirt") as the contest winner.

This is the first episode that Estelle Harris appears as Estelle Costanza. John F. Kennedy Jr., like Joe DiMaggio before him, only appears in our imaginations. Jerry Seinfeld has cited "The Contest," along with "The Marine Biologist" and "The Invitations," as his three favorite episodes in the series.

Episode 51: "The Airport" (original air date: November 25, 1992)

Written by Larry Charles, this episode contains not a single scene in any of the characters' apartments or in Monk's Café, which didn't happen very often during the show's nine seasons. Rather, we find Jerry and Elaine on their way home from St. Louis—he had a gig there, and she was visiting her sister—and George and Kramer on their way to John F. Kennedy International Airport to pick them up.

When their flight to JFK is canceled, Jerry and Elaine are compelled to catch another one to LaGuardia Airport. One of their two tickets, however, is in coach, while the other is in first class. Jerry insists that Elaine ride in the former, because he is so accustomed to the latter that he couldn't possibly go back. The end result: he parties during the entire flight with a model named Tia Van Camp, played by Jennifer Campbell, while Elaine has a miserably uncomfortable experience in the recesses of the plane.

Meanwhile, George and Kramer find themselves running back and forth between airports. George's perfect airport pick-up plan is a distant memory. And while he is purchasing the last available copy of *Time* magazine in an airport gift shop, he encounters a convict in shackles who wants the magazine for himself because his picture, along with the blaring headline "Caught," is on the cover. George refuses to turn it over, all the while taking pleasure in the convict's predicament.

While this is transpiring, Kramer sees a man he believes to be John Grossbard, boarding a plane. Grossbard, a former roommate of his from twenty years ago, owes him two-hundred-forty dollars. He asks George to purchase a ticket for him so that he can get on the plane and confront Grossbard. George agrees to the plan only when Kramer reassures him that he will exit the plane before takeoff and get a refund. In fact, George sees the whole thing as a win-win situation for him because he will not only get his money back, but frequent flier miles for the purchase. Why not then purchase *two* tickets? he reasons. Kramer, though, procures non-refundable tickets because the counterperson informs him that they are the best deal.

On the plane, Kramer confronts Grossbard (played by Alan Wasserman), who claims not to know him. Ultimately, Kramer is arrested after a contentious scene and ushered off the plane. Waiting to use the bathroom on the same plane, George is surprised when the door opens to see the convict in shackles—the very same man who wanted his *Time* magazine. He is pulled inside by him and pummeled. Wily Kramer somehow eludes the security people and winds up coming down a baggage chute, where Jerry and Elaine are there to greet him. George, though, is not so lucky and seen on a plane taking off to someplace unknown—bruised and battered, in despair, and plaintively mouthing the word *Kramer!* through a window.

Episode 52: "The Pick" (original air date: December 16, 1992)

Larry David originally wanted to call this episode "The Nipple," but decided against it because of likely network censor objections. He wrote the teleplay with story help from Marc Jaffe. The central plotline of "The Pick" revolves around a Christmas card photograph taken of Elaine by Kramer that inadvertently exposes her nipple. Another plot twist finds George obsessing on getting back together with Susan, and even seeing a therapist about it. Then there's Jerry dating Tia Van Kamp, a Calvin Klein model, whom he met on the plane trip home in the previous episode. Exactly where George's unplanned plane ride took him is never addressed in this episode. Finally, when Kramer turns up in Jerry's apartment to borrow his friend's Dustbuster, he meets Tia, who is wearing a familiar fragrance that he cannot, at first, readily identify.

Kramer, though, quickly realizes that she's wearing Calvin Klein's "The Ocean" perfume, a knockoff of "The Beach" that he had unsuccessfully pitched to them in the episode "The Pez Dispenser." Spitting mad at this injustice, he visits the offices of Calvin Klein to set them straight. He gets no redress with regard to the perfume piracy, but does land a job as an underwear model.

Meanwhile, Jerry's relationship with Tia comes to an abrupt end when she catches him—from her perspective, at least—picking his nose. Jerry explains that he was merely scratching it and that there was no "nostril penetration," but she doesn't buy his explanation. George gets his wish and is back together with Susan, but he fast concludes that it was a mistake. He decides to let her catch him picking his nose, which ends the relationship once more.

Nicholas Hormann played Calvin Klein, who is bowled over by Kramer's physique, masculinity, and charm.

Episode 53: "The Movie" (original air date: January 6, 1993)

Written by the troika of Steve Skrovan, Bill Masters, and Jon Hayman, "The Movie" is another *Seinfeld* episode about nothing much, this one containing a series of miscommunications in the age before cell phones. We find the gang planning to see the movie *Checkmate* together. George and Elaine are at the theater awaiting the arrival of both Jerry and Kramer.

Before meeting his friends, Jerry is slated to perform in two comedy clubs and has everything perfectly timed out. But when the first of his two gigs runs late, his best laid plans have indeed gone agley. He decides not to skip the first show and arrives at the second one too late. On top of that, he shares a cab with Buckles (played by Barry Diamond), a wannabe comedian who is forever annoying him.

At the theater, George stands in the wrong line to buy tickets, which—with all the waiting around—makes it almost certain that they'll get a poor choice of seating by the time they get into the movie. Kramer arrives, but insists on leaving to visit nearby Papaya King for a hot dog. A movie theater frankfurter is, to him, a repulsive notion. Kramer's entrance and then exit merely continues the waiting and miscommunication game. Finally, George and Elaine decide to go to a theater around the corner, where they purchase tickets to see *Rochelle, Rochelle*, a movie that George will subsequently rent from the video store and that, in its Broadway adaptation, will star Bette Midler.

When all is said and done, only Kramer sees the movie that the foursome had originally planned on viewing together.

Episode 54: "The Visa" (original air date: January 27, 1993)

Written by Peter Mehlman, this episode finds George winning over an attractive Asian lawyer named Cheryl with his delicious sense of humor. Coincidentally, she is also the cousin of Ping, the Chinese delivery boy who was injured by Elaine's mad dash in "The Virgin." He is suing her and being represented by Cheryl.

George takes Cheryl out to dinner and, to his utter dismay, Jerry and Elaine turn up in the same restaurant. George fears that Jerry will outshine him in the humor department. When Cheryl excuses herself to make a phone call, George implores Jerry not to be funny around her. Jerry then assumes an ultra-serious demeanor, which—to George's great displeasure—appeals to Cheryl.

Meanwhile, Elaine's been holding Jerry's mail that she picked up for him when he was out of town. It's been weeks and she still hasn't brought it over. Also, Babu Bhatt is now living in Jerry's apartment building and working in Monk's Café. He is grateful that Jerry both got him a job and found him a nice place to live. When they learn that immigration officials have taken Babu away, Jerry visits him in jail. Babu tells him that the immigration bureaucrats never received his visa-renewal application, which he himself hadn't received. Jerry then breaks the news to Babu that the application had been delivered to his mailbox by mistake, and that Elaine had possession of his mail for weeks. Babu is very upset upon hearing this, but Jerry promises to get him legal help. He asks Cheryl to take on Babu's case.

However, when George learns that Cheryl has taken quite a shine to Jerry and his dark, brooding personality, he comes clean and tells her that it was all an act, and that he, George, is really the unfunny, depressed, deeply troubled guy. Highly insulted at this duplicity, Cheryl storms off.

While all this is going on, Kramer returns from a New York Yankees baseball fantasy camp with big news: he accidentally punched out Mickey Mantle and sent him to the hospital. Kramer then visits the baseball legend's Manhattan restaurant to apologize, but gets unceremoniously tossed out.

The episode closes with Babu Bhatt back in Pakistan and ruing the day he ever met that "very, very bad man" Jerry Seinfeld. He vows revenge. Apparently, after George made his revelation, Cheryl didn't lift a finger for Babu. The Ping lawsuit against Elaine, which she had previously convinced her client to drop, is also back on the docket.

Maggie Han played Cheryl. Prior to appearing on *Seinfeld*, Han had a recurring role on *Murphy's Law* as Kimiko Funnuchi.

Episode 55: "The Shoes" (original air date: February 4, 1993)

Jerry Seinfeld and Larry David collaborated on the writing of this episode that continues the story arc of Jerry and George laboring on their sitcom pilot. While in Monk's Café, Gail Cunningham, a former girlfriend of Jerry's who never allowed him to kiss her on their three dates, complains that she was just snubbed by Kramer. She believes, therefore, that Jerry must have spread lies about their relationship to him, which would explain the snub. Gail also comments on Elaine's Botticelli shoes, implying that the latter is hoity-toity for wearing them.

Embarrassed by Gail's discourteous behavior toward her, Elaine calls on the restaurant where she is employed as a chef to *let her have it*. While there, she accidentally sneezes on a plate of pasta primavera that had been ordered by the president of NBC, Russell Dalrymple. Afterwards, when Jerry and George visit Russell with their newly completed script, they find him suffering from a stomach ailment—presumably the result of eating a sneezed-upon dinner—and running back and forth to the bathroom. After George is caught red-handed staring at his fifteen-year-old daughter's cleavage, they are abruptly kicked out of the NBC honcho's office.

Jerry and George realize now that they desperately need to see Russell, who refuses to return their calls. They devise a plan that involves accidentally bumping into him in his favorite restaurant, which is also where Gail is employed. They ask Gail to call them when he shows up. She agrees to help out but only on the condition that she gets Elaine's shoes in return for the favor.

In Kramer's world, he succeeds where Jerry failed. He kisses Gail and claims that women are attracted to a good snub. Kramer believes that the snubbing affair turned her on to him. George, though, disagrees that snubbing a woman would make him more attractive to her.

The episode ends with Elaine asking that the character based on her be given more lines in the *Jerry* sitcom script. Jerry and George had earlier realized that they hadn't given her character a single line, owning up to the fact that they had no idea how to write dialogue for women.

"The Shoes" marked an important milestone in *Seinfeld* history, as the show moved from Wednesday night to Thursday night at 9:30 p.m., following the highly rated *Cheers*. This move brought the show an ever-increasing audience for the remainder of season four. Anita Barone portrayed Gail in this episode. Among her multiple television credits are *The Jeff Foxworthy Show* (1995–1997), as Karen Foxworthy; *The War at Home* (2005–2007), as Vicky Gold; and *Shake It Up!* (2010–2013), as Georgia Jones.

Episode 56: "The Outing" (original air date: February 11, 1993)

This episode delivered one of the most popular catchphrases in the entire series: "Not that there's anything wrong with that." Written by Larry Charles, the central storyline revolves around Jerry and George being presumed gay.

A writer named Sharon, a graduate student at New York University, is doing a feature article on Jerry for the school newspaper. While in Monk's Café, Elaine notices a woman eavesdropping on their conversation and, as a gag, addresses Jerry and George as if they were a closeted gay couple.

The woman turns out to be Sharon of NYU, who now believes that the subject of her interview is gay, especially after she calls on Jerry at his apartment and finds George there. Despite their unequivocal denials, Sharon publishes an article underscoring the gay angle. The Associated Press picks up the story and so does the *New York Post*, which prompts Jerry to say: "I've been outed. I wasn't even *in*."

Largely as an attempt to prove that he is indeed heterosexual, Jerry subsequently dates Sharon. In an effort to break up with his girlfriend, Allison, George hopes to use the story for his benefit. In the final analysis, though, she is not convinced that George is gay, and Sharon is not convinced that Jerry is straight.

Busy character actress Paula Marshall played Sharon, and the equally indus-
trious Kari Coleman was Allison.

Episode 57: "The Old Man" (original air date: February 18, 1993)

It's unusual to find Jerry, George, and Elaine involved in volunteer work, but
that's the case in this episode written by Larry Charles, with the story by Bruce
Kirschbaum. They are working with the elderly. Jerry is entrusted with Sid
Fields, an irascible old coot with a Senegalese housekeeper that George ultimately falls for because she can't speak a word of English.

George, meanwhile, is assisting Ben Cantwell, who quickly tires of the
behavior of his more youthful companion. He informs George in no uncertain
language: "Life's too short to waste on you." Elaine, too, is having problems
with the woman she visits, nauseated by the sight of her goiter. However, she
discovers that she was once Mahatma Gandhi's lover, which intrigues her.

In a completely unrelated storyline, Kramer and Newman attempt to make
a killing selling old LPs to a music store. They first attempt to peddle Jerry's
old records, but come away disgusted with the lowball price offered for them.
Later, they take some of Sid Fields's records to the same place. Again, Kramer
and Newman are dissatisfied with what they are offered and a fight ensues, with
all of the records and potential profits lost.

Veteran character Bill Erwin as Sid Fields with his LP collection and less-than-
enthusiastic caretaker Jerry.   *NBC/Photofest*

In the big picture, the gang does a lousy job in bringing companionship to their elderly charges, with Jerry responsible for both losing Sid Fields's dentures and the man himself.

Veteran character actor Bill Erwin played Sid Fields in this episode and was nominated for an Emmy Award. He passed away in 2010 at the age of ninety-six. The character name of Sid Fields pays tribute to the actor and writer best known for his recurring role on *The Abbott and Costello Show* (1952–1953). Robert Donley played Ben. Most people are unaware that he was the original Joseph "Rocky" Rockford—Jim Rockford's dad—in *The Rockford Files*'s pilot episode (1974), starring James Garner.

Episode 58: "The Implant" (original air date: February 25, 1993)

Peter Mehlman wrote this episode where Jerry dumps yet another girlfriend, Sidra, this time because he's convinced she's had breast implants. Kramer has a Salman Rushdie sighting at the health club and claims he's living under the assumed name of "Sal Bass." An unhappy camper, George is flying to Detroit to attend a wake and funeral service.

As things turn out, Jerry is completely wrong about Sidra's breasts. Elaine, who was chiefly responsible for planting the seed of doubt in Jerry's head—she said that "this chick's playing with Confederate money"—is the one who breaks the news that they are the genuine articles. Slipping in a health club sauna room, and grabbing hold of Sidra's breasts to keep from falling down, removed any and all doubt.

Meanwhile, George is with his girlfriend, Betsy (played by Megan Mullally), at her aunt's wake. He's endeavoring, too, to secure a death certificate, which will enable him to get a discount on the airfare. Also, George quarrels with Betsy's brother, Timmy, over the former's penchant for double-dipping chips.

The episode climaxes with Sidra, played by Teri Hatcher, offering Jerry a well-deserved parting salvo: "Oh, by the way, they're real . . . *and they're spectacular.*"

Jerry's Not Necessarily Top Ten Reasons for Dumping a Girlfriend

10. Jillian had "man hands" ("The Bizarro Jerry").
9. Christie wore the same dress every day ("The Seven").
8. Melanie ate her peas one at a time ("The Engagement").
7. Gwen was two-faced: attractive one day, not attractive the next day ("The Strike").
6. Jodi, a masseuse, refused to give him a massage ("The Masseuse").
5. Audrey wouldn't sample his apple pie ("The Pie").
4. Jeannie was too much like him ("The Foundation").
3. Donna liked a Docker's TV commercial that he didn't like ("The Phone Message").
2. Margaret had previously dated and been dumped by Newman ("The Big Salad").
1. Sidra was suspected of having fake breasts ("The Implant").

Hatcher, who went on to play Lois Lane in *Lois and Clark* (1993–1997) and Susan Mayer in *Desperate Housewives* (2004–2012), was long credited with ad-libbing the "and they're spectacular" tag to the line. Recently, she revealed that Larry David fed her the unscripted line at the last moment. Actor and writer Kieran Mulroney portrayed Timmy, who took George to task for his boorishness.

Episode 59: "The Junior Mint" (original air date: March 18, 1993)

Physician and writer Andy Robin penned this teleplay, which fittingly has scenes in a hospital milieu. One storyline involves Jerry, with George's assistance, vainly attempting to guess the first name of his girlfriend (played by Susan Walters), which he doesn't know. She, though, has supplied him with a key clue: her name rhymes with a part of the female anatomy. This leads the boys to conjure up various possibilities, including Aretha, Bovary, Celeste, and Mulva.

In another plot thread, Elaine calls on her ex-boyfriend Roy (played by Sherman Howard), who is in the hospital and awaiting the removal of his spleen. Roy is an artist who was dumped by Elaine because of his excessive girth. When she sees him in his hospital bed, however, she is duly impressed with his weight loss and is interested in dating him again. He attributes the shedding of pounds to the depression he suffered in the aftermath of their breakup.

During Roy's operation, Jerry and Kramer, who are on the premises, opt to watch the whole thing from a viewer's gallery. The latter offers the former a Junior Mint candy during the spectacle and one accidentally lands in Roy's open body cavity. When word gets out that Roy has developed a post-operative infection, George opts to purchase some of his paintings. Figuring that Roy's death is imminent, he anticipates the paintings will fast appreciate in value. Roy lives to paint another day, though, and credits George's munificent support for his turnaround. In "The Junior Mint," George is caught weepy-eyed while watching *Home Alone*, the 1990 movie starring Macaulay Culkin.

Finally, when Jerry is put on the firing line at last to guess his girlfriend's first name, he selects "Mulva," which causes her to storm away in disgust. In one last attempt to make amends, Jerry hollers out the window to her: "Dolores." Her name is never revealed, although it is presumed that Jerry got it right in the end. Lastly, Elaine spies the post-surgery Roy pigging out in his room and decides not to pursue getting back together.

Episode 60: "The Smelly Car" (original air date: April 15, 1993)

This Larry David and Peter Mehlman collaboration finds Jerry and Elaine returning to his pricey BMW after dining out and encountering horrendous body odor therein, presumably from a restaurant valet parking attendant. Elaine subsequently has problems with her boyfriend, Carl (played by Nick Bakay), who is not too happy with the scent of her hair—because of riding in the malodorous car—and informs her that he's got to get up early the next morning. Translation: Elaine is not welcome to stay the night.

Meanwhile, George and Kramer encounter Susan Ross holding hands with another woman in their favorite video store. George learns that Susan began dating Mona (played by Viveka Davis) just as soon as she and George broke up. Kramer is getting on well with Mona, too, which displeases Susan, who—with sufficient reason—loathes the sight of him. After all, he vomited on her and his carelessness led to the total destruction of her family's beloved country cabin. Ultimately, Mona samples a man for the first time—*a man named Kramer.* George, on the other hand, can't help but feel attracted to Susan again because of her lesbianism and his belief that he drove her to it.

Meeting with little success in ridding the body odor trapped in his vehicle, Jerry intends on getting the responsible party to pony up for at least half the cleaning bill. When the restaurant maître d' refuses to share the cost, Jerry locks him in the smelly car until he relents. After a thorough cleaning, though, Jerry discovers that the stink endures. He can't even sell the vehicle.

The smelly car factor continues to impact the lives of all who ride in it and even—in Kramer's case—of those who borrow clothing from one of its passengers. He has borrowed the jacket Jerry had worn on the night in question and Mona ends their relationship because of the nasty scent. With seemingly no other option at his disposal, Jerry abandons his very expensive but incredibly stinky set of wheels. But even on the street, it's hard to find takers for a car in the grips of this mysterious and seemingly indestructible body odor.

Episode 61: "The Handicap Spot" (original air date: May 13, 1993)

Larry David wrote this episode—one that, in many respects, underscored what separated *Seinfeld* from its sitcom competitors. The show's willingness in prime-time to poke fun at people who were not normally the objects of ridicule—in situations, too, that were not normally considered funny—defined the show. It's also what added fuel to the ratings, which would continue to grow until it reached number one in season six.

For openers, Jerry, George, Elaine, and Kramer find themselves at a shopping mall in Lynbrook, New Jersey, where they are looking for an engagement present for a mutual friend, "The Drake." Upon their arrival in the mall's overly crowded parking lot, Kramer convinces George to park in a handicap reserve spot, which he agrees to do. His rationale for taking the spot is that they won't be very long anyway. They are pressed for time, too, with an engagement party later that day. Nonetheless, Jerry, George, Elaine, and Kramer take their sweet time and, upon their return to the vehicle, encounter an angry mob. It seems that a legitimately disabled woman in a wheelchair, who couldn't access the handicap spot, suffered an accident as a result of parking a fair distance from the store entrance. For their own health and welfare, the foursome pretend not to know whose car it is and continue on their merry way. After the riled crowd dissipates, they return to the car, which George had borrowed from his father, and find it pulverized beyond recognition.

George hurriedly concocts a phony story to tell his father, but his lie doesn't hold up when Frank Costanza is arrested, ironically, while being feted for his charitable works with the handicapped. He, as the car's legal owner, was traced. Meanwhile, Kramer visits the accident victim, a woman named Lola, in the hospital and falls head over heels in love with her. His love, though, is unrequited in the end because he is not good-looking enough for her.

As punishment for destroying his car, Frank Costanza enlists George as his butler, which is akin to George's sitcom idea that so impressed NBC executives. In the episode's waning moments, Lola is seen losing control of her wheelchair. George and Kramer had purchased her a replacement one on the cheap that, from the looks of things, had faulty brakes.

Veteran television and stage actor John Randolph played Frank Costanza in the first appearance in the series of George's father. The character that Jerry Stiller infused with such hysteria and rage was not yet born. The fact that Frank Costanza is being given an award for helping others in need is just not something that would have happened to the Frank Costanza of later episodes. John Randolph's scenes, in fact, were re-shot with Stiller for the show's syndication because of the comedian's strong identification with the character. It is nonetheless very strange seeing Stiller in this episode, which clearly was not written for him and the character that he single-handedly established.

Episode 62: "The Pilot" (original air date: May 20, 1993)

The last episode of the fourth season, written by Larry David, aired in a one-hour format. It also was the lead-in for the final episode of *Cheers*, at 9:00. Moving up a half hour on the Thursday-night schedule, *Seinfeld* would assume that premium time slot at the start of its fifth season.

"The Pilot" revolves around Jerry and George at long last getting the go-ahead to produce their sitcom pilot, *Jerry*. Actors are cast to play the various parts based on George, Elaine, and Kramer. Meanwhile, NBC president Russell Dalrymple becomes fixated on Elaine, who is not interested in pursuing a relationship with him. George suffers from a fixation of his own, fearing that a white spot on his lip is cancer and that he won't live long enough to see the almost certain monetary windfall that a future *Jerry* series will generate.

Elaine has other things on her mind and is concerned with matters beyond Russell's obsession with her. She doesn't like the fact that only ample-breasted women comprise the entire wait staff at Monk's Café. When she herself gets turned down for a waitress job, she files a discrimination lawsuit against her preferred eatery. She later learns that the buxom waitresses are the owner's daughters.

To try to let Russell down easily, Elaine says that she could never, ever be in a relationship with a corporate executive in the dog-eat-dog business world, preferring instead men who contribute to the betterment of the planet, like those who work with Greenpeace. To prove his fealty to her, Russell ultimately joins the organization, but gets lost at sea. The *Jerry* pilot script is, in fact, seen floating away in what apparently is a shipwreck.

The *Jerry* pilot is filmed and aired, but the new NBC president, unlike her predecessor, is not a fan and cancels it forthwith, without even waiting to see the ratings. Jerry and George blame Elaine for driving Russell Dalrymple away, along with their chances of getting the show picked up for a full season. The actors cast in *Jerry* were Michael Barth as George, played by Jeremy Piven; Tom Pepper as Kramer, played by Larry Hankin; and Sandi Robbins as Elaine, played by Elena Wohl. Ironically, the six-foot-four-inch Hankin auditioned for the Kramer role in *Seinfeld*, and ended up playing the fictional Kramer—a fictional character to begin with—in a fictional TV show.

23

Season Five

Almost Number One

The second half of season four found *Seinfeld* slowly but surely becoming a real ratings grabber. The show would finish number three in the Nielsen ratings this season, trailing only Tim Allen's *Home Improvement*—a decidedly different brand of comedy, for sure—and the venerable CBS newsmagazine *60 Minutes*.

The *Seinfeld* phenomenon was undeniably in full swing at the start of season five, and it didn't hurt that it moved up a half hour to fill the vaunted Thursday night 9:00 slot long held by the popular *Cheers*. For his efforts in the new season, Michael Richards won his second Emmy Award in a row for "Outstanding Supporting Actor in a Comedy Series," besting his co-star, Jason Alexander, who was also nominated. The show garnered twelve Emmy nominations for season five, including Jerry Seinfeld, nominated for "Outstanding Lead Actor in a Comedy Series," and Julia Louis-Dreyfus, nominated for "Outstanding Supporting Actress in a Comedy Series." Tom Cherones once again directed the entire season's twenty-two episodes.

Episode 63: "The Mango" (original air date: September 16, 1993)

Written by Larry David and Lawrence H. Levy, with the story by the latter, the first episode of season five is vintage *Seinfeld*, with its multiple, interwoven storylines. Its working title was "The Orgasm," which underscored the central plotline: Elaine's admission that she never, ever had one in her past relationship with Jerry. Not surprisingly, this revelation unnerves Jerry, who wants one more chance to deliver the goods. He gets that chance, but doesn't rise to the occasion, so to speak. George, meanwhile, becomes so fixated on the possibility of women faking orgasms that it negatively impacts his relationship with Karen, his latest girlfriend, played by Lisa Edelstein. Ultimately, he is unable to perform in bed at all.

A counter story here involves Kramer and a matter of fruit, which he buys from Joe's neighborhood market. While the fruit is typically top notch there, he samples a "sub-par" peach and, without delay, brings it back to Joe for full restitution. The shopkeeper, played by Leonard Termo, not only refuses

Kramer's request, but bans him from his store altogether. Kramer then enlists Jerry to do his fruit shopping for him, which he dutifully does for his friend. However, Joe is wise to the subterfuge and bans Jerry as well. George is finally asked to do the shopping at Joe's, which he admirably performs. The deliciously juicy mangoes from Joe's fruit store appear, too, to behave as an aphrodisiac and vanquish George's virility issues.

Episode 64: "The Puffy Shirt" (original air date: September 23, 1993)

Larry David wrote this teleplay that finds Kramer dating Leslie, a clothing designer who also happens to be a "low-talker." When Jerry and Elaine dine with the happy couple, the former inadvertently agrees to wear one of Leslie's new designs on television. Her low volume is responsible for Jerry consenting to sport a "puffy shirt"—just like the pirates wore—in a *Today* show interview with Bryant Gumbel, who plays himself. When the host can't help but continually ridicule the shirt, Jerry lets loose on it, too. Backstage, Leslie roars out, "You bastard!" in stark contrast to her usual hushed tones.

"I heard that!" Jerry replies.

Jerry, with Kramer, preparing for his *Today* show appearance in "The Puffy Shirt." The titular blouse is now in the Smithsonian's National Museum of American History.

NBC/Photofest

Meanwhile, George is back home living with his parents and optimistic at embarking on a new career as a hand model. He's already received a nice paycheck for his first shoot. Meeting Jerry backstage at NBC after his appearance on *Today*, he is positively aglow but cannot help, too, mocking the puffy shirt. Unbeknown to George, though, is that its designer is within earshot. Leslie pushes him in anger and his bare hands come into contact with a hot iron—the one that Kramer had used to press Jerry's puffy shirt before he appeared on the show. His promising career as a hand model ends in its infancy.

"The Puffy Shirt" marks the very first episode with Jerry Stiller in the role of Frank Costanza. (In syndication, he is seen in an earlier episode, "The Handicap Spot," having re-shot John Randolph's scenes.) Canadian actress Wendel Meldrum, who was born in Rome, Italy, played Leslie. One final postscript to this memorable episode is that the puffy shirt itself is now on display at the National Museum of American History and keeping company with Archie Bunker's chair and the ruby slippers belonging to Dorothy from *The Wizard of Oz*.

Episode 65: "The Glasses" (original air date: September 30, 1993)

The prolific comedy-writing duo of Tom Gammill and Max Pross penned this episode—their first of multiple contributions they would make through season eight. The principal storyline revolves around George and his missing eyeglasses, which he believes were stolen at the health club.

While not sporting his spectacles, George is nonetheless convinced that he saw Amy, Jerry's girlfriend, kissing Jeffrey, Jerry's cousin and devoted employee of the New York City Parks Department. When Jerry confronts Amy about this serious allegation, she heatedly denies that she did any such thing. Jerry then begins to wonder whether George—even though he's an accomplished squinter sans his glasses—could have really seen what he claims to have seen. When he plucks an onion, assuming that it's an apple, out of Jerry's refrigerator and bites into it, George's eyewitness account appears on even shakier ground.

At Kramer's friend and optometrist Dwayne's place of business, meanwhile, a man's dog takes a healthy bite out of Elaine, initiating a visit to the emergency room. Later, Jerry's new air conditioner falls out the window, injuring the same canine that bit Elaine, and he gets stuck with a considerable veterinarian's bill. When George finally gets his new pair of glasses, he spies a homely policewoman planting a wet kiss on her horse, which he realizes was what he had mistaken for Amy kissing Jeffrey, who always "wears a long face."

Stage and screen actress Anna Gunn portrayed Jerry's wrongfully accused girlfriend. Timothy Stack played Dwayne, the optometrist.

Episode 66: "The Sniffing Accountant" (original air date: October 7, 1993)

Written by Jerry Seinfeld and Larry David, this episode is based on the former's bad experience with an accountant who stole approximately fifty thousand dollars from him to support a cocaine habit.

The story gets rolling with Jerry, George, and Elaine chatting in Monk's Café. One subject of conversation revolves around an old sweater that Jerry is wearing, which he found in the back of his closet. Elaine, too, recounts the tale of meeting her new boyfriend, author Jake Jarmel, at Pendant Publishing. They then notice Jerry's new accountant, Barry Prophet, outside of the café and he is invited to join them. But Barry's perpetual sniffing during their brief exchange alarms Jerry, who fears that his accountant may have a substance abuse problem along with a lot of his money.

Meanwhile, George's father gets him a job interview with Sid Farkus, who sells bras. Farkus is impressed with George and offers him a job on the spot. Excited, George brazenly touches a woman's shirt on the way out—a woman who happens to be Farkus's superior. She demands that George be fired. The Costanzas, one and all, are unhappy at this turn of events.

On the other side of town, Elaine chastises her boyfriend, Jake, for not using exclamation points on some of the phone messages he jotted down for her. Jake storms out of her apartment with the words, "I'm *leaving*!" emphasizing that the sentence he just uttered ended with an exclamation point.

By staking out his office and following him into a bar, Kramer and Newman—who also have some money tied up with Barry Prophet—assist Jerry in getting to the bottom of the "Does he?" or "Doesn't he?" question. Kramer's undercover work confirms more sniffing and he snaps a photo of Prophet in the bathroom. As a result, Jerry opts to terminate his relationship with his accountant. He entrusts Newman with mailing a letter stating that it's over, but it never reaches its intended destination—a mailbox. Subsequently, Jerry believes he might have been mistaken concerning the origins of the sniffing, thinking that Prophet was only doing so because of the old sweater of his, which caused a pizza delivery guy to sniff, too.

In the end, though, Prophet declares bankruptcy, presumably because of his drug use. Had Newman delivered the letter as promised—prior to the declaration of bankruptcy—Jerry could have gotten his money back from him.

John Kapelos played accountant Barry Prophet, and Patrick Cronin was bra salesman Sid Farkus. Cronin would reprise the role in "The Doorman." Marty Rackham portrayed Jake Jarmel in the first of three episodes. He would also appear in "The Opposite" and "The Scofflaw."

Episode 67: "The Bris" (original air date: October 14, 1993)

Larry Charles wrote this episode that finds Jerry, George, Elaine, and Kramer at the hospital. They are visiting friends who just welcomed a new bundle of joy into the world. George, too, is strutting around like a male peacock because he secured the ideal parking spot so very near the hospital entrance. Kramer is a late arrival because he can't find the right hospital room and ends up crashing the wrong one with, he claims, a half man–half pig—a Pig Man, as it were—patient. He fervently believes this creature is the result of government experimentation.

During the gang's visit, a mentally unstable patient leaps to his death and lands on George's car—the one parked in the picture-perfect location. He later tries to collect from the hospital the damages incurred to his vehicle, but is thrown out of an administrator's office and denounced for his utter insensitivity to the suicide.

As the just anointed godparents, Jerry and Elaine are busy, too, preparing for their friends' new baby's bris. They are responsible for hiring the mohel, the man who performs the circumcision, and Jerry is expected to hold the child during the procedure. The mohel entrusted to do the job turns out to be a cantankerous, neurotic basket case who doesn't like children. He accidentally sends Jerry to the hospital after slashing his finger. Upon a second sighting, Kramer realizes that the hospital's Pig Man is not a government-created mutant but merely a "fat little mental patient." In the episode's waning moments, Jerry and Elaine are dismissed as the godparents and replaced by Kramer because of the great concern that he showed for the child. He had earlier expressed opposition to the practice of circumcision. In this episode, Elaine describes seeing an uncircumcised penis for the first time: "It had no face, no personality. It was like a Martian."

Reflecting on the series at large, Jason Alexander said that "The Bris" is the only episode that he wished he had never done. He cited as the reason the mohel's inexcusable behavior, notably his disdain for children. (Charles Levin played the ill-tempered, bungling mohel.) This episode also marks the final time that the audience applauded Michael Richards's frenetic entrances as Kramer. Larry David thereafter importuned the show's audiences to refrain from the applause because it was simultaneously throwing off the actors' timing and eating into the episode's time allotment.

Episode 68: "The Lip Reader" (original air date: October 28, 1993)

Carol Leifer wrote this episode, the first of six with her byline in the series. Leifer once dated Jerry Seinfeld and is often cited as the model for the Elaine Benes character.

"The Lip Reader" storyline commences with Jerry and George at a U.S. Open tennis match in Flushing Meadows, in Queens. The former is attracted to a lineswoman at the match, who appears to be ignoring him, while the latter is captured by television cameras—unbeknown to him—with chocolate syrup all over his face from an ice cream sundae he purchased at a concession stand.

Jerry soon realizes that the lineswoman, Laura, is deaf. And George is upset that his girlfriend, Gwen (played by Linda Kash), has broken up with him with what he considers an unexpressed reason. She said, "It's not you; it's me." George says that *he* invented that line. Elaine, meanwhile, is riding in a limo on business and feigns being deaf to avoid talking with the driver, played by Christopher Darga. She ultimately is compelled to end her ruse when she hears a radio communiqué that the driver is slated to pick up actor Tom Hanks.

Jerry dates Laura but lip-reading miscommunications trigger a few problems. When Jerry asks, "How about six?" in reference to picking her up for a party, Laura thinks he said, "How about sex?" Further lip-reading miscommunications ensue as Laura tries to help George get to the bottom of why Gwen broke up with him. He believes that she must have seen him on television with chocolate syrup all over his face. Kramer, in a sidebar story, lands a job as a ball boy at the U.S. Open, where he, in his enthusiasm, unintentionally knocks tennis star Monica Seles out cold.

Marlee Matlin, who is deaf in real life, portrayed Laura in this episode and was nominated for an Emmy. Among her many achievements on the Hollywood scene, Matlin won an Academy Award for "Best Actress" in the movie *Children of a Lesser God* (1986).

Episode 69: "The Non-Fat Yogurt" (original air date: November 4, 1993)

Written by Larry David, this episode was timed to coincide with the 1993 New York City mayoral race between incumbent David Dinkins and challenger Rudy Giuliani. It aired two days after the election and two different versions of its ending were filmed—one with Dinkins having won re-election, and another, with Giuliani having unseated him. Rudy Giuliani emerged the winner and a taped segment of him was made specifically for this episode. The more prim and proper Dinkins had declined to do something similar.

The main plotline revolves around a non-fat yogurt shop in which Kramer has invested money. One and all are enamored with the delightful-tasting product being sold there. However, when Kramer detects that Jerry and Elaine have gained some weight, the latter is very suspicious about the yogurt's ingredients and sends it to a laboratory to be analyzed. Jerry, meanwhile, gets himself in trouble by using some bad language around the yogurt shop owner's boy, Matthew, who adds some choice words to his own vocabulary.

Elaine, in an unrelated storyline, is dating Lloyd Braun, George's childhood nemesis, who is on Mayor Dinkins's staff. She offers Lloyd a policy suggestion

Elaine, Jerry, and George delighting in the non-genuine article in "The Non-Fat Yogurt."

NBC/Photofest

that the mayor could use in his re-election campaign—New Yorkers wearing name tags so that they could all get to know one another. It would then be like a small town, Elaine reasons. Lloyd likes the idea and it is adopted by the campaign. It is, however, widely ridiculed and believed to have been a deciding factor in the close election.

Despite Kramer's best efforts in trying to sway the lab technician analyzing the yogurt to falsify her findings—he wants to protect his investment—word gets out that the scrumptious-tasting yogurt has fat in it after all. The alternate yogurt made without it doesn't taste very good and business plummets, causing the shop owner's son, Matthew, to lob an F-bomb Jerry's way for destroying his father's business. The F-bomb was, of course, censored.

Peter Keleghan played Lloyd Braun. The character shares the same name as Larry David's lawyer and manager, which was intended as an inside joke. Matt McCoy would assume the Lloyd Braun role in future episodes "The Gum" and "The Serenity Now."

Episode 70: "The Barber" (original air date: November 11, 1993)

A somewhat unusual episode written by Andy Robin, "The Barber" employs Gioachino Rossini's famous *Barber of Seville* overture throughout it. The main storyline involves Jerry getting a haircut. In fact, Elaine asks him to get one so

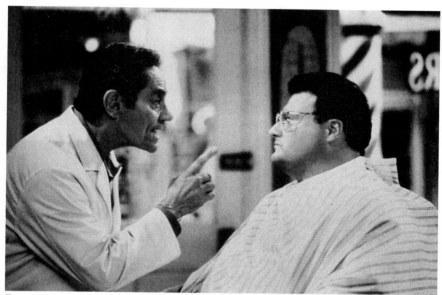

Enzo the Barber (Antony Ponzini) and Newman (Wayne Knight) in "The Barber."

NBC/Photofest

that he will look his best for the impending bachelor auction he had agreed to attend. George, on the other hand, is sitting through another job interview, this time with a man named Mr. Tuttle (played by Jack Shearer), who inadvertently leaves him hanging as to whether or not he's got the job. While Mr. Tuttle is on vacation, George decides to show up for work as if he was hired.

Kramer, meanwhile, recommends that Jerry not get his haircut by Enzo, his regular barber, but by Gino, his nephew, instead. He claims that the younger Gino is a more competent cutter and furnishes Jerry with information on Enzo's day off. Jerry turns up for a haircut from Gino, but Enzo unexpectedly materializes and gives him one that makes him look like a schoolboy. In an effort to rectify the problem, Kramer arranges for Gino to do it on the sly at the latter's apartment but, without warning, Enzo shows up there, compelling Jerry to hide in a closet. Enzo, though, detects hair on the floor that he suspects belongs to Jerry. He enlists another one of his clients, Newman, to get a sample of Jerry's hair for him so that he can compare that with what he found in Gino's apartment. When Enzo confirms that the two samples belong to one and the same person, he seeks revenge on his traitorous former barber shop client and ends up in a serious row with Gino at Jerry's place. Fortunately, *Edward Scissorhands*, starring Johnny Depp, is playing on the television. The two barbers lay down their arms and become transfixed by the movie. They sob together, with Enzo forgetting all about his disagreement with Jerry.

Jerry nonetheless looks like a little kid with his bad haircut, and Kramer is compelled to substitute for him at the bachelor auction. George, on the other hand, has little luck in keeping the job he wasn't certain he really had. Believing that he had a better offer from a client of theirs, Mr. Pensky (played by Michael Fairman), he subsequently learns that the company's board members have been indicted lock, stock, and barrel and they are unable to hire George or anyone else for that matter.

Antony Ponzini played Enzo, and David Ciminello was Gino.

Episode 71: "The Masseuse" (original air date: November 18, 1993)

Peter Mehlman returns as writer of this episode with vintage *Seinfeld* plot twists and references to current events and people in the news. Elaine, for starters, is dating a man named Joel Rifkin, who, alas, shares the same moniker with a recently arrested serial killer. Jerry is involved with a woman, Jodi, a licensed masseuse, who spurns his multiple entreaties for a massage of his own. It's an especially tough pill to swallow because she supplies Kramer with one. Jodi, too, doesn't much like George, and he becomes obsessed by this. He, meanwhile, gives short shrift to Karen, his girlfriend (played by Lisa Edelstein), and they break up because of it.

There is a scene in "The Masseuse" with Elaine and Joel at Giants Stadium, where the latter is paged over the public-address system. When his name is mentioned—Joel Rifkin—the crowd nervously stirs, fearing that a serial killer is in their midst. Bob Sheppard, the longtime announcer for both the New York Yankees and the Giants football team, furnished the voice-over. This event opened Joel Rifkin's eyes that, perhaps, he really should change his first name.

Jennifer Coolidge played Jodi, Jerry's masseuse girlfriend. Among her many acting credits is the role of Stifler's mother in *American Pie* (1999) and Polish bombshell Sophie Kaczynski on *2 Broke Girls* (2012–present). Anthony Cistaro played the boyfriend with the unfortunate name of Joel Rifkin.

Episode 72: "The Cigar Store Indian" (original air date: December 9, 1993)

Another Tom Gammill and Max Pross collaborative effort, this episode finds Jerry with his sights set on a Native American woman named Winona (played by Kimberly Guerrero), and George bringing a lady friend to his parents' house while they are away and pretending that it's his own.

"The Cigar Store Indian" commences at the Costanzas' house, with George insisting that Jerry help him take the Costanza living room coffee table to an antique and furniture-refinishing shop to remove a stain. Elaine and Kramer are thus out of luck and compelled to take the subway home. The former is particularly annoyed with Jerry, who has the car, because she needs to be home to host a girls'-night-out poker game. As subway reading material, Elaine is given an old *TV Guide* with New York weatherman Al Roker gracing its cover.

To make amends for this inconvenience, Jerry subsequently buys Elaine a gift from the antique shop: a cigar store Indian. With Winona as witness—he doesn't yet know her ethnicity—Jerry makes stereotypical Indian sounds and gyrations when presenting it to her. Winona is not amused.

Ultimately, Jerry dates Winona. He learns her heritage, too, but finds it incredibly difficult not to say things that might offend her. George, meanwhile, has sex with the woman who works in the antique store. Along the way, he accidentally leaves a condom wrapper in Frank and Estelle Costanza's bed. When the unhappy couple return home, it is discovered, and so is the fact that one of Frank's *TV Guide*s is missing. He has a complete collection containing every issue and accuses Elaine of stealing from him. This leads to Herculean efforts to get Frank a clean replacement copy, which doesn't come easily. Elaine, in fact, encounters a man on the subway who assumes possession of Frank's original *TV Guide* and turns it into a paper bouquet of flowers for her. As if she doesn't have problems enough, Kramer wants her to pitch his coffee table book about coffee tables to the big shots at Pendant Publishing.

George's latest deception comes to a crashing end, too, when Estelle Costanza visits the shop that employs his new girlfriend. She sets her straight on George: he is, she explains, *not* a homeowner, he has *no* job to speak of, and he is back living with his parents. In other words: her son is a total loser.

Al Roker appears as himself in this episode and snatches a gyro from Jerry's hand after said hand gets stuck in a subway door. Earlier in the episode, Kramer had lost a gyro to similar circumstances. Sam Lloyd played Ricky, the strange subway rider fixated on Elaine. He would reprise his role in the episode "The Pie."

Episode 73: "The Conversion" (original air date: December 16, 1993)

Written by newcomer Bruce Kirschbaum, the episode's chief storyline revolves around George and his new girlfriend, Sasha, who is Latvian Orthodox. When Sasha, played by Jana Marie Hupp, tells him that her parents absolutely forbid her from dating anyone outside of the Latvian Orthodox faith, George considers converting to the religion. After wading through copious Latvian Orthodox texts, he successfully converts, even though he cheats on the tests to make the grade.

Meanwhile, Jerry is dating Tawni, a neighbor (played by Kimberly Campbell), whose medicine cabinet contains an ointment for an unknown fungal condition. This unsolved mystery greatly unsettles Jerry—so much so that he needs to know the ointment's true purpose before forging a relationship with her. Elaine, on the other hand, is dating a podiatrist. There is much discussion on whether or not a podiatrist merits being called a *doctor*. Kramer's magnetism, too, is on display in "The Conversion" as he sweeps Sister Roberta of the Latvian Orthodox order (played by Molly Hagan) off her feet. She considers leaving the church for him but, in the end, does not. Kramer is said to have the *kavorka*, a Latvian word that translates into "lure of the animal." Kramer's *kavorka* is believed to make him completely irresistible to the opposite sex.

Sidebar plot twists involve Frank and Estelle Costanza learning of George's conversion and fearing that he's both joined a cult and lost his marbles. And Jerry ultimately discovers that the fungal medicine is not for Tawni's personal use, but for her cat. To his dismay, George discovers, too, that his conversion was for naught when Sasha reveals that she is moving back to Latvia.

Bruce Kirschbaum, the episode's writer, admitted that when he wrote the script he was blissfully unaware that a Latvian Orthodox religion existed. It was his intention to create a fictitious one. Nonetheless, the Latvian Orthodox sect was pleased as punch to get the publicity. Character actor Kay E. Kuter appeared in the episode as a Latvian Orthodox priest. Baby boomers remember him for his recurring role as Newt Kiley in both *Green Acres* (1965–1971) and *Petticoat Junction* (1963–1970). Kuter died in 2003 at the age of seventy-eight.

Episode 74: "The Stall" (original air date: January 6, 1994)

Written by Larry Charles, this episode focuses upon the myriad love interests of Jerry, Elaine, and Kramer, too, if one considers phone sex a "love interest." Jerry is dating Jane, who by chance finds herself in a movie theater bathroom stall beside Elaine. When the latter notices that there is no more toilet paper in her stall, she requests some of it from the former through the partition, but is coldly turned down with the words "Can't spare a square."

Elaine, who is in the movie theater with her date, Tony (played by Dan Cortese), is unaware that Jane, the woman in the adjoining stall who refused her toilet paper entreaty, is Jerry's date. Jerry dubs Elaine's Tony a *mimbo*, his word for "male bimbo." Back at the apartment, Kramer is accused—with ample evidence to bolster the accusation—of using Jerry's phone to place telephone sex calls. When Kramer meets Jane for the first time, he's certain that he's heard her voice before, and concludes that it sounds an awful lot like "Erika," from the telephone sex line.

George immerses himself in the current scene by becoming unduly impressed with the good looks and athletic prowess of Tony—a man crush, as it were. When Tony invites him to go rock climbing, George jumps at the chance. Kramer, too, gets an invite, which annoys George, who hoped to have Tony all to himself. Meanwhile, Jerry realizes that Jane was the woman in the stall next to Elaine and fears a future confrontation.

On their rock-climbing afternoon, George and Kramer's negligence cause Tony to fall off a mountain cliff and seriously damage his handsome face. The accident leaves Elaine pondering whether she could possibly love Tony without his pretty-boy looks. It also presents her with a real moral dilemma: how long should she have to remain his girlfriend while he is convalescing? Tony, for one, wants nothing to do with George, who visits him in the hospital with a Whitman Sampler and Superman comic book in a futile attempt to make amends.

As it turns out, Kramer is correct that Jane and Erika are one and the same person. By making a date with her, the cat is out of the bag when she shows up at Monk's Café. When Jane, a.k.a. Erika, retreats to the café bathroom, Elaine gets even with a little toilet paper legerdemain of her own.

Actress Jami Gertz played the dual roles of Jane and Erika. Gertz's television and movie credits span decades, including recurring roles in series ranging from *The Facts of Life* (1979–1988) to *Ally McBeal* (1997–2002) to *The Neighbors* (2012–2014).

Episode 75: "The Dinner Party" (original air date: February 3, 1994)

Written by Larry David, "The Dinner Party" is another *Seinfeld* episode that could be classified as being about nothing—or nothing especially important. Jerry, George, Elaine, and Kramer have been invited to a dinner party. Elaine, though, insists that they not go empty-handed and should bring something— specifically, a bottle of wine and a cake. George suggests an alternative: a bottle of Pepsi and box of Ring Dings. Jerry and Elaine are charged with the cake part and call on Schnitzer's Bakery with the intention of purchasing a chocolate babka, whereas George and Kramer are responsible for the wine.

By not taking a number in the bakery, Jerry and Elaine encounter the first in a series of snafus. The last remaining chocolate babka is sold before they are served. They are thus compelled to purchase a cinnamon babka instead, which Elaine considers vastly inferior to its chocolate cousin. When they discover that their cinnamon babka has a hair on it, they exchange it. A not-so-happy counterperson, played by Kathryn Kates, replaces it with another one, which she disgustingly coughs upon. (Kates would return as the bakery counterperson in the episode "The Rye.")

George and Kramer, meanwhile, attempt to procure the bottle of wine with a hundred-dollar bill, which the liquor store owner refuses to accept. This forces them to break the bill someplace else. They try a nearby newspaper stand and buy a pack of chewing gum, but the newspaper stand proprietor doesn't feel that's a significant enough purchase to justify making change for the big bill. They buy a few more items, receive their change, and return for the bottle of wine.

With their mission finally accomplished, they discover that a double-parked car has blocked their vehicle. It being bitterly cold outside, George and Kramer retreat to the liquor store to stay warm while awaiting the double-parker's return. However, the liquor store owner kicks them out, saying that his business establishment is not a hangout. Upon their exit, George's recently purchased, oversized, and warm winter parka—made of Gore-Tex—knocks over several bottles of wine, which he is compelled to pay for with the very same coat. When the double-parker at last turns up, it's a man who bears an uncanny resemblance to Iraqi dictator Saddam Hussein, who tells George that he is seriously underdressed for the extremely cold weather.

When Jerry, George, Elaine, and Kramer at long last arrive at the dinner party, they drop off the cinnamon babka and bottle of wine but choose not to attend the party.

Episode 76: "The Marine Biologist" (original air date: February 10, 1994)

Written by newcomers Ron Hauge and Charlie Rubin, this episode has the distinction of being the first one not to climax with Jerry performing standup. It is also one of Jerry Seinfeld's personal favorites. The plot twists and turns are multifold, including Jerry meeting Diane (played by Rosalind Allen), an old friend from their college days. When she inquires about George and what he's up to, Jerry lies and says that he's a marine biologist. George wishes that he would have told her that he was an architect instead, because he always wanted to lie about being that.

Meanwhile, Elaine and Pendant Publishing are wooing Russian author Yuri Testikov, an exceptionally testy man who tosses her electronic organizer out of a limousine window because of its excessive beeping. It ends up striking a woman named Corinne, who tracks down Jerry via his phone number in the organizer. She demands that her hospital bills be paid.

In a separate plot twist, Kramer ventures to the ocean to hit the six hundred golf balls he's acquired into the surf. Maintaining the deception that he is a marine biologist, George happens to be in the vicinity with Diane. When a whale in distress is reported nearby, a voice (belonging to Larry David) from the beach throng is heard crying out: "Is anyone here a marine biologist?" George, who is believed to be one—by Diane at least—must act decisively, and he does so by diving into the ocean waters to reach the whale. He finds a golf ball lodged in its blowhole and removes it, saving the whale's life. Kramer, it seems, who had hit only one golf ball out of the hundreds, is the responsible party. He takes some solace that at least he hit a hole in one.

Back on the Manhattan scene, Jerry and Elaine confront Testikov at his hotel concerning the hospital bills of the woman who was struck by the electronic organizer. Testikov believes that Elaine is secretly recording the conversation with the tape recorder in her bag, and he tosses it out the hotel window. It hits the very unlucky Corinne, who is waiting outside.

Carol Kane played Corinne in this episode. Although she has many television and movie credits, she is probably most remembered for playing Simka Dahblitz-Gravas, the wife of Latka Gravas, played by Andy Kaufman, for two seasons on *Taxi* (1981–1983). Veteran character actor George Murdock portrayed the ill-tempered Yuri Testikov. His lengthy list of television credits dates back to *The Twilight Zone* (1959–1964) and includes appearances on *Bonanza* (1959–1973), *The Streets of San Francisco* (1972–1977), *Barney Miller* (1974–1982), and *Little House on the Prairie* (1974–1983). Murdock passed away in 2012 at the age of eighty-one.

Episode 77: "The Pie" (original air date: February 17, 1994)

The team of Tom Gammill and Max Pross wrote this episode's teleplay with its principal plotline based on an actual occurrence from Jerry Seinfeld's life. For openers, Jerry is perplexed why his girlfriend, Audrey (played by Suzanne Snyder), refuses to sample a piece of his apple pie. On another front, Kramer spies a mannequin in a chic clothing store that bears a striking resemblance to Elaine. He tells her: "It's like they chopped off your arms and legs, dipped you in plastic, then screwed you all back together again and stuck you on a pedestal. It's really quite exquisite." Kramer is also dealing with an inscrutable itch on his back and employs Jerry's spatula to scratch it. Fortunately, Olive, a waitress at Monk's Café with long fingernails, solves that problem for him and renders the spatula obsolete.

Meanwhile, George is in the market for a new suit. He finds one that strikes his fancy, but wants to wait for the store's upcoming sale to purchase it. With another customer keenly interested in the suit as well, George hides it until the sale date and buys it under the nose of the competing suitor. This man who was outsmarted by George, though, vows to get even someday.

Still smarting over the pie affair, Jerry accompanies Audrey to Poppie's, her father's restaurant. While there he discovers that Audrey has enjoyed all the desserts on Poppie's menu, including the apple pie. He discovers, too, that Poppie doesn't wash his hands after going to the bathroom and that the restaurant is rather unsanitary as a result.

After all the trouble he had gone through in acquiring the suit, George realizes that it makes a whooshing noise when he moves. He fears that these sounds could impact whether or not he gets the new job for which he is interviewing. His prospective employer, though, is not bothered by the sounds emanating from George's garments. In fact, he invites George out to dinner. Unfortunately, the chef at the restaurant is the very man who competed with George for the suit—the one who, in no uncertain terms, vowed revenge. He couldn't, therefore, take the chance of eating anything prepared by him. George doesn't get the job but—looking on the bright side—he doesn't get sick either.

On the mannequin front, a furious Elaine steals her waxen doppelgänger from the clothing store. She learns that the man who designed the mannequin, which has become a smashing success all over town, is Ricky, the peculiar fellow she met on the subway in "The Cigar Store Indian"—the one who cut up Frank Costanza's *TV Guide* and turned it into a bouquet of flowers for her.

Reni Santoni made his first of three appearances as Poppie. Of Spanish-French heritage, Santoni began his career as a comedy writer and subsequently appeared in a long roster of movies and television shows, including *The Rockford Files* (1974–1980), *Hill Street Blues*, and *Murder, She Wrote* (1984–1996). The intriguingly named Sunday Theodore played Olive, the waitress with the magical fingernails.

Episode 78: "The Stand-In" (original air date: February 24, 1994)

Larry David is back as sole writer of this episode that finds Jerry and George on a bus and bumping into an old friend, Al Netche, played by W. Earl Brown. Al informs them that a mutual friend of theirs, Fulton, is hospitalized and in need of a pick-me-up. He suggests that Jerry visit him in the hospital and tell him some jokes.

George, meanwhile, is increasingly restless in his relationship with Daphne, his latest girlfriend (played by Karla Tamburrelli), and wants to end it. However, when Daphne tells him that Al Netche suggested to her that she end the relationship—citing George's inability to commit to anything—he abruptly changes his tune. In fact, George wants to keep the relationship going just to spite Al. He'd even go so far as to marry her to prove that he can commit. In another plot twist, Jerry sets Elaine up on a date with another old friend, Phil Tatola, played by Mark Tymchyshyn. Things go well at first until he "whips it out" on their second date.

On a different front altogether, Kramer goes to work. He lands a job as a stand-in on *All My Children*, the long-running and popular soap opera, as does his little friend, Mickey. When Mickey expresses the concern that he will be incapable of keeping up with the growth of the eight-year-old kid he is standing in for, Kramer suggests that he wear lifts. Mickey goes along with the plan, but fellow little people ostracize him for doing so. Frustrated, he physically attacks Kramer for getting him into such a bind.

Jerry does, in fact, visit Fulton in the hospital but, despite his best efforts, fails to get even a smile out of him. Al shows up, too, and is equally unsuccessful in getting a rise out of Fulton. On a return visit, Jerry tries out some new material and Fulton finally laughs—hysterically this time out—but he also breathes his last.

Danny Woodburn played Mickey, Kramer's good pal, for the very first time. He would reprise his character in "The Race," "The Wait Out," "The Yada Yada," "The Burning," and "The Finale."

Episode 79: "The Wife" (original air date: March 17, 1994)

Peter Mehlman wrote this teleplay that revolves around Jerry's lifetime 25 percent discount at his preferred cleaners. Things get interesting when his girlfriend, Meryl, wants in on the cleaning discount by masquerading as Mrs. Jerry Seinfeld. Jerry is compelled to tell Uncle Leo that he is married. Meanwhile, at the health club, George is caught urinating in the shower by Greg (played by Scott LaRose), a man on whom Elaine has set her sights.

Dearly missing his favorite quilt while it's at the cleaners, Kramer is in a quandary, too. He has difficulty getting a good night's sleep without it and is expected, on top of that, to meet his new African-American girlfriend's parents. To restore his natural glow—which has taken a huge hit because of his lack of sleep—Kramer visits a tanning salon but falls asleep under a lamp. He emerges with a black face. His girlfriend's folks are anything but amused when he turns up.

Jerry's "marriage" to Meryl seriously strains their relationship and it ends altogether when he offers to share his cleaning discount with another woman. Meryl discovers this when she goes to pick up her clothes. Still reeling from his shower indiscretion, George worries that he will be expelled from the health club if Greg reports him. However, when he notices a violation of the club rules committed by Greg, George sees this as his saving grace.

Courteney Cox played Meryl. She is best known for her role as Monica Geller, Ross's younger sister, on the popular series *Friends* (1994–2004).

Episode 80: "The Raincoats" (original air date: April 28, 1994)

This episode originally aired as a single hour show, but in syndication it is shown in two parts. Credited with writing the teleplay are Tom Gammill, Max Pross, Larry David, and Jerry Seinfeld. "The Raincoats" gets rolling with Jerry grumbling about his parents staying over at his place for three whole days before their big trip to Paris. Without question, they are cramping his style vis-à-vis the advancement of his relationship with Rachel, his new girlfriend.

Meanwhile, Alec, the head of a local Big Brother outfit, ropes George into taking a young boy named Joey under his wing. Later, George tries to weasel out of this mentoring arrangement by concocting a tale that he's flying to Paris. To attest to his veracity, the Seinfelds will mail a letter from Paris—ostensibly from him—to New York. George also invites Morty and Helen Seinfeld to the Costanza house for a paella dinner, which, citing prior plans, they decline. The fact that they didn't actually have any other plans surprises Jerry, who was unaware of their disdain for Frank and Estelle.

Elaine has a new boyfriend to contend with—Aaron, a "close-talker," who violates people's space when speaking to them. When Aaron offers to give Morty and Helen Seinfeld a very special tour of the Metropolitan Museum of Art, Elaine and Jerry find it odd. He subsequently invites the Seinfelds to attend the Broadway play *My Fair Lady* with him and Elaine, but without her knowledge. They also do lunch and ride in a hansom cab together.

In another plot turn, Kramer shows up in Jerry's apartment wearing a trench coat sans a belt, and Morty immediately recognizes it as his invention from many years ago. Kramer informs him that they are a red-hot item in Rudy's Antique Boutique. He and Morty become business partners on the spot with plans of resurrecting the beltless trench coat, known as "The Executive." Morty telephones his Florida neighbor Jack Klompus and asks him to promptly ship to New York the boxloads of Executives that he has stored in his garage. Kramer will then peddle them to Rudy at the antique shop. When George learns of this new business arrangement, he realizes that the Seinfelds had lied about having plans the previous night, and intentionally avoided having dinner with his parents. He also sells a boxload of his father's old vacation clothes to Rudy.

With his apartment occupied by his folks, and Rachel living with her parents, Jerry takes his girlfriend to see *Schindler's List*. He is caught making out with her during the somber film by none other than Newman, who later tells the elder Seinfelds about the incident. George is in hot water, too, when Frank Costanza discovers that his garments are missing. He is compelled to buy them back and returns the money to Rudy, who takes the cash but then informs George that his father's clothes had all been burned because of a moth infestation.

Meanwhile, Morty cancels his Paris trip to await shipment of the Executives. George's Paris ruse comes back to haunt him when he's informed that Joey, his brother in the program, has a father living in the City of Light. And since George is going there anyway, he can accompany Joey, who always feared traveling alone. George seizes the opportunity to use Morty and Helen's plane tickets to get both a free trip to Paris and to impress those involved in the Big Brother organization.

When Morty's shipment finally arrives, Kramer learns that Rudy—after the bad experience with Frank Costanza's clothes—will no longer purchase old clothing from people off the street. Having missed their trip to Paris, Morty and Helen return home to Florida, which causes Aaron genuine anguish as he wonders whether or not he did enough for them while they were in New York. The Seinfelds go on a cruise as a substitute for their aborted Paris vacation—the same cruise, coincidentally, with passengers Frank and Estelle Costanza. George lands in Paris with Joey, who is not making his life easy on foreign terra firma. And Jerry finds out that his making out during *Schindler's List* has some serious repercussions. Rachel's father—after getting a descriptive account from his postman, Newman—forbids his daughter from ever seeing him again. (Jerry does, however, see her again in the episode "The Hamptons.")

Actor Judge Reinhold played close-talking Aaron. He achieved his first measure of fame as Brad Hamilton in the 1982 film *Fast Times at Ridgemont High*, starring Sean Penn.

Episode 81: "The Fire" (original air date: May 5, 1994)

Larry Charles returns as the writer of this episode that finds George dating Robin, and Kramer dating Toby, who works with Elaine at Pendant Publishing. Kramer is also pitching his coffee table book about coffee tables to the publisher, which Toby thinks is a wonderful idea and Elaine thinks is absolutely ridiculous.

In Jerry's world, he is preparing a new standup routine, which he hopes will impress a certain magazine critic.

Meanwhile, George's girlfriend, Robin, who has a child, is hosting a birthday party for her boy. George is on hand and so is a clown named Eric, who is there to perform for the kids. George believes Eric is a terrible name for a clown and tells him so. When a small fire breaks out in the kitchen, he panics and races out of the apartment, pushing away Eric the Clown, an old lady with a walker, and a gaggle of little kids to make his escape. Confronted afterwards about his cowardly behavior, George explains that *he* was really the brave one, leading the way out of the apartment. Nobody believes him.

Kramer and Toby attend Jerry's performance with the magazine critic on hand. Initially, Toby is pleased with the comedy routine, but eventually turns hostile and mercilessly heckles Jerry. Her behavior ruins his act and he exacts revenge by showing up at her place of work and heckling *her*. Toby bolts from the Pendant Publishing work scene in tears and gets clipped by a street sweeper that lops off one of her toes. Providentially, Kramer is able to locate the severed toe and get it to the hospital in the nick of time, where it is reattached. Because of Mr. Lippman feeling sorry for her ordeal, Toby gets the promotion that Elaine was counting on.

In the arena of second chances, Jerry invites the magazine critic to another performance, and George asks Robin to attend as well. But things go awry when George panics once more—this time at the sight of a fake-gun-toting comedian—and the comedy club empties in the resulting hysteria.

Melanie Chartoff played Robin, George's girlfriend. She starred in the late-night sketch comedy show *Fridays* with, among others, Michael Richards and Larry David. Actress Veanne Cox portrayed Toby.

Episode 82: "The Hamptons" (original air date: May 12, 1994)

Co-written by Peter Mehlman and Carol Leifer, this episode finds Jerry, George, Elaine, and Kramer venturing beyond the cozy confines of New York City and visiting the upscale Hamptons on the eastern end of Long Island. They have come to this scenic beach community on the Atlantic Ocean to see a friend's baby, which the gang unanimously concludes is one of the most ugly newborns they have ever seen. In fact, the episode's working title was "The Ugly Baby."

What is most memorable about "The Hamptons" is the scene in which George is seen naked by Jerry's girlfriend, Rachel, after getting out of a pool. He screams, "I was in the pool! I was in the pool!" hoping that she'll understand that what she just chanced upon was the result of "shrinkage," which happens to men after swimming and showering. When Rachel informs Jane, George's girlfriend, of what she laid eyes on, he exacts his revenge. George tricks Rachel, who doesn't violate kosher strictures, into eating lobster in a breakfast omelet. Shellfish are not kosher. Earlier, Jerry had spied Jane sunbathing topless on the beach. This sighting prompted Kramer to blurt out, "Yo-Yo Ma!" and Jerry to return fire: "Boutros-Boutros Ghali!" Later, Kramer gets arrested for poaching lobsters from a fisherman's trap and is sentenced to community service—i.e., picking up garbage along the area's roads.

Meanwhile, Elaine takes a fancy to the ugly baby's pediatrician and is initially pleased when he refers to her as "breathtaking," but then is left wondering whether it was a compliment when he uses the very same adjective to describe the ugly baby.

The word *shrinkage* went on to become one of the most popular *Seinfeld* catchphrases; writer Peter Mehlman is credited with having coined it. Melanie Smith reprised her role as Rachel; Melora Walters played Jane.

Episode 83: "The Opposite" (original air date: May 19, 1994)

The final episode of the season proved a fitting end for what had been a stellar year for *Seinfeld*. Written by the triumvirate of Jerry Seinfeld, Larry David, and Andy Cowan, "The Opposite" nicely sets the table for the following season. Its story centerpiece involves George ruing the fact that every instinct he has ever had augured disaster. Jerry tells him to do exactly the opposite of what he would normally do and let the chips fall where they may. George gives it a try by going against every grain of his personality and, surprisingly, it works like a charm.

Meeting an attractive woman in his travels, he doesn't lie as he normally would. He tells women point-blank that he's unemployed and back home living with his parents. When the woman agrees to go out with him, George senses that he might be on to something and continues being the anti-George. Meanwhile, Elaine rekindles her relationship with Jake Jarmel, but it abruptly ends when he lands in the hospital after an accident. Jake is not too happy that Elaine purchased a box of Juicy Fruit before rushing to his bedside.

Kramer, with his coffee table book about coffee tables in print, is riding high and appears on *Live with Regis and Kathie Lee* to promote it. However, when he burns his mouth on hot coffee and spits it out on Kathie Lee, his promotional tour is put on ice. George, though, continues to enjoy positive fortune, including landing a good job with the New York Yankees as their assistant traveling secretary. He moves out of his parents' house, too, and—continuing to be the anti-George—tells them that he loves them.

In stark contrast with George, Elaine's life is heading in the wrong direction. She learns that she is being evicted from her apartment for a whole host of reasons, including using Canadian quarters in the building's washing machines and buzzing in unsavory types. On the job front, things aren't much better—Pendant Publishing is merging with a Japanese company. But when Elaine neglects to tell Mr. Lippman, her boss, that he forgot his handkerchief, things get a bit awkward when he sneezes into his hand and then refuses to shake hands with his Japanese counterparts. They consider this a colossal insult and cancel the merger, which causes Pendant Publishing to go out of business.

While Elaine laments that she has "become George," Jerry can't help but look at the ups and downs of his friends' lives and smile—for his life remains, as always, on an even keel.

Regis Philbin and Kathie Lee Gifford appear as themselves in "The Opposite." This is also the first appearance of George Steinbrenner as voiced by Larry David. In all his appearances on the show, we see him only from the back. The real George Steinbrenner actually filmed a scene for "The Invitations," but Larry David concluded that his acting skills left a lot to be desired. His scene with Julia Louis-Dreyfus ended up being excised from the episode. Steinbrenner had previously showcased his dreadful acting when he hosted *Saturday Night Live* on October 20, 1990.

24

Season Six

Number One

Season six saw *Seinfeld* reach number one in the Nielsen ratings for the first time, besting runners-up *Home Improvement* and *ER*. In the show's remaining three seasons it would finish either first or second. Andy Ackerman assumed the directorial duties for this season, with the sole exception being the ninth episode, "The Secretary," which was directed by David Owen Trainor. Ackerman, in total, directed eighty-seven episodes of *Seinfeld* from season six on. His other directorial credits include *The New Adventures of Old Christine* (starring Julia Louis-Dreyfus), *The Ellen Show* (2001–2002), and *Two and a Half Men* (2003–2015).

Episode 84: "The Chaperone" (original air date: September 22, 1994)

Larry David, Bill Masters, and Bob Shaw collaborated on the writing of season six's inaugural episode, which finds Jerry dating Miss Rhode Island, a contestant in the Miss America beauty pageant. Having lost her job at Pendant Publishing when the company went bust at the close of season five, Elaine is interviewing with Doubleday. It is her hope to take over where Jackie Kennedy Onassis left off: the former first lady had passed away on May 19, 1994. "The Chaperone" aired just four months later. Here again, *Seinfeld* proved quite topical with its blending of the real world with the not-quite-real-world of Jerry, George, Elaine, and Kramer.

Meanwhile, in his new job with the Yankees, George decides to replace their polyester uniforms with the hot cotton that former greats Babe Ruth and Joe DiMaggio donned. Yankees manager Buck Showalter and outfielder Danny Tartabull guest star as themselves.

Plot twists therein find Miss Rhode Island needing a chaperone on her date with Jerry, and none other than Kramer fills in admirably (and then some), as he becomes the beauty's tutor and trainer. Elaine does not get the job she covets, but instead is hired on as a personal assistant to the elderly and eccentric Mr. Justin Pitt. This work proves to be very unfulfilling and frustrating for Elaine, who is essentially the old publishing executive's gofer and nanny. Respected British actor Ian Abercrombie played Mr. Pitt throughout season six.

Episode 85: "The Big Salad" (original air date: September 29, 1994)

Larry David wrote the teleplay of this episode that revolves around George purchasing for Elaine, at her request, a "big salad" from Monk's Café. But when his girlfriend, Julie (played by Michelle Forbes), gets involved—as the individual who physically hands the salad to Elaine—the meltdown begins. Elaine thanks Julie and the latter accepts the thanks without noting that George was actually the one who bought the salad. This eventually leads to a serious disagreement between the couple. George cannot understand how Julie could accept Elaine's thank you under such overtly "false pretenses."

Also on the dating front is Jerry, who discovers that his new girlfriend, Margaret, dated Newman in the past, and that Newman was the one who broke it off. This piece of historical information haunts him because he's absolutely convinced that there must be something seriously wrong with her. Why else would Newman dump such an attractive woman? Meanwhile, Elaine is running errands for Mr. Pitt and encounters a stationery store employee (played by Jerry Levine) who takes a real shine to her.

On a different front altogether, Kramer plays a game of golf alongside a former Major League baseball player named Steve Gendason, who is later suspected of having murdered a dry cleaner. This episode's finale is a satire of O. J. Simpson and the infamous slow-speed police chase that he was involved in before his arrest on suspicion of murder. Kramer drives Gendason's white Bronco—just like O. J.'s—with police in pursuit on the New Jersey Turnpike. O. J. Simpson's Los Angeles highway chase occurred on June 17, 1994, approximately three months prior to the airing of "The Big Salad." Marita Geraghty played Margaret, Jerry's girlfriend and Newman's ex. Dean Hallo portrayed Gendason.

Episode 86: "The Pledge Drive" (original air date: October 6, 1994)

Tom Gammill and Max Pross renewed their *Seinfeld* writing partnership in their first episode of season six, which finds Jerry assuming the hosting duties of a PBS fundraiser. "The Pledge Drive" likewise features Elaine's boss, the eccentric and cantankerous Mr. Pitt, eating his Snickers candy bar with a knife and fork, a pioneering way to consume one that somehow catches the fancy of the city at large. And at Jerry's urging, George brings Yankee outfielder Danny Tartabull to the fundraiser taping.

Other plot twists and turns include Jerry taking Kramer's advice and depositing several old checks given to him from Nana, his grandmother, for his birthday. This delayed action results in her account going into the red. Jerry and Elaine are having problems, too, with two different people, Dan and Noreen, who sound eerily alike on the telephone—i.e., they are both "high-talkers."

Noreen is Elaine's girlfriend, and Dan, her boyfriend, sounds like a woman. This confusion leads to many unwanted outcomes, including Elaine telling off Jerry's grandmother on the telephone. Later, at Kramer's urging—he has volunteered to man the telephones at the pledge drive—Nana pledges fifteen hundred dollars to PBS, which she cannot afford.

Brian Reddy played Dan, the high-talker, although the high-pitched woman's voice that comes out of his mouth is not is own, but that of an unnamed actress. Kelly Coffield, who is best known for being an original cast member in the popular comedy ensemble show *In Living Color*, played Noreen, which she would reprise for the next episode. Billye Ree Wallace portrayed Jerry's Nana. She would also appear in "The Kiss Hello" and "The Doodle." Wallace passed away in 1999 at the age of seventy-three.

Episode 87: "The Chinese Woman" (original air date: October 13, 1994)

Peter Mehlman wrote this episode that finds the Costanzas, Frank and Estelle, contemplating divorce. Frank Costanza is also seen in the company of a man wearing a cape—his lawyer in the impending divorce case. When George learns that his parents are possibly splitting up, it deeply disturbs him as he worries, first and foremost, about having to visit two parents in two separate locations on Thanksgiving.

Meanwhile, Kramer calls on the fertility clinic because of a low sperm count; Elaine causes problems for her friend Noreen's new relationship; and Jerry makes a date with a woman he assumes is Chinese. After all, her name is Chang, and he likes Chinese women. However, he subsequently discovers that she had changed her name from Changstein to Chang and is not Chinese at all. Angela Dohrmann portrayed Donna Chang.

A postscript to this episode places a distraught Noreen on the Queensboro Bridge and contemplating leaping to her death in the East River. Fortunately, a man in a cape appears—Frank Costanza's lawyer—in the nick of time and convinces her not to take the plunge. Larry David played the man in the cape.

Episode 88: "The Couch" (original air date: October 27, 1994)

Larry David wrote this episode with its zigzagging storylines, including Kramer going into the pizza business with Poppie, the restaurateur, and a trailblazing concept to allow customers to make their own pizza pies from scratch. Meanwhile, Jerry is getting a new couch and giving Elaine his old one. George is active as well, having joined a book club in an effort to impress his new girlfriend, Lindsay, played by Jessica Hecht.

George's troubles begin when the first reading assigned in the book club is *Breakfast at Tiffany's*, a novella by Truman Capote. This short book is nonetheless too big a task for George, and he attempts to circumvent the reading part by renting the movie version instead. This ploy on his part hits a snag when he's apprised at the video store that it's been rented and is unavailable. When the video store clerk refuses to tell him who rented the movie, George sneaks a peek at the man's name and address in the shop's computer database. He then heads over to Joe Temple's apartment to try to procure the videotape for himself, but is unsuccessful. George ultimately watches the movie with Joe and Remy, the man's less-than-pleased-at-the-circumstances daughter.

Further developments find Elaine getting into a serious row with Poppie at his restaurant over the subject of abortion. Poppie is pro-life, and she is pro-choice. She also dates the man who delivered Jerry's new couch, but breaks up with him because of his pro-life position on abortion. Later, Kramer and Poppie feud over their pizza concept, with the latter objecting to the former utilizing cucumbers as a topping. They also debate on when the life of a pizza begins—when it's being prepared to go in the oven or when it comes out fully formed and cooked. This dispute of theirs is a riff on the abortion debate about whether life begins at conception or birth.

When all is said and done, George doesn't get to see the end of the movie after he spills grape juice all over the Temples' couch and is kicked out of the apartment. (Veteran television and movie actor Robert Hooks played Joe Temple.) George thus fails to impress his girlfriend and the others with his knowledge of *Breakfast at Tiffany's*. Jerry's old and new couches alike are cursed with Poppie urinating on the latter and, while it's being returned to him, Elaine spilling grape juice on the former.

Episode 89: "The Gymnast" (original air date: November 3, 1994)

A new team of *Seinfeld* writers, Alec Berg and Jeff Schaffer, are credited with this teleplay, which has Jerry dating an Olympic gymnast from Romania named Katya; George getting a second chance with Lindsay, his girlfriend from the previous episode; and Kramer in real distress with a painful kidney stone.

As the episode unfolds, Kramer implores Jerry to go for broke with Katya because, as a gymnast, she's no doubt a very flexible woman. Jerry, though, is thinking entirely too much about recently deposed Romanian dictator Nicolae Ceausescu when in her presence, but he ultimately goes the distance with her. He claims, however, the experience was anything but gymnastic. But Katya, too, is equally disappointed, citing her great expectations because of the Romanian legend of the libidinous comedian. George, on the other hand, is making headway in his rapprochement with his girlfriend and winning over her mother, too, until he is caught eating a discarded éclair from the kitchen garbage pail.

On the Elaine front, she is attending a corporate meeting in place of Mr. Pitt and gets into an argument over the proposed new name—"Moland Springs"—for merged companies Morgan Springs and Poland Creek.

In this episode, George's penchant for taking off his shirt while in bathrooms is also revealed. He wishes to feel "no encumbrances" while in them. And Kramer's fear of clowns comes to the fore, too. Romanian-born actress Elina Löwensohn played Katya. Veteran character actress Lois Nettleton portrayed Mrs. Enright, the mother of George's girlfriend, who catches him sampling a pastry from the garbage. Nettleton, whom *Twilight Zone* fans remember from the classic episode "The Midnight Sun," passed away in 2008 at the age of eighty.

Episode 90: "The Soup" (original air date: November 10, 1994)

Fred Stoller, a standup comedian and comedy writer, penned the teleplay for "The Soup." Stoller's most memorable acting credit was his recurring role on *Everybody Loves Raymond* as the whiny and meek Gerard, Raymond's cousin. He also penned a memoir entitled *My Seinfeld Year*, which recounts his experiences working on the show alongside Jerry Seinfeld and Larry David. It is available as an e-book.

This episode introduces Kenny Bania (played by Steve Hytner), a fellow standup comedian who Jerry regards as an unlikable hack. Kramer, recovering from his painful kidney stone from the previous episode, "The Gymnast," opts to trash everything in his refrigerator and consume only freshly bought foods thereafter. Meanwhile, George has his eye on Kelly, a waitress at Monk's Café, and tells her about his fascination with the word "manure." When she informs him soon after this tête-à-tête that she's got a boyfriend, George wonders if the "manure" topic of conversation was the reason. Later, he learns from Hildy, Kramer's girlfriend, that Kelly doesn't have a boyfriend. Tracy Kolis played Kelly, and Linda Wallem was Hildy.

On Kramer's new dietary front are minefields, including the extremely hungry Hildy looking for something to eat when he's got nothing in his refrigerator to offer her. He is compelled to repeatedly raid Jerry's apartment for foodstuffs. And in a major faux pas that comes back to haunt him, Jerry accepts a free Armani suit from Kenny Bania, who only wants a restaurant meal in return. But at Mendy's restaurant, Bania orders only a bowl of soup and claims that it doesn't constitute a meal. Jerry disagrees. In order to rid himself of Bania once and for all, Jerry gives the suit to Simon, an Englishman who came to the States—with the help of Elaine's frequent flier miles—on the return end of a business trip to London with Mr. Pitt.

Kramer's relationship with Hildy comes to an end when his constant calls to her place of employment, Reggie's diner, lead to her termination. George employs the excessive phone calls bit with Kelly—who he feels has spoken against him—at Monk's, but the plan backfires. He gets banned from Monk's and ends up dining alone in Reggie's as a result.

Episode 91: "The Mom and Pop Store" (original air date: November 17, 1994)

Writing duo Tom Gammill and Max Pross penned this episode that is partially based on the real-life experiences of the former, who thought that he had purchased a car previously owned by actor Jon Voight. However, Gammill subsequently discovered that this wasn't the case.

In "The Mom and Pop Store," George does likewise and later learns that the car's former owner was a man by the name of John Voight, although not the actor Jon Voight. In this episode, the actual car that Tom Gammill once thought belonged to Jon Voight is used as George's wheels. And, as a bonus, Jon Voight makes a cameo.

In another story thread, Elaine continues her labors as Mr. Pitt's dutiful assistant. She helps him live his dream when he wins the right to be one of the Woody Woodpecker balloon's line handlers in the Macy's Thanksgiving Day Parade. Elaine also expresses interest in Jerry's dentist, Dr. Tim Whatley, but inadvertently turns down a date from him because of a temporary hearing glitch caused by overly loud music. Kramer, meanwhile, brings all of Jerry's sneakers to a mom-and-pop shoe-repair shop that is fighting for its life. While his intentions are noble—he just wants to help them avoid closure with some added business— the place shuts down and the proprietors peddle Jerry's sneakers in a garage sale in Parsippany, New Jersey. Jerry is left with only a pair of cowboy boots, which cause him endless grief.

On a different frontier, Kramer bumps into Jon Voight on the street and queries him about the lineage of George's car, but the actor bites him on the arm and makes a getaway without answering any questions. Later, George and Kramer

Times Square subway turnstile ad featuring Bryan Cranston, *Seinfeld*'s Dr. Tim Whatley and *Breaking Bad*'s Walter White. The character of Tim Whatley debuted in season six's "The Mom and Pop Store." The versatile actor more recently played President Lyndon Baines Johnson in *All the Way* on Broadway.

Photo by Thomas Nigro

compare the bite mark on the arm with a chewed-on pencil found in the car's glove compartment.

Bryan Cranston makes his first appearance as Tim Whatley. Cranston would go on to win three Emmy awards as Walter White in the AMC series *Breaking Bad* (2008–2013).

Episode 92: "The Secretary" (original air date: December 8, 1994)

This is the sole episode in the sixth season that is not directed by Andy Ackerman. David Owen Trainor, who had previously been with the show as a technical coordinator, assumed the reins. Carol Leifer and Marjorie Gross collaborated on the teleplay of "The Secretary," which finds George in the position of hiring a secretary for the first time in his life. So as not to distract him from his workload, his plan is to hire an unattractive woman.

Meanwhile, after seeing the owner of the dry cleaners that he patronizes at the movies, Jerry is convinced that he was wearing his jacket. Kramer bumps into actress Uma Thurman and writes her telephone number down on Jerry's cleaning ticket. (We don't see this encounter, nor does Uma Thurman appear in the episode.) Later, Jerry spies the dry cleaner's wife in his mother's fur coat. In another plot twist, Elaine is convinced that the fashionable clothier, Barneys in Manhattan, is utilizing "skinny mirrors" to make their clothes look better on wearers while they're trying them on in the store than when they get home.

Kenny Bania is also back and in the market for a new suit. Kramer sells him his entire wardrobe while the two are in Barneys. Jerry, though, needs a cleaning ticket to get his stuff back, which Kramer had in his possession until he sold his clothes to Bania. Jerry is compelled to buy them back from Bania, who wants *two* dinners this time for the privilege. They end up in Mendy's for an encore and Bania again orders only soup.

On the George–secretary front, he hires a woman named Ada, played by Vicki Lewis, and they end up having sexual intercourse in the office. During their roll in the hay, George promises her a raise. When he goes to ask his boss, George Steinbrenner, about the possibility, he discovers that Ada has already gotten a raise—one for twenty-five thousand dollars—and is now getting paid more than George himself. When George expresses his incredulity at the notion of a secretary making more money than her superior, Ida sets him straight.

Episode 93: "The Race" (original air date: December 15, 1994)

The troika of Larry David, Tom Gammill, and Max Pross wrote this multifaceted episode. Along with its trio of writers, Sam Kass is credited with developing the story that finds Jerry interested in Lois, who, as things turn out, works for an old high school rival of his named Duncan Mayer, played by Don McManus. The rivalry is rooted in a foot race the duo waged in the ninth grade—one where Jerry bested the heavily favored Mayer by inadvertently getting an unfair head start. But Jerry prefers to allow the legend of his victory to endure. Mayer, however, knows that somehow he was cheated that day but has no proof to back it up.

Meanwhile, Elaine is dating a man named Ned (played by Todd Kimsey), who is rightly suspected of being a Communist when a copy of the *Daily Worker* is discovered in his apartment. George, in fact, answers a personal ad in the paper from a woman who claims "appearance is not important." Kramer, too, involves himself with Ned when he takes some of the man's Communist literature. This presents a problem when he starts passing it out to children in his new job as a department-store Santa. Mickey, acting as his elf, warns him that it is a bad idea, and it is. Both men get fired. Further troubles include Elaine getting blacklisted by a Chinese takeout-delivery restaurant Hop Sing's and, much to her chagrin—"She named name"—getting Ned blacklisted, too. (Hop Sing, by the way, was the Cartwrights' excitable cook on *Bonanza*.)

With George receiving calls at work from Natalie, the woman from the personal ad, Ada, his secretary, suspects that he's a Communist and alerts George Steinbrenner. "The Boss," though, thinks it's a good idea to have a Communist on the payroll because it will help the team recruit Cuban baseball players. George is dispatched to Cuba and gets an earful from Fidel Castro.

In the end, Jerry is compelled to run a rematch race with his high school rival, because, if he doesn't, Lois will lose her job. As the race is about to commence on the street, the backfiring of Kramer's car causes Jerry to mistake it for the starting gun and prematurely take off—something akin to what had happened in high school—and he emerges victorious once more. The race is run with John Williams's *Superman* movie theme playing in the background. This is the only episode, outside of "The Chronicle" (the clip show), where the so-called Fourth Wall is broken—with an actor talking directly to the audience, à la George Burns on the Burns and Allen television show and the title character in *Ferris Bueller's Day Off*. Jerry gives the camera a knowing wink—like George Reeves as Superman often did—at the show's conclusion, saying, "Maybe I will, Lois . . . maybe I will." This shattering of the Fourth Wall was utilized frequently in *The Adventures of Superman* (1951–1957), and Superman references were frequent throughout *Seinfeld*, particularly in this episode. Renee Props played Lois.

Episode 94: "The Switch" (original air date: January 5, 1995)

Bruce Kirschbaum and Sam Kass wrote this teleplay wherein Jerry's latest girlfriend, Sandy, is a "non-laugher," and George's latest girlfriend, Nina (played by Charlotte Lewis), is possibly suffering from bulimia. Elaine, on the other hand, encounters problems by lending a special Bruline tennis racket that belongs to her crotchety employer, Mr. Pitt, to a Mrs. Landis—also from Doubleday— whom she hopes to impress and land a better job.

Elaine de-salting pretzel sticks for her well-heeled and eccentric boss, Justin Pitt (Ian Abercrombie).   *NBC/Photofest*

When Jerry and George compare notes about their respective girlfriend issues—George had heard a distinctive retching sound emanating from a bathroom visited by Nina—they toss around ideas on what to do about them. George wants to engage the services of a certain restaurant matron to definitively uncover whether or not his girlfriend is bulimic. Coincidentally, the matron he has in mind is Kramer's mother, who, for the very first time, reveals her son's first name: Cosmo. Meanwhile, Jerry, who gets a bellyful of laughs from Laura, Sandy's roommate, is advised by George to suggest a ménage à trois, which he believes will simultaneously disgust Sandy, who will break up with him, and flatter Laura when she learns about it. Neither comes to pass when Sandy and Laura consent to the threesome. Jann Karam played Sandy, and Heather Medway was Laura.

With the assistance of the matron, Mrs. Kramer, denied, George takes matters into his own hands and enters the women's restroom. He ends up mistaking a retching sound from another woman as Nina's. Nina leaves him posthaste. Elaine, on the other hand, has to get back the racket she lent to Mrs. Landis—who suffered a serious injury while on the courts—because Mr. Pitt has a tennis date with Ethel Kennedy.

In the show's waning moments we see Mrs. Kramer, as played by veteran character actress Sheree North, in bed with Newman. North had a busy career in television, appearing on such shows as *The Mary Tyler Moore Show* (1970–1977), *Medical Center* (1969–1976), and *The Golden Girls* (1985–1992). She also had a supporting role in John Wayne's last (and quite apropos) movie, *The Shootist* (1976). Born Dawn Shirley Crang, Sheree North passed away in 2005 at the age of seventy-three.

Episode 95: "The Label Maker" (original air date: January 19, 1995)

Alec Berg and Jeff Schaffer co-wrote this teleplay. Berg not only wrote for *Seinfeld* but also directed numerous episodes of Larry David's *Curb Your Enthusiasm*. He served, too, as the show's executive producer.

"The Label Maker" revolves around two Super Bowl tickets that Jerry has acquired but cannot use due to the fact that he must attend a wedding—"The Drake's" wedding, which is coming to pass after all. (The couple had split up in "The Handicap Spot.") He thus gives the tickets to his dentist friend, Dr. Tim Whatley, the very man believed to be guilty of being a "re-gifter." That is, Jerry received a label maker from him for Christmas, which is the exact same thing Elaine had gotten *him* as a present.

Meanwhile, George is dating a woman named Bonnie (played by Jessica Tuck), who has a male roommate who bears an uncanny resemblance to him. She also has a velvet couch in her apartment that George just adores. On an entirely different front, Kramer and Newman are involved in a highly competitive game of Risk. They leave the unfinished game board in Jerry's apartment—neutral territory—so it cannot be tampered with. The concern about cheating, though, finds Kramer chasing after a tow truck that is towing his car away with the Risk board game in his possession: he is that concerned Newman will cheat in his absence. Newman, too, feels the same way and frantically shadows Kramer.

Later, Jerry learns that The Drake's wedding has been postponed due to the Super Bowl and—horror of horrors—that Newman has been given one of Dr. Whatley's tickets to the game. Intrigued by the re-gifting mystery, Elaine seeks to find out if the aforementioned Whatley is, in fact, a re-gifter; to do this, she agrees to go on a date with the man. He invites her to the Super Bowl, which means that Newman is out of luck.

In George's personal soap opera, he asks Bonnie to lose her roommate, Scott, as a condition to remain in a relationship with him. She consents to his demand and Scott takes all of his possessions from the apartment, including the velvet couch that George loved so much. After getting what he ostensibly desired, George feels trapped and wants to break up with Bonnie. He proposes a ménage à trois with Scott, figuring that she will dump him on the spot for suggesting such a thing, but both she and Scott like the idea. This ménage à trois maneuver didn't work in "The Switch," either.

Finally, Elaine concludes that Dr. Tim Whatley is only interested in one thing—seducing her if she attends the Super Bowl with him. Strange bedfellows Jerry and Newman ultimately attend the big game together.

Episode 96: "The Scofflaw" (original air date: January 26, 1995)

Peter Mehlman is back as the writer of this classic *Seinfeld* episode with its numerous plot twists and turns, beginning with George bumping into an old friend, Gary Fogel, who, from the looks of things, has been receiving chemo-therapy treatments in an ongoing battle with cancer. George subsequently learns that Jerry knew about Gary's illness but was asked not to tell him about it because of his inability to keep secrets. Later, George discusses with Gary this very thing and, to make amends, the latter offers the former a coveted garage parking space. And he also tells George the biggest secret of them all: he never had cancer in the first place.

Not one to keep a secret, George promptly tells Jerry that Gary has been lying all along about having cancer. This news upsets Jerry because he had given Gary an expensive gift certificate for a toupee. However, to maintain George's prized parking-spot gift from Gary, Jerry agrees to keep his mouth shut about having learned the truth. When Gary tells George that he cannot, in fact, relin-quish the parking spot to him, Jerry is no longer obligated to remain silent and he plucks the toupee off Gary's head.

Kramer, in a separate plot twist, tangles with a cop after calling a litterbug a *pig*. The policeman, sporting an eye patch, wrongly assumed that he was the recipient of that unfortunate epithet. When Kramer explains the truth of the matter, the cop tells him that an egregious scofflaw he has been tracking for some time—his "white whale"—has gotten away from him yet again. Kramer is later seen wearing an eye patch and claiming, "I wanna be a pirate," unlike Jerry, who bemoaned looking like one in "The Puffy Shirt."

Elaine, meanwhile, is waging a battle with an ex-boyfriend, writer Jake Jarmel. During a book signing, Kramer made the faux pas of telling Jake that "Elaine says, 'Hi,'" which she believes completely destroyed her advantage vis-à-vis their contentious breakup. A strange battle thus ensues with Elaine attempt-ing to find a pair of eyeglasses, just like Jake's, which will render his pair less than unique. The one-of-a-kind nature of his glasses means an awful lot to him.

In the end, it is revealed that Newman is the scofflaw whom the eye patch–wearing policeman has been after for a seeming eternity, and that he is the one who is getting George's parking space. Having been sentenced by a judge, Newman must keep his car parked in the spot until all his parking tickets are paid in full.

Saturday Night Live alumnus Jon Lovitz played Gary Fogel with unctuous élan in this episode. Some of his memorable *SNL* characters include Tommy Flanagan, The Pathological Liar, The Master Thespian, and Harvey Fierstein. In the episode "The Face Painter," we learn that Gary Fogel passed away—not of a cancer, but in a car accident while adjusting his toupee.

Episode 97: "The Highlights of 100" (original air date: February 2, 1995)

This episode originally aired as an hour-long special. It is introduced by Jerry Seinfeld (the actor) and is a retrospective look back at the show's nearly one hundred episodes. (There are, in fact, discrepancies in *Seinfeld* episode counts based on exactly how they are tallied. Often, hour-long episodes are counted as two shows, instead of just one longer version, because they play as separate shows in syndication. For the purposes of this book, however, one-hour *Seinfeld* episodes are counted as one, with two-part episodes—shown a week apart—counted as two. One exception is "The Pitch" and "The Ticket," which originally aired as a one-hour episode. However, they are widely seen now as two distinct episodes, with monikers of their own.)

Clips shown in this celebration of comedic genius leading to the show's reaching the number-one slot in the Nielsen ratings include Kramer declaring matter-of-factly, "I'm out" in "The Contest"; Jerry and Elaine entering the former's malodorous car for the first time in "The Smelly Car"; Elaine laughing uncontrollably when the Tweety Bird Pez dispenser is placed on her knee during a piano recital in "The Pez Dispenser"; Kramer unknowingly torpedoing George's "Vandelay Industries" job ruse in "The Boyfriend"; and Jerry and George trying to quell the misperception that they're gay in "The Outing."

The retrospective show covers a lot of ground, from Kramer accidentally dropping a Junior Mint candy into a body on the operating table, to Jerry upsetting an elderly relation with an offhanded aside, and George frantically escaping a small fire while barreling over young and old alike.

Episode 98: "The Beard" (original air date: February 9, 1995)

Carol Leifer returned as the writer of this episode that finds Elaine with tickets to the ballet *Swan Lake* and acting as a beard for a gay man, Robert, played by Robert Mailhouse. Robert feels that his boss—also in attendance—could not accept discovering the truth about him. On another frontier altogether, George is sporting the toupee that he had originally donned in "The Scofflaw," and Kramer is attempting to set him up on a date with a woman he knows named Denise, played by Joan Scheckel. However, without a picture of her to show him, George and Kramer visit the police station, where the latter's friend, Lou, a sketch artist, quickly composes an image of Denise. Upon poring over the finished product, George likes what he sees and agrees to go out on a date with her.

En route to the stationhouse, Kramer had bestowed his leftover Chinese takeout on a homeless man, and Jerry, who had tagged along, took a shine to police Sergeant Cathy Tierney, played by Katherine LaNasa. On their return trip, Kramer attempts to reclaim the Tupperware dish that contained the Chinese food given to the homeless man, but has no luck in doing so.

Meanwhile, Jerry continues to ridicule George's toupee, even after the latter expresses excitement at meeting Denise. On the Elaine-bearding front, she nobly plays the role as Robert's girlfriend at the ballet, becomes interested in him as a real romantic partner, and hopes to get him to "change teams."

Later, Kramer and Jerry visit the police station once more. Kramer earns fifty dollars for posing in a police lineup and Jerry meets with the latest object of his affection, Sergeant Tierney, who wants him to take a lie-detector test regarding his claim that he has never once watched *Melrose Place*. George at last meets Denise in person and discovers that she is bald. Surprised by this revelation, Kramer nonetheless tells George that he is bald, too. "I *was* bald!" George cries. This remark prompts Elaine, who has had enough of George's new hair, to snatch the rug off his head and toss it out the window. The homeless man to whom Kramer gave the Chinese food picks it up. Denise, the bald woman, subsequently casts George aside.

As the plot twists and turns resolve themselves, Jerry is unmasked as a prevaricator with respect to watching *Melrose Place*. He just didn't possess George's wily proficiency in beating lie-detector tests. Elaine, in the end, doesn't have long-term success with Robert, who goes back to his original "team." Continuing to appear in police lineups, Kramer gets fingered as a jewel thief by the wig-wearing homeless man who didn't return his Tupperware container.

Episode 99: "The Kiss Hello" (original air date: February 16, 1995)

The show's creators, Jerry Seinfeld and Larry David, collaborated for the first time this season in the writing of "The Kiss Hello," in which the gang (minus Kramer) bumps into Wendy, a physical therapist and friend of Elaine's. Jerry is compelled to kiss Wendy "hello" on the cheek, a precedent that he regrets establishing. George, meanwhile, wants to make an appointment with her to address his sore arm. Wendy, too, is notorious for sporting an antiquated 1960s hairdo that Elaine detests, but she doesn't quite know how to tell her. By introducing her to the always-blunt Kramer, she hopes that he will do it for her. However, this plan backfires big time when Kramer compliments her on her hairstyle.

As the myriad plot turns unfold, George is perturbed at being charged by Wendy's office one hundred dollars for missing his appointment. He did not know of the twenty-four-hour cancellation policy. So as to establish a friendlier environment with everybody addressing one another by their first names, Kramer has come up with the bold idea of putting all of the building's tenants' pictures in the lobby. Jerry is less than happy with having to kiss "hello" more and more people and, when he starts avoiding them, becomes an outcast in the building. His picture is even defaced.

Jerry also learns from Nana that Uncle Leo owes his mother, Helen, fifty dollars from their youth. When Morty finds out about this unpaid debt, he calculates the interest on what Uncle Leo now owes his wife. Lastly, Elaine goes on a skiing trip with Wendy, who, rather than drop Elaine off at her door with her heavy skiing equipment upon their return, deposits her a block away due to a one-way street traffic conundrum. Elaine strains her arm on the long walk home and is not particularly happy when Wendy charges her to treat it.

Carol Leifer, a sometime *Seinfeld* writer and comedienne, appeared as Wendy's secretary in this episode. Wendie Malick, who portrayed Nina Van Horn on the NBC hit comedy *Just Shoot Me!* (1997–2003), played Wendy.

Episode 100: "The Doorman" (original air date: February 23, 1995)

Written by Tom Gammill and Max Pross, this episode finds Elaine looking after Mr. Pitt's apartment while he is away in Europe. Visiting her there, Jerry encounters the building's very peculiar doorman and later bumps into him on the street, standing in front of the building that he calls home. Jerry is accused of stalking him, but he believes the doorman is "playing mind games."

Meanwhile, George has his father as a roommate—a situation that has existed since Frank and Estelle's separation—and Kramer notes that Mr. Costanza has man breasts. This observation—that his father has some "serious hooters"—instills the fear in George that he, too, will become ample breasted with the passage of time.

The always-entrepreneurial Kramer, though, sees an opportunity on the horizon and sets to inventing a man's bra. He partners with Frank Costanza, who wants to call the support device "The Manssiere," although Kramer prefers "The Bro." The new partners strike a deal with bra salesman Sid Farkus, but Frank puts the kibosh on the whole thing when he learns that Sid has his eye on Estelle.

Jerry's problems with the doorman escalate when he agrees to stand in for him for a short spell while the latter runs an errand. During Jerry's fill-in duty, he leaves his post and a couch is stolen from the building's lobby. Jerry is compelled to make good on the stolen couch and George offers his as the replacement. George's couch was formerly Jerry's—the one that Poppie had urinated on in "The Couch." He had merely flipped the cushions on it. By giving away the couch, George hopes that his father—who will have no place

> What a turnaround! Your embarrassing upper body has landed you the gig of spokesmodel for the Bro, aka the Manssiere. Mazel tov!
>
> *Move forward one space and pray it doesn't get cold in here.*

The *Seinfeld* Scene It trivia game resurrects some of the show's greatest moments, such as Frank Costanza's invention—a brassiere for men: the "Manssiere." Card from the *Seinfeld* Scene It game.

to sleep—will go elsewhere. However, in the show's waning moments, we see that George's plan didn't work as expected. Frank is now sharing his son's bed.

Comedian, writer, and voice-over talent Larry Miller played the strange, malevolent doorman. A good friend of Jerry Seinfeld's in real life, Miller experienced a serious fall in late 2012 and, having been put on life support, nearly died from a brain injury. He has since fully recovered.

Episode 101: "The Jimmy" (original air date: March 16, 1995)

The collaborative writing duo of Gregg Kavet and Andy Robin penned their first of eight *Seinfeld* episodes. "The Jimmy" finds Jerry, George, and Kramer in a competitive game of basketball at the health club with Jimmy, a guy who always refers to himself in the third person. George also admires the special training footwear that Jimmy wears. Both he and Jimmy anticipate making money selling similar sneakers, which improve agility on the basketball court and elsewhere, to the general public.

Meanwhile, Elaine, who has an eye on a handsome blond down at the club, runs into Jimmy for the first time. Because of his penchant for speaking in the third person, she believes that Jimmy is acting as a go-between for her and the man she's interested in. When she makes the date, she doesn't realize that it's with Jimmy and not the object of her affections.

In a separate plot thread, Kramer's visit to Dr. Tim Whatley leaves him wandering the streets under the influence of Novocain. Still under the sway of the drug, he drools all over the health club floor, causing Jimmy to slip and seriously injure himself. Kramer quickly learns that "Jimmy holds grudges" when the man who speaks solely in the third person vows revenge. Later in the day, Kramer is mistaken for an Able Mentally Challenged Adult (AMCA) and taken to a benefit in their honor. Elaine, in fact, has tickets to the event, which features crooner Mel Tormé as the show's master of ceremonies. (Tormé died in 1999 at the age of seventy-three.)

Other plot twists and turns include Jerry waking up from the effects of nitrous oxide at Dr. Tim Whatley's office and seeing the doctor and his nurse hastily putting their clothes back on. On the job front, George is accused of stealing Yankees baseball equipment and must face "The Boss," George Steinbrenner. Back at the health club, Elaine learns that the guy she had set her sights on is gay and settles for dating Jimmy, whom she finds somewhat intriguing with his inimitable speech pattern. Finally, Kramer revels in his role as guest of honor at the Able Mentally Challenged Adults benefit, with Mel Tormé dedicating a song to him.

Richard Herd played Mr. Wilhelm, George's superior with the Yankees, in the first of eleven appearances, including "The Finale." Anthony Starke played Jimmy. Among his many television roles was gunfighter Ezra Standish in the television series *The Magnificent Seven* (1998–2000), which he described as "every boy's fantasy" in that he got to wear nifty threads, ride a horse, fire a gun, and win over the hearts of pretty girls.

Episode 102: "The Doodle" (original air date: April 6, 1995)

Writers Alec Berg and Jeff Schaffer collaborated on this teleplay that finds Jerry and George with Shelly and Paula, their new girlfriends, dining out as a foursome. There, George quietly alerts his old friend that the pecans he just placed in his mouth were previously in Shelly's. Jerry's violent reaction in spitting them out disgusts his new lady friend.

Meanwhile, George's girlfriend, Paula, sketches a doodle of him, which he finds very unflattering. Elaine thinks that it resembles Mr. Magoo. George thereafter becomes obsessed with whether or not Paula likes him and his appearance. Paula concedes that looks aren't that high on her agenda.

In another storyline, Elaine is interviewing for a new job, this time with Viking Press. So that she can stay at the publisher's suite in the Plaza Hotel, she lies to the powers-that-be by saying that she is coming in from out of town for the interview. Elaine supplies Jerry's parents' address in Florida as her own. Jerry, though, pleads with her to allow Morty and Helen Seinfeld to stay in the suite when they come to town. His apartment is being fumigated because of a flea infestation caused, as things turns out, by Newman. She agrees and the Seinfelds, plus Uncle Leo and Nana, go hog wild in their luxurious digs, taking full advantage of all the hotel's amenities, including expensive meals from room service, adult movies, and massage services.

In Kramer's world, his sense of taste vanishes because of the apartment fumigation. He can no longer taste his Mackinaw peaches, which he says are "like having a circus in your mouth." Jerry, too, is compelled to stay elsewhere and crashes with Shelly, his girlfriend. She kicks him out when he refuses to use her toothbrush. As part of Elaine's interview process, she is asked to interpret a manuscript, but must rely on Kramer's unconventional reading of it. In the end, the publisher likes what she has to say regarding the manuscript, but she loses the would-be job when the considerable hotel tab run up by the Seinfelds, Uncle Leo, and Nana materializes.

Christa Miller played Sherry, and Dana Wheeler-Nicholson was Shelly.

Episode 103: "The Fusilli Jerry" (original air date: April 27, 1995)

Marjorie Gross wrote the teleplay of this episode. Sadly, Gross died of ovarian cancer a year later at the age of forty. The premiere episode of *Seinfeld*'s eighth season, "The Foundation," was dedicated to her memory. Jonathan Gross, Ron Hauge, and Charlie Rubin contributed to the story.

"The Fusilli Jerry" introduces David Puddy, Jerry's auto mechanic, as Elaine's boyfriend. Their on-again, off-again relationship will persist to the end of the series. When Jerry learns that Puddy is using one of his patented sex moves—albeit with a slight deviation—he takes his car-repair business elsewhere. Later, he returns to Puddy because of his lower rates.

Intrigued by the sex move, George asks Jerry if he can teach it to him. He tries it on his girlfriend but gets dumped when she discovers written instructions of the move on his bare hand. Meanwhile, Kramer is driving Estelle Costanza home after having work done on her eyes. When he hits a pothole and his arm inadvertently touches her, Estelle sees it as one of her husband Frank's moves—i.e., "stopping short." Frank is not too happy when he hears about this and confronts Kramer in Jerry's apartment. A brief tussle causes Frank to land smack-dab on a pasta statue of Jerry made by Kramer called the "Fusilli Jerry."

At the Department of Motor Vehicles, Kramer receives new license plates that read "ASSMAN." He believes the plates were likely meant for a proctologist, but takes advantage of the blunder by parking in "Doctors Only" spots.

Patrick Warburton portrayed David Puddy in the first of ten appearances on the show, including "The Face Painter" and "The Finale."

Episode 104: "The Diplomat's Club" (original air date: May 4, 1995)

Tom Gammill and Max Pross wrote this episode—their fifth teleplay credit in season six—with its multiple storylines, including Jerry anxiously awaiting his scheduled liaison with his new girlfriend, a supermodel, at the airport upon his return from a gig in Ithaca. However, with a new handholding agent named Katie (played by Debra Jo Rupp of *That '70s Show* fame) along with him, things don't go quite as planned. For starters, Jerry's comedy act bombs big time after Katie invites the pilot of the plane, who flew them to Ithaca, to the show. Afterwards, she ham-handedly excoriates the pilot for ruining Jerry's performance by making him nervous. This leads to both Jerry and her being ushered off the plane on their return trip to New York, which is being flown by the same pilot. When Katie endeavors to drive Jerry back to New York, she gets hopelessly lost, lands in somebody's swimming pool, and becomes a local news item.

George, meanwhile, insults his African-American superior, Morgan (played by Tom Wright), by noting that he bears a strong resemblance to boxer Sugar Ray Leonard. He endeavors thereafter to prove that he hasn't a racist bone in his body and tries to conjure up a black friend as proof. George asks Joe Temple from "The Couch" to masquerade as his friend, but he declines, so George attempts to enlist Karl, the exterminator of Jerry's apartment in "The Doodle." In Elaine's world, she is on the verge of telling her boss, Mr. Pitt, that she is quitting her job as his assistant, until she learns that he is including her in his will.

Hanging out at the Diplomat's Club—the airport lounge where Jerry is supposed to meet his date—Kramer awaits his friend by betting on airport arrival and departure times with a wealthy Texan named Earl, played by O'Neal Compton. Mr. Pitt, in another plot twist, almost dies from a bad reaction to cough medicine that he purchased in a drug store—from a bottle, in fact, that was handed to him by Jerry, who happened to be in the same store at the time. Mr. Pitt had confused Jerry for the pharmacist and subsequently connects Jerry with Elaine. This leads him to believe that they are in cahoots in trying to bump him off for Elaine's inheritance. The end result is a one-two punch in which Elaine loses both her future inheritance and her job.

When Jerry, at long last, arrives at the Diplomat's Club and begins to canoodle with his girlfriend, he is frightened when a plane pulls up just outside the airport lounge's window, with the very same pilot, who refused to let him fly on his plane, in the cockpit and glowering his way.

Episode 105: "The Face Painter" (original air date: May 11, 1995)

Larry David returned as the sole writer of this episode, with story help from Fred Stoller, which revolves around Elaine's boyfriend, David Puddy, and a predilection for painting his face devilish red while attending the games of his favorite hockey team, the New Jersey Devils. This act disturbs Elaine, who voices her dismay with the practice and threatens to end their relationship over it. Puddy agrees not to paint his face the next time they attend a game together, but instead paints his chest red. Puddy's face painting also unnerves a priest he encounters. The man of the cloth believes he has seen the devil himself.

Meanwhile, George is dating Siena (played by Katy Selverstone), who works at the Central Park Zoo. At the zoo, Kramer gets into a row with a chimpanzee who tosses a banana peel at him. Later, George tells Siena that he loves her, but gets no response. This upsets him until he discovers that she has serious hearing loss in one ear—the ear side that he was on when he bared his heart. Assuming that she didn't hear his expressed sentiment the first time, he tries again on the good ear side. As things turn out, she had indeed heard him the first time.

In the episode's closing moments, Elaine calls on the priest who thought he encountered the devil on earth. Bedecked in white, with streaming light filtering through her garments, the same priest now believes he has had a vision of the Virgin Mary.

Episode 106: "The Understudy" (original air date: May 18, 1995)

Written by Marjorie Gross and Carol Leifer, the final episode of season six features singer-actress Bette Midler as herself. The principal storyline finds Jerry dating Gennice, Midler's understudy in the Broadway adaptation of *Rochelle, Rochelle*. He is also playing in a softball game—on the "Improv" team, which includes George on the roster—against the cast and crew of *Rochelle, Rochelle*.

During the highly competitive and spirited game, George barrels hard into Bette Midler, her team's catcher, and injures the diva, who is compelled to miss a couple of weeks' worth of shows while she recovers. This twist of fate permits Gennice to get her shot, which is what she has always wanted. However, when it becomes known that Jerry is dating Gennice, it is suspected that George purposely caused Midler's injury. "The Understudy" parodied the Tonya Harding–Nancy Kerrigan scandal that played out during the U.S. Figure Skating Championships that winter in Detroit. There, it was discovered that Harding's ex-husband had hired some goon to break Kerrigan's leg in order to give his gal pal a leg up in the competition. An attempt was, in fact, made that didn't quite break Kerrigan's leg but nonetheless caused a bad bruise that forced her to drop out of the championships. Both Harding and the fully recovered Kerrigan made the 1994 Olympic team.

In another plot thread, Elaine enlists the help of Frank Costanza to interpret for her at a nail salon run by Koreans. His knowledge of the language, she hopes, will get to the bottom of what kinds of jokes the staff is making at her expense. Elaine also learns that Frank had a Korean girlfriend—a true love named Kim—who now works in the salon. In the end, Elaine is kicked out of the place for spying and Frank tries to rekindle his old love affair, but to no avail.

Kramer, meanwhile, has devoted all his time and energy into helping Bette Midler recuperate and is not too happy with what he believes to be Jerry and George's complicity in causing her injury. In her first performance as Midler's replacement in *Rochelle, Rochelle*, Gennice is rattled by the all the catcalls that she receives from an audience that is very definitely not in her corner. On a couple of positive notes, Kramer and Bette Midler are heard singing in his apartment, and Elaine runs into J. Peterman on the street, where she is offered a job.

This episode marks the first appearance of John O'Hurley as Jacopo Peterman, owner of the J. Peterman Catalog. It is also the first episode that contains none of Jerry's standup. Actress and comedienne Amy Hill played Gennice, Midler's understudy, who had a penchant for crying at little things, like dropping her hot dog in the park, and not shedding a tear for seemingly more important events in life, like the death of a family member.

25

Season Seven

Goodbye, Larry

Season seven proved to be a milestone year for *Seinfeld*, with co-creator and lead writer Larry David leaving the show after the final episode, "The Invitations," aired. Without exception, Andy Ackerman directed the season's twenty-two episodes, which included many that are regarded as classics, including "The Soup Nazi," "The Rye," and "The Invitations." Season seven ranked number forty-one on *TV Guide*'s list of the "100 Greatest Television Seasons" ever.

Episode 107: "The Engagement" (original air date: September 21, 1995)

Larry David wrote the season's first episode, which inaugurates the important story arc for the season wherein George gets back with his old flame, Susan Ross, after breaking up with his latest girlfriend because she beat him in a game of chess. It is then that both he and Jerry decide it's time to radically amend the direction of their lives and, perhaps, settle down.

This spanking-new outlook prompts George to ask Susan to marry him, which she agrees to do after some persuading. Jerry, though, breaks up with his girlfriend, Melanie, because she eats her peas one at a time.

Meanwhile, Elaine is having difficulty getting a good night's sleep because of a perpetually barking dog in her apartment building. Kramer tells her that he knows someone who can fix that problem for her—a canine assassin named Newman. However, the caper, which is downgraded to a dognapping, goes awry when the dog makes its way back home with damning evidence of the abductors on its person—a piece of Kramer's clothing. Police locate and arrest the dognapping conspirators: Elaine, Kramer, and Newman. Newman is heard exclaiming to the cops when they show up at his door, "What took you so long?" This is what serial killer and fellow postman David Berkowitz is said to have uttered when he was arrested in the summer of 1977.

In the end, George and Susan are engaged, with the latter seeming quite happy about it and the former already questioning why he opened Pandora's Box with the marriage proposal.

Episode 108: "The Postponement" (original air date: September 28, 1995)

Larry David wrote the second episode of the season, too, which picks up where the first episode left off. George, for one, is desperate to postpone his wedding date and will go to great lengths to accomplish that end. Rabbi Glickman (played by Bruce Mahler), who lives in Elaine's building, at long last resolves the dog-barking problem that the botched dognapping failed to accomplish in the prior episode. Said rabbi, though, has a fondness for gossip, and a cable show on top of that, where he reveals on the air—naming names—what Elaine had said to him about feeling insecure because her loser friend George is engaged to be married and she's not. She had assumed that her confession would be held in confidence.

Meanwhile, Kramer sneaks a cup of gourmet coffee into a movie theater and accidentally scalds his hand after spilling it. He promptly envisions a huge lawsuit settlement. In the news at the time was a piping-hot legal case: Stella Liebeck v. McDonald's. After spilling some of the fast-food chain's coffee on herself, and sustaining serious burns that necessitated an eight-day hospital stay and skin grafting, Liebeck sued McDonald's. Although from the preponderance of the evidence, it does seem that McDonald's coffee was on the scalding-hot side, the case nonetheless inspired much debate on frivolous lawsuits and supplied ample fodder for comedians, including Larry David.

Episode 109: "The Maestro" (original air date: October 5, 1995)

More of the ongoing story arcs are on display in this episode—once again written by Larry David—with Kramer, for one, taking his spilled-coffee lawsuit to the next level by hiring an attorney named Jackie Chiles. Alas, from his lawyer's perspective, Kramer agrees to accept a settlement: free coffee for life at any of the gourmet coffee chain's stores. Chiles believed that both he and his client could have won a considerable monetary settlement had this first offer been rejected.

On the George front, his relationship with Susan, his fiancée, continues unabated. He also expresses concern for a security guard, who must be on his feet all day, in Susan's uncle's place of business. Uncharacteristically generous, George purchases the man a rocking chair. However, this random act of kindness leads to the security guard falling asleep in the chair and the store getting robbed because of it.

Meanwhile, Elaine has a new boyfriend, bush league music conductor Bob Cobb, who prefers to be called "The Maestro." When he offhandedly says that there are no house rentals in Tuscany—where he is headed with Elaine—a skeptical Jerry consults Poppie's cousin as to whether or not this is true. With the credits rolling in the show's waning moments, we see Elaine and "The Maestro" in his Tuscany digs, where they are vacationing, and Jerry and Kramer arriving in a taxicab directly across the street from them.

Mark Metcalf played "The Maestro," and Phil Morris assumed the role as Jackie Chiles, Kramer's lawyer. From this point forward, Morris would appear in a recurring role as Chiles, a parody of lead O. J. Simpson lawyer Johnnie Cochran. Morris even reprised the character in television commercials after *Seinfeld* ended its nine-year run.

Episode 110: "The Wink" (original air date: October 12, 1995)

Tom Gammill and Max Pross collaborated to pen their first episode of season seven and the first teleplay not credited to Larry David. "The Wink" revolves around Jerry's healthy dietary habits, which preclude him from making headway with Elaine's cousin Holly (played by Stacey Travis), who cooks mutton and pork chops. His good eating ways are also responsible for a squirt of his breakfast grapefruit pulp lodging in George's left eye.

This turn of events—and burning sensation—causes George to periodically wink throughout the day. Unfortunately, the winking from the grapefruit pulp is constantly misinterpreted and engenders all kinds of unforeseen problems, including Kramer selling off a birthday card signed by the entire Yankees team—and meant for George Steinbrenner—and Morgan, George's superior, losing his job.

In an effort to get back the birthday card he mistakenly sold because of a George wink, Kramer promises Bobby, a hospitalized boy and the card's new owner, that his favorite Yankee star, Paul O'Neill, will hit two home runs in a game for him. Yankee outfielder Paul O'Neill guest stars as himself, and Thomas Dekker played Bobby.

Kramer requesting that New York Yankees outfielder Paul O'Neill pull a Babe Ruth and hit two home runs for a sick boy in "The Wink."   *NBC/Photofest*

Episode 111: "The Hot Tub" (original air date: October 19, 1995)

Gregg Kavet and Andy Robin joined forces in writing this teleplay, which finds George hosting his compatriots from the Houston Astros front office and subsequently adopting their earthy lingo as his own. With the New York City Marathon on the horizon, Elaine is also playing host, but to a runner from Trinidad and Tobago named Jean-Paul, played by Jeremiah Birkett. When Jean-Paul hears George liberally using his newly acquired vocabulary—swear words—he thinks that they are both commonplace and terms of endearment in America. In an effort then to get on well with Americans, Jean-Paul parrots George and calls Elaine's neighbor's baby a "bastard" and the building's super a "son of a bitch." Jean-Paul had previously missed an important race at the past Olympic games because he overslept, and Jerry wants to make certain that never happens again.

Meanwhile, Kramer's installation of a hot tub in his apartment leads to a series of ill-timed events, including shorting out the electricity in the entire building. This causes Jean-Paul to almost miss the marathon.

Episode 112: "The Soup Nazi" (original air date: November 2, 1995)

First-time *Seinfeld* writer Spike Feresten, who would remain with the show to its end, is the man responsible for this very memorable episode—one that spawned the unforgettable catchphrase "No soup for you!"

Based on a real-life soup peddler in New York City, "The Soup Nazi" revolves around a local shop that sells delicious-tasting soups, but whose proprietor is not quite as delicious, with his litany of strict rules and extremely brusque behavior toward his clientele. The fun begins when Jerry, George, and Elaine visit the soup stand. Jerry, who is privy to the place's myriad rules, lays them out for his two friends. But when George doesn't get a piece of bread with the soup, which others had gotten, he has the temerity to ask for it and is rudely told that it'll cost him two dollars extra. When he further objects, the price of the bread rises to three dollars. Finally, his soup is snatched away from him with a curt "No soup for you!" as the cashier refunds his money.

Later, Jerry's girlfriend, Sheila, is kicked out of the soup stand for talking back to the proprietor after he vehemently chided her for canoodling with Jerry while in line. Elaine, too, gets booted from the Soup Nazi's place and banned for an entire year for not playing by the rules.

In another plot thread, Elaine purchases an armoire, which she cannot move into her building on a weekend. In the interim, she enlists Kramer to stand guard over it on the street, which he does admirably until it is stolen from him by two somewhat effete street toughs. When he relays the tale of the theft to his new friend, Yev Kassem, a.k.a. the Soup Nazi, the man is surprisingly

Larry Thomas poses as his "Soup Nazi" alter ego with the Seinfeld "No Soup for You" Food Truck in New York City in 2012.

Christopher Black/ Everett Collection Inc./ Alamy

sympathetic to Kramer's plight and offers him—free of charge—an armoire from his basement. Elaine, who was enraged by her prior treatment at the soup stand, has a change of heart when she learns of the Soup Nazi's munificence. She even goes down to his business to thank him in person, but is treated even more rudely than before, with the man telling her that he would have destroyed the piece of furniture before turning it over to her. The Soup Nazi did not know that Elaine was the intended recipient of the armoire.

Later, Jerry finds assorted papers in an armoire drawer, which turn out to be the Soup Nazi's collection of recipes for his coveted soups. Elaine sees this as an opportunity to get even with the man who humiliated her on two separate occasions. She returns to the shop and waves the recipes under the Soup Nazi's nose and threatens to destroy his business, which she does when he closes down the soup stand and returns to his native Argentina.

The actual New York City soup entrepreneur who inspired this episode is a man named Al Yeganeh, who was not too happy with how he was portrayed. The character of the Soup Nazi did not reveal his name in this episode but did, in "The Finale," as Yev Kassem. The actor who portrayed him was Larry Thomas, who received an Emmy nomination for "Outstanding Guest Actor in a Comedy Series."

There were some mildly controversial particulars surrounding this episode. One involved the character's pejorative nickname of "Soup Nazi," which some Jewish groups thought trivialized the Holocaust. Another involved the armoire thieves being portrayed as gay. Larry David had determined that this was the humorous route to take because "only gay guys would steal an armoire." Played by John Paragon and Yul Vazquez, the street thugs were unnamed in "The Soup Nazi," but in subsequent episodes would be known as Cedric and Bob. In "The Sponge" they are summoned to compel by force Kramer to sport a ribbon in an AIDS Walk fundraiser.

Episode 113: "The Secret Code" (original air date: November 9, 1995)

Alec Berg and Jeff Schaffer collaborated on this teleplay revolving around George and his ATM password, which he refuses to divulge to Susan, firmly believing that a man has the right to maintain *some* secrets in a relationship.

The multiple storylines in this episode include Elaine going out to dinner with her boss, J. Peterman, and inviting Jerry to tag along. Jerry, in turn, invites George, who ends up having dinner alone with Peterman. After a rather uncomfortable dining experience, Peterman receives a call that his mother is not long for this earth and both he and George rush to her bedside. George reveals his ATM code to the dying woman. It's "Bosco," and that ends up being the last word she utters in this life, which greatly befuddles her son.

Meanwhile, Jerry gets together with Leapin' Larry, an appliance peddler, to discuss the possibility of appearing in his television commercials. Larry wears a prosthetic leg and—when Jerry's foot falls asleep—becomes convinced that he is being mocked. At their next meeting the very same thing happens to Jerry with respect to the sleepy foot, but instead of walking it off—he does not want to offend Larry again—he stomps it down real hard, which causes a can of paint thinner to tumble to the floor and ignite a fire.

In Kramer land, he is more than happy to be of assistance to the fire department with his new emergency band radio. When the department learns of a blaze at Leapin' Larry's, Kramer is there to lend a hand, but accidentally knocks out the on-call driver. He then gets to experience one of his dreams: navigating a fire truck through the streets of Manhattan. However, his lack of training for the role causes the vehicle to crash. Due to Kramer's ineptitude, the fire at Leapin' Larry's rages unmolested, without a fire truck on the scene.

The firehouse shown in this episode is the historic Hook & Ladder 8 at 14 North Moore Street in the Tribeca section of lower Manhattan. The building is also renowned as the firehouse used in *Ghostbusters*, the 1984 hit movie starring Bill Murray and Dan Aykroyd. Hook & Ladder 8 is the second-oldest firehouse in New York City.

Fred Stoller, who wrote the episode "The Soup," appears here as the very forgetful Fred Yerkes. Elaine dates him because she is intrigued that he didn't remember that they had met and spoken before at length. In fact, she had told Fred all about her uncle who worked in the Texas School Book Depository with Lee Harvey Oswald, and how—after being informed the president had been shot—the assassin winked at him and said he was off to the movies. Oswald was subsequently arrested in a movie theater. Elaine, though, comes to regret her date with the forgetful Fred. A final twist finds a man with his sleeve caught in an ATM machine vestibule near the raging fire at Leapin' Larry's. George is compelled to reveal his ATM password and hand over his card to free the man.

Veteran character Lewis Arquette played Leapin' Larry. At the time of his passing in 2001, Arquette had a lengthy list of television credits, including a recurring role as J. D. Pickett on *The Waltons* (1971–1981). He was the son of comedian Cliff Arquette, a.k.a. Charley Weaver, and the father of Rosanna, Patricia, and David.

Episode 114: "The Pool Guy" (original air date: November 16, 1995)

David Mandel wrote this episode with its main storyline focused on Ramon, a pool guy at the health club, who wants nothing more than to pal around with Jerry and be part of the gang. Jerry is thus in the awkward position of trying to make short work of Ramon without offending him.

Meanwhile, Elaine has a spare ticket to a fashion show and decides to invite Susan, George's fiancée, in an attempt to get to know her better. This meeting of female minds—Elaine and Susan—makes George very uncomfortable. He cannot help but worry about what is being said about him.

In the world of Kramer, he receives a new phone number, 555-FILK, which is very similar to 555-FILM, the movie hotline. This coincidence leads to many erroneous phone calls made to Kramer concerning movies and movie times. Kramer, though, takes it upon himself to supply all the callers who dialed his number—the wrong one—with the most up-to-date and accurate movie information possible. George even experiences talking with the Kramer version of the movie hotline. After a series of prompts—"enter the first three letters of your movie title now"—lead to nowhere, an exasperated Kramer blurts out, "Why don't you just tell me the name of the movie you've selected?"

Carlos Jacott plays Ramon, the pool guy, who almost drowns at the end of the episode while Jerry and Newman dicker over who is more responsible for his predicament, and who should give him mouth-to-mouth resuscitation. The role was originally to be played by Danny Hoch, who ended up refusing to do the part as written, claiming that it was an antiquated and ugly ethnic stereotype. Mr. Moviefone himself, Russ Leatherman, plays himself. In 1989, Leatherman co-founded Moviefone with its familiar greeting: "Hellooo and welcome to Moviefone!" AOL bought the outfit in 2000, making Leatherman a very wealthy man indeed.

Episode 115: "The Sponge" (original air date: December 7, 1995)

Peter Mehlman wrote this teleplay that finds Jerry, Kramer, and Elaine at Monk's Café discussing, among other things, a contraceptive—the Today Sponge—that is being taken off the market. This news prompts Elaine to go on a major safari to locate as many of the sponges as possible before they go the way of the dinosaur. She finds a caseload's worth at Pasteur's pharmacy but now must carefully evaluate each and every one of her boyfriends as to whether or not they are "sponge-worthy."

Kramer, meanwhile, is planning to participate in the charity AIDS Walk New York and is acquiring sponsors. Jerry takes down a woman's phone number from

Elaine tackling a monumental dilemma—which men are "sponge-worthy"—in "The Sponge."   NBC/Photofest

Kramer's list of sponsors—an individual whom he casually remembers. Against his pal's wishes, George tells Susan how Jerry procured his new girlfriend, Lena, and the gossip grapevine eventually reaches her ears. Lena, however, doesn't seem bothered by the news and Jerry frets about her seemingly rosy nature and easygoing personality. He later discovers that she has a closet full of contraceptive sponges.

At the AIDS Walk, Kramer's principles stand in the way of his wearing an AIDS ribbon. He'll not knuckle under to "ribbon bullies." This stance, though, augurs trouble from an angry mob, including Bob and Cedric, the toughs who stole Elaine's armoire in "The Soup Nazi."

Episode 116: "The Gum" (original air date: December 14, 1995)

Tom Gammill and Max Pross teamed up to write this episode that brings back Lloyd Braun, who had suffered a nervous breakdown after disastrously advising Mayor Dinkins in his losing re-election effort. Kramer, though, takes him under his wing and Lloyd offers Jerry and George a piece of gum that he got from a pal in Chinatown. Jerry accepts the gum, feeling that declining it might possibly offend him and set back his mentally fragile recovery. George, however, says no because he doesn't chew gum.

So as to avoid sitting next to Lloyd, her old flame, later at the movies, Elaine says that she must sit with Jerry close to the screen because he forgot to wear his glasses. This charade is maintained whenever Lloyd is around, with Jerry always sporting a pair while in his presence. In the movie theater, Elaine also loses a button on her blouse, exposing some cleavage, which gives Lloyd the wrong idea.

Meanwhile, George is convinced that Ruthie Cohen, the cashier at Monk's Café, has purloined a twenty-dollar bill of his. At his parents' house, he encounters an old friend named Deena Lazzari (played by Mary Jo Keenen) and her father, "Pop" Lazzari (played by Sandy Ward), both of whom, like Lloyd, recently suffered nervous breakdowns. While Pop tinkers with George's car, Deena begins to suspect that George has some serious mental issues of his own. She is absolutely convinced of this when she spies George dressed as Henry VIII at the re-opening of the Alex Theater, which Kramer had been instrumental in bringing back.

Pop's fiddling with George's car—the Jon Voight car—ultimately leads to it catching fire on the street. Ruth Cohen appears as Ruthie Cohen, the cashier. She has the distinction of appearing in more episodes than any recurring character, including Susan Ross, Morty and Helen Seinfeld, and Frank and Estelle Costanza. For the first and only time in "The Gum," she turns up in a location other than Monk's Café. With the character being harangued by George concerning the twenty-dollar bill, she bears witness to his vehicle catching fire. Ruth Cohen passed away in 2008 at the age of seventy-eight.

Episode 117: "The Rye" (original air date: January 4, 1996)

Carol Leifer returns as the writer of this teleplay that finds the Costanzas, Frank and Estelle, having dinner with Mr. and Mrs. Ross, George's fiancée's folks, for the very first time. Not unexpectedly, things go awry when Frank complains to George and Estelle that the marble rye he bought for the dinner was never brought to the table. Unbeknown to his hosts and his son, Frank takes the loaf of bread back with him when he leaves.

A subplot to the main one of the dinner party involves Jerry going to Schnitzer's Bakery to purchase another loaf of marble rye, which George hopes to clandestinely replace in the Rosses' kitchen before they notice it's missing. Jerry, though, runs into problems of his own when an elderly woman named Mabel Choate purchases the last loaf of its kind and refuses to sell it to him, even for the inflated sum of fifty dollars. Getting nowhere with the woman, Jerry ultimately snatches the bread from her and brands her an "old bag" as he makes his getaway. Mabel Choate would, however, exact her revenge on Jerry in the episodes "The Cadillac" and "The Finale." All the trouble in securing this second loaf of marble rye goes for naught when George is caught with a fishing pole, reeling the loaf up to the Rosses' third-floor window.

Meanwhile, Elaine is dating John Jermaine, a jazz saxophonist, who apparently is averse to oral sex. When Jerry blabs to one of John's band mates about the relationship between Elaine and John, the former is embarrassed because she doesn't want to put any undue pressure on the man. Having taken over his friend's hansom cab duties for a week, Kramer is busy, too, and furnishes the Rosses with a romantic ride through Central Park on their anniversary. However, the horse's flatulence, caused by Kramer giving it a can of "Beef-a-Reeno" prior to the ride, casts asunder the romantic ambience.

Canadian actress Frances Bay played Mabel Choate, the victim of the marble rye heist. Courtesy of a lobbying effort, which included a letter from Jerry Seinfeld, Bay was elected into the Canada Walk of Fame in 2008; she passed away three years later. Warren Frost and Grace Zabriskie reprised their roles as Mr. and Mrs. Ross in this episode. Busy television character actor Jeff Yagher played John Jermaine.

Episode 118: "The Caddy" (original air date: January 25, 1996)

The writing duo of Gregg Kavet and Andy Robin penned this teleplay that finds Elaine encountering an old nemesis of hers, Sue Ellen Mischke, played by actress and yoga guru Brenda Strong. Courtesy of being the heiress to the Oh Henry! candy bar fortune, Sue Ellen is now quite wealthy. She also is referred to as a "braless wonder," which inspires Elaine to buy her—what else?—a bra as a birthday gift. When Sue Ellen sports the bra and the bra alone, she starts—much to Elaine's dismay and many men's viewing pleasure—a new fashion trend.

Meanwhile, George desires a job promotion and leaves his car parked in the Yankee Stadium garage in the hopes that his superiors, including George Steinbrenner, will conclude that he is a tireless employee willing to burn the midnight oil for the team. His ruse fails when Jerry and Kramer borrow the car and get into an accident, which is caused by taking their eyes off the road and placing them on the solely bra-wearing Sue Ellen. When the car is returned to the parking garage severely damaged with traces of blood on it, too, the New York Yankee superiors fear that George has been in a horrific accident. After an unsuccessful search for him, "The Boss," George Steinbrenner, declares him dead and breaks the bad news in person to Mr. and Mrs. Costanza. (The real George Steinbrenner is, as always, never seen. We hear only Larry David's voice as Steinbrenner.)

At Elaine's urging, Kramer agrees to bring suit against Sue Ellen for damages and again enlists the help of attorney Jackie Chiles. Things are looking pretty good for them until his new caddy friend, Stan (played by actor and voice specialist Armin Shimerman), tells him that Sue Ellen should try on the bra in the courtroom. Reluctantly, Jackie Chiles makes the request to the judge, who consents. Sue Ellen puts on the bra over her clothing, which Chiles knew would not fit. In a parody of the O. J. Simpson trial and Johnnie Cochran's verbiage, Chiles says: "You can't let the defendant have control of the key piece of evidence. Plus, she's trying it on over a leotard. Of course a bra's not gonna fit on over a leotard. A bra's gotta fit right up against a person's skin, like a glove!"

Episode 119: "The Seven" (original air date: February 1, 1996)

Alec Berg and Jeff Schaffer wrote this teleplay that finds George contemplating a name—when and if that blessed day ever comes—for his first child. He tells his fiancée, Susan, that he would like to name their firstborn "Seven," the number worn by baseball great Mickey Mantle. Susan is not warm to the idea, but tells her cousin Carrie, who is expecting a baby, what George proposed. Surprisingly, Carrie and her husband, Kevin (played by Shannon Holt and Ken Hudson Campbell, respectively), love the name. Kevin is a big Mickey Mantle fan, too, and the couple plan on assigning the name Seven to their newborn. This piece of news greatly upsets George and he tries, without success, to convince Carrie and Kevin to select another name like "Soda" or "Six" or "Fourteen."

Meanwhile, Elaine wrenches her neck while taking down a bicycle from a rack in an antique store—a pink Schwinn Sting-Ray for girls. Jerry doesn't assist her because he is more interested in Christie, a fellow store browser whom he ultimately dates. Because of her intense pain, Elaine impetuously offers her newly purchased old bicycle to anyone who can relieve it, which Kramer does with chiropractic élan. He asks for the bicycle as payment and Elaine, both very surprised and very unhappily, turns it over to him. But when the pain in her neck returns worse than ever, she asks for the bicycle back—the retro-girlie bicycle that Kramer's been riding around the streets of New York with great fanfare.

Kramer thus enlists Newman as an arbiter to determine who is the rightful owner of the bicycle. Based on the Judgment of Solomon, his decision is to split it by half. However, rather than see it destroyed by Newman's decree, Kramer decides to return the bicycle to Elaine. In the immediate wake of this benevolent act, Newman then changes his decision and determines that Kramer should keep the bicycle because only its true owner would not want it harmed in any way, shape, or form.

In a separate story thread, Kramer tells Jerry that he's going to record everything that he takes from the latter's apartment, which he wants to be billed for at the end of each week. When Jerry presents him with a fifty-dollar tab for week number one, Kramer sells the bicycle to Newman to help pay it off.

Jerry's overriding dilemma throughout "The Seven" is not Kramer poaching his food; it is his attempts at unraveling the mystery of why his new girlfriend, Christie (played by Lisa Deanne Young), is always wearing the same outfit. Perhaps she's like Superman, with a closet full of matching outfits. When she catches him rummaging through her closets, Jerry is sent on his way before he uncovers the truth.

Episode 120: "The Cadillac" (original air date: February 8, 1996)

This episode originally aired in an hour-long format. Its writers were Jerry Seinfeld and Larry David. This would mark the final time in the series that Seinfeld was awarded a writing credit. The main storyline revolves around Jerry returning from a very lucrative comedy gig and feeling in an especially generous mood. In fact, he buys his folks, Morty and Helen, a brand new and very expensive Cadillac Fleetwood.

The Not Necessarily Top Ten Celebrities Who Appeared on Seinfeld as Themselves

10. Keith Hernandez ("The Boyfriend")
9. Mel Tormé ("The Jimmy")
8. Candice Bergen ("The Keys")
7. David Letterman ("The Abstinence")
6. Al Roker ("The Cigar Store Indian")
5. Rudy Giuliani ("The Non-Fat Yogurt")
4. Geraldo Rivera ("The Finale")
3. Raquel Welch ("The Summer of George")
2. Derek Jeter ("The Abstinence")
1. Marisa Tomei ("The Cadillac")

Meanwhile, Elaine's friend knows actress Marisa Tomei and George frets that if he wasn't engaged he might have had a shot with her. Apparently, Tomei likes quirky, funny, bald guys. Despite his engagement, George becomes totally obsessed with meeting the actress. He eventually does and she takes a shine to him until she finds out that he is "sort of engaged." Tomei, who played herself, punches George. Later, Susan, who believes that her fiancé is having an affair with Elaine, punches him as well.

Meanwhile, Kramer is waging a battle with the cable company, which he feels is not providing proper service. He plays a cat-and-mouse game with a cable guy, who unsuccessfully tries to confront Kramer. In the end, the cable guy owns up to the problems with the cable service and promises more customer-friendly days ahead. He and Kramer even embrace.

Back in Florida, the Seinfeld elders—with Morty driving around in his new set of fancy wheels—are suspected of having come into money. Jack Klompus accuses Morty, who is the president of the condo board, of embezzling condo funds. A vote is taken to impeach him. Morty is counting on a woman friend on the board to save his hide. Her name is Mabel Choate, the very woman from whom Jerry stole the loaf of marble rye bread in "The Rye." When she puts two and two together that Jerry is Morty's son, Mabel votes to impeach. Morty leaves the condo grounds akin to the way President Richard Nixon left Washington, D.C., after resigning from the presidency in August 1974. He turns to the crowd, smiles an exaggerated smile, and holds up both arms, flashing two "V for Victory" salutes as the Seinfelds depart.

Episode 121: "The Shower Head" (original air date: February 15, 1996)

A Peter Mehlman–Majorie Gross writing collaboration, "The Shower Head" places Morty and Helen Seinfeld in New York City, a temporary stopover after leaving their Florida condo under a cloud of suspicion. They take possession of Uncle Leo's apartment while he moves in with Lydia, his lady friend. It doesn't take Jerry very long, though, to become annoyed with his parents living in such close proximity and—because the phone calls are local ones—calling him incessantly.

Jerry thus encourages Uncle Leo to break up with Lydia and move back to his old apartment, compelling Morty and Helen Seinfeld to leave. The Seinfelds contemplate moving to a new condo in Florida called Del Boca Vista until they receive an irate call from Frank Costanza, informing them that he and Estelle are considering the same thing. Ultimately, the Costanzas abort their moving plans because they don't want to leave George. The Seinfelds can then move back to the Sunshine State without trepidation.

Uncle Leo's penchant for accusing everyone and anyone of being an anti-Semite is on display in this episode, too, including the cook at Monk's Café for overcooking his hamburger. Later, Jerry appears on *The Tonight Show with Jay Leno*, which is taping in New York, and jokes about Uncle Leo and his ubiquitous anti-Semitism accusations. Lydia finds the material highly amusing. Branding *her* an anti-Semite, Uncle Leo calls an end to their relationship.

Meanwhile, testing positive for opium, Elaine is in a pickle after a work-mandated drug test. Poppy seeds from her favorite muffins are the culprits. A urine switcheroo with Helen Seinfeld doesn't afford her much better results, when it tests positive for osteoporosis. And new showerheads in Jerry, Kramer, and Newman's apartments are low pressure and driving them batty. Kramer and Newman locate black-market showerheads with more *oomph*—ones used for elephants—and they are powerful indeed.

Episode 122: "The Doll" (original air date: February 22, 1996)

Tom Gammill and Max Pross once again employed their collective talents by writing this teleplay with ample Seinfeldian plot twists and turns, including George complaining that a doll in Susan's impressive collection is a dead ringer for his mother. In fact, he becomes so fixated on the doll that he comes to believe it is speaking to him. Later, when Frank Costanza sees the doll for the first time, he, too, hears the voice of Estelle, and beheads it.

Jerry, meanwhile, is returning from a road trip with a wedding gift from Susan's friend Sally and a case full of barbecue sauce with a picture of a man resembling actor and talk-show host Charles Grodin on it. Jerry planned on presenting them to Grodin as part of a comedy bit when he appeared on his show, but they got smashed on the flight back home. He gets a second chance with the barbecue sauce when he hears that Sally is flying into New York to visit with Susan. However, she brings him another brand. Later, he asks her to bring over the doll that resembles Estelle Costanza—as a comedic substitute for the barbecue sauce bottle bit—but Sally brings another one, which she finds much funnier, and foils Jerry's plans again.

In "The Doll," Elaine is back from Tuscany, where she had been with "The Maestro," and desperately trying to replace an autographed picture of the "third tenor," which she had damaged. It was a personal favorite of "The Maestro's" and she hopes to secure another one when the third tenor appears alongside Jerry on *The Charles Grodin Show*. She does, in fact, get it and present it to "The Maestro," but—alas—ruins it again. (The three tenors—a popular teaming in the 1990s opera scene—were, in actuality, Luciano Pavarotti, Plácido Domingo, and "the other guy" José Carreras.)

Comedienne Kathy Griffin played Sally, and John Lizzi, the third tenor—the "other guy" with a name that nobody can seem to remember. Interestingly, Griffin and Jerry Seinfeld had something of a contentious relationship after this episode aired when the big-mouthed comedienne made some negative comments about the show's star in her Comedy Central standup routine. *Seinfeld* writers nonetheless couldn't pass up a good thing and Griffin returned to the show again as Sally, a "standup comedienne who made her living talking smack about Jerry Seinfeld," in the episode "The Cartoon."

Episode 123: "The Friars Club" (original air date: March 7, 1996)

David Mandel wrote this episode that revolves around Jerry's lost Friars Club jacket and Elaine's interactions with Bob, a new employee with apparent hearing problems, played by *Saturday Night Live* alumnus Rob Schneider. Meanwhile,

George has gotten his wedding date postponed for a few more months and Kramer is involved with a woman named Connie, who never seems to want to leave his apartment.

Further developments find Jerry and George hunting for the former's lost jacket at a magic show, where it had gone missing. Their efforts get them in all kinds of hot water. Elaine, too, is at the magic show with Bob, who she is convinced may not really have a hearing problem after all. When he loses his hearing aid upon being ushered out of the place for inappropriate behavior—groping Elaine—she tries it on to see if it really is a working hearing aid and discovers, the hard way, that it is.

Kramer and Connie's relationship ends in dramatic fashion when he falls asleep and she believes that he is dead. Connie calls up some unsavory individuals to get rid of the body and Kramer is placed in a sack and dumped in the Hudson River, which is really an estuary with currents flowing in two directions. He survives the strong estuarial currents and the police turn up at Connie's apartment, where Kramer identifies her as the woman who tried to do him in.

Lisa Arch Kushell, comedienne and *MADtv* alumnus, played Connie, Kramer's mafia gal pal, and comedian Pat Cooper, the man who promised to sponsor Jerry's induction into the Friars Club, appeared as himself.

Episode 124: "The Wig Master" (original air date: April 4, 1996)

This episode is Spike Feresten's baby. It finds Jerry shopping at an upscale clothier's store with Elaine, who gets involved with a pony-tailed sales clerk named Craig after the man promises her a great price on a yet-to-arrive Nicole Miller dress that she's been champing at the bit to own.

Meanwhile, George and Kramer cannot believe their good fortune when they find a parking lot with decidedly non–New York City rates. However, when George uncovers a used condom in his vehicle, the picture becomes increasingly clear that something is rotten in the Jiffy Park. To compound George's misery, he's entertaining a houseguest that he didn't bargain for: Susan's friend Ethan, who is working with the Broadway play *Joseph and the Amazing Technicolor Dreamcoat* as its "wig master."

Later, Kramer, who had borrowed the technicolor dreamcoat from the show's costume designer, discovers a prostitute and her client conducting business in his car. Courtesy of both where he is and the way he's dressed, the police—believing that he is a pimp—arrest him. The über-affordable parking lot utilized customers' cars as assignation hot spots.

Finally, in the show's waning moments, Elaine deduces that Craig has been pulling her strings and holding a dress, which he had all along, until she slept with him. She exacts her revenge on him by snipping off his prized ponytail while he's asleep.

Actor and director Patrick Bristow played the "wig master," Ethan. He had recurring roles in multiple television series, including *Mad About You*

(1992–1999), *Head Over Heels* (1997), and *Ellen* (1994–1998). Bristow also appeared as Bolton, Virtucon Tour Guide, in *Austin Powers: International Man of Mystery* (1997). English actor Harry Van Gorkum portrayed the ponytailed Craig.

Episode 125: "The Calzone" (original air date: April 25, 1996)

Another Alec Berg and Jeff Schaffer collaboration, this episode finds George Steinbrenner admiring the aroma of George's lunch, a pepperoni and eggplant calzone from Paisano Restaurant, and then expecting one at lunchtime every single day thereafter. Problems arise, though, when George gets caught dipping his hand into the restaurant counter's tip jar. Naturally, he is presumed to be stealing from it when, in fact, he was attempting to retrieve the buck tip that he dropped in there because the counterperson had not seen him do so. George merely wanted to repeat the gesture for his intended audience and get due credit for the tip.

In order to stay in George Steinbrenner's good graces, George enlists Newman to make the daily calzone purchases for him. His postal route takes him past the place every day anyway. Newman agrees to help but with a few stipulations, including a complimentary daily calzone, slice of pepperoni pizza, and a little more as compensation. When Newman takes off from work on a rainy day, which is customary, George asks Kramer to make the purchase for him. Things go awry when Kramer's clothes get wet in the rainstorm and he dries some of them in Paisano's pizza oven.

Meanwhile, Elaine is dating a man named Todd (played by John D'Aquino), despite the fact that he never officially asked her out on a date. On the other hand, Jerry is pleased with his attractive girlfriend, Nicki, who utilizes her good looks to get what she wants, including talking a police officer out of giving him a speeding ticket.

Danette Tays played Nicki in this episode. Her other *Seinfeld* connection involved a television commercial that both she and Jason Alexander appeared in for Rold Gold pretzels.

Episode 126: "The Bottle Deposit" (original air date: May 2, 1996)

Gregg Kavet and Andy Robin wrote this episode that originally aired as an hour-long show, but—like others before it—has been split into two separate episodes for syndication. "The Bottle Deposit" contains multiple plot threads and Seinfeldian twists and turns, including Kramer and Newman valiantly trying to determine how they can cash in on the state of Michigan's ten-cent bottle deposit, which is double New York's paltry five-cent amount.

Other goings-on find Elaine bidding on a set of golf clubs once owned by President John F. Kennedy for her boss, J. Peterman. After loaning out his vehicle to Kramer and Newman, Jerry encounters car trouble and takes his vehicle to an extremely dedicated auto mechanic named Tony. Meanwhile, George is having all sorts of problems at work, with his superior, Mr. Wilhelm, accusing him of needing work assignments repeated to him time and again.

Despite being under orders to bid no more than ten thousand dollars to win Kennedy's golf clubs, Elaine doubles the amount to impress the heir to the Oh Henry! candy bar fortune, braless wonder Sue Ellen Mischke, who also attends the auction at Sotheby's. In the matter of the bottle deposits, the wily Newman, it seems, has come up with a viable plan to get all the bottles and cans that he and Kramer have collected to Michigan. They'll employ a U.S. mail truck, which Newman has generously volunteered to drive for his employer.

Jerry's car problems take a new turn and, because of Tony's overzealousness, he decides to take his business elsewhere. Not too happy about the situation, Tony takes off with Jerry's vehicle as well as the historic twenty-thousand-dollar presidential golf clubs, which were in its back seat.

On the trip to Michigan in the mail truck, Kramer and Newman spy Jerry's stolen car on the road. They debate whether or not to pursue Tony and the car or continue on their appointed rounds, which include delivery of the bottles and cans. Ultimately, Kramer takes control of the truck and pursues Tony, lessening his load by tossing out the bottles, cans, and then Newman. Tony retaliates by tossing the golf clubs at the truck, which eventually cause Kramer to throw in the towel. After getting tossed out of the mail truck, Newman stumbles upon a farm, replete with a farmer's daughter who takes a real shine to him. Newman, however, goes too far with the farmer's daughter, and her gun-toting father is compelled to drive him—and Kramer, who has turned up—away.

When Elaine finally presents the damaged golf clubs to J. Peterman, he assumes that JFK was a bad sport on the links—a man who tossed around his clubs in fits of anger. And due to a report that he handed in, about which he was completely clueless as to what he was supposed to do, George, as per George Steinbrenner's orders, lands in a mental institution. Exhibiting signs of dementia, Mr. Wilhelm inadvertently contributes to George's workplace woes.

The six-foot-eight Brad Garrett played Tony, the auto mechanic. The busy actor, comedian, and voice-over talent is best known for playing Robert Barone on *Everybody Loves Raymond*, which starred Ray Romano. This episode also marked the first time that cell-phone technology appeared on *Seinfeld*. "The Bottle Deposit" contains a faux pas as well, which was made by actress Karen Lynn Scott, the farmer's daughter, who famously said, "Goodbye, Norman," as Newman was being driven away from her farm. It was left in the final cut because it was thought to be funny, and not—as some viewers presumed—a revelation of Newman's first name.

Episode 127: "The Wait Out" (original air date: May 9, 1996)

Written by Peter Mehlman, with story contributions from Matt Selman, this episode finds George and Susan's wedding fast approaching, with the former still hoping to get out of it someway or another. "The Wait Out" gets cranking with George making an off-handed remark to a couple, David and Beth Lookner, who separate thereafter. He had merely said, in a light-hearted tone, that Beth could do better. David, however, blames George for the breakup. While George tries to straighten things out with Beth, Jerry and Elaine hope that there will be no reconciliation. Jerry is interested in Beth, played by Debra Messing, and Elaine has her sights set on David, played by Cary Elwes.

David, in fact, subsequently gets back at George by making a similar remark to Susan. When George's fiancée reacts as Beth did, George hopes that this will lead to the wedding being called off. To George's utter dismay, it doesn't.

Meanwhile, Kramer has taken to wearing very tight jeans—so tight, in fact, that he is unable to take them off. When he is asked to babysit for neighbor Mrs. Zanfino's kid, Joey, he frightens the boy because of his stilted, awkward gait in the overly tight pants. Joey, played by Todd Bosley, thinks that Kramer is the Frankenstein monster and runs off into the night. Kramer goes after him but not before getting his pint-sized friend, Mickey, to substitute for the boy.

Episode 128: "The Invitations" (original air date: May 16, 1996)

This episode, written by Larry David, marked the end of an era—the end of David's *Seinfeld* tenure as a writer, although he would return for "The Finale" two years later. It is no stretch to say that Larry David went out with a bang with "The Invitations," which is considered an absolute classic. This particular episode was also steeped in some controversy and actually caused a percentage of the *Seinfeld* audience to question if the show had finally gone too far.

"The Invitations" begins with a morose George and his fiancée, Susan, thumbing through wedding invitations. At George's urging, the couple settles upon the cheapest ones available. When the soon-to-be-married pair bump into Kramer on the street, he calls Susan "Lily," which riles her. She thus bars Kramer from being an usher at the wedding.

Meanwhile, Jerry and Elaine ruminate over the fact that after George's nuptials, their foursome will be down to three. She reveals her plans for leaving the group as well. Later, a daydreaming Jerry is almost hit by a car, but is saved by Jeannie Steinman, played by Janeane Garofalo.

With the wedding fast approaching, George is desperate to have Susan call it off. He employs various plans, including smoking in her presence, knowing full well that she detests smoking. The cigarette makes him sick, though, and that effort fast flames out. He then demands a pre-nuptial agreement, believing that such a request will insult his bride-to-be, but it doesn't. She makes more money than he does, in fact, and laughs the whole thing off.

Finally, Susan is preparing to get out the wedding invitations and licking the various envelopes shut. A bad taste is immediately left in her mouth and, as she continues the licking process, she gets dizzier and dizzier until she passes out.

Last licks for Susan Biddle Ross (Heidi Swedberg) in "The Invitations."

NBC/Photofest

Finding her unconscious, George rushes her to the hospital. We also learn that Jerry has proposed marriage to Jeannie, who is a lot like him.

At the hospital, a doctor informs George that his fiancée is dead. The cause of her untimely passing, he says, is very likely the licking of toxic glue on the wedding envelopes. Only Kramer expresses a measure of sadness at Susan's death when he exclaims, "Poor Lily!" Jerry is more concerned that he proposed to Jeannie, part of the quasi-pact that he and George had established at the beginning of the season. With George internally ecstatic that he is off the wedding hook, the gang goes off for coffee and thus ends the seventh season.

Susan's sudden and unexpected death being treated so callously is what caused a wave of indignation in certain elements of the fan base. But for most *Seinfeld* aficionados, it was appreciated as pure *Seinfeld*, with its wickedly funny dearth of sympathy and sentiment.

Season Eight

The Post–Larry David Difference

With the departure of Larry David and his unique creative impulses, Jerry Seinfeld now reigned supreme over the show's direction. It is widely held that the last two seasons of *Seinfeld* took a noticeably different comedic path, veering toward the more absurd and off-kilter. This is the first season, too, without any Jerry Seinfeld standup segments during the show's openings or closings. The comedian noted that he didn't have the time to develop the material because of the additional workload he had assumed after Larry David's departure. The *Seinfeld* logo also looked a little different, with a black and white checkered background, because it was initially believed this season would be the show's last. With the sole exception of "The Comeback," Andy Ackerman directed the entire season's episodes.

Episode 129: "The Foundation" (original air date: September 19, 1996)

Alec Berg and Jeff Schaffer wrote season eight's initial volley, which picks up from where season seven left off. George, for one, is seen at the grave of Susan, his late fiancée. Her parents would like to keep their daughter's memory alive by creating a foundation in her honor and putting George on its board of directors. This notion doesn't exactly sit well with him.

Jerry, meanwhile, who had become engaged to Jeannie Steinman in "The Invitations," puts the kibosh on that and reunites with Dolores, a former girlfriend—whose name rhymes with a part of the female anatomy—from the episode "The Junior Mint." This relationship redux quickly dissolves when Dolores concludes that Jerry hasn't matured one iota, which she was counting on.

In Elaine's life and times, she receives a major career boost when her boss suffers a nervous breakdown, goes to Burma, and leaves her in charge of the J. Peterman Catalog. Her fashion idea of the "urban sombrero," though, does not go over well when it's placed on the catalog's front cover. Elaine discovers, too, that actions have consequences and that others were negatively impacted by her disastrous decision. Kramer, in another plot thread, becomes a martial-arts expert in a karate academy for kids. He is at first revered by the youths but, after seeing Elaine knock him for a loop, the very same kids, who once stood in awe of his prowess, rough him up.

To compound his miseries, George discovers that had he married Susan, he would have come into an awful lot of money. Now, however, he must watch in silence as the foundation auctions off all her property, including her vast collection of valuable dolls.

"The Foundation" pays homage to *Star Trek* on multiple occasions, with references to dialogue and characters in *Star Trek II: The Wrath of Khan* (1982) and *Star Trek III: The Search for Spock* (1984).

Episode 130: "The Soul Mate" (original air date: September 26, 1996)

Written by Peter Mehlman, this episode picks up where "The Foundation" left off and finds George greatly concerned that the lawyer for the Susan Ross Foundation believes he had something to do with Susan's untimely passing. To find out whether or not this is the case, George leaves his unattended briefcase in the boardroom with a running tape recorder inside of it. When he returns, the briefcase is damaged and the tape recorder is no longer working. While the paranoid George suspects foul play, it turns out that it was indeed an accident. Nevertheless, he *is* suspected of having murdered Susan.

Meanwhile, Kramer has fallen head over heels for Jerry's girlfriend, Pam, and has Newman clandestinely feed him some romantic verse in a riff on *Cyrano de Bergerac*. In Elaine's love life, she meets a man named Kevin, who shares her belief in not having children. He goes so far as to have a vasectomy to prove the extent of his love for her. When it's discovered that Pam, too, doesn't want to have children, Kramer and Jerry go for a vasectomy to show their fealty to the woman they both desire. Because of his fixation on Elaine, Newman also joins them. In the end, though, only Kramer goes through with the procedure, and Kevin has his vasectomy reversed.

Guest stars in this episode include Tim DeKay as Kevin, who would reprise his role in "The Bizarro Jerry." DeKay would later appear as Julia Louis-Dreyfus's boyfriend in three episodes of *The New Adventures of Old Christine*. Actress Kim Myers played Pam, the object of both Jerry's and Kramer's affections.

Episode 131: "The Bizarro Jerry" (original air date: October 3, 1996)

The title of this episode, which was written by David Mandel, is derivative of *Superman* of DC comics. In the comics, "Bizarro" is Superman's doppelgänger, whose actions reflect the polar opposite of what the Man of Steel would do and say.

Among the plot twists and turns in "The Bizarro Jerry" is Elaine's breakup with Kevin. They agree, however, to remain friends—just like Jerry and Elaine did after ending their romantic relationship. In many ways, Elaine sees Kevin as a more steadfast friend than Jerry. She begins hanging out with him and his two best buddies, Gene and Feldman. Gene and Feldman are the flip sides of George and Kramer. This arrangement works out well until she rubs Kevin, Gene, and Feldman the wrong way with her "make yourself at home" attitude and behaviors, such as raiding Kevin's refrigerator without asking permission and pushing him too hard with her patented and playful "Get out!"

Meanwhile, Jerry is dating the beautiful Gillian with her "man hands," and Kramer accidentally lands a non-paying job at a place called Brandt-Leland. His going to work every day and Elaine's new friends in the Bizarro world leave Jerry feeling lonely and frightened, worried that the old gang is splintering apart. Further, in trying to get back into the game in his post-Susan world, George uses a picture of the very attractive Gillian—she's extraordinarily eye-catching beyond the hands—to gain entry into Forbidden City, a club rife with attractive, available women.

In keeping with the Bizarro mood of the show, the *Seinfeld* theme music is played backwards. Kristin Bauer played the fine-looking-but-man-handed Gillian. The hands shown are not hers, of course; they belong to actor James Rekart. Kyle T. Heffner played Gene, the Bizarro George, and *MADtv*'s Pat Kilbane was Feldman, the Bizarro Kramer.

Episode 132: "The Little Kicks" (original air date: October 10, 1996)

Written by Spike Feresten, this episode finds Elaine and George attending the former's company party. Looking to meet someone, George attempts to make headway with Anna (played by Rebecca McFarland), but gets nowhere with her until Elaine tells her to stay away from him because he's a "bad seed." This prohibition supplies George with a "bad boy" image that makes him perversely attractive to her.

Meanwhile, Elaine takes to the dance floor and makes a fool of herself in front of her underlings at the J. Peterman Catalog. She erroneously speculates that the reason her staff has turned on her is because of George's attendance at the party, not her incontestable lack of dancing acumen.

On the Jerry and Kramer front, they are prepping to attend a sneak preview of the movie *Death Blow*. Kramer, however, invites a pal of his named Brody (played by Neil Giuntoli), who brings a video camera into the theater to make a bootleg copy of the film. When he gets sick during the showing—from consuming entirely too many snacks—he asks Jerry to finish the filming of the movie for him. Jerry declines but changes his mind in a hurry when Brody brandishes a gun. Subsequently, Jerry becomes the stuff of legend in the bootleg underworld for his filming expertise.

When, at long last, Elaine is convinced that she's a bad dancer—it took videotape evidence to prove it—she apologizes to Anna, saying that George is really a good guy. No longer appealing in Anna's eyes, George attempts to resurrect his old image by picking up where Jerry left off in filming movies for the bootleg market. The plan backfires when he gets arrested. The episode climaxes with Elaine and Frank Costanza about to come to blows.

Episode 133: "The Package" (original air date: October 17, 1996)

Newcomer Jennifer Crittenden wrote this teleplay. Prior to this *Seinfeld* effort, she touted five episodes of *The Simpsons* on her résumé. She would subsequently work as a writer and producer on such shows as *Everybody Loves Raymond*, *The Drew Carey Show* (1995–2004), and *The New Adventures of Old Christine*. She has also been nominated for five Emmy Awards.

"The Package" finds Elaine bedeviled by both a nagging rash and a past notation on her medical records labeling her a "difficult" patient. George, meanwhile, is convinced that Sheila (played by Heather Campbell), who works at the one-hour photo shop, has been lustily poring over his pictures. And Kramer's got a foolproof idea how Jerry can have his malfunctioning stereo—with its expired warranty—fixed free of charge.

One thing leads to another with George, now certain that Sheila slipped a sexy photo of herself into his pack of pictures. Kramer suggests that he reciprocate the gesture and volunteers to take photos of George in various seductive poses. On another front, Kramer's plan for Jerry's stereo repair involves mail fraud. This puts the latter on the hot seat with United States Postal Service employee Newman, his number-one nemesis. Finally, Elaine's medical dilemma—of having her rash treated and seeing what exactly is written on her medical records—has her enlisting the help of both Kramer and Uncle Leo. Their assistance, though, leads to naught and she remains on a medical service provider's blacklist.

Episode 134: "The Fatigues" (original air date: October 31, 1996)

Gregg Kavet and Andy Robin collaborated on this teleplay that finds Jerry with a new girlfriend, Abby, who has a mentor named Cynthia. While this mentor concept initially intrigues Jerry, he is taken aback when he learns that Abby's mentor is dating none other than Kenny Bania. Meanwhile, George is compelled to lecture on the topic of risk management, but finds that he cannot properly prepare for it because reading the requisite books is well-nigh impossible for someone like him who's been spoiled by books on tape. However, when he learns that the blind have access to any and all books on tape, he purposely fails an eye test.

On the Elaine job front at the J. Peterman Catalog, she contemplates firing an employee named Eddie Sherman (played by Ned Bellamy), who is just not working out, but fears doing so because of both his brusque manner and penchant for wearing military fatigues all the time. Promoting him not once but twice, Elaine angers others in the office who are more deserving of the promotions and finds herself—without any choice—working closely with the man she really wanted to fire.

In Kramer's world, he is organizing a Jewish singles night at Frank Costanza's Knights of Columbus lodge. He needs help, though, in the cooking department and enlists the assistance of Frank, who was a cook in the Korean War. The problem is, Frank hasn't picked up a spatula since then because of a traumatic incident: he had sickened his entire outfit by serving them overly spiced, less-than-prime beef. He finally relents, though, to Kramer's coaxing, cooks again, and sees that his food is a big hit, which makes him very happy indeed. However, when Eddie Sherman, who accompanies Elaine to the affair, shows up in his fatigues and begins choking on a piece of food, Frank suffers a harrowing flashback and begins turning over the buffet tables and importuning those in attendance not to take another bite.

Episode 135: "The Checks" (original air date: November 7, 1996)

The writing troika of Steve O'Donnell, Tom Gammill, and Max Pross was responsible for this multi-layered teleplay. The episode marks Steve O'Donnell's first *Seinfeld* credit. After *Seinfeld*, O'Donnell assumed the role as head writer of *Jimmy Kimmel Live!* when it debuted in 2003. Other writing credits on his résumé include *The Simpsons* and *Late Night with David Letterman*.

The myriad storylines of "The Checks" include Elaine encountering problems with her new boyfriend, Brett, who is fixated on furniture designed by a man named Karl Farbman and, too, the Eagles song "Desperado." In fact, whenever the song plays he insists on absolute silence in deference to it. Meanwhile, Jerry is receiving oodles of twelve-cent royalty checks from a past appearance on a Japanese television show, *The Super Terrific Happy Hour*, and acquires a serious case of writer's cramp from endorsing them. Furthermore, he spies a street umbrella salesman both peddling his wares and using his technique "the twirl" to drum up sales. When he mentions to the man that *he* was the originator of "the twirl," he is told in no uncertain terms that it was Teddy Padillac, an umbrella salesman whom Jerry worked alongside in his younger days before making it as a comedian, who introduced it. Padillac later refuses to sell Jerry, who is caught in the rain, an umbrella at the going rate—instead, he wants two hundred dollars for it—because he is peeved that he is trying to take credit for having invented "the twirl."

Kramer's world finds him hosting Japanese tourists and showing them the sights of New York. Courtesy of an exchange-rate misunderstanding, he spends almost all of their money on miscellaneous luxuries and they are compelled to stay as guests in his apartment, including sleeping in the dresser drawers of a Karl Farbman piece of furniture given to him by Brett. Kramer also warns George that the carpet cleaners he has hired to clean his apartment, and later the offices at Yankee Stadium, are members of a religious cult. Intrigued, George attempts to be recruited by them, but, instead, they take on his boss, Mr. Wilhelm, who assumes the name "Tania," which was the name that the kidnapped and brainwashed Patty Hearst took with the Symbionese Liberation Army in the 1970s. George also tries to sell his and Jerry's failed sitcom pilot to Japanese TV, but to no avail.

In a final bit of business, a Japanese guest of Kramer's gets stuck in a dresser drawer due to the humidity in the apartment generated by the hot tub. Still suffering from writer's cramp, Jerry comes to the rescue brandishing an axe and breaks the thing to pieces, which both frightens the Japanese guests and knocks out Brett, who had unsuccessfully tried to stop him from destroying a vaunted piece of Karl Farbman furniture.

James Patrick Stuart played Brett, who, in the show's coda, is seen on an operating table while his surgeon becomes preoccupied by the Eagles song "Witchy Woman." We are left to speculate on what ultimately happens to Brett when a nurse utters, "We're losing him."

Episode 136: "The Chicken Roaster" (original air date: November 14, 1996)

"The Chicken Roaster" is an Alec Berg and Jeff Schaffer collaboration that finds Kramer distracted by a large red neon chicken sign that is part of a new Kenny Rogers Roasters fast-food place that has opened across the street from both his and Jerry's apartment building. Unable to get a good night's sleep because of it, he convinces Jerry to switch apartments with him. Living in Kramer's old space, Jerry finds himself acting more like his old friend, and vice versa.

Established in his new digs, Kramer invites Newman over, who brings a box of Kenny Rogers Roasters chicken to celebrate the move. Despite the chicken joint being public enemy number one from his perspective, Kramer becomes absolutely addicted to its product.

Meanwhile, Elaine is in hot water for liberally using the J. Peterman Catalog expense account. She's got a lot of explaining to do, particularly regarding the purchase of an eight-thousand-dollar sable Russian hat for George. She travels to Burma to locate J. Peterman, but he won't approve the purchase until he sees the hat himself, which George doesn't have but knows is at his date Heather's house—because he purposely left it there. When Heather, played by Kymberly Kalil, denies that the hat is in her apartment, George naturally assumes that she is lying and swipes a clock of hers in retaliation. He later concludes that she is, in fact, telling the truth about the hat and is surprised, too, that she actually likes him and wants to date him again. Heather, though, promptly casts him aside upon discovering that he stole her clock.

In the end, the health department shuts down the Kenny Rogers Roasters restaurant, which distresses the now-addicted Kramer. What Jerry inadvertently left behind—feathers from a knockoff sable Russian hat—was the cause of the closure.

It was a genuine concern of the Kenny Rogers Roasters chain that this episode would make their restaurants look bad—being closed down by the health department and all. But in the end, Kenny Rogers himself gave the episode his blessing, reasoning that it was a heaping helping of free publicity to be an integral part of a *Seinfeld* episode at the height of the show's popularity.

Episode 137: "The Abstinence" (original air date: November 21, 1996)

Queens-born Steve Koren wrote this teleplay that finds George abstaining from sexual relations for six weeks due to his girlfriend's presumed mononucleosis. Elaine, meanwhile, has met a medical intern studying to get his doctor's license. To help him attain this goal, she likewise abstains from sex. While practicing abstinence, George's chaste path makes him a whole lot smarter—genius level in intelligence. He completes a Rubik's Cube in no time flat and can answer all the questions on *Jeopardy*. Elaine, on the other hand, gets measurably dumber. To get back her mojo, she even asks Jerry to have sex with her, which he declines after giving the notion some thought.

George gives Yankee stars Bernie Williams (second from left) and Derek Jeter (right) some batting tips in "The Abstinence."   *NBC/Photofest*

Kramer's dilemma of not being allowed to smoke cigars in Monk's Café is solved when he converts his apartment into a smoking lounge for himself and like-minded souls. However, the excessive smoke in such close quarters turns his face gruesomely leathery and his teeth yellow. With the help of attorney Jackie Chiles, Kramer sues the tobacco interests for his travails. However, he backtracks and permits the tobacco powers-that-be to use his distinct visage on a Times Square billboard as a veritable Marlboro Man.

While exhibiting real smarts, George offers Yankee players Derek Jeter and Bernie Williams batting advice and hits balls several hundred feet, too. (The Yankee stars appear as themselves.) Jerry also takes advantage of George's newfound intelligence by asking him to help with an assembly presentation at their former grade school, Edward R. Murrow Junior High. However, when George arrives at the school no longer behaving super-intelligently, Jerry correctly surmises that he has had sex, which he had with a Portuguese waitress from Monk's Café. Without George's help, Jerry's act bombs at the assembly. A scheduled appearance on *Late Night with David Letterman* is canceled because of it. Letterman makes a cameo to deliver the bad news. Debra Jo Rupp reprises her role as Katie, Jerry's flighty agent.

Episode 138: "The Andrea Doria" (original air date: December 19, 1996)

Spike Feresten wrote this episode, wherein George is overly excited about the new apartment he is slated to move into; Elaine is prepping for a blind date; and Jerry and Kramer uncover a backlog of mail in the former's storage space.

George's dream apartment, however, runs into a snag when the tenant association opts to give it to Clarence, a survivor of the SS *Andrea Doria*. Elaine's blind date, Alan (played by Tom Gallop), causes her a few problems, too, when she concludes that he is a "bad breaker-upper." When, in fact, she breaks up with him, he calls her "Big Head." And Jerry discovers that, rather than delivering his route's mail, Newman has been storing it in his space. Why? Because he didn't get his dream job—a transfer to Hawaii. Seeing that it is in both of their interests, Jerry agrees to help Newman deliver the backlog of mail when the Hawaii position becomes available again. He desperately wants Newman to get the new job and leave both the building and his life for all time.

Meanwhile, Kramer gets involved with Smuckers, a dog who suffers from a nagging cough very much like his own. He takes the canine to a veterinarian and receives antibiotics, which he takes himself. This action causes Kramer to develop dog-like characteristics, including biting Newman on the ankle. Not one to give up without a fight, George requests a hearing with the tenant association regarding the apartment. While recounting his life story and countless hardships—everything from the "shrinkage" moment to Susan's untimely death from licking wedding invitation envelopes that he picked out—George appears to be winning the day. However, the apartment goes to Alan, Elaine's blind date, because, it turns out, he bribed the building's super. Confronting Alan about the unseemly affair, George is called "chinless."

Episode 139: "The Little Jerry" (original air date: January 9, 1997)

Written by Jennifer Crittenden, this episode received its moniker based on a real-life chicken named "Little Jerry Seinfeld." New York Mets pitcher Tim Byrdak purchased the bird in Chinatown in response to his teammate Frank Francisco calling the cross-town rival New York Yankees a "bunch of chickens." Byrdak pretended Little Jerry Seinfeld was a *gift* from the Yankees.

The episode's multiple storylines commence with Kramer alerting Jerry that a local bodega run by Marcelino (played by Miguel Sandoval) has a bounced check written by him prominently displayed. Meanwhile, George is all excited that the Susan Ross Foundation has contributed a not inconsiderable sum of money to a women's prison, which he plans to visit. In Elaine's world, she's got a new boyfriend, Kurt, who regularly shaves his head. Later, she is dismayed to learn that he is going bald as well.

In trying to make some headway with Marcelino regarding the bounced check, Jerry gets nowhere despite giving the man full restitution. At the prison, George takes a shine to Celia, the prison's librarian, and asks her out on a date, so to speak. He is fixated on the notion of "conjugal visit" sex. Cagey as always, Kramer purchases what he believes is a hen that he names "Little Jerry." He anticipates Little Jerry supplying him with all his future egg needs. Little Jerry doesn't deliver, though, when Kramer discovers that he's got a rooster on his hands. Marcelino, however, has got his eyes on Little Jerry for cockfighting and agrees to take Jerry's bounced check down in exchange for Kramer's rooster.

Back at the prison, George learns that Celia is up for parole, but he does everything in his power to stop it because he prefers a relationship with Celia the prisoner, not Celia on the outside. She is, in fact, denied parole, but then escapes. George is now turned on by the idea of "fugitive sex." Celia is ultimately recaptured and Kurt, having been mistaken for George, is arrested and sentenced to ten to fourteen months in prison for his role in the prison break. Having previously received an engagement ring from him, Elaine opts to end her relationship with the imprisoned Kurt.

Andrea Bendewald played Celia. She is best known for her role as Maddy Piper in the television series *Suddenly Susan* (1996–2000), which starred Brooke Shields.

Episode 140: "The Money" (original air date: January 16, 1997)

Peter Mehlman returned as the writer of this teleplay that, in true Seinfeldian fashion, harks back to past stories. For starters, Morty and Helen Seinfeld sell the Cadillac that Jerry bought for them to Jack Klompus for six thousand dollars. They do this to help out their son, who they believe is financially strapped. Jerry is naturally upset by this transaction—the vehicle is worth a lot more—and intends on buying it back from the slippery Klompus. He flies to Florida and—when all is said and done—ends up paying Jack (who initially asked for twenty-two thousand dollars) fourteen thousand dollars to get it back. Klompus, though, drives the car into a swamp before turning it over to Jerry, who must assume the entire tab on the damages.

Meanwhile, Morty and Helen discuss possible new career ventures for their son, including working at Bloomingdale's. Morty, too, convinces a very reluctant Elaine to give him a job at J. Peterman Catalog. This comes on the heels of J. Peterman himself returning from Burma, which knocks Elaine off her pedestal as the catalog's impresario. She is back at her old job and old salary, and not too happy about it.

A further plot thread involves Kramer and his girlfriend, Emily, played by Sarah Silverman. He complains about her "jimmy legs" in bed. In George's world, he is seriously speculating on his parents' net worth—since he's never actually seen them spend any money—and a potential future inheritance. Questions proffered by George to Frank and Estelle Costanza about their health history, however, convince them that they don't have too much time left. They begin spending their money, including making a big move to Florida. These actions run counter to George's hopes of being the sole beneficiary of a considerable inheritance. After the Costanzas' relocation, Kramer—because of fears of a neighborhood prowler—moves into the Costanza house in Queens.

The Costanzas ultimately move back to Queens, though, after Frank spies what he presumes is a homeless man living in a car. But, unbeknown to him, it was Jerry sleeping in the Cadillac. Because Jack Klompus wouldn't let him stay at his place, Jerry, suffering from a temporary cash and credit crunch, had little choice but to temporarily call home the car that he would soon be returning to his parents.

Episode 141: "The Comeback" (original air date: January 30, 1997)

"The Comeback" marks the only episode not directed by Andy Ackerman in season eight. David Owen Trainor assumed the reins in this teleplay, written by Gregg Kavet and Andy Robin.

George's storyline revolves around him not having a worthy comeback line for a co-worker of his who, upon seeing him feasting on shrimp cocktail at a meeting, said: "Hey, George, the ocean called; they're running out of shrimp." He thereafter makes it his life mission to utter this comeback, which he thought of a wee bit too late: "The Jerk store called and they're running out of you."

Meanwhile, Elaine is in the video store and checking out employee "Vincent's picks"—recommended movies that are just up her alley. She becomes fascinated with the mysterious Vincent, whom she has never met, and—after speaking with him on the telephone—envisions dating him. Elaine ultimately agrees to meet Vincent at his apartment, where she discovers that he is a fifteen-year-old boy.

After watching the beginning of a movie called *The Other Side of Darkness*, Kramer has a living will drawn up with the assistance of an attorney named Shellbach, played by Ben Stein. However, the movie's climax reveals a woman coming out of a coma, which prompts Kramer to reverse course concerning his living will, where Elaine could have made the decision whether or not to pull the plug on him.

Having purchased an expensive tennis racket, Jerry is in a pickle, too, after taking pro-shop employee Milos's advice. As things turn out, Milos, played by Mark Harelik, is a pathetically awful tennis player. One thing leads to another, with Milos asking Jerry to take a dive for him in a tennis match to save his marriage.

Joel Polis played Reilly, George's co-worker and nemesis with the acid tongue. Danny Strong played Vincent in an ultra-brief appearance. Strong made a name for himself years later as Jonathan Levinson on *Buffy the Vampire Slayer* (1997–2003). The voice of Vincent in this episode, however, belongs not to Strong but to actor Robby Benson, whose track record of voice work includes Disney's *Beauty and the Beast* (1991).

Episode 142: "The Van Buren Boys" (original air date: February 6, 1997)

Darin Henry wrote this episode featuring a fictional New York City street gang known as the "Van Buren Boys," who took its name from the persnickety Martin Van Buren, the eighth president of the United States, and the first to hail from the state of New York. It is Kramer who initially encounters the gang and gets out of potential trouble by inadvertently flashing their secret sign, the number eight. George, meanwhile, is considering candidates for the first-ever scholarship offered by the Susan Ross Foundation. He is not impressed with what he perceives as the various candidates' cocksure attitudes and braggadocio until Steven Koren, played by Jed Rhein, comes along. Steve reminds George of himself as a younger man. The choice of the moniker Steven Koren is an homage to the *Seinfeld* writer of the same name.

In Jerry's world, he is dating Ellen (played by Christine Taylor), who seems almost perfect—too perfect, in fact—and he worries that there might be something wrong with her. On the job front, Elaine has been given the honor of ghostwriting J. Peterman's autobiography. She's not too pleased, though, when he purchases stories from Kramer's life and times to include as his own. Elaine is thus compelled to interview Kramer ad nauseam.

After championing Steven Koren for the scholarship, George rescinds his support because of the audacity of the young man wanting to be a city planner and not just an architect, which is George's dream occupation. It riles him that an idler with a 2.0 grade point average would set his sights so high. Subsequently, Steven joins the Van Buren Boys, who apply pressure on George to give him back the scholarship.

In the relationship game, Jerry sees the light vis-à-vis Ellen after his parents come to town and take a real shine to her. From his perspective, this is the kiss of death and proof positive that Ellen is *anything* but perfect.

Episode 143: "The Susie" (original air date: February 13, 1997)

David Mandel wrote this episode that finds Kramer admitting to a serious gambling problem. For some time he has been betting through Jerry with an old friend and a fledgling bookie named Mike, the same man who labeled Jerry a "phony" in season three's "The Parking Space." Meanwhile, a co-worker, Peggy, is calling Elaine "Susie" for some inexplicable reason, and George is on tenterhooks while prepping for a big pinstriped ball being thrown by George Steinbrenner at Tavern on the Green. He anticipates sauntering into the event arm in arm with his very attractive girlfriend, Allison (played by Shannon Kenny), and wowing his co-workers in the process.

However, George gets wind that Allison is intent on breaking up with him, so he endeavors to avoid her altogether, reasoning that she can't officially end their relationship if he doesn't see her. In his clever dodging game, George utilizes his anwering machine to screen her calls. His unique message is an amusing parody of the song "Believe It or Not," the theme song of the 1981–1983 TV show *The Greatest American Hero*: "Believe it or not, George isn't at home." Via Jerry, Kramer comes up a considerable betting winner. When Mike can't deliver Jerry's winnings, the former fears that the latter is out to do him physical harm. The "Susie" impasse reaches a new level when Peggy, believing that she is speaking to Susie, trashes Elaine. A row ensues that J. Peterman intends on patching up.

Tired of playing along as Susie, Elaine determines that the only way out is by eliminating Susie altogether. She informs Peterman that Susie has committed suicide. A memorial service is held, and he creates a foundation—in the tradition of the Susan Ross Foundation—in her name, which he expects Elaine to oversee. George, in the end, does not go to the ball with Allison, who employed Kramer as the go-between to break up with him. Kramer attends the ball in her place.

Megan Cole played Peggy, Elaine's co-worker. The entire episode was a riff on "The Invitations" and the mini-controversy it spawned. In "The Susie," Mike accuses Jerry of murdering Susie.

Episode 144: "The Pothole" (original air date: February 20, 1997)

This Steve O'Donnell and Dan O'Keefe collaboration sees Jerry unintentionally knock the toothbrush belonging to his girlfriend, Jenna, into the toilet bowl. And before he can get around to tell her about the little mishap, she uses it. The unsettling image haunts Jerry as he devises various ways to sterilize her mouth.

Meanwhile, George has received a special key ring from George Steinbrenner that honors Phil Rizzuto's induction into the Hall of Fame by the veterans committee. He loses both the key ring and his keys, which end up buried in a newly filled pothole. In Kramer's world, he has adopted a stretch of highway and takes it upon himself to see that the road is properly maintained. Elaine's storyline finds her hankering for a Chinese takeout special, the "Supreme Flounder," but—alas—she's just outside the restaurant's delivery range. Her solution to the dilemma has her masquerading as the janitor in the building across the street.

Eventually, Jenna discovers Jerry's "toothbrush in the toilet bowl" secret. To get back at him, she informs Jerry that she has evened the score by marinating something of his in the toilet, but doesn't tell him what it is. This revelation inspires him to throw out virtually everything in his apartment that could fit into the toilet. On Kramer's Adopt-a-Highway front, things go from bad to worse, with Newman's mail truck, courtesy of Kramer's negligence, catching fire. Newman is heard exclaiming, "Oh, the humanity!" as he observes the conflagration. This line spoofs radio reporter Herbert Morrison's emotional live account of the *Hindenburg* passenger zeppelin going up in flames as it crashed to the ground at the Lakehurst Naval Air Station on May 6, 1937.

Kristin Davis, who is perhaps best known for starring in HBO's *Sex in the City* (1998–2004) as Charlotte York Goldenblatt, played Jerry's girlfriend Jenna. Interestingly, she also starred as Brooke Armstrong in *Melrose Place* (1992–1999), which Jerry had so vehemently denied watching in "The Beard."

Episode 145: "The English Patient" (original air date: March 13, 1997)

Written by Steve Koren, "The English Patient" pokes fun at the Academy Award–winning movie that was praised by some as the perfect film and mocked by others as a colossal bore. The episode's storylines and twists parallel those in *The English Patient.*

Foremost, George is mistaken as the boyfriend of a very attractive woman named Danielle (played by Chelsea Noble), who tells him that he bears quite a resemblance to her Neil. In fact, George is taller and in better shape. Thus, it becomes George's mission—come hell or high water—to meet Neil. Meanwhile, Elaine is at the movies with her date, Blaine, and pines to see a comedy called *Sack Lunch*, starring Dabney Coleman. He, though, wants to see *The English*

Patient, for which he purchases tickets. When Elaine expresses her disdain for the film after viewing it, Blaine thinks there's something wrong with her and their relationship ends because of it. Later, at the office, Elaine pretends that she never saw the film so as not to say anything that would upset J. Peterman, who absolutely loved it. He, though, promptly takes her to the theater to see the movie, but she cannot hold back her contempt this time and makes a big scene. Peterman fires her on the spot, but gives her a second chance if she agrees to go to Tunisia, where *The English Patient* was filmed, and live for a spell in a cave.

Meanwhile, Jerry is visiting his parents in Florida to give them a hand in moving out of their old condo. While down there, he meets the ultra-competitive senior citizen Izzy Mandelbaum, who challenges him to a weightlifting contest. Mandelbaum hurts his back in the process. Jerry has also been entrusted to bring back some "Cubans" for Kramer. They turn out not to be cigars but real people. Kramer's got the grand idea of making Cuban cigars. The Cubans, though, are Dominicans, and things don't go quite as planned.

At long last, George gets the opportunity to meet Neil, who is in the hospital with bandages on his face caused by burns—Kramer's Cubans were actually responsible. He sees the opportunity now to win over Danielle—with no strings attached—and hopes to move in with her. She, though, is sticking with Neil and plans on traveling with him to England and a clinic that can help him with his medical woes. "I win," a prostrate Neil says to George on his way out of the hospital room. Always a sore loser, George pulls out his IV tubes before exiting. Finally, Kramer's Dominicans hijack Elaine's Tunisian flight to Cuba. What most upsets her is not the hijacking, per se, but that they have the flight's movie, *Sack Lunch*, turned off.

Veteran actor Lloyd Bridges played Izzy Mandelbaum and reprised the role in the episode "The Blood." He died a year later, in 1998, at the age of eighty-five.

Episode 146: "The Nap" (original air date: April 10, 1997)

The writing pair of Gregg Kavet and Andy Robin returned for this episode that finds George napping at work under his desk, which he had custom made for the purpose, and Kramer taking to the East River for his swims because health club pools really cramp his style. On the relationship front, Elaine receives a mattress from her boyfriend, Hal Kitzmiller, a gesture that she initially takes the wrong way. Because he suffers from chronic back problems, he requires a specially designed mattress. Hal, played by Vince Grant, merely wanted to help Elaine ward off similar back troubles with a mattress just right for her size and weight. Unfortunately, she had given the mattress to Kramer before discovering the truth. When he returns it to her, it reeks of the East River.

Meanwhile, Jerry has hired a contractor named Conrad (played by Stephen Lee, who passed away in 2014) to put in new kitchen cabinets for him, but is finding the experience agonizingly slow and less than satisfying. Ultimately,

Conrad does a total makeover of the kitchen space, which one and all dislike. Jerry then asks him to return the kitchen to its former state.

Looking for George, "The Boss," George Steinbrenner, decides to wait around in the former's office for him. Unfortunately, George is napping under his desk. Ultimately, he has Jerry call in a bomb threat to get Steinbrenner out of his office. However, this plan doesn't pay long-term dividends for George when the bomb squad smashes his special desk to pieces courtesy of a ticking sound inside it—his alarm clock.

Episode 147: "The Yada Yada" (original air date: April 24, 1997)

Peter Mehlman and Jill Franklyn collaborated on the writing of this episode that finds Dr. Tim Whatley converting to Judaism and promptly telling Jewish jokes, which doesn't sit well with Jerry, who is offended, not so much as a Jew but as a comedian.

On the dating frontier, George is seeing Marcy (played by Suzanne Cryer), a woman who has the habit of shortening her sentences with the tag "yada, yada, yada," which leaves an awful lot unsaid. Kramer and Mickey Abbott double date but have difficulties figuring out which of the two women—Karen or Julie—is right for them. Mickey ultimately commits to and marries Karen but, as things turn out, she really loved Kramer. It was Julie who loved Mickey.

In Elaine's world, her friends Beth and Arnie ask her to serve as a character reference as they attempt to adopt a child. In her inimitable style, though, she blows their chances when she tells the adoption agent an anecdote about Arnie's explosive temper. Not only does the couple's adoption fall through, but Beth and Arnie split up, with the former accompanying Jerry to Mickey's wedding. Jerry discovers, too, that he is perceived as an "anti-Dentite." He is treated hostilely by the dental set, which includes Mickey's father, a dentist, played by Robert Wagner. Actress Jill St. John (Robert Wagner's longtime partner in real life), portrayed little Mickey's mother.

"The Yada Yada" has the distinction of not only disseminating a popular catchphrase—even though it's not a *Seinfeld* original—but also running longer than the usual thirty-minute allotment on the primetime schedule. NBC specifically promoted the episode as running long.

Episode 148: "The Millennium" (original air date: May 1, 1997)

Jennifer Crittenden wrote this episode with its reference to the impending new millennium. The storylines include Kramer and Newman planning competing parties to ring in the year 2000. Newman has dubbed his party the "Newmannium" and has already booked singer-songwriter Christopher Cross of "Sailing" and "Arthur's Theme" renown. Ultimately, Kramer and Newman agree to host one party.

Speed-dial ranking wars with Lauren Graham as Valerie in "The Millennium."   *NBC/Photofest*

Meanwhile, George has a chance to get a more prestigious, better-paying job as head scout of the cross-town rival New York Mets. The only caveat to accepting this new position is that he must get fired from his job with the New York Yankees. However, his efforts fail spectacularly, including quasi-streaking through the ballpark during a game. When, at last, he seems to have succeeded—by trashing a World Series trophy and members of the organization, too—Mr. Wilhelm intercedes, claiming that George was merely acting on his orders. He is the one who gets fired and the better job with the Mets.

Elaine's got problems of her own with a clothing store called Putumayo, which she intends on putting out of business—à la the Soup Nazi—because of its horrible customer service. She enlists Kramer's help in doing so, but he proves hopelessly inept and inadvertently drops a desiccant package into a bowl of salsa in the shop, which customers partake of, including Jerry's girlfriend Valerie's stepmother, who gets poisoned.

A plot twist finds Jerry, in fact, doing battle with the stepmother as to who merits a higher position on Valerie's speed dial. A classic popular-culture moment is referenced when Jerry and the stepmother meet in an automobile, reminiscent of Mrs. Robinson and Benjamin Braddock in *The Graduate* (1967). Lauren Graham played Valerie; Louan Gideon played her stepmother, Mrs. Hamilton. Graham is best known for her role as Lorelai Gilmore on *Gilmore Girls* (2000–2007).

Episode 149: "The Muffin Tops" (original air date: May 8, 1997)

David Sims of *The A.V. Club* dubbed this episode written by Spike Feresten "spoof heavy." He noted how "The Muffin Tops" was so "chockablock with references that the plot gets a little lost."

Indeed, there are many plot twists and turns here, with George entrusted to watch a tourist's suitcase for a short spell that turns into a long one. So long, in fact, that George begins wearing clothes from the suitcase and is mistaken for a tourist himself. George tells a woman, Mary Anne, that he is from Little Rock, Arkansas, and employed as a hen supervisor with the Tyler Chicken Company. When he adds that he's considering moving to New York, she says he'll be "eaten alive" in the Big Apple. These words compel George to prove otherwise and they visit the office of his *new* job at Yankee Stadium and *new* apartment. George Steinbrenner gets wind of his employee's other "job" with Tyler Chicken, prompting him to call them. Steinbrenner just doesn't want to share George with anybody. Mr. Tyler offers Steinbrenner a complete overhaul of the Yankees concessions in exchange for George Costanza. This would entail chicken dogs instead of hot dogs, chicken twists in lieu of pretzels, and alcoholic chicken replacing beer.

Meanwhile, when Elaine casually mentions to her former boss at Pendant Publishing, Mr. Lippman, that she believes a shop that sold just muffin tops would be a winner, he opens up a place called Top of the Muffin to You! Disposing of the rest of the muffins—the stumps—becomes a weighty problem. When Kramer gets wind from Elaine that J. Peterman's just-published autobiography contains Kramer-supplied life stories after all, even though their deal in "The Van Buren Boys" had fallen through, he interferes with a Peterman book signing and then inaugurates The Peterman Reality Tour in a yellow school bus. This reality tour was a play on Kenny Kramer's Reality Tour, which he was conducting through the streets of New York at the time. (In fact, the three-hour tour is going strong all these years later. It commences from the Producer's Club Theater at 358 West 44th Street between Eighth and Ninth Avenues.) Peterman's autobiography is entitled *No Placket Required*, a riff on the name of the 1985 best-selling Phil Collins album *No Jacket Required*.

Jerry's problem in "The Muffin Tops" is his chest hair, which he inadvertently shaved off, leaving him with serious itching problems. He ultimately howls like the wolf man upon the moon's rise.

Episode 150: "The Summer of George" (original air date: May 15, 1997)

Alec Berg and Jeff Schaffer had the honor of penning season eight's final episode, which finds George out of his Yankees job and collecting a severance package that he calculates will see him through the summertime. His initial plans to lead a very active summer, though, quickly degenerate into sheer indolence.

Kramer takes home a Tony Award and takes it to Sardi's restaurant, too, in "The Summer of George." It's fire Raquel Welch or relinquish the Tony.

Photo by Thomas Nigro

Meanwhile, Jerry is going to the Tony Awards with his perky date, Lanette, played by Amanda Peet. He is an invited guest while Kramer is in attendance, too, in the role of seat filler. At the awards, circumstances see Kramer hurried to the stage, where he mistakenly receives a Tony Award for the musical *Scarsdale Surprise*, which stars the voluptuous Raquel Welch. Later, at Sardi's restaurant, producers—who know Kramer is not a legitimate winner of the award—ask him to fire Welch because she doesn't move her arms when she dances; only then can he keep his prized Tony. The idle-arms problem is one that Elaine's co-worker Sam, played by Molly Shannon, shares. When, in fact, Elaine informs Sam that she walks like a caveman, she goes ballistic, destroys Elaine's office, and leaves a series of hostile messages on her answering machine. Kramer has as little luck as Elaine in this regard. When he fires Raquel Welch, she physically attacks him and destroys his Tony Award. Elaine gets attacked by Welch as well, who thinks she's being made fun of when she spies her speaking with police and mimicking Sam's walk. The cops and the other men in Elaine's world are not especially interested in solving her problem, but more intrigued by a good catfight.

George's active summer, which has been anything but, comes to an end when he trips over party invitations, of all things—the irony of ironies—and falls down a flight of stairs. He had gotten them for Jerry in his role as his friend's dating assistant. Lanette's active lifestyle—she lived with a "dude"—was tiring Jerry out, so George agreed to pitch in. His accident lands him in the very hospital where Susan Ross passed away. The same doctor, in fact, who broke the news that Susan had died, advises Jerry, Elaine, and Kramer this time that George might never walk again due to the sorry shape of his body after such a languid summer. The gang of three takes the news as nonchalantly as they received the news of Susan's untimely passing.

The final scene of the season finds George receiving physical therapy and learning to walk again. Sam, too, is there and learning to swing her arms.

27

Season Nine

Going Out on Top

Seemingly, the *Seinfeld* years flew by. Like no other show on the air, it defined the 1990s: it was emblematic of the entire decade. And in its final year on the air, *Seinfeld*, very fittingly, was number one in the ratings. Despite some critics claiming that the last couple of years of the show were not vintage *Seinfeld*, viewers obviously thought otherwise. Andy Ackerman was once again in the director's chair for the entire season.

Going out a winner.

Episode 151: "The Butter Shave" (original air date: September 25, 1997)

The triumvirate of Alec Berg, Jeff Schaffer, and David Mandel penned the teleplay that inaugurated the last season of *Seinfeld*. The episode is dedicated to NBC executive Brandon Tartikoff, who had passed away a month earlier, on August 27, from Hodgkin's lymphoma, the insidious form of cancer that he had battled for years.

"The Butter Shave" sets the tone for the remainder of the season, with Jerry believing that he and George's sitcom idea might not be dead and buried after all. Appearing on an *NBC Showcase*, Jerry is endeavoring to catch the eyes and ears of executives. He is unhappy, though, that the annoyingly bad comic Kenny Bania has been riding his coattails and would again be appearing after him in the showcase lineup.

Meanwhile, George is still not completely up to snuff after "The Summer of George" and is getting around with a cane. He does, though, land a job at Play Now, a playground-equipment company, and is elated that he is presumed handicapped and can use the handicapped bathroom.

In Kramer's world, he's discovered that shaving with butter works for him. He likes the feel so much that he spreads it all over his body as a skin beautifier. However, the heavily buttered Kramer leads to Newman imagining cannibalistic acts—with his friend as the main course. Elaine is returning from a European vacation with her boyfriend, David Puddy, but breaks up with him on the plane, then gets back together while still airborne. They break up after that.

Courtesy of Kenny Bania taking the stage directly after him, Jerry purposely sabotages his own act to torpedo Bania, who he feels always basks in his glow. His plan backfires big time when Bania gets offered a sitcom, the result of Kramer and Newman inadvertently disrupting his act. Attending the event, Kramer accidentally spills Parmesan cheese and oregano on his already-buttered body, which is more than Newman can bear. He attacks Kramer and the pair interrupt Bania's performance. Assuming that the antics were all scripted, NBC executives leap at the opportunity to sign up Jerry's comedic nemesis. And things go no better for George, who is seen by his boss at Play Now behaving—most definitely—like a non-handicapped person.

Kristin Davis appears again as Jenna in this episode, only this time she is Kenny Bania's girlfriend.

Episode 152: "The Voice" (original air date: October 2, 1997)

In a repeat performance, Alec Berg, Jeff Schaffer, and David Mandel are back as the writing trio for episode two, which finds Play Now, George's employer, attempting to get rid of him because of his deception in masquerading as a handicapped person. He won't leave voluntarily, though, and his contract explicitly states that if he shows up for work, he gets paid. Mr. Thomassoulo, George's boss at Play Now, nonetheless plays hardball to make his showing up for work extremely difficult. The always-dexterous George, however, manages to cling to his job despite all the slings and arrows.

Jerry's love du jour in "The Voice" is Claire, played by Sara Rose Peterson. He tells George about imagining a voice—the sounds of the stomach—emanating from Claire's belly button at night. While George appreciates "the voice," Claire doesn't and breaks up with him because of it. Elaine's on-again, off-again romance with David Puddy continues unabated, with Jerry betting her that she will be on-again very soon, which, of course, she is.

Meanwhile, Kramer intends on seeing through one of his grandest inventions and enlists the help of an intern at New York University. Kramerica Industries will develop the oil tank bladder and put an end to toxic oil spills once and for all. But it doesn't quite work out as planned, with NYU pulling the plug on Kramer's intern, Darren, when the school realizes that Kramerica consists of one man in a messy apartment. Darren is, nonetheless, undeterred and desires to help Kramer make the oil tank bladder a reality. When the invention is at long last tested—from George's office at Play Now—a considerable rubber ball loaded with oil is dropped from the window. Unfortunately, it lands on Claire, who had agreed to give Jerry a second chance if he'd jettison "the voice." Claire sues Play Now and puts the company out of business. George, too, is out of a job. The wily Kramer manages to shift the blame of the fiasco on to Darren, who is sentenced to prison "for a long, long time."

Veteran character actor Gordon Jump played Mr. Thomassoulo, George's boss. He is best known for his role as Arthur "Big Guy" Carlson in *WKRP in Cincinnati*, a popular CBS sitcom that ran from 1978 to 1982. He reprised the role a decade later in the short-lived *The New WKRP in Cincinnati*. Jump died in 2003 at the age of seventy-one. Actor and comedian Jarrad Paul portrayed Darren, Kramer's idealistic intern.

Episode 153: "The Serenity Now" (original air date: October 9, 1997)

Steve Koren penned this teleplay in which Frank Costanza, in one of its storylines, utters the self-help phrase "Serenity now!" whenever he gets very angry, which is quite often. Koren recalled a real-life incident wherein his parents were engaged in an argument and his father cried out, "Serenity now!" He thought it odd—this wrath-control exercise—and very memorable, too. Hence, this episode.

Other plot twists in "The Serenity Now" find Frank Costanza inaugurating a business: the peddling of personal computers out of his garage. He employs the anything-but-dynamic duo of his son, George, and Lloyd Braun as salesmen. In Kramer's unique sliver of the world, he's in the process of converting his apartment into a cozy house in Small Town, USA, replete with a screen door and front porch festooned with potted plants, wind chimes, and Old Glory hanging in the hallway. And Jerry undergoes something of a personality metamorphosis after his girlfriend, Patty, gives away his New York Knicks tickets and enlightens him to the fact that he never—on the surface at least—gets "real mad." Delving into his unexpressed anger enables Jerry to get in touch with a mother lode of deep-seated feelings. He even proposes to a stunned Elaine.

Meanwhile, Elaine experiences a further dilemma at Mr. Lippman's son's bar mitzvah when the boy, played by Ross Malinger, gives her an unexpected French kiss. Other Lippman men express great interest in her, too, which George attributes to Elaine's "Shiks-appeal." A visit to Rabbi Glickman on this bedeviling subject matter proves unhelpful when he, too, makes a play for her. After giving it serious thought, Elaine accepts Jerry's marriage proposal. However, it turns out that Jerry's newfound "emotional" personality was a short-lived phenomenon and the proposal is null and void.

In other episode wrap-ups, Kramer undergoes a nervous breakdown and irreparably damages George's computer-sales career. And it seems that Lloyd Braun's salesmanship never took flight: he hadn't even bothered to plug in his telephone. Lloyd cites his mental health as the stumbling block and Frank Costanza's oft-repeated "Serenity now!" phrase, which he described as "Serenity now, insanity later."

Busy character actress Lori Loughlin played Jerry's girfriend Patty in this episode. Her myriad television credits include a regular role on the sitcom *Full House* (1988–1995). She played Becky Donaldson, who became Becky Katsopolis, after marrying Jesse Katsopolis, played by John Stamos. Reprising their characters were Richard Fancy as Mr. Lippman, and Matt McCoy as Lloyd Braun.

Episode 154: "The Blood" (original air date: October 16, 1997)

Returning as Izzy Mandelbaum in this episode written by Dan O'Keefe, Lloyd Bridges makes his final television appearance. We find Jerry's concerned parents hooking up their son with a personal trainer, Mandelbaum, to assist him in regular workouts and getting in better shape. After smelling his girlfriend's vanilla-scented incense during lovemaking, George decides that he needs to incorporate food into his sex life. However, it gets out of hand when he attempts to kiss his lover while simultaneously devouring a pastrami sandwich. Jerry attempts to educate him that "sex is about love between a man and a woman, not a man and a sandwich."

Meanwhile, Kramer, who had been storing blood at the blood bank, takes matters into his own hands—storing the blood in his apartment—after a cost-prohibitive rate increase. Elaine's quandary is not about blood storage but responsibility. That is, she takes great offense when her friend Vivian, played by Kellie Waymire, suggests that she isn't a suitable babysitter for Jimmy, her son. Worse still, Vivian thinks Kramer is qualified for the job. When Elaine forces

Kramer to relinquish his sitting duties to her, she comes to regret it when she sees what a bratty kid Jimmy is.

Later, Jerry suffers a freak injury and receives some of Kramer's blood in a needed transfusion. Jerry is not particularly happy to learn that his friend's blood is now coursing through his veins. Worse things are on the horizon, though, when his last workout under the supervision of Izzy Mandelbaum augurs another transfusion. This go-round he doesn't receive his "blood brother" Kramer's blood, but Newman's instead.

Episode 155: "The Junk Mail" (original air date: October 30, 1997)

Spike Feresten wrote this teleplay that finds Jerry on the receiving end of a thank-you gift from a childhood friend, "Fragile" Frankie Merman, who operates a car dealership. While Jerry anticipated a more practical vehicle for helping Merman out with a show on behalf of his business, he takes ownership of a conversion van.

Meanwhile, George learns that his parents are, in effect, "cutting him loose," when they give him short shrift in their weekly telephone call and his visits to their home. With Pottery Barn sending him a surfeit of their catalogs in the mail, Kramer's got problems of his own. Getting nowhere with them vis-à-vis the catalogs, he wages war with the big kahuna, the United States Postal Service, by first bricking up his mailbox and then canceling his mail altogether. Commandeered by the postmaster general, played by Wilford Brimley, Kramer is set straight in the matter of the post office. In Elaine's love life she's back with David Puddy, but has her eyes focused on a man named Jack, whose résumé includes playing "The Wiz," the eponymously named mascot for the electronics chain. (The chain is no more.)

As the storylines unfurl, Jerry clearly has no use for the van, but he does not want to hurt Frankie's feelings by getting rid of it. Kramer agrees to help him sell it via a unique classified advertisement. George continues to take his parents' abandonment decision hard and begins dating his cousin, Rhisa, in hopes of keeping them in his life circle. He surmises that canoodling with Rhisa will rattle their cages. But George never gets that chance to perform for his parents. Circumstances intervene when George, Rhisa, Jerry, and Frankie stumble upon the Costanzas having sex in the back of Jerry's van. There is no more dickering on Jerry's part now about the fate of the van. He *will* sell it.

Toby Huss, best known for his role as Artie, the "Strongest Man in the World," in the Nickelodeon series *The Adventures of Pete & Pete* (1993–1996), played Jack. Standup comedian Dana Gould portrayed "Fragile" Frankie Merman.

Episode 156: "The Merv Griffin Show" (original air date: November 6, 1997)

Only *Seinfeld* could pull off an episode with one of its chief plotlines featuring a major character—Kramer, in this instance—finding the old set from *The Merv Griffin Show* in the trash and recreating the long-running interview program in his apartment. Bruce Eric Kaplan, a.k.a. BEK, wrote the teleplay. Kaplan is better known as a cartoonist with a penchant for dark humor. His work has frequently appeared in *The New Yorker*.

Meanwhile, George's girlfriend Miranda, played by Arabella Field, is upset that he ran over some pigeons while driving. Jerry's got a new gal pal, Celia (played by Julia Pennington), who has a vintage toy collection that she won't let him near. And Elaine is quietly battling with a co-worker named Lou (played by Brent Hinkley), whom she has deemed a "sidler"—a person who ultra-quietly, almost imperceptibly, goes about his business at the office.

With Kramer now hosting a daily version of *The Merv Griffin Show*, his guests include Jerry, who reveals his plan for getting to play with Celia's toys. When he admits to drugging her, Kramer—with his co-host, Newman—ushers Celia out from backstage to both lay into Jerry and to break up with him. Animal authority Jim Fowler—who plays himself—and a hawk, also appear as guests on the show. When George shows up with an injured squirrel—he had hit it in an attempt to avoid pigeons and had been nursing it back to health—Fowler's hawk makes a beeline toward it.

Kramer giving Oprah a run for her money with his reassembled *Merv Griffin Show* set.
NBC/Photofest

Episode 157: "The Slicer" (original air date: November 13, 1997)

Gregg Kavet and Andy Robin wrote the teleplay of this episode, with Darin Henry contributing to the story. "The Slicer" finds George with a new job at Kruger Industrial Smoothing. The only problem is that his boss has a picture of his family at the beach on the wall of his office from 1989, with a decidedly less hair-challenged George in the backdrop. On that very day, George had assumed the Kruger kids stole all of his belongings while he was taking a swim and, in retaliation, threw their boom box into the surf. However, it turned out that the tide had washed his things into the ocean. Mr. Kruger demanded that George recompense his family for the boom box. George, though, furnished him with a phony name and address, and now is concerned that Kruger—these many years later—will recognize him in the picture and make the unwanted connection. He goes to great lengths to airbrush himself out of the picture.

Meanwhile, Kramer has had enough of malformed meats in his sandwiches and purchases a meat slicer to solve the problem. Elaine uses the slicer to even heels on her shoes. And Jerry's latest girlfriend is Dr. Sara Sitarides (played by Marcia Cross), who gets under his skin by incessantly talking about being a lifesaver in her work. He gets even more perturbed when he discovers that she's a dermatologist and thus, from his perspective at least, hardly a lifesaver. In fact, he calls her a "Pimple Popper MD," which—when all is said and done—ends their relationship.

Further developments find Elaine locked in her apartment and Kramer mistaken for a dermatologist—due to his white "meat-slicing" butcher's coat—and examining George's boss, Mr. Kruger, for a cancer screening. Kramer refers to moles as the "freckle's ugly cousin."

Daniel von Bargen played Mr. Kruger, as he would for the reminder of the ninth season.

Episode 158: "The Betrayal" (original air date: November 20, 1997)

Peter Mehlman and David Mandel wrote the teleplay of this completely distinctive *Seinfeld* episode that employs the reverse-chronology device. That is, the final scene plays first, as "The Betrayal," in effect, runs backward. The episode's moniker pays homage to Harold Pinter's play and 1983 film *Betrayal*, which turned the story's chronology on its head. In fact, the wedding that Jerry, George, and Elaine travel to India to attend features a groom named Pinter Ranawat.

The beauty of this episode is that the comedic drama inherent in the storylines is unfurled at the onset, with Kramer deathly afraid of dropping dead; Elaine going to Sue Ellen Mischke's wedding in faraway India; and George sporting spray-painted Timberland boots to make him appear a shade taller.

The backward nature of episode includes flashbacks, one of which has Jerry telling George and his fiancée, Susan Ross, that Nina, his girlfriend at the time, might just be the one. In the present, however, a chance encounter with Nina—whom Jerry never slept with—finds George desiring a date with her and hoping that his friend will set them up. Jerry, though, at long last, has that previously elusive sex with Nina, and the news is kept from George for as long as possible.

Kramer's fear of imminent death, we learn, is the byproduct of a "drop dead" curse put on him by his friend, Franklin Delano Romanowski, a.k.a. FDR. Thereafter, Kramer desperately endeavors to break the curse, even asking Newman to use his one birthday wish in protecting him from that awful fate.

As for the wedding in India between Sue Ellen Mischke and Pinter Ranawat, the latter's parents try to convince Elaine not to attend the wedding. They aren't going and, as things turn out, nobody else from the United States is, with the notable exceptions of Jerry, George, and Elaine. At the wedding, Elaine realizes that she knew the groom and had had sex with him. George also learns that Jerry and Nina went the distance. And, for good measure, Sue Ellen Mischke calls off the wedding.

Back from the dead, as it were, Heidi Swedberg reprised her role as Susan Ross in a flashback scene. Brenda Strong returned as Sue Ellen. Michael McShane played FDR. Justine Miceli, who portrayed Detective Adrienne Lesniak in *NYPD Blue*, played Nina, Jerry's girlfriend for one brief shining moment, George's desire, and a "great conversationalist," too. "The Betrayal" also clears up the nagging discrepancy of why Kramer was called Kessler in "The Seinfeld Chronicles." During a flashback scene, we relive the very first time Jerry met Kramer. Upon his move into the building, Kramer comes over to welcome him.

"You must be Kessler?" Jerry says. "I saw your name on the buzzer."

"No, it's *Kramer*," he replies.

Episode 159: "The Apology" (original air date: December 11, 1997)

Jennifer Crittenden wrote this teleplay that weaves together multiple storylines, including Kramer plotting to spend the preponderance of his waking hours in the shower because he loves the experience so much.

Jerry's dilemma is that his girlfriend, Melissa (played by Kathleen McClellan), engages in casual nudity while in the apartment. The practice disturbs him but he nonetheless gives the nudity bit the old college try. Melissa, however, sets Jerry straight on the difference between male nudity and female nudity. The former is "bad nudity." After Jerry convinces her to tone down the nudity, he comes to regret it because he can't help but think about her *au naturel*. She, too, has the image of Jerry in the buff lodged in her brain, which turns her off and casts asunder their relationship.

Meanwhile, Elaine is waging battle with a co-worker, Peggy, a bona fide germophobe, who is particularly turned off by Elaine, who she feels is a walking and talking germ carrier based on her licentious lifestyle. We learn here, too, that David Puddy is a germophobe and has long had problems with Elaine in this area.

"The Apology" received its episode title due to an old friend of George's, who is a recovering alcoholic. James Hanky, a.k.a. "Stanky Hanky," is in the Alcoholics Anonymous (AA) twelve-step program and on step nine, which asks individuals to apologize to those in their circle of family and friends who have been in any way aggrieved by their years of drinking and irresponsible ways. George, for one, feels that he merits an apology for an instance when Hanky insulted him. Hanky refused to let George wear his sweater at a party, claiming that his oversized head would stretch it out. After much badgering by George, Hanky apologizes: "I'm sorry that I didn't want your rather bulbous head struggling to find its way through the normal-size neck hole of my finely knit sweater." George doesn't take this "apology" very well and ends up attending Rageaholics Anonymous meetings.

James Spader played the smarmy James Hanky. Spader, whose movie career had ground to a virtual halt at the time, would soon be a familiar television face by starring in *The Practice* (1997–2004) and *Boston Legal* (2004–2008), the latter alongside William Shatner. Spader landed in another hit on NBC, *The Blacklist* (2013–present). Megan Cole, who also appeared in "The Susie," portrayed Peggy.

Episode 160: "The Strike" (original air date: December 18, 1997)

This episode introduced to the popular culture and the vernacular the alternative holiday to Christmas called Festivus, which is celebrated on December 23. Written by Alec Berg, Jeff Schaffer, and Dan O'Keefe, "The Strike" was ranked number three by *TV Guide* in its top-ten list of holiday episodes.

For starters, Jerry, George, and Elaine are guests at a Hanukkah party thrown by Dr. Tim Whatley, who gives each of them a gift—a note advising them that a donation has been made in each of their names to a charity called The Children's Alliance. George finds this rather insulting, but then utilizes the same approach on the job at Kruger's, when he is expected to give gifts to his fellow employees. However, his charity, "The Human Fund," is bogus.

At Whatley's party, Jerry meets Gwen, whom he finds very attractive. But he later concludes that she is a "two-face"—somebody who looks really good in some situations and locations and categorically less so in others. Meanwhile, Kramer is ecstatic at having been called back to work after a twelve-year strike at H&H Bagels. His work experience doesn't quite go as planned, however, and is short-lived. Elaine's problems begin when she gives a fake telephone number to a guy she doesn't want to see, but inadvertently uses the card that would have enabled her to get a free submarine sandwich at her favorite sub shop.

Naturally, George's duplicity comes to haunt him when Mr. Kruger makes a twenty-thousand-dollar donation to the non-existent Human Fund. George's explanation for the ruse is that he doesn't celebrate Christmas, which compels him to invite his boss to the Festivus gathering at the Costanza house. There, the family patriarch spells out the particulars of the Festivus holiday—the antithesis of Christmas commercialism and over-spending—including the "airing of grievances" and "feats of strength," during which George is expected to pin down his father. This act officially brings to a close the Festivus festivities. Ben & Jerry's Ice Cream honored this episode with a flavor of its own called "Festivus."

Actor and playwright Tracy Letts makes a cameo appearance in this episode. Letts went on to receive the Pulitzer Prize for Drama for his play *August: Osage County*. For his role as George in a revival of Edward Albee's *Who's Afraid of Virginia Woolf?*, Letts won a Tony Award for "Best Actor in a Play" in 2013.

Episode 161: "The Dealership" (original air date: January 8, 1998)

David Puddy's got a new job as a car salesman in this episode written by Steve Koren. He's promised Jerry a super deal on a Saab 900 NG convertible. And Elaine is agog now having a "salesman boyfriend," but this "please don't let this feeling end" moment ends when they break up one more time.

Meanwhile, George is ravenously hungry while at the car dealership and, left with few options, patronizes a candy vending machine to get a Twix bar. Having all kinds of problems with his wrinkled dollar bill not working in the machine, he asks a mechanic on duty to exchange it, but receives no help. When George finally gets change to use in the machine, his Twix bar fails to drop, leaving him without his candy bar pick-me-up and in a confrontation with the staff at the dealership, who he believes procured his bought-and-paid-for Twix bar.

There's more action at the dealership when Kramer takes Jerry's prospective car for an extended test drive with another salesman. They are seemingly on the verge of a *Thelma and Louise*–style road trip. And as is so often the case with car salesmen, David Puddy's super deal looks less and less so as time passes, as many extra charges are added to the final price.

Episode 162: "The Reverse Peephole" (original air date: January 15, 1998)

Spike Feresten returns as writer of this episode that finds Kramer and Newman reversing the peepholes on their apartment doors without getting permission from Silvio, the building's super. Silvio blames Newman for the breach of protocol and wants him evicted. Not knowing that Newman is involved in an extramarital affair with Silvio's wife, Svetlana, Kramer goes to bat for his friend. As a result, Newman can stay in the building.

Meanwhile, Elaine is not too happy that her on-again boyfriend, David Puddy, is wearing "man fur." Impulsive as always, she throws the coat out a window during a birthday party for Joe Mayo, but, alas, throws out the wrong one—Joe's fur, not Puddy's. At the party, too, Jerry, George, and Elaine don't have a gift for Joe, because the always-parsimonious George refused to pay for overnight delivery on the massage chair that they had agreed to get him. Before turning over the chair to Joe, George uses it himself after experiencing excruciating back pain caused by his overly stuffed wallet.

Further troubles arise when Newman finds the discarded fur coat. When Elaine demands it back, he refuses because he has already given it to Svetlana. To keep the über-suspicious Silvio from connecting the dots, Jerry claims the coat as his own. He even wears it in front of Silvio. Upon seeing Jerry in "man fur," Puddy says that he looks like a "dandy" and agrees that's it's not the coat for him. His new sartorial selection, though, doesn't make Elaine any happier. Later, to again deflect suspicions from Newman, Kramer tells Silvio that Svetlana and Joe Mayo are having an affair.

Jon Polito played Silvio, and busy character actor Pat Finn portrayed Joe Mayo. Finn's television credits include recurring roles in *Ed* (2000–2004), *Marvin Marvin* (2012–2013), and *The Middle* (2009–present).

Episode 163: "The Cartoon" (original air date: January 29, 1998)

Cartoonist Bruce Eric Kaplan fittingly wrote this episode that not so delicately mocks the cartoons that appear in *The New Yorker*—cartoons that often leave readers, especially Elaine, scratching their heads in befuddlement.

For starters, "The Cartoon" finds Kramer's trademark candor getting Jerry in hot water with Sally Weaver, Susan Ross's old roommate, played by Kathy Griffin. The comedienne's return to *Seinfeld*—she had previously appeared in "The Doll"—was rooted in a feud that she had initiated during a standup routine on HBO. Griffin mocked Jerry and claimed that he was not especially nice to her when she initially appeared on his show. Jerry figured that he could have some fun with their public spat and made it part of a storyline, with Sally performing a one-woman show called "Jerry Seinfeld: the Devil."

Kramer, meanwhile, determines that the only way his very frank and always-flapping tongue can be silenced is to be entirely silent. Meanwhile, Elaine is utterly confused over a particular cartoon in *The New Yorker*. Her obsessing over the cartoon leads her to the magazine's offices and the cross-examining of Mr. Elinoff, the editor responsible for publishing the cartoon, who—when all is said and done—doesn't know what it means either. The upside to Elaine's quest is that she has a cartoon published in *The New Yorker*, one that J. Peterman immediately detects as a not-so-subtle ripoff of a *Ziggy* comic strip.

George is dating a girl named Janet (played by Tracy Nelson), who, according to general consensus, looks a lot like Jerry. Kramer's perpetual noting of their similarities—before he turned off the sound—drives George up the wall. Kramer though, reassures George that just because his girlfriend and Jerry resemble one another is not proof positive that George is in love with his best friend. Paul Benedict played Mr. Elinoff, the editor at *The New Yorker*. He is best known for having played neighbor Harry Bentley during the entire run of *The Jeffersons* from 1975 to 1985. Benedict died in 2008 at the age of seventy.

Episode 164: "The Strongbox" (original air date: February 5, 1998)

Written by Dan O'Keefe—with story-concept help from Billy Kimball—this episode finds George attempting to break up with his latest girlfriend, Maura, but having little success: Maura just won't let him do it. Elaine's affairs of the heart are a bit different than George's, as she is dating a mystery man, Glenn (played by Nicholas Walker), who, she believes, may be secretly married. As things turn out, his big secret is that he is impoverished and on welfare. He is married, too.

Meanwhile, with a rash of crimes in the building, Kramer purchases a strongbox to house his valuables. He becomes obsessed, too, with hiding its key in a location known only to him. He tries everywhere, from a shirt of Jerry's to the building's intercom, which malfunctions because of it. In fact, courtesy of the non-working intercom and crime wave, Jerry refuses to let a man named Phil, played by Louis Mustillo, into the building because he doesn't recognize him. Phil, however, lives on the same floor as Jerry.

Further plot twists see George scheming to cheat on Maura in hopes that the act facilitates a breakup. Kramer's key dilemma continues until he hides it in neighbor Phil's parrot's dish. Unfortunately, the parrot, Fredo, eats it, chokes, and dies. When Jerry is searching for a special pair of cufflinks—the ones Jerry Lewis wore in his 1960 film *Cinderfella* that he intends on wearing to the Friars Club—he remembers that Kramer had locked them in the strongbox, with its key now inside a dead parrot that is buried in a pet cemetery. With no alternative, Jerry and Kramer visit the cemetery with the intention of exhuming the bird and the key, but Phil catches them in the act.

In a classic popular culture reference to *Godfather II*, Kramer, after being accused of causing Fredo's death, tells Jerry: "Fredo was weak and stupid. He shouldn't have eaten the key."

Alex Kapp Horner played Maura, George's not-so-easy-to-get-rid-of girlfriend. Mary Scheer, an original cast member in *MADtv*, portrayed Glenn's welfare caseworker, Mrs. Smoth.

Episode 165: "The Wizard" (original air date: February 26, 1998)

Newcomer Steve Lookner wrote this teleplay. While it was his only *Seinfeld* credit, Lookner's résumé includes writing for *Saturday Night Live*, *MADtv*, *The Late Late*

Kramer's Not Necessarily Top Ten Work Experiences

10. Department store Santa Claus ("The Race")
9. Movie actor with one line—"These pretzels are making me thirsty"—in a Woody Allen picture ("The Alternate Side")
8. Sitcom actor with a guest appearance on *Murphy Brown* ("The Keys")
7. Inventor of a beach-scented cologne ("The Pez Dispenser")
6. Model for Calvin Klein underwear ("The Pick")
5. Tennis ball boy ("The Lip Reader")
4. Soap opera stand-in ("The Stand-In")
3. Police lineup stand-in ("The Beard")
2. Author promoting his book: *The Coffee Table Book of Coffee Tables* ("The Opposite")
1. Pretend patient suffering from a pretend disease—gonorrhea—at the hospital ("The Burning")

Show with Craig Kilborn, *The Man Show,* and *Last Call with Carson Daly.*

In this episode, Jerry gives his father a fancy "Wizard" organizer as a gift and Kramer has his coffee table book about coffee tables optioned to Hollywood, which enables him to retire to Florida. He winds up living in the same condo complex as Morty and Helen Seinfeld. There, he runs for condo board president, with Morty's backing. Morty hopes to install a puppet regime with Kramer out front and him behind the scenes, pulling all the strings.

Meanwhile, Elaine is dating a man named Darryl (played by Samuel Bliss Cooper), who might—or might not—be black. Nevertheless, the uncertainty of his race intrigues her. George gets an invitation to an event hosted by the Susan Ross Foundation, but makes the excuse that he cannot attend because he is closing escrow on a house in the Hamptons. His deception is revealed when Susan's parents run into him on the street—and not in the Hamptons. In a battle of wills, George sticks to his story and drives the Rosses to the Hamptons to see who will give in first. He eventually blinks and confesses to his lie.

In Kramer's campaign for board president, he comes up short after giving board members knockoff copies of the Wizard organizer that malfunction—notably in doing tip calculations. In the end, Elaine discovers that her boyfriend is *not* black, although he thought *she* was Hispanic. And Mr. and Mrs. Ross have harvested further evidence that George is a bad seed and reaffirm their belief that he is responsible for Susan's death.

Episode 166: "The Burning" (original air date: March 19, 1998)

With the final season winding down comes "The Burning," written by Jennifer Crittenden, in which Elaine discovers that David Puddy is not only very religious-minded, but believes that non-believers, like Elaine, will burn in Hell for eternity.

Other storylines in this episode find George's seemingly clever machinations on the job saddling him with more work than ever. And Jerry's got a new girlfriend, Sophie, whose voice he does not recognize after an "it's me" message

Kramer and Mickey (Danny Woodburn) "playing sick" for cash as Jerry looks on in "The Burning." *NBC/Photofest*

is left on his answering machine. As things turn out, she doesn't recognize his voice on the telephone, either, believing instead that she is talking with a friend named Rafe. She reveals to Rafe, who's actually Jerry, that she has not apprised Jerry of a certain incident in her life dubbed the "tractor story."

Meanwhile, Kramer and his little friend, Mickey, have landed acting jobs. They are playing hospital patients. Kramer gives a bravura performance as a man suffering from gonorrhea and is asked to do an encore. He worries about being typecast. Later, we learn that Sophie's "tractor story" involved her contracting the disease while wearing a bathing suit on a tractor. Jerry had wrongly assumed the story had something to do with a scar on her leg.

As the myriad plot twists work their way to Seinfeldian conclusions, Elaine and Puddy visit a priest to clarify a spiritual matter. The man of the cloth tells them that they are *both* going to Hell because premarital sex is a sin. Elaine is happy to hear this and witness Puddy's religious certainty knocked for a loop.

Cindy Ambuehl played Sophie, the girl with the "tractor story." She is best known for her recurring role as Rene Peterson in *JAG* (1995–2005).

Episode 167: "The Bookstore" (original air date: April 9, 1998)

Spike Feresten wrote this teleplay, with story concept credits awarded to Feresten, Darin Henry, and Mark Jaffe. Fittingly, as *Seinfeld* neared its closing act, we get a rare glimpse of what Kramer actually does in Jerry's apartment when the latter isn't on the premises. As the episode opens, we see him preparing a smoothie drink for himself and then spilling it, riding Jerry's bicycle around, partying, and even redecorating the place. Miraculously, he manages to get just about everything back to the way it was before Jerry returns.

Meanwhile, Jerry and George are shopping at Brentano's, an area bookstore. George makes the mistake of taking a book with him into the bathroom and is compelled to buy it. He thereafter tries to return it, and even give it away, but discovers that it has been flagged everywhere he goes as having been in a bathroom. Jerry's dilemma is that he spies his Uncle Leo shoplifting in the bookstore, then confronts him about it, and later turns him in. Uncle Leo, who believes it's a perk of being a senior citizen to shoplift, naturally feels betrayed by his nephew. He vows never to forget it. Jerry has a terrible nightmare involving Uncle Leo behind bars and doing chin-ups, a parody of a scene in the 1962 movie *Cape Fear*.

At a J. Peterman party, Elaine has one too many but doesn't get up to dance it off. Rather, she necks with an equally besotted co-worker named Zach. Elaine worries that, if she's not officially dating him, she will be thought of as the "office skank." And never ones to pass up a potential business opportunity, Kramer and Newman are planning to operate a rickshaw business on the streets of Manhattan. They need someone to pull the rickshaw, however, and interview homeless men as potential candidates. When one of them makes off with the rickshaw, Kramer and Newman decide that the homeless man idea is not feasible. Kramer ends up with the job of pulling the rickshaw.

In the waning minutes of "The Bookstore," Kramer loses control of the rickshaw while pulling it up a hill and it runs down Zach. Still trying to get rid of his book, George decides to steal another copy of it—one that hasn't been flagged as being in the bathroom. His luck is no better this go-round and, like Uncle Leo before him, he is branded a common thief.

Episode 168: "The Frogger" (original air date: April 23, 1998)

Gregg Kavet and Andy Robin wrote the teleplay of this episode, with story help from Steve Koren and Dan O'Keefe. "The Frogger" finds Elaine mentally exhausted from office birthday parties and the unnatural socializing that comes with them. Her plan: call in sick when a birthday party is on the docket. In another plot thread, Jerry and George call on Mario's Pizza place—a hangout of theirs during the high school years—for one last slice before it closes its doors forever. While at Mario's, George discovers that the Frogger, the video game that he used to play with élan, is still there, and that his high score of 860,630 points has never been surpassed. George is intent on buying the Frogger game as an enduring shrine, of sorts, that will maintain, in perpetuity, evidence of his supreme accomplishment.

Meanwhile, Kramer is spreading the word that a serial killer—known as "The Lopper"—is on the loose in nearby Riverside Park, and that the killer's most recent victim was a dead ringer for Jerry. And speaking of Jerry, he's dating a friend of Elaine's named Lisi, played by Julia Campbell. However, he finds a certain habit of hers off-putting. She's a serial sentence finisher, which Jerry gripes is "like dating Mad Libs!"

Elaine's avoidance of birthday and other celebrations at the office leads her astray to get that sugar fix that she is no longer enjoying at the parties; she decides to raid J. Peterman's refrigerator for a piece of cake. Elaine, though, is unaware that Peterman won the cake at a Sotheby's auction for the not-inconsiderable sum of twenty-nine thousand dollars. A collector's item, the prized dessert originated from the 1937 wedding of the former King Edward VIII and Wallis Simpson. When Elaine finds out what she did, she replaces the cake with an Entenmann's. Peterman's security camera, though, ultimately unmasks her sweet tooth–induced crime of passion.

Finally, George's noble attempt to get the Frogger game from the pizza parlor to his apartment—with the assistance of "Slippery Pete" and battery power to maintain the score—comes up short as he artfully dodges busy traffic just like the frog in the video game. Across the street at last and almost home, George attempts to lift the Frogger above the curb, but a speeding truck whizzing by doesn't allow that to happen. Jerry is heard to exclaim, "Game over!"

Swedish actor Peter Stormare played "Slippery Pete." His most famous role is that of Gaear Grimsrud in the Academy Award–winning movie *Fargo* (1996).

Episode 169: "The Maid" (original air date: April 30, 1998)

The trio of Alec Berg, David Mandel, and Jeff Schaffer wrote this teleplay, with story contributions from Kit Boss and Peter Mehlman. The episode's original title was "The Long-Distance Relationship," which refers to Kramer's love life and his girlfriend's move all the way downtown, causing him to bemoan the difficulties inherent in a "long-distance relationship."

Meanwhile, Jerry's hired a maid named Cindy (played by Angela Featherstone), who becomes more than household help to him. Elaine's big problem is a new New York City area code—646—which she cannot abide as part of her phone number. When she gets her old phone 212 area code number back—courtesy of the death of Mrs. Krantz—she is besieged with phone calls from Bobby, the woman's grandson. To put an end to his incessant calls, Elaine feigns her own death for Bobby's benefit, but he phones 911 and firemen break down her apartment door. In George's life, he's hoping to get nicknamed "T-Bone" on the job, but the name gets affixed, much to his annoyance, to a co-worker. He gets nicknamed "Coco the Monkey" instead.

As Jerry's relationship with Cindy deepens, he realizes that he is still paying her for maid services that he is not getting. Kramer candidly informs him that he has now become a john. Jerry talks to Cindy about the money and maid thing, and she ends their relationship. But he must now deal with Cindy's pimp-like boss, who demands the monies owed to her.

Episode 170: "The Puerto Rican Day" (original air date: May 7, 1998)

This episode marks the last traditional foray before "The Finale." The following *Seinfeld* episode would be a retrospective of the show's nine seasons. Fittingly, the writing credits for "The Puerto Rican Day" are a lengthy roster of names: Alec Berg, Jennifer Crittenden, Spike Feresten, Bruce Eric Kaplan, Gregg Kavet, Steve Koren, David Mandel, Dan O'Keefe, Andy Robin, and Jeff Schaffer.

Foremost, "The Puerto Rican Day" is notorious in *Seinfeld* lore for the controversy it engendered when Kramer inadvertently set the Puerto Rican flag on fire with a sparkler and then attempted to stomp it out with his feet. Despite it being the highest rated show to date, NBC never repeated the episode.

Controversy notwithstanding, "The Puerto Rican Day" returned to the show's roots with storylines that were, in essence, about nothing overtly important. The gang is coming home from a Mets game at Shea Stadium a little early—in an attempt to beat the usual traffic snarl in the stadium parking lot—but encounter an unexpected logjam on the streets of Manhattan courtesy of the Puerto Rican Day Parade and a certain driver of a maroon Volkswagen Rabbit, who will bedevil them repeatedly.

Getting nowhere, George and Elaine exit the car, with the latter hailing a taxi and the former visiting a movie theater playing *The Blimp*, which chronicles the *Hindenburg* disaster. Elaine's cab driver has no better luck with all the traffic and she commences walking, navigating her way underneath the parade viewing stands with equally aggrieved parties in a spoof of the 1972 action film *The Poseidon Adventure*, in which Gene Hackman's character leads the way in a capsized ocean liner.

Meanwhile, Kramer's got to go to the bathroom and he spies an apartment with a "For Sale" sign in the window. Utilizing his alias of H. E. Pennypacker, a wealthy industrialist and potential buyer, he gains access to the apartment and use of the bathroom. Jerry ultimately joins him there to watch the end of the Mets game. Left unattended, their vehicle is subsequently trashed by parade revelers. When the bumbling Kramer sets fire to the Puerto Rican flag with his sparkler, an angry mob, led by none other than belligerent gay couple Bob and Cedric (from "The Soup Nazi" and "The Sponge") descend upon him. The voice of legendary New York Mets broadcaster Bob Murphy is heard in this episode.

Episode 171: "The Chronicle" (original air date: May 14, 1998)

This episode serves as a retrospective of *Seinfeld*'s nine seasons. Jerry Seinfeld breaks the Fourth Wall here and speaks directly to the audience. George, Elaine, and Kramer do not step out of character. Darin Henry is credited as the writer of "The Chronicle," also known as "The Clip Show," which ran as an hour-long episode and lead-in to "The Finale."

"The Chronicle" reprises classic moments from the show played to composer John Williams's *Superman* theme, particularly fitting considering all the Man of Steel references throughout the series. Everything from George's "shrinkage" problem to Elaine's unique style of dancing to the Soup Nazi is included. Fun looks at hairstyles and sartorial expressions are also highlighted in the clips, including moments from "The Puffy Shirt," "The Barber," and "The Wig Master."

28

The Finale

A Vociferous Last Shout

The final *Seinfeld*, aptly titled "The Finale," aired May 14, 1998, to a considerable audience of 76.3 million viewers. To keep the show's contents a perplexing riddle and unsolved mystery until its airing, the show's working title was "A Tough Nut to Crack." Only the last episodes of *M*A*S*H* and *Cheers* were bigger draws. When it aired on CBS on February 28, 1983, *M*A*S*H*'s "Goodbye, Farewell and Amen" reached 105.9 million viewers. And on May 20, 1993, *Cheers*'s "One for the Road" on NBC garnered 84.4 million viewers. *Seinfeld*'s "The Pilot" was the lead-in for this final episode of *Cheers*.

"The Finale" was a much-heralded event that captured viewers who weren't necessarily fans and some people, too, who'd never before seen the show. Ol' Blue Eyes, Frank Sinatra, died on the evening of *Seinfeld*'s exit from the prime-time stage. Nancy Sinatra admitted to *Entertainment Weekly* that she missed visiting her father for the last time because of *Seinfeld*. "I got so involved in watching the damn show," she said, "that I never got over to my dad's."

Hello, Larry

Appropriately, Larry David returned to write this long-anticipated sendoff to the series that brought back so many of the show's memorable characters. Jerry's standup routines also returned for the first time since the close of season seven. The principal plotline finds Jerry and George on the receiving end of very good news. Courtesy of a change in the managerial hierarchy, NBC wants to produce thirteen episodes of *Jerry*, their sitcom. As an added perk, Jerry has the network's private plane at his disposal and takes the gang with him to Paris for what is widely regarded as "one last hurrah." For Jerry and George will thereafter be leaving for the West Coast to oversee the new show.

En route to Gay Paree, Kramer contends with leftover water in his ear from an earlier visit to the beach. His manic efforts to dislodge it cause the pilots to lose control of the aircraft and it begins to nosedive. For a fleeting moment, Jerry, George, Elaine, and Kramer believe that the end is near. Before the plane rights itself, Elaine is on verge of telling Jerry that she still loves him, and George lets the cat out of the bag that he had cheated in "The Contest." Happily for all concerned, the plane safely lands in Latham, a small village in Massachusetts.

As the four friends await the requisite plane repairs, they observe a carjacking. An obese man is held up at gunpoint while they stand idly by and crack jokes about the victim's excessive girth. A police officer summoned to the scene is told about the four onlookers' callous and indifferent behavior and they are arrested for violating a "duty to rescue" city statute, a Good Samaritan law, which requires eyewitnessses to assist their fellow citizens in distress.

On trial now in the courtroom of Judge Arthur Vandelay, Jerry, George, Elaine, and Kramer are represented by Jackie Chiles. George feels that having Judge Vandelay preside over the affair is a positive sign, as that surname has always been a favorite alias of his. And Chiles sums up the overriding importance of the case this way: "You don't have to help anybody. That's what this country is all about." He also queries the jury: "Have you ever heard of a guilty bystander? No. Because you cannot be a bystander and be guilty." The prosecution, however, is loaded for bear, bringing witness upon witness from their pasts to reveal the true character of the accused.

Marla Penny, for one, recounts on the witness stand how her then boyfriend, Jerry, told her all about a contest—abstaining from masturbation—that he and his friends had entered into. Mabel Choate tells of being mugged by Jerry for a loaf of marble rye bread. Even the pharmacist who sold Elaine a caseload of sponges—and "not the kind you clean your tub with"—testifies. Dr. Wilcox, who broke the news that Susan Ross was dead, is on hand, too, as a prosecution witness to describe the look of "restrained jubilation" on George's face when he first got word of her passing.

Phil Morris as Jackie Chiles with client Jerry, armed and ready for the defense, in "The Finale."

NBC/Photofest

The Not Necessarily Top Ten *Seinfeld* Crimes and Misdemeanors, Alleged and Otherwise

10. Shoplifting (Uncle Leo and George, "The Bookstore")
9. Public urination (Jerry and George, "The Parking Garage")
8. Serial murder (Kramer, "The Trip")
7. Dognapping (Elaine, Kramer, and Newman, "The Engagement")
6. Pimping (Kramer, "The Wig Master")
5. Mail fraud (Jerry, "The Package")
4. Soliciting prostitution (Jerry, "The Stranded")
3. Jewel theft (Kramer picked out in a police lineup, "The Beard")
2. Library book delinquency (Jerry, "The Library")
1. Good Samaritan law violation (Jerry, George, Elaine, and Kramer, "The Finale")

Library cop Joe Bookman calls Jerry "a criminal." Lola, the woman in the wheelchair who couldn't park in a handicap spot because of them, describes the various trials and tribulations brought on by Jerry, George, Elaine, and Kramer.

The parade of witnesses for the prosecution is long indeed. Robin, George's former girlfriend, describes his cowardice in mowing down women and children to escape a small fire. Donald Sanger, the bubble boy, testifies to George's poor character, too, while recollecting their game of Trivial Pursuit and the literal bursting of his bubble. The shopping mall security guard, who caught Jerry urinating in parking garage, is even there to enlighten the court of Jerry's spurious excuse for committing the act: he "could get uromysitisis poisoning and die." Babu Bhatt is back as well to exact his promised revenge on Jerry. Justin Pitt conveys to the somber assemblage how Elaine attempted to smother him with a pillow to collect an inheritance. And Yev Kassem, the Soup Nazi, tells one and all of Elaine's spiteful and ruthless actions in destroying his business.

In the end, the preponderance of the evidence is overwhelming. Even Estelle Costanza's attempt at seducing Judge Vandelay comes up short in altering the sentence, which is one year in jail for Jerry, George, Elaine, and Kramer. Incarcerated in a jail cell—before heading off to prison—Jerry and George engage in a conversation that sounds awfully familiar. It's about nothing too important. Jerry observes the buttons on George's shirt and remarks: "The second button is the key button. It literally makes or breaks the shirt. Look at it. It's too high. It's in no-man's land." George responds, "Haven't we had this conversation before?" And indeed they had, in "The Seinfeld Chronicles." The episode and series concludes with Jerry performing standup for his fellow inmates—with topical material—but only Kramer is amused.

The Other Verdict

As things turned out, the long-awaited and hyped final *Seinfeld* episode was not everyone's cup of tea. In fact, it received its fair share of negative reviews, with some critics claiming that "The Finale" veered far from the *Seinfeld* concept and what made it so unique and special.

The *Newark Star-Ledger*'s Alan Sepinwall wrote: "It's not that it didn't work because the characters were revealed to be selfish and shallow and awful human beings. We all already knew that they were. That was part of the joke, particularly in the later seasons. It didn't work because Larry [David] clearly worried that his audience hadn't figured this out on their own, and that he needed to tell them, and to judge the characters—and, by proxy, the viewers who liked them—in the finale."

Larry David would vehemently disagree that this was his intention.

Starpulse contributing writer Mike Ryan complained ten years after its airing: "The final episode of any long running series should be the proverbial exclamation point. Take what the series has always done successfully, do it one last time—only better—since the character arcs are all coming to an end. . . . *M*A*S*H* and *Cheers* both had outstanding final episodes. *Seinfeld* went away from their basic formula and, instead, paraded a herd of every guest star that ever appeared on the series through a convoluted trial accusing the main characters of 'doing nothing.'"

The A.V. Club summarized "The Finale" as such: "The episode is heavy on the plot, which wouldn't be a bad thing if it was one of those graceful, complicated *Seinfeld* plots like 'The Betrayal,' where things line up nicely by the end. But that's not what's going on here. The plot of 'The Finale' isn't complicated—it's not even that dense. It's actually kind of boring."

Caryn James reviewed "The Finale" for the *New York Times* and had a decidedly different take. "The hilarious final episode was everything *Seinfeld* was at its best: mordant, unsentimental, and written by Larry David," she wrote. "Wildly self-referential and slightly surreal, the final episode revels in petty details, turns clichés on their heads, and reveals why *Seinfeld* worked so well. . . . The parade of witnesses might not have made much sense to people who had never seen the show, but for fans it was an uproarious parade in which all the pettiness that Jerry, George, Elaine and Kramer had enacted over the years catches up with them: the Soup Nazi, the bubble boy, the woman whose marble rye Jerry stole."

In fact, based on reviews of the show on IMDb, Netflix, and other venues where fans can express their opinions, "The Finale," when all is said and done, gets a thumbs up. More fans approve of how the show exited the stage than disapprove, although "The Finale" was, without question, polarizing. That is, the fans who didn't like the show's finish *really* didn't like it, sometimes pathologically so.

Larry Thomas, who played the Soup Nazi and who appeared in "The Finale," told CNN: "I thought it was every bit as it should have been. I thought Larry did an incredible job with the script. Whether people will be satisfied after all the hype is hard to say." "Hard to say" is an understatement. Nonetheless, Larry David has no regrets and remains a fan of "The Finale" and believes it was a very fitting ending. When the *Seinfeld* cast—Jerry Seinfeld, Jason Alexander,

Character actors with character: John O'Hurley as Peterman, Patrick Washburton as Puddy, and Wayne Knight as Newman in "The Finale."   *NBC/Photofest*

Julia Louis-Dreyfus, and Michael Richards—reunited on Larry David's HBO show *Curb Your Enthusiasm* in 2009, some in the media deemed it an attempted "do-over." In fact, Jerry says in the *Curb Your Enthusiasm* episode called "Seinfeld": "We already screwed up one finale." It was a joke referring to the critical tsunami that occurred in some quarters after "The Finale" aired eleven years earlier. Larry, however, replies: "We didn't screw up a finale. That was a good finale."

The Gang's All Here

Whether one loved or hated "The Finale," it brought back a considerable cast of characters and the actors who played them: Wayne Knight as Newman; Jerry Stiller as Frank Costanza; Estelle Harris as Estelle Costanza; Barney Martin as Morty Seinfeld; Liz Sheridan as Helen Seinfeld; Len Lesser as Uncle Leo; John O'Hurley as J. Peterman; Phil Morris as Jackie Chiles; Danny Woodburn as Mickey; Ian Abercrombie as Mr. Pitt; Richard Fancy as Mr. Lippman; Patrick Warburton as David Puddy; Richard Herd as Mr. Wilhelm; Kevin Page as Stu Chermak; Warren Frost as Mr. Ross; Grace Zabriskie as Mrs. Ross; Steve Hytner as Kenny Bania; Brian George as Babu Bhatt; Philip Baker Hall as library detective Joe Bookman; Victor Raider-Wexler as Dr. Wexler; McNally Sagal as Carol; Reni Santoni as Poppie; Peter Blood as Jay Crespi; Frances Bay as Mrs. Choate; Brian Doyle-Murray as Mel Sanger; Jon Hayman as Donald Sanger, the "bubble boy"; Teri Hatcher as Sidra; Melanie Chartoff as Robin; Keith Hernandez as himself; Wendle Josepher as Susie; Jane Leeves as Marla; Bruce Mahler as Rabbi Glickman; Wendel Meldrum as Leslie, the "low-talker"; Carlos Jacott as Ramon, the pool guy; Miguel Sandoval as Marcelino; Larry Thomas as the Soup Nazi; Sheree North as Babs Kramer; Robert Katims as Arnold Deensfrei; and David Byrd as the pharmacist.

John Pinette played Howie, the portly fellow who not only gets carjacked but mocked by the gang as well. (Pinette died unexpectedly in 2014 at the age of fifty.) Stanley Anderson played Judge Vandelay, and James Rebhorn, District Attorney Hoyt. Other cast members in "The Finale": James Pickens Jr. as Detective Hudson; Ed O'Ross as Detective Blake; Peter Riegert as NBC president James Kimbrough; Myra Turley as the jury foreman; Steve Carlson as Captain Maddox, the airplane pilot; Gay Thomas Wilson as flight attendant O'Neal; Geoffrey Ewing as the baliff; Scott Jaeck as Officer Vogel; Jim Zulevic as Bernie; Geraldo Rivera as himself; and Jane Wells as herself. In fact, real-life reporters Rivera and Wells both covered the trial and offered commentary throughout the proceedings.

No Credit Where Credit Is Due

Through the years on *Seinfeld*, there were often actors in very small roles and background extras who were not listed in the credits. The show's writers and members of the production team were occasionally called before the cameras. In "The Finale," writers Spike Feresten, Darin Henry, and Steve Koren are members of the jury sitting in judgment of Jerry, George, Elaine, and Kramer. Carol Brown, a *Seinfeld* production assistant, also sits on the jury along with Daena E. Title, Jason Alexander's wife. Tom Cherones, who directed seventy-eight episodes of *Seinfeld* in its early years, has a cameo as a customer in a coffee shop. And, of course, Larry David, who provided the voice of George Steinbrenner and so many others through the years, is uncredited for his extracurricular contributions to "The Finale." *Seinfeld* ranked number one in the ratings in its last season on the air. Only *I Love Lucy* and *The Andy Griffith Show* can make such a claim. They went out on top in their final seasons: 1956–1957 and 1967–1968, respectively.

Part VI
The Legacy

29

A Tough Act to Follow

Life After *Seinfeld*

einfeld wasn't just on the air for nine seasons—it was a phenomenon. The characters were unique in the annals of television. They talked about things and behaved like no other sitcom characters before them. When it was officially announced that *Seinfeld*'s ninth season would be its last, it was front-page news in the *New York Times*. The big question on fans' minds was: What next? What next for Jerry, Jason, Julia, and Michael? Could they ever equal or surpass playing Jerry, George, Elaine, and Kramer in future projects? Would they ever be able to capture the magic of *Seinfeld*, or anything close to that magic, in the years ahead?

Initially, things looked pretty bleak for the actors in achieving post-*Seinfeld* success. In fact, the *Seinfeld* curse was mentioned as possibly at play as the gang navigated the new terrain.

The Curse at Work

Larry David once said of the so-called *Seinfeld* curse: "It's so completely idiotic. . . . It's very hard to have a successful sitcom." Nonetheless, the talk of the curse established roots when Michael Richards, Jason Alexander, and Julia Louis-Dreyfus flopped in their new sitcom projects. Jerry Seinfeld, for the most part, eschewed television and returned to his roots as a standup comedian.

The Michael Richards Show debuted in October 2000, with Richards playing an unconventional Kramer-esque private detective named Vic Nardozza. The last name paid homage to Michael's mother, whose maiden name was Nardozza. In fact, the NBC brass insisted that the lead character maintain a certain level of the offbeat wackiness that made Cosmo Kramer a television icon. Creators of the show included *Seinfeld* alumni Spike Feresten, Gregg Kavet, and Andy Robin. William Devane co-starred as Brady McKay, owner of McKay's Investigative Services, which employed the bumbling Nardozza. The show lasted a mere eight episodes before NBC pulled the plug on it, citing poor ratings and the considerable savings it would reap in not making any more shows. The *Seinfeld* stars didn't come cheap.

Jason Alexander, too, tried his hand with his own sitcom, *Bob Patterson*, in which he played a motivational speaker and self-help guru. The show, which co-starred comedian Robert Klein, debuted on the ABC fall lineup in 2001, but got the hook after just five episodes. In fact, it lasted the month of October, premiering on October 2 and riding into the sunset after its October 31 airing. *Bob Patterson* got almost universally bad reviews for commiting the worst sitcom sin of all: it wasn't funny.

Alexander then played a big-mouthed sports talk-show host named Tony Kleinman, with co-stars Malcolm-Jamal Warner, Will Rothhaar, and Daniella Monet, in the CBS sitcom *Listen Up!* It survived twenty-two episodes and the entire 2004–2005 television season, but the ratings were weak and it was canceled.

Julia Louis-Dreyfus, too, initially bombed with a sitcom, this one called *Watching Ellie*, which was created by her husband, Brad Hall. It lasted two abridged seasons in two different incarnations. Directed by Ken Kwapis, *Watching Ellie* debuted on NBC as a non-traditional sitcom. The early episodes were filmed with a single camera and employed no studio audience. On top of that, they featured a clock ticking down in the corner of the screen as the individual shows portrayed specific happenings in Ellie's life. The clock device proved more of a distraction than anything else, revealing for one that the thirty-minute sitcom was actually only twenty-two minutes with copious commercial interruptions. The show was then retooled to follow the more traditional sitcom formula—multiple cameras and a studio audience—but it wasn't enough to save *Watching Ellie*. Nineteen episodes were produced, with three of them never airing, between February 2002 and May 2003.

Curse Busters

If one single person is responsible for turning the *Seinfeld* curse on its head, it's Julia Louis-Dreyfus, who hit pay dirt after *Watching Ellie* with two successful sitcoms: *The New Adventures of Old Christine*, wherein she played with comedic flair a divorced mother named Christine Campbell—a neurotic character who owns a women's fitness club. The show ran for five seasons on CBS, from March 13, 2006, to May 12, 2010. In 2006, she won an Emmy Award for "Outstanding Lead Actress in a Comedy Series."

After the show's cancellation, Louis-Dreyfus assumed the role of Selina Meyer, the vice president of the United States, in the HBO comedy series *Veep*, which debuted April 22, 2010. For her work on this highly acclaimed series, two more Emmy Awards came her way, in 2012 and 2013, for "Outstanding Lead Actress in a Comedy Series." Julia Louis-Dreyfus is the only individual to win Emmys in three different roles on three different sitcoms. In 2014 she bared all—well, almost all—by posing nude for *Rolling Stone* magazine. She sported only the words of the U.S. Constitution's preamble.

Jason Alexander, too, has been a busy actor post-*Seinfeld* and, despite the two sitcom flops, has very definitely broken free from the curse. He's been back on the stage, which he loves above all else, and has varied television and voice-over credits on his ever-growing résumé. A sampling of his eclectic work includes playing Principal Edwards on *Everybody Hates Chris* and Dr. Palmer on *The New Adventures of Old Christine*. He's supplied the voice of Mr. Nibbles on the animated series *Fish Hooks*. Alexander has served as a guest judge on the Bravo reality show *Step It Up & Dance*. He also appeared on Larry David's *Curb Your Enthusiasm* multiple times, including for the *Seinfeld* reunion in 2009, which many critics claimed was how *Seinfeld* should have drawn its curtain in 1998.

Jerry Above the Fray

After the incredible success of *Seinfeld*, Jerry Seinfeld did not return to television in acting roles. When he did appear he was—as is the norm with him—playing Jerry Seinfeld. Immediately after the show ended, Seinfeld toured the country with new standup material and was an extremely popular draw. On August 9, 1998, just a few months after the airing of "The Finale," he appeared live at the Broadhurst Theatre in New York City for an HBO comedy special called *I'm Telling You for the Last Time*. The show was subsequently released as an album and became available on VHS and DVD, too. Seinfeld also vowed that his future standup routines would always break new ground and not recycle old jokes over and over.

During the first decade of the new millennium, Jerry Seinfeld could also be seen promoting Apple as part of its "Think different" advertising campaign. He appeared in American Express web advertisements—called webisodes—that were dubbed *The Adventures of Seinfeld & Superman*. Seinfeld, in fact, fulfilled his fantasy by appearing alongside the Man of Steel in the commercials, albeit an animated version of him. Actor Patrick Warburton, who had played David Puddy, supplied the voice of Superman. While the clever commercials aired largely via the Internet, they did appear on regular television in 2004. He was also the main subject, along with other standup comedians, in a behind-the-scenes documentary of their unusual business. It was called *Comedian* and highlighted the pressures involved in developing winning standup material and living a life on the road. *Comedian* debuted in theaters in 2002.

On May 13, 2006, Jerry turned up on *Saturday Night Live*. He interrupted host Julia Louis-Dreyfus's monologue about the *Seinfeld* curse and its sheer ridiculousness with a literal bang. That is, a stage light nearly falls on Julia. Jerry is seen backstage with a scissors in hand and murmuring, "Dammit!" He has been highly visible, too, in commercials for Windows Vista, appearances at the Academy Awards, and, of course, on *Curb Your Enthusiasm* for the reunion with his *Seinfeld* castmates.

In 2007, Jerry Seinfeld penned the script—with Spike Feresten, Barry Marder, and Andy Robin—for *Bee Movie*, an animated children's movie. He also provided the voice of the restless and humorous lead bee, Barry B. Benson.

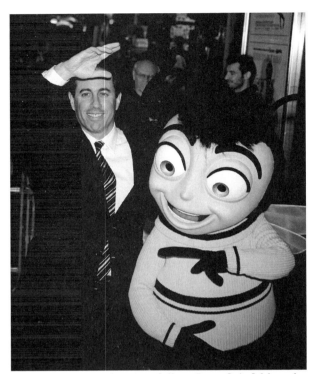

Other voices in the film included Renée Zellweger, Matthew Broderick, Patrick Warburton, John Goodman, Chris Rock, and Kathy Bates. *USA Today* said of *Bee Movie*: "It's so unfunny, it almost stings," which was the general consensus. In 2010, Seinfeld took part in a TV reality show called *The Marriage Ref*, which brought real-life bickering married couples before a panel of celebrity judges to weigh in on who is right and who is wrong in their domestic disputes. To say that the show got panned would be an understatement. The *Newark Star-Ledger* dubbed it an "ugly, unfunny, patronizing mess" and National Public Radio described it as "painfully bad."

Seinfeld was a tough act to follow. Jerry Seinfeld at the UK premiere of *Bee Movie*, which got stung by the critics.
Entertainment Press/Shutterstock.com

After the less-than-successful *Bee Movie* and the *Marriage Ref* debacle, Seinfeld inaugurated an intriguing web series in 2012 called *Comedians in Cars Getting Coffee*. It has been well received with its simple premise of two comedians getting together and having both good coffee and good conversation. Seinfeld told the *Guardian*: "My goal was to make it the effortless talk show, where you don't have to show up, you don't have to think about what you're wearing, there's no makeup, no prep—there's nothing. It's literally getting in a car."

The premise of the show involved Seinfeld picking up one of his peers in a different vehicle for each episode. They then travel to a restaurant or diner for coffee and a bite to eat. In episode fourteen, entitled "You'll Never Play the Copa," Jerry picked up legendary tart-tongued Don Rickles in a 1958 Cadillac Eldorado and they visited Factor's Famous Deli in Los Angeles. In episode nineteen, entitled "Comedy Is a Concealed Weapon," Seinfeld met Jay Leno in a 1949 Porsche 356/2 and the pair shared some java at Jones Coffee in Pasadena. Other comedians with whom Jerry has kibitzed over coffee include Larry David, Michael Richards, Chris Rock, Carl Reiner, Mel Brooks, Louis C. K., Ricky Gervais, Sarah Silverman, and David Letterman.

The Camera Never Blinks

When Jerry picked up his old *Seinfeld* pal Michael Richards in a 1962 Volkswagen Bus, the pair headed over to the Malibu Kitchen in Malibu, California, for a cup of joe and some conversation. Seinfeld and Richards chatted about what it was like working on their hit show together. They also discussed Richards's infamous meltdown while performing standup at the Laugh Factory on November 17, 2006, in West Hollywood. Responding to a couple of African-American hecklers, who claimed that he was completely unfunny apart from the *Seinfeld* show, Richards went off the deep end. The racial epithets poured out of his mouth like a fusillade of bullets. It wasn't just a slip of the tongue but an extended barrage of N-words. And in this day and age, virtually everything is recorded for posterity via cell phones. When the incident went viral on YouTube, Richards had a lot of explaining to do.

"It was a selfish response," Richards told Seinfeld. "I took it too personally, and I should have just said: 'Yeah, you're absolutely right. I'm not funny. I think I'll go home and work on my material and I'll see you tomorrow night.'"

Michael admitted to Jerry that perhaps he didn't enjoy working on *Seinfeld* as much as he should have. He said he worked "selfishly" instead of "selflessly." Jerry wisely replied: "Our job was not for us to enjoy it. Our job was to make sure *they* enjoy it."

If there's something positive that came out of the Laugh Factory tirade, it's that Richards saw who his real friends were—particularly the ever-loyal Jerry Seinfeld. "Thanks for sticking by me," Richards told him. "It really meant a lot to me." He wistfully added, "But inside, it still kicks me around a bit." To which his buddy responded: "That's up to you to say, 'I've been carrying this baggage long enough. I'm going to put it down.'"

By 2013, it looked like Michael Richards had, in fact, put down the baggage—at least the lion's share of it. A proud husband and father, he was seen publicly with his new wife, Beth Skipp, and their blond-haired boy, Antonio Baz. Richards also landed a co-starring role in the 2013 TV Land original sitcom *Kirstie*, starring Kirstie Alley.

Curb Your Enthusiasm

In 1999, HBO aired the one-hour special *Larry David: Curb Your Enthusiasm*. Because it was so well received, David was asked to develop a series based on the same concept. That is, Larry David essentially playing himself, albeit a fictionalized version of himself in the grand tradition of Jerry Seinfeld playing a character named Jerry Seinfeld. The fictional Larry David, like the real one, is a semi-retired television writer and producer who calls Los Angeles and, later, New York, home. With a general plot outline crafted by David, *Curb Your Enthusiasm*'s dialogue is, by and large, improvised, which is what makes the show so unique and so funny. Cheryl Hines plays Larry's wife, Cheryl, and Jeff

The Gang's all here: the 2009 *Seinfeld* reunion on *Curb Your Enthusiasm.*
HBO/Photofest

Garlin, his manager, Jeff Greene, who is married to Susie, played by Susie Essman.

Philosophically opposed to a *Seinfeld* reunion, Larry David nonetheless thought that it would work within the framework of *Curb Your Enthusiasm.* That is, the fictionalized Larry David writing the script for the show and casting his now ex-wife Cheryl—in hopes of winning her back—as Amanda, George Costanza's ex-wife.

The reunion features all four leads of the original ensemble entering the world of *Curb Your Enthusiasm* to shoot the show. Scenes include Julia Louis-Dreyfus hosting a book party for Jason Alexander, whose new tome, *Acting Without Acting,* has just hit the bookstores. Jerry and Larry gripe that the book is too short. Julia later accuses Larry of staining her antique table with his drink. He denies culpability and intends on hunting down the guilty party.

The reunion show itself—the show within the show—has a story thread revolving around George's desire to get back together with his ex, Amanda, who had left him some time ago and received half of his fortune in the divorce settlement. George had made a mint devising an iPhone application known as the iToilet, which could locate the nearest and the finest public restroom facilities any place in the world.

Unfortunately for George, investing his monies with Bernie Madoff left him indigent once more and living with Jerry. Elaine now has a child of her own—a girl who refers to Jerry as "Uncle Jerry" until she learns that he is, in fact, her biological father (Jerry had donated sperm to Elaine several years earlier); he is thereafter "Daddy." Meanwhile, Amanda will consider taking George back providing he sign a pre-nuptial agreement to ensure that his intentions are honorable and not merely a money grab. The *Curb Your Enthusiasm* episode entitled "Seinfeld" aired on November 22, 2009, and got mostly positive reviews. Ken Tucker wrote in *Entertainment Weekly* that the reunion "amounted to a regular *Seinfeld*, with George having lost a lot of money in the Bernie Madoff scandal. There was some fine, fresh *Seinfeld* observational humor conducted in Jerry's apartment, as when Elaine started reading her Blackberry messages. Jerry's petulant indignance was impeccable: 'Oh, you're gonna do the Blackberry head-down thing on me now!'" *Seinfeld* writer Peter Mehlman told the *Hollywood Reporter* that the *Curb Your Enthusiasm* reunion worked. "I thought it was where they should be," he said. "Still not really advanced much. Circumstances changed, but they didn't. It seemed like the logical place where they'd be."

The 2014 Super Bowl Commercial

After all the mystery surrounding what Jerry Seinfeld, Larry David, and Jason Alexander were doing in Tom's Restaurant in Manhattan in January 2014, it turned out not to be the "big, huge, gigantic" project that Seinfeld had cryptically spoke of in a radio interview. They were, in fact, shooting a television ad there, which was aired during the February 2, 2014, Super Bowl between the Seattle Seahawks and the Denver Broncos. Speculation was rife that a *Seinfeld* reunion was in the works.

More specifically, it was a commercial for Seinfeld's *Comedians in Cars Getting Coffee*. It featured Jerry chatting with his old buddy George Costanza. So, actually, it *was* a reunion, of sorts. In the ad, Jerry and George discuss a Super Bowl party that Jerry had been invited to but not George, who had become persona non grata at the hosts' home because of unacceptable behavior—over-cheering—at a past Super Bowl gathering. Wayne Knight, as Newman, also appeared in this funny promo for *Comedians in Cars Getting Coffee*—one in which Jerry picks up George Costanza to shoot the breeze over a cup of coffee. Jerry meets his old friend in a 1976 AMC Pacer and remarks: "I love this car for three reasons: it

The almost-billionaire Jerry Seinfeld now calls home the historic and über-expensive Beresford on Central Park West between 81st and 82nd Streets.   *Photo by Thomas Nigro*

doesn't work, looks ridiculous, and falls apart. Which makes it the perfect car for my guest today, Mr. George Costanza. George was my best friend for almost every single day of the 1990s."

With Jerry Seinfeld back in the spotlight after this Super Bowl ad, he was grilled in an interview on *CBS This Morning* why most of his guests in *Comedians in Cars Getting Coffee* are white males. Seinfeld angrily replied to the question, saying, "It really pisses me off." He further went on to point out that comedy is about being funny, not a "census" count or "actual pie chart of America." He closed with these words: "Funny is the world that I live in. You're funny, I'm interested. You're not funny, I'm not interested. And I have no interest in gender or race or anything like that."

Syndication Gold

In the spring of 2013, fifteen years after "The Finale" aired and *Seinfeld* rode off into the syndication sunset, it was estimated that the show had reaped $3.1 billion in repeat fees, with individual episodes generating on average more than $17 million a piece. Like the ever-growing National Debt Clock near

Manhattan's Union Square Park, these big numbers are growing bigger and bigger as you read these words.

Jerry Seinfeld and Larry David's take on this syndication bonanza is somewhere in the ballpark of $400 million. The show's amazing popularity in reruns and in DVD sales is testament to its large fan base and evidence that its brand of humor transcends time, even if Jerry, George, Elaine, and Kramer didn't own iPhones or have GPS in their cars. In retrospect, they certainly would have benefited from—in more than a few episodes—such modern technology at their disposal.

Unfortunately for Jason Alexander, Julia Louis-Dreyfus, and Michael Richards, they have no stake in syndication rights with Warner Bros., who owns the show, but they did hold out for DVD royalties when they negotiated their season-nine contracts. This gives them an income stream from the show for as far as the eye can see. *Seinfeld*'s cult status ensures that future generations will discover the show in reruns. They'll want to know what all the fuss was about in the 1990s when this sitcom was all the rage. Only *The Simpsons* in syndication is expected to surpass the *Seinfeld* money train, and this is because of the sheer number of episodes—more than five hundred—that will be available in the syndication package. Coincidentally, *The Simpsons* debuted in 1989, the very same year the pilot episode "The Seinfeld Chronicles" premiered.

30

The Post-*Seinfeld* World

An Altered Sitcom Landscape

When *Seinfeld* hit its stride in the mid-1990s as both a top-rated TV show and cultural phenomenon, there was a palpable sense in the ether that the creative genie was out of the bottle—that any and all sitcoms would thereafter be compared with what made the show so unique and so successful. Indeed, when *Seinfeld* drew the curtain after nine seasons in 1998, it had left an indelible mark on the television sitcom and its future, but also a vacuum as well.

TV Guide television critic Matt Roush wrote in 2009: "The TV comedy is so depleted now. There's nothing that has that kind of buzz around it [like *Seinfeld* had]. No matter how many awards you give *30 Rock*, it's never going to be *Seinfeld*. It's just too strange a show. It's brilliant for sure, but it's not what *Seinfeld* is. Everybody got *Seinfeld*. When it went away, it was almost like we didn't want to settle for anything that wasn't *Seinfeld*. It changed what we wanted TV comedy to be."

Joel Rubinoff said in the *Toronto Star*: "*Seinfeld*—as anyone who watched TV in the '90s can attest—was the great white whale of sitcoms, the last non-cable, mass audience comedy to triumph both critically and commercially before it signed off in '98. . . . The truth is, fifteen years after Jerry and company stopped complaining about Soup Nazis and 'man hands,' no one has succeeded in taking comedy to the next level on the mainstream stage."

Legacy

Undeniably, the overriding *Seinfeld* legacy is that the TV sitcom concept in its wake is a markedly different animal. Jerry Seinfeld and Larry David effected change—a sea change, as a matter of fact—on the sitcom frontier. Even if it doesn't always appear so today—with all that has transpired since it went off the air—*Seinfeld*, in the 1990s, was cutting-edge comedy. By repeatedly pushing the envelope, it dramatically raised the bar vis-à-vis what subject matter could be played for laughs. NBC was very leery of airing "The Contest," which dealt with the subject of masturbation without ever uttering the M-word, in primetime.

Yet the censors and the network brass relented as new sitcom ground was charted. *Seinfeld* paved the way for future sitcoms to navigate controversial waters without the all-consuming fear of running aground.

In the February 2014 edition of *Reader's Digest*, *Seinfeld* writer Peter Mehlman authored an essay entitled, "Will Write for Laughs." He wrote: "In 1992, when *Seinfeld* struggled for Wednesday night ratings, 'The Virgin' episode featured a plotline in which George Costanza inadvertently caused his girlfriend, Susan, to lose her job. NBC executives took offense, calling George callous and unlikable. The writing staff tinkered, making George more regretful and less unlikable. A mere four years later, when *Seinfeld* was a hit on Thursdays, an episode called 'The Invitations' featured a plotline in which George inadvertently caused Susan to . . . *die*. The same executives had no objections."

The *Seinfeld* sitcom legacy is really all about lasting influence. Almost single-handedly, *Seinfeld* legitimized the total "jerk" and "heel" sitcom character for the very first time in the annals of television. True, American television history going back to its infancy is littered with sitcom characters who exhibited more than a few character flaws—some of them quite egregious. In the final analysis, though, they almost always managed to reveal a redeeming quality or two. Even the bigoted Archie Bunker in *All in the Family* (1971–1979) was—when all was said and done—likable. To fans of the show, Archie was viewed—above all else—as a put-upon working stiff who really meant no harm. *Seinfeld*'s immense popularity proved that sitcom characters could go about their business sans consciences and moral underpinnings and still be loved and faithfully watched week in and week out. Their perverted ethical standards and inability to learn from their mistakes and transgressions was not in the least bit a liability that negatively impacted ratings. Pre-*Seinfeld* American sitcoms, on the other hand, were hopelessly wedded to happy endings and characters who—at the end of the day—recognized the errors of their ways and expressed remorse when appropriate.

It was never, ever necessary for Jerry, George, Elaine, and Kramer to prove that they were good folks at heart. *Seinfeld*, too, further raised the sitcom to a new level by addressing the ordinariness of everyday life—with mundane reality, as it were. Unlike the sitcoms that preceded it, *Seinfeld* worked with multiple, overlapping storylines wending to and fro through each episode. Typically, each character was involved in a unique plot twist, and often more than one. Pre-*Seinfeld* sitcoms habitually unfurled with linear, A and B plotlines that were neatly and predictably resolvable in twenty-two minutes.

Seinfeld's use of the multi-camera—pioneered by Desi Arnaz on *I Love Lucy* (1951–1957)—worked well in supplying the show, with its ever-twisting and turning plotlines, a theatrical air. The single-camera sitcom, which is presently in vogue, couldn't have cut the mustard with the *Seinfeld* brand of humor and the show's filming on predominantly interior sets like Jerry's apartment and Monk's Café. *Seinfeld* very literally brought the sitcom as an unfolding play to its pinnacle.

If you're visiting Tom's Restaurant on a nice day and opt to dine alfresco, be prepared to have your picture taken. You have been warned.

Photo by Thomas Nigro

Popular shows from the mid-1990s to the present—such as *Friends* (1994–2004), *How I Met Your Mother* (2005–2014), and *The Big Bang Theory* (2007–present), for instance—have clearly employed the *Seinfeld* playbook in mining laughs from a decidedly disparate non-family unit. This is yet another *Seinfeld* contribution to the television sitcom, which for decades revolved around family units. *The Office* (2005–2013), too—a mock-reality show that spoofed the current reality TV obsession—also incorporated the Seinfeldian non-family-unit-as-a source-of-comedy foundation, while also harvesting laughs from life's seeming trivialities and everyday occurrences.

So many of the shows that debuted during the mid-1990s were clearly derivative of *Seinfeld*. The aforementioned *Friends* is maybe the most overtly Seinfeldian, with its main characters—a pack of six friends—doing a lot of hanging out together while warding off life's daily problems. It should be said, however, that Rachel, Monica, Phoebe, Joey, Chandler, and Ross were hardly Jerry, George, Elaine, and Kramer. While the latter four were friends, they did an awful lot of *unfriendly* things to one another. The characters on *Friends* cared for one another in ways that were absolutely foreign to the *Seinfeld* gang.

Everybody Loves Raymond, starring Ray Romano, Patricia Heaton, Brad Garrett, Peter Boyle, and Doris Roberts, is another show born in the *Seinfeld* glory days. It featured a cast of characters with a penchant for saying and sometimes doing less-than-nice things to one another. The Barones—Ray, Debra,

Robert, Frank, and Marie—were more than just a dysfunctional television family. Despite on the surface constituting a traditional family unit—multiple generations and all—its comedic style was more *Seinfeld* than, say, Danny Thomas's *Make Room for Daddy* (1953–1965). *Everybody Loves Raymond* even shared the talents of Len Lesser. Uncle Leo on *Seinfeld* appeared as the Uncle Leo-esque Garvin in nine episodes. *Just Shoot Me* (1997–2003), starring Laura San Giacomo, George Segal, David Spade, Wendie Malick, and Enrico Colantoni, is worth including among the heavily *Seinfeld*-influenced sitcoms. It debuted in *Seinfeld*'s final season and introduced a quipping ensemble of co-workers on the job— Maya, Jack, Dennis, Nina, and Elliot—who were not loath to cruelly insulting one another or even sabotaging people they considered friends. Other sitcoms were born in *Seinfeld*'s shadow and influenced by what made it successful, included *The Drew Carey Show* (1995–2004), *Spin City* (1996–2002), and *Suddenly Susan* (1996–2000).

Television Sea Change

While the sitcoms that have followed in *Seinfeld*'s impossible-to-duplicate footsteps have built upon the show's trailblazing comedic boldness, the television landscape has irrefutably undergone a metamorphosis in recent years. In so many ways, *Seinfeld* reflected the abiding culture of the 1990s. In retrospect, that decade was the last of its kind—a transitional epoch before the encroachment of a brand new, less innocent reality. Consider all that's come down the pike in *Seinfeld*'s aftermath. Since the show's finale aired in the spring of 1998, we've collectively lived through both 9/11 and a Great Recession. We've witnessed technological advancements amend the very fabric of our lives, including both how and what we watch on television. Viewing tastes are diametrically at odds with what they were when *Seinfeld* lorded over the primetime lineup. Despite its superlative syndication and DVD sales success, it's hard to conceive of *Seinfeld* on today's primetime schedule. It was a show that defined its time in such a big way—a big way that could not be replicated now because of snowballing technologies and cable channels galore. We have what seems like infinite choices as to what we choose to watch, where we choose to watch it, and even when we opt to tune in.

With its wending tentacles that extend far beyond the traditional three network lineups, the scope of contemporary television make *Seinfeld*—these many years later—appear almost innocent in its simplicity. Throughout the 1990s— and in the preceding decades—the highest-rated TV shows always included a fair number of sitcoms in the mix. When *Seinfeld* led the ratings pack during the 1994–1995 television season, the top twenty shows were awash in sitcoms like *Home Improvement, Grace Under Fire, Friends, Roseanne, Mad About You, Ellen, Frasier,* and *Murphy Brown.* A mere two decades later finds the American sitcom— with a few notable exceptions—on something akin to life support. Nowadays, the highest-rated TV shows are dominated by intense police procedurals and dour crime dramas like *NCIS, The Blacklist, CSI: Crime Scene Investigation, Castle,* and *Blue Bloods.* Reality shows such as *Dancing with the Stars* and *The Voice* attract faithful audiences week after week. Water cooler chitchat at the office is more likely to be about *The Walking Dead* or *Game of Thrones* than any sitcom on the air.

Nevertheless, shows like *The Big Bang Theory* and *Two and a Half Men* (2003–2015) are ratings grabbers in a sea of non-sitcoms. They are clearly *Seinfeld* progeny in that they've followed in the *I Love Lucy*–*Seinfeld* tradition of utilizing both the multi-cam and the laugh track, which seem positively quaint by today's different standards. Many of the popular post-*Seinfeld* sitcoms—such as *Arrested Development* (2003–present), *The Office, 30 Rock* (2006–2013), *Modern Family* (2009–present), and *Parks and Recreation* (2009–2015)—employed the more hip single-camera approach. They come across as more movie-like in the process.

Celebrating Diversity

Among the criticisms of *Seinfeld* chronicled in this book is that the show was lily-white and not only didn't celebrate diversity but unmercifully mocked it with buffoonish characters and situations that were the worst kinds of stereotypes. It has been said now that the three networks—CBS, NBC, and ABC—are the last bastion of the mostly white-bread sitcoms. Indeed, how *Seinfeld* portrayed certain races, religions, and ethnicities likely wouldn't pass muster in the brave new world of television. That is, shows today—from the sitcom to the drama—regularly address identity issues such as sexual preference and race. It's so embedded in the modern television playbook that diversity matters in presentation. Shows like *Modern Family*, which debuted in 2009, more than a decade after *Seinfeld* left the air, is at once a sitcom and mockumentary, with its characters often addressing the camera directly. *Modern Family* features a gay couple with an adopted Vietnamese child in its portrayal of family units.

Ty Burrell, who plays Phil Dunphy on the show, fervently believes *Modern Family* is making the world a better place by including a gay couple as a legitimate family—one that is no different from any so-called traditional family. It's this social consciousness that is deeply rooted in the current culture. Jerry Seinfeld and Larry David weren't motivated in making the world a better place, only a funnier one. They weren't interested in depicting characters as role models. Advancing social justice wasn't on their agendas, either.

Not that there's anything wrong with all that.

It's just that the times have changed since *Seinfeld*'s farewell. The creators and the writers of contemporary sitcoms and dramas more often than not seek out diversity as part of their job responsibilities, and that includes establishing characters that represent the whole of society in all its hues, backgrounds, and lifestyles. *Seinfeld* was unashamedly non-diverse, with its New York City Jewish flavor and thirty-something white yuppies living on Manhattan's Upper West Side. It took great pleasure in being anti-PC, which was beginning to make serious inroads in the 1990s.

These four have left an indelible mark on television.

Over and Over

Despite *Seinfeld* having a certain dated quality—the whole 1990s thing—it is nonetheless enormously popular in reruns. DVD sales of the show's nine seasons have added to the creators' sizable bottom lines. What makes a show an enduring classic is its fan base's capacity to watch reruns over and over and never tire of them. The classic thirty-nine episodes of *The Honeymooners* (1955–1956), starring Jackie Gleason, Art Carney, Audrey Meadows, and Joyce Randolph, fit into this category. Thirty-nine episodes watched time and again that remain funny despite knowing what's coming in the storylines and the dialogue—and despite the fact that the episodes were filmed sixty years ago. *Seinfeld* is, likewise, a show that fans can never get enough of, even after they've watched the individual episodes dozens of times. Yet another reason that *Seinfeld* has legs is its strong supporting characters who carry many episodes with memorable performances.

In the 2008 *Newsweek* article "Is *Seinfeld* a Legend After 10 Years?" Marc Peyser wrote: "The truth is, even we loyal fans can get a little tired of the three yuppie leads and their hipster-doofus buddy nattering on about nothing. But when we do, there are plenty of other great characters to keep us watching, especially the deranged trio of Frank Costanza (Jerry Stiller), Estelle Costanza (Estelle Harris) and Newman (Wayne Knight). How deeply disturbed these folks are, how extraordinary the actors who bring their pathologies to life."

So, is there a possibility of an official *Seinfeld* reunion—outside of *Curb Your Enthusiasm* and the Super Bowl commercial—in the future? Because of the show's enormous and enduring popularity, there's always that speculation being bandied about, even if today's television tastes and menu are so different from what they were in the *Seinfeld* era.

While visiting *Late Night with Jimmy Fallon*, Jerry Seinfeld was asked if a reunion of the old gang was possible. He stated unequivocally: "No. It ended fifteen years ago. It's depressing already. It would be like an old people reunion." Larry David didn't mince words either when he told *The Huffington Post*: "I never considered it and I never will consider it."

While a reunion, or series of reunion specials, has great appeal to the fans, once again the show's creators seem to know what's best for the *Seinfeld* franchise. They realize that inevitably a reunion show or series of specials wouldn't live up to the hype or the high quality of the series. Speaking to Louis C. K. in *Comedians in Cars Getting Coffee*, Jerry noted that *Seinfeld* had "an expiration date" based on its premise and cast of single characters who are serial daters in New York City. When the "Seinfeld Chronicles" pilot first aired, Jerry was thirty-five and looked younger than that. Now he's a sixty-one-year-old man who can rest on his laurels and appreciate what *Seinfeld* was and will always be. Why haul out the director's chairs and the actors today? So we can all say, "Boy, they've gotten old!"

No!

Why tinker with perfection?

Appendix A
Episode Chronology

Pilot/Season One (1989–1990)

Episode 1: "The Seinfeld Chronicles" (original air date: July 5, 1989)
Episode 2: "The Stakeout" (original air date: May 31, 1990)
Episode 3: "The Robbery" (original air date: June 7, 1990)
Episode 4: "Male Unbonding" (original air date: June 14, 1990)
Episode 5: "The Stock Tip" (original air date: June 21, 1990)

Season Two (1991)

Episode 6: "The Ex-Girlfriend" (original air date: January 23, 1991)
Episode 7: "The Pony Remark" (original air date: January 30, 1991)
Episode 8: "The Jacket" (original air date: February 6, 1991)
Episode 9: "The Phone Message" (original air date: February 13, 1991)
Episode 10: "The Apartment" (original air date: April 4, 1991)
Episode 11: "The Statue" (original air date: April 11, 1991)
Episode 12: "The Revenge" (original air date: April 18, 1991)
Episode 13: "The Heart Attack" (original air date: April 25, 1991)
Episode 14: "The Deal" (original air date: May 2, 1991)
Episode 15: "The Baby Shower" (original air date: May 16, 1991)
Episode 16: "The Chinese Restaurant" (original air date: May 23, 1991)
Episode 17: "The Busboy" (original air date: June 26, 1991)

Season Three (1991–1992)

Episode 18: "The Note" (original air date: September 18, 1991)
Episode 19: "The Truth" (original air date: September 25, 1991)
Episode 20: "The Pen" (original air date: October 2, 1991)
Episode 21: "The Dog" (original air date: October 9, 1991)
Episode 22: "The Library" (original air date: October 16, 1991)
Episode 23: "The Parking Garage" (original air date: October 30, 1991)
Episode 24: "The Café" (original air date: November 6, 1991)
Episode 25: "The Tape" (original air date: November 13, 1991)
Episode 26: "The Nose Job" (original air date: November 20, 1991)
Episode 27: "The Stranded" (original air date: November 27, 1991)

Episode 28: "The Alternate Side" (original air date: December 4, 1991)
Episode 29: "The Red Dot" (original air date: December 11, 1991)
Episode 30: "The Subway" (original air date: January 8, 1992)
Episode 31: "The Pez Dispenser" (original air date: January 15, 1992)
Episode 32: "The Suicide" (original air date: January 29, 1992)
Episode 33: "The Fix-Up" (original air date: February 5, 1992)
Episode 34: "The Boyfriend" (original air date: February 12, 1992)
Episode 35: "The Limo" (original air date: February 26, 1992)
Episode 36: "The Good Samaritan" (original air date: March 4, 1992)
Episode 37: "The Letter" (original air date: March 25, 1992)
Episode 38: "The Parking Space" (original air date: April 22, 1992)
Episode 39: "The Keys" (original air date: May 6, 1992)

Season Four (1992–1993)

Episode 40/41: "The Trip" (original air dates: August 12/August 19, 1992)
Episode 42: "The Pitch" (original air date: September 16, 1992)
Episode 43: "The Ticket" (original air date: September 16, 1992)
Episode 44: "The Wallet" (original air date: September 23, 1992)
Episode 45: "The Watch" (original air date: September 30, 1992)
Episode 46: "The Bubble Boy" (original air date: October 7, 1992)
Episode 47: "The Cheever Letters" (original air date: October 28, 1992)
Episode 48: "The Opera" (original air date: November 4, 1992)
Episode 49: "The Virgin" (original air date: November 11, 1992)
Episode 50: "The Contest" (original air date: November 18, 1992)
Episode 51: "The Airport" (original air date: November 25, 1992)
Episode 52: "The Pick" (original air date: December 16, 1992)
Episode 53: "The Movie" (original air date: January 6, 1993)
Episode 54: "The Visa" (original air date: January 27, 1993)
Episode 55: "The Shoes" (original air date: February 4, 1993)
Episode 56: "The Outing" (original air date: February 11, 1993)
Episode 57: "The Old Man" (original air date: February 18, 1993)
Episode 58: "The Implant" (original air date: February 25, 1993)
Episode 59: "The Junior Mint" (original air date: March 18, 1993)
Episode 60: "The Smelly Car" (original air date: April 15, 1993)
Episode 61: "The Handicap Spot" (original air date: May 13, 1993)
Episode 62: "The Pilot" (original air date: May 20, 1993)

Season Five (1993–1994)

Episode 63: "The Mango" (original air date: September 16, 1993)
Episode 64: "The Puffy Shirt" (original air date: September 23, 1993)
Episode 65: "The Glasses" (original air date: September 30, 1993)
Episode 66: "The Sniffing Accountant" (original air date: October 7, 1993)

Episode 67: "**The Bris**" (original air date: October 14, 1993)

Episode 68: "**The Lip Reader**" (original air date: October 28, 1993)

Episode 69: "**The Non-Fat Yogurt**" (original air date: November 4, 1993)

Episode 70: "**The Barber**" (original air date: November 11, 1993)

Episode 71: "**The Masseuse**" (original air date: November 18, 1993)

Episode 72: "**The Cigar Store Indian**" (original air date: December 9, 1993)

Episode 73: "**The Conversion**" (original air date: December 16, 1993)

Episode 74: "**The Stall**" (original air date: January 6, 1994)

Episode 75: "**The Dinner Party**" (original air date: February 3, 1994)

Episode 76: "**The Marine Biologist**" (original air date: February 10, 1994)

Episode 77: "**The Pie**" (original air date: February 17, 1994)

Episode 78: "**The Stand-In**" (original air date: February 24, 1994)

Episode 79: "**The Wife**" (original air date: March 17, 1994)

Episode 80: "**The Raincoats**" (original air date: April 28, 1994)

Episode 81: "**The Fire**" (original air date: May 5, 1994)

Episode 82: "**The Hamptons**" (original air date: May 12, 1994)

Episode 83: "**The Opposite**" (original air date: May 19, 1994)

Season Six (1994–1995)

Episode 84: "**The Chaperone**" (original air date: September 22, 1994)

Episode 85: "**The Big Salad**" (original air date: September 29, 1994)

Episode 86: "**The Pledge Drive**" (original air date: October 6, 1994)

Episode 87: "**The Chinese Woman**" (original air date: October 13, 1994)

Episode 88: "**The Couch**" (original air date: October 27, 1994)

Episode 89: "**The Gymnast**" (original air date: November 3, 1994)

Episode 90: "**The Soup**" (original air date: November 10, 1994)

Episode 91: "**The Mom and Pop Store**" (original air date: November 17, 1994)

Episode 92: "**The Secretary**" (original air date: December 8, 1994)

Episode 93: "**The Race**" (original air date: December 15, 1994)

Episode 94: "**The Switch**" (original air date: January 5, 1995)

Episode 95: "**The Label Maker**" (original air date: January 19, 1995)

Episode 96: "**The Scofflaw**" (original air date: January 26, 1995)

Episode 97: "**The Highlights of 100**" (original air date: February 2, 1995)

Episode 98: "**The Beard**" (original air date: February 9, 1995)

Episode 99: "**The Kiss Hello**" (original air date: February 16, 1995)

Episode 100: "**The Doorman**" (original air date: February 23, 1995)

Episode 101: "**The Jimmy**" (original air date: March 16, 1995)

Episode 102: "**The Doodle**" (original air date: April 6, 1995)

Episode 103: "**The Fusilli Jerry**" (original air date: April 27, 1995)

Episode 104: "**The Diplomat's Club**" (original air date: May 4, 1995)

Episode 105: "**The Face Painter**" (original air date: May 11, 1995)

Episode 106: "**The Understudy**" (original air date: May 18, 1995)

Season Seven (1995–1996)

Episode 107: "The Engagement" (original air date: September 21, 1995)
Episode 108: "The Postponement" (original air date: September 28, 1995)
Episode 109: "The Maestro" (original air date: October 5, 1995)
Episode 110: "The Wink" (original air date: October 12, 1995)
Episode 111: "The Hot Tub" (original air date: October 19, 1995)
Episode 112: "The Soup Nazi" (original air date: November 2, 1995)
Episode 113: "The Secret Code" (original air date: November 9, 1995)
Episode 114: "The Pool Guy" (original air date: November 16, 1995)
Episode 115: "The Sponge" (original air date: December 7, 1995)
Episode 116: "The Gum" (original air date: December 14, 1995)
Episode 117: "The Rye" (original air date: January 4, 1996)
Episode 118: "The Caddy" (original air date: January 25, 1996)
Episode 119: "The Seven" (original air date: February 1, 1996)
Episode 120: "The Cadillac" (original air date: February 8, 1996)
Episode 121: "The Shower Head" (original air date: February 15, 1996)
Episode 122: "The Doll" (original air date: February 22, 1996)
Episode 123: "The Friars Club" (original air date: March 7, 1996)
Episode 124: "The Wig Master" (original air date: April 4, 1996)
Episode 125: "The Calzone" (original air date: April 25, 1996)
Episode 126: "The Bottle Deposit" (original air date: May 2, 1996)
Episode 127: "The Wait Out" (original air date: May 9, 1996)
Episode 128: "The Invitations" (original air date: May 16, 1996)

Season Eight (1996–1997)

Episode 129: "The Foundation" (original air date: September 19, 1996)
Episode 130: "The Soul Mate" (original air date: September 26, 1996)
Episode 131: "The Bizarro Jerry" (original air date: October 3, 1996)
Episode 132: "The Little Kicks" (original air date: October 10, 1996)
Episode 133: "The Package" (original air date: October 17, 1996)
Episode 134: "The Fatigues" (original air date: October 31, 1996)
Episode 135: "The Checks" (original air date: November 7, 1996)
Episode 136: "The Chicken Roaster" (original air date: November 14, 1996)
Episode 137: "The Abstinence" (original air date: November 21, 1996)
Episode 138: "The Andrea Doria" (original air date: December 19, 1996)
Episode 139: "The Little Jerry" (original air date: January 9, 1997)
Episode 140: "The Money" (original air date: January 16, 1997)
Episode 141: "The Comeback" (original air date: January 30, 1997)
Episode 142: "The Van Buren Boys" (original air date: February 6, 1997)
Episode 143: "The Susie" (original air date: February 13, 1997)
Episode 144: "The Pothole" (original air date: February 20, 1997)
Episode 145: "The English Patient" (original air date: March 13, 1997)

Episode 146: "The Nap" (original air date: April 10, 1997)
Episode 147: "The Yada Yada" (original air date: April 24, 1997)
Episode 148: "The Millennium" (original air date: May 1, 1997)
Episode 149: "The Muffin Tops" (original air date: May 8, 1997)
Episode 150: "The Summer of George" (original air date: May 15, 1997)

Season Nine (1997–1998)

Episode 151: "The Butter Shave" (original air date: September 25, 1997)
Episode 152: "The Voice" (original air date: October 2, 1997)
Episode 153: "The Serenity Now" (original air date: October 9, 1997)
Episode 154: "The Blood" (original air date: October 16, 1997)
Episode 155: "The Junk Mail" (original air date: October 30, 1997)
Episode 156: "The Merv Griffin Show" (original air date: November 6, 1997)
Episode 157: "The Slicer" (original air date: November 13, 1997)
Episode 158: "The Betrayal" (original air date: November 20, 1997)
Episode 159: "The Apology" (original air date: December 11, 1997)
Episode 160: "The Strike" (original air date: December 18, 1997)
Episode 161: "The Dealership" (original air date: January 8, 1998)
Episode 162: "The Reverse Peephole" (original air date: January 15, 1998)
Episode 163: "The Cartoon" (original air date: January 29, 1998)
Episode 164: "The Strongbox" (original air date: February 5, 1998)
Episode 165: "The Wizard" (original air date: February 26, 1998)
Episode 166: "The Burning" (original air date: March 19, 1998)
Episode 167: "The Bookstore" (original air date: April 9, 1998)
Episode 168: "The Frogger" (original air date: April 23, 1998)
Episode 169: "The Maid" (original air date: April 30, 1998)
Episode 170: "The Puerto Rican Day" (original air date: May 7, 1998)
Episode 171: "The Chronicle" (original air date: May 14, 1998)
Episode 172: "The Finale" (original air date: May 14, 1998)

Appendix B
Characters in
Seinfeld Land

All of the following characters appeared in two or more episodes.

Family

Frank Costanza: George's irascible father and inventor of "Festivus," celebrated on December 23 as an alternative to the Christmas holiday.

Estelle Costanza: George's histrionic and insufferable mother.

Morty Seinfeld: Jerry's father, a former raincoat salesman, who is now retired in Florida.

Helen Seinfeld: Jerry's practical mother, who lives in Florida with her husband, Morty.

Uncle Leo: Jerry's beady-eyed uncle on his mother's side and the father of Jeffrey, who works for the NYC Parks Department.

Nana: Jerry's maternal grandmother.

Barbara "Babs" Kramer: Kramer's mother, who reveals her son's first name: Cosmo.

Friends and Neighbors

Newman: Jerry's neighbor and number-one nemesis, who toils as a mail carrier for the United States Post Office.

Mickey Abbott: Testy little person, actor, and Kramer's friend.

Jack Klompus: The elder Seinfelds' petulant and unctuous neighbor in their retirement village.

Dr. Tim Whatley: Dentist and friend of Jerry, George, Elaine, and Kramer.

Carol: Friend of Jerry, George, Elaine, and Kramer; she has two babies—a cute one and an ugly one.

Noreen: Elaine's friend who dates Dan, the high-talker, and later attempts suicide by jumping off a bridge.

Deena Lazzari: George's childhood friend, who is convinced he is mentally unstable.

Scott Drake, a.k.a. "The Drake": Friend of Jerry, George, Elaine, and Kramer who gets engaged but never married.

Izzy Mandelbaum: Neighbor of the elder Seinfelds at Del Boca Vista and a highly competitive physical fitness buff.

Joe Mayo: Friend of Jerry, George, and Elaine—but not Kramer—and the recipient of a massage chair as a belated birthday gift.

Alec Berg: Jerry's friend who gives him hockey tickets and—apparently—doesn't get a sufficient number of "thank you" follow-ups for doing so.

Franklin Delano Romanowski, a.k.a. "FDR": Kramer's peculiar friend who uses a birthday wish in a nefarious way to settle a score with him.

Ruthie Cohen: Cashier at Monk's Café, whom George once accuses of a little legerdemain regarding a twenty-dollar bill of his.

Mike Moffit: Kramer's friend (and, later, his bookie), who calls Jerry a "phony" and subsequently comes to believe that he wanted him dead.

Mrs. Zanfino: Jerry's neighbor, who asks Kramer to babysit her son, Joey.

Joey Zanfino: Young boy who is frightened by his babysitter, Kramer, and runs away.

Matthew: Yogurt shop proprietor's young son, who picks up a few choice curse words from Jerry.

Boyfriends and Girlfriends

Susan Ross: George's fiancée, who dies an untimely death after ingesting toxic glue from her wedding invitation envelopes.

Mrs. Ross: Susan Ross's mordant mother and an accomplished tippler.

Henry Ross: Susan Ross's wealthy father, who once had a homosexual affair with novelist John Cheever.

David Puddy: Auto mechanic (and then car salesman) and Elaine's on-again, off-again boyfriend.

Lloyd Braun: George's childhood adversary who dates Elaine and subsequently suffers a mental breakdown.

Jake Jarmel: Star author who dates Elaine and who eschews the use of exclamation points.

Bob Cobb, a.k.a. "The Maestro": Elaine's boyfriend and a B-level conductor.

Leslie: Kramer's "low-talker" girlfriend and designer of the puffy shirt that Jerry wears on the *Today* show, hosted by Bryant Gumbel.

Marla Penny: Jerry's girlfriend who loses her virginity to John F. Kennedy, Jr.

Sidra Holland: Jerry's well-endowed girlfriend whose breasts are wrongly presumed to be counterfeits.

Kevin: Elaine's boyfriend, and then just friend, who is dubbed the "Bizarro Jerry."

Dolores: Jerry's girlfriend whose mysterious first name rhymes with a part of the female anatomy.

Rachel Goldstein: Jerry's girlfriend with whom he necks during *Schindler's List*, and who sees George in a state of "shrinkage."

Jenna: Jerry's girlfriend who later dates Kenny Bania.

Tina Robbins: Elaine's roommate, who dates Kramer.

Vanessa: Jerry's girlfriend with whom he snares a date by "accidentally" bumping into her after they had previously met at a party.

Tia Van Kamp: Calvin Klein model whom Jerry meets on a flight from St. Louis and who later dumps him for seemingly picking his nose.

Lindsay: George's girlfriend and fellow member of a book club, whose mother catches him eating a discarded éclair from the trash.

Employers and Co-workers

Jacopo Peterman, a.k.a. J. Peterman: Elaine's unconventional boss and owner of the J. Peterman Catalog.

Matt Wilhelm: George's superior while working with the New York Yankees, who sometimes exhibits signs of dementia.

George Steinbrenner: The blustering "Boss" of the New York Yankees.

Mr. Kruger: George's boss at Kruger Industrial Smoothing.

Mr. Morgan: George's co-worker for the New York Yankees who resembles boxer Sugar Ray Leonard.

Mr. Lippman: Elaine's superior at Pendant Publishing, who later opens up a shop—Top of the Muffin to You!—that sells only muffin tops.

Justin Pitt: Elaine's post–Pendant Publishing boss with innumerable idiosyncracies, including eating Snickers bars with a knife and fork.

Mr. Thomassoulo: George's boss at Play Now, who attempts to get rid of his employee after discovering that he's faked being handicapped.

Katie: Jerry's bumbling agent, who can't seem to do anything right.

Dugan: Co-worker of Elaine's at the J. Peterman Catalog.

Peggy: Elaine's J. Peterman co-worker who refers to her as Susie.

Walter: Another of Elaine's J. Peterman co-workers.

Nemeses

Kenny Bania: Lame standup comedian, who gets under Jerry's skin.

Sue Ellen Mischke: The "bra-less wonder," heiress to the Oh Henry! candy bar fortune, and Elaine's longtime rival.

"Crazy" Joe Davola: Mentally disturbed NBC writer, who attacks Kramer and stalks both Jerry and Elaine.

Lt. Joe Bookman: Gruff and dedicated library detective, who tracks down Jerry for a long-overdue book, *Tropic of Cancer*.

Donald Sanger, a.k.a. the Bubble Boy: Ill-tempered young man who lives inside a plastic bubble and both plays Trivial Pursuit and gets into a nasty scuffle with George.

Bob and Cedric: Gay couple and street toughs who steal Elaine's armoire and beat up Kramer for refusing to wear an AIDS ribbon.

Mabel Choate: Old lady from whom Jerry purloins a loaf of marble rye; she later casts the deciding vote to oust Morty Seinfeld as president of their condo board.

Ramon: Exasperating pool boy, who desperately wants to be friends with Jerry, and who nearly dies when Jerry pulls him into the pool and Newman lands on top of him.

Businesspersons and Professionals

Russell Dalrymple: President of NBC, who gives Jerry and George's sitcom pilot the green light and then perishes at sea while working with Greenpeace.

Jackie Chiles: Attorney who represents Kramer in a couple of cases and then Jerry, George, Elaine, and Kramer after their arrests for violating a "Good Samaritan" law.

Babu Bhatt: Pakistani restaurateur, whose business goes bust and who gets deported—he believes—because of Jerry, a "very, very bad man."

Yev Kassem, a.k.a. "the Soup Nazi": Soup peddler with stringent rules for ordering his product.

Poppie: Incontinent restaurateur who urinates on Jerry's new couch.

Acquaintances

Rabbi Glickman: Resident of Elaine's building who, on his cable show, blabs what she said to him in confidence.

Joe Temple: Man in whose living room George watches *Breakfast at Tiffany's*.

Remy Temple: Joe Temple's daughter, who is not too happy about having George in her home.

Ricky: Man who makes a bouquet of flowers out of Frank Costanza's *TV Guide* and later designs a mannequin that looks exactly like Elaine.

Rusty: Homeless man recruited to pull Kramer and Newman's rickshaw; he later picks the former out as a jewel thief in a police lineup.

Rebecca DeMornay: Thrift store employee with a short fuse.

Appendix C
Awards

Primetime Emmy Awards

1992

Outstanding Writing in a Comedy Series, Elaine Pope and Larry Charles, "The Fix-Up"
Outstanding Editing for a Series, Janet Ashikaga, "The Subway"
Outstanding Supporting Actor in a Comedy Series, Michael Richards
Outstanding Writing in a Comedy Series, Larry David, "The Contest"

1993

Outstanding Comedy Series
Outstanding Supporting Actor in a Comedy Series, Michael Richards

1994

Outstanding Individual Achievement in Editing for a Series, Janet Ashikaga, "The Opposite"

1995

Outstanding Individual Achievement in Editing for a Series, Janet Ashikaga, "The Diplomat's Club"
Outstanding Supporting Actress in a Comedy Series, Julia Louis-Dreyfus

1996

Outstanding Supporting Actor in a Comedy Series, Michael Richards

Golden Globe Awards

1993

Best TV Series Comedy/Musical
Best Performance by an Actor in a TV Series Comedy/Musical, Jerry Seinfeld

1994

Best Performance by an Actress in a Supporting Role in a Series, Mini-Series, or Motion Picture Made for Television, Julia Louis-Dreyfus

Screen Actors Guild Awards

1995

Outstanding Performance by an Ensemble in a Comedy Series
Outstanding Performance by a Male Actor in a Comedy Series, Jason Alexander

1997

Outstanding Performance by an Ensemble in a Comedy Series
Outstanding Performance by a Female Actor in a Comedy Series, Julia Louis-Dreyfus

1998

Outstanding Performance by an Ensemble in a Comedy Series
Outstanding Performance by a Female Actor in a Comedy Series, Julia Louis-Dreyfus

People's Choice Awards

1996

Favorite TV Comedy Series

1997

Favorite TV Comedy Series

1998

Favorite TV Comedy Series

1999

Favorite TV Comedy Series (tied with *Frasier*)

Writers Guild of America Awards

1994

Episodic Comedy, Larry David, "The Contest"

1995

Episodic Comedy, Larry David and Lawrence H. Levy, "The Mango"

1997

Episodic Comedy, David Mandel, "The Pool Guy"

1998

Episodic Comedy, Gregg Kavet and Andy Robin, "The Fatigues"

Directors Guild of America Awards

1992

Outstanding Directorial Achievement in a Comedy Series, Tom Cherones, "The Contest"

1996

Outstanding Directorial Achievement in a Comedy Series, Andy Ackerman, "The Rye"

1997

Outstanding Directorial Achievement in a Comedy Series, Andy Ackerman, "The Betrayal"

ASCAP Film & Television Awards

1994

Top TV Series, Jonathan Wolff

1995

Top TV Series, Jonathan Wolff

1996

Top TV Series, Jonathan Wolff

1997

Top TV Series, Jonathan Wolff

1998

Top TV Series, Jonathan Wolff

1999

Top TV Series, Jonathan Wolff

ACE Eddie Awards

1997

Best Edited Half-Hour Series for Television, Skip Collector

Appendix D
The *Seinfeld* Production Team

Jerry Seinfeld, executive producer/producer (1990–1998)
Larry David, executive producer/producer (1990–1998)
George Shapiro, executive producer (1990–1998)
Howard West, executive producer (1990–1998)
Jeffrey Stott, executive producer in charge of production (1990–1998)
Fred Barron, executive producer (1990)
Andrew Scheinman, executive producer (1991–1993)
Alec Berg, executive producer/supervising producer (1996–1998)
Jeff Schaffer, executive producer/supervising producer (1996–1998)
Tom Cherones, producer/supervising producer (1990–1994)
Tim Kaiser, producer/associate producer/coordinating producer (1990–1998)
Larry Charles, producer/supervising producer (1991–1994)
Suzy Mamann-Greenberg, producer/associate producer (1992–1998)
Tom Gammill, producer/supervising producer/consulting producer (1993–1997)
Peter Mehlman, producer/co-producer/co-executive producer/supervising producer (1993–1997)
Max Pross, producer/supervising producer/consulting producer (1993–1997)
Marjorie Gross, producer (1995–1996)
Andy Ackerman, producer (1996–1998)
David Mandel, producer/co-producer/ supervising producer (1996–1998)
Joan Van Horn, line producer (1991–1994)
Nancy Sprow, associate producer/coordinating producer (1992–1998)
Morgan Sackett, associate producer (1994–1995)
Rick Corcoran, associate producer (1996–1998)
Elaine Pope, co-producer (1991–1992)
Carol Leifer, co-producer (1995–1996)
Spike Feresten, co-producer/supervising producer (1996–1998)
Gregg Kavet, co-executive producer/supervising producer (1996–1998)
Andy Robin, co-executive producer/supervising producer (1996–1998)
Jennifer Crittenden, co-producer (1997–1998)
Steve Koren, co-producer (1997–1998)

Selected Bibliography

Articles

Achenbach, Joel. "Seinfeld Leaves His Mark on History." *Washington Post*, November 19, 2004.

"A Conversation with Heidi Swedberg." *Dadnabbit*, Dadnabbit.com, April 28, 2011.

Adams, Erik. "Patrick Warburton on *Rules of Engagement*, *Seinfeld*, and Why *Family Guy* Upsets His Parents." *The A.V. Club*, AVClub.com, February 4, 2013.

"America's Billionaires in the Making." *Forbes*, September 24, 2010.

Arena, Salvatore. "Kenny's Roasters Have Him Boiling." *New York Daily News*, February 16, 1996.

"Ask Me Anything" Q&A with Jerry Seinfeld. Reddit.com, January 6, 2014.

"Barney Martin, TV Father of *Seinfeld*, Dead at 82." *Associated Press*, March 24, 2005.

Bogdanovich, Peter. "*Seinfeld* Battles Actor Danny Hoch." *New York Observer*, March 9, 1998.

Buckley, William F., Jr. "The Murphy Brown Law." *Baltimore Sun*, May 27, 1992.

Burkeman, Oliver. "Jerry Seinfeld on How to Be Funny Without Sex or Swearing." *The Guardian*, January 5, 2014.

Callebs, Sean, and Reuters. "*Seinfeld* Finale Touches Some, Bothers Others." CNN.com, May 15, 1998.

Cerasaro, Pat. "Jason Alexander Talks *Reprise!*, *Lucky Stiff*, *Two by Two*, *Seinfeld*, Sondheim & More." InDepth InterView, Broadwayworld.com, December 15, 2012.

Couch, Aaron. "Ex-*Seinfeld* Writer on *Curb*, His Book and Why *Girls* Is the Only Comedy He Can Stand." *The Hollywood Reporter*, April 3, 2013.

"Doctor Says Voice on TV Caused Seizures." *New York Times*, July 11, 1991.

Dowd, Kathy Ehrich. "Jerry Seinfeld Says the *Seinfeld* Reunion Is Real." *People*, January 30, 2014.

Dowd, Maureen. "Yada Yada Yuppies." *New York Times*, May 14, 1997.

Dunlap, David. "Rockefeller Center Quietly Closes Theater." *New York Times*, October 19, 1999.

"Estelle Harris Talks About Being *Seinfeld*'s Mrs. Costanza." CTV News, March 30, 2012.

Evans, Bradford. "The Lost Roles of *Seinfeld*." Splitsider.com, April 14, 2011.

"Forever *Seinfeld*." *People*, May 14, 1998.

France, Lisa Respers. "Jerry Seinfeld Takes Heat Over Race Remarks." CNN, February 5, 2014.

Fussman, Cal. "What I've Learned: Jerry Stiller." *Esquire*, May 1, 2005.

Gallagher, Pat. "John O'Hurley—The 7th Most Interesting Man in the World." *Huffington Post*, March 2, 2015.

Gay, Verne. "*Seinfeld*'s Lee Bear: The Man Who Was Steinbrenner." *Newsday*, July 13, 2010.

Givens, Ron. "Not Part of the Wild Bunch During Turbulent Period in U.S., Jerry Went His Own Way." *New York Daily News*, November 24, 1997.

Gliatto, Tom. "Jerry Engaged? Get Out!" *People*, November 22, 1999.

Goh, Melisa, and the NPR staff. "Not Funny Enough? *New Yorker* Gives *Seinfeld* Cartoon a Second Chance." NPR.org, July 22, 2012.

Grace, Melissa. "Helmer Toro, Owner of H&H Bagels, Gets 50 Weekends in Jail for Stealing $500,000 in Employee Taxes." *New York Daily News*, July 22, 2010.

Harnick, Chris. "Lee Garlington Reflects on Lost *Seinfeld* Role, Lengthy Hollywood Career for 'Isn't That . . . ?'" *Huffington Post*, April 2, 2013.

Harris, Will. "Wayne Knight Talks About *The Exes*, Newman, and Working in the Mud for *Jurassic Park*." *The A.V. Club*, AVClub.com, July 25, 2012.

Hurd, R. Wesley. "Postmodernism." Gutenberg College, McKenzie Study Center, msc.gutenberg.edu, June 1998.

"Interview with Jason Alexander." *UVU Review*, March 5, 2012.

Israel, David K. "An Interview with Jason Alexander." *Mental Floss*, March 18, 2010.

Itzkoff, Dave. "*Curb Your Enthusiasm*: The Other *Seinfeld* Finale." *New York Times*, November 23, 2009.

Jacobs, A. J. "Mr. Seinfeld's Neighborhood." *Entertainment Weekly*, May 4, 1998.

James, Caryn. "Television Review: *Seinfeld* Goes Out in Self-Referential Style." *New York Times*, May 15, 1998.

Kaplan, Ben. "Remembering Uncle Leo: Len Lesser Was Frail but Funny." *National Post*, February 17, 2011.

Kehr, Dave. "New DVDs." *New York Times*, November 23, 2004.

Kendrick, Deborah. "Actor Pushes Film Industry to Measure Up." Enquirer.com, February 15, 2004.

King, Susan. "With an Eye On . . . : The Dinosaurs *Really* Liked Wayne Knight—and So Do TV Producers." *Los Angeles Times*, October 31, 1993.

Konow, David. "*Fridays*: A Look Back at L.A.'s Answer to *Saturday Night Live*." *Dallas Observer*, July 31, 2003.

"Larry David Talks Dating Post-Divorce, *Seinfeld*, and Wealth." *Rolling Stone*, July 20, 2011.

Laskow, Michael. "Jonathan Wolff, TV Composer." Taxi.com.

Leco, Mike. "*Seinfeld*'s New York." USATourist.com.

Lipton, Michael A. "An Affair to Remember." *People*, June 24, 1996.

Locker, Melissa. "Jerry Seinfeld and Jason Alexander Reunited at the *Seinfeld* Diner." *People*, January 14, 2014.

Loftis, Ryan. "Jerry Seinfeld: One of TV's Most Successful Sitcom Stars Ever." Celebrity Biographies, Entertainmentscene360.com.

Marsellos, Michael M. "Brother Michael A. Richards: Renaissance Man, Not 'Kramer.'" *Scottish Rite Journal*, September 2000.

Marshall, Kelli. "A Friendly Reminder: *Seinfeld* Was Criticized Too." Kellimarshall.net, March 5, 2013.

McLemee, Scott. "*Seinfeld* and the Culture of Narcissism." Mclemee.com, May 3, 1998.

McShane, Larry. "Game Over for Mickey Mantle's Restaurant." *New York Daily News*, June 5, 2012.

Mehlman, Peter. "Will Write for Laughs." *Reader's Digest*, February 2014.

"Michael Richards." *People*, May 14, 1998.

Miller, Nod. "Applying Insights from Cultural Studies to Adult Education: What *Seinfeld* Says About the AERC." Adult Education Research Conference Proceedings, January 1, 1999.

"NBC Apologizes for *Seinfeld* Episode on the Puerto Rican Day Parade." *New York Times*, May 9, 1998.

O'Connor, John J. "Television View: A Few Qualms from a Fan of *Seinfeld*." *New York Times*, May 30, 1993.

Patterson, John. "Julia Louis-Dreyfus: Bucking the *Seinfeld* Curse." *The Guardian*, June 15, 2012.

"Paul Shaffer as Seinfeld Sidekick: Not That There's Anything Wrong with That." *New York Daily News*, June 11, 2009.

Peyser, Marc. "Television: Is *Seinfeld* a Legend After 10 Years?" *Newsweek*, May 3, 2008.

Pisner, Noah B. "15 Questions with Jason Alexander." *Harvard Crimson*, April 15, 2013.

Pogrebin, Robin. "1st Amendment Protection for a Restaurant's Critic." *New York Times*, April 26, 1996.

Puig, Claudia. "Seinfeld's *Bee Movie* Deserves a Good Swat." *USA Today*, November 2, 2007.

Reuters. "Seinfeld's *Marriage* Gets Big Ratings, Bad Reviews." March 1, 2010.

"Review: *Dizzy & Jimmy*." *Publishers Weekly*, Reed Business Information, 2000.

Riley, Naomi Schaefer. "The Post-Racial World of Jerry Seinfeld." *New York Post*, February 11, 2014.

Rose, Lacey. "Emmys: Jerry Seinfeld on Why He May Never Go Back to TV (Q&A)." *The Hollywood Reporter*, August 21, 2013.

Rosenthal, Phil. "NBC Executive Stands Apart by Taking Stands." *Chicago Tribune*, August 21, 2005.

Rothschild, Richard. "*Seinfeld*'s John O'Hurley Talks About J. Peterman's Management Style." *Workforce*, Workforce.com, June 21, 2012.

Rubinoff, Joel. "Post-*Seinfeld*, TV Comedy Tries to Find Itself." *Toronto Star*, November 13, 2013.

Rusoff, Jane Wollman. "Kramer's Birth." *Chicago Tribune*, April 7, 1993.

Ryan, Mike. "Ten Years Later: Still Bitter About *Seinfeld* Finale, Reunion Needed." Starpulse.com, September 18, 2008.

Schneider, Karen S. "The Game of Love." *People*, March 28, 1994.

Segall, Rebecca, and Peter Ephross. "Critics Call Show 'Self-Hating': Was *Seinfeld* Good for Jews?" Jweekly.com, May 8, 1998.

Sepinwall, Alan. "*Curb Your Enthusiasm*, 'Seinfeld': The Finale Is the Reunion." *Newark Star-Ledger*, November 22, 2009.

Sepinwall, Alan. "*The Marriage Ref*: Jerry Seinfeld's Unfunny, Painful New Series." *Newark Star-Ledger*, March 1, 2010.

Shuster, Fred. "Behind the Silly Symphony of *Seinfeld*." *Los Angeles Daily News*, December 2, 1993.

Silverstein, Frank. "J. Peterman Rides Again." NBCNews.com, January 25, 2009.

Sims, David. "*Seinfeld*: 'The Finale.'" *The A.V. Club*, AVClub.com, April 19, 2012.

Slate, Libby. "Setting the Tone: Jonathan Wolff Has Been Creating Music for TV Since 1982; His Biggest Latest Hit Is the Theme for *Seinfeld*." *Los Angeles Times*, December 23, 1994.

Storer, Natasha. "Top Ten *Seinfeld* Locations in NYC." Guest of a Guest, Guestofaguest.com, July 21, 2010.

Thoma, Peter. "The Show About Nothing and Everything (and Me): *Seinfeld*, Political Correctness, and Serfdom." *The History Roll*, Historyroll.com, July 30, 2010.

Torrance, Kelly Jane. "The Joys of Being Julia Louis-Dreyfus." *Capitol File*, December 12, 2011.

Warnett, Gary. "A Complete Guide to Seinfeld's Sneakers." Complex Sneakers, Complex.com, April 5, 2011.

Weiner, Jonah. "Jerry Seinfeld Intends to Die Standing Up." *New York Times Magazine*, October 20, 2012.

Windolf, Jim. "Master of His Domain: With His Creative Partner Larry David Gone, Will Jerry Seinfeld Still Embody the Neurotic Nineties?" *New York Observer*, September 16, 1996.

Zinoman, Jason. "On Stage, a Comic's Still at Home." *New York Times*, October 14, 2012.

Books

Dunne, Sara Lewis. *Seinfeld: Master of Its Domain*. London: Bloomsbury Academic, 2006.

Levine, Josh. *Jerry Seinfeld: Much Ado About Nothing*. Toronto: ECW Press, 1993.

Shaffer, Paul. *We'll Be Here for the Rest of Our Lives*. New York: Anchor, 2010.

Sheridan, Liz. *Dizzy & Jimmy*. New York: HarperEntertainment, 2000.

Stiller, Jerry. *Married to Laughter*. New York: Simon & Schuster, 2000.

Media

Blogtalkradio.com, "Liz Sheridan Interview," July 29, 2008.

Blogtalkradio.com, "Liz Sheridan Returns," June 11, 2009.

Clash, Jim. "*Seinfeld*'s J. Peterman" *Adventurer* interview of John O'Hurley, Forbes.com YouTube video, November 13, 2007.

Comedians in Cars Getting Coffee, Jerry Seinfeld and Larry David, September 19, 2012.

Comedians in Cars Getting Coffee, Jerry Seinfeld and Louis C. K., January 2, 2014.

Comedians in Cars Getting Coffee, Jerry Seinfeld and Michael Richards, December 2, 2012.

EmmyTVLegends.org, interview with George Shapiro, July 19, 2011.

Late Night with Jimmy Fallon interview of Jerry Seinfeld, June 18, 2013.

Late Show with David Letterman interview of Larry David, September 6, 2007.

Phil Donahue Show, Andy Griffith Show cast reunion interview, March 28, 1986.

Seinfeld Volume 1 (Seasons 1 & 2), Inside Look, Commentary, Notes About Nothing, Sony Pictures Home Entertainment, November 23, 2004.

Seinfeld Volume 2 (Season 3), Inside Look, Commentary, Notes About Nothing, Sony Pictures Home Entertainment, November 23, 2004.

Seinfeld Volume 3 (Season 4), Inside Look, Commentary, Notes About Nothing, Sony Pictures Home Entertainment, May 17, 2005.

Seinfeld Volume 4 (Season 5), Inside Look, Commentary, Notes About Nothing, Sony Pictures Home Entertainment, November 22, 2005.

Seinfeld Volume 5 (Season 6), Inside Look, Commentary, Notes About Nothing, Sony Pictures Home Entertainment, November 22, 2005.

Seinfeld Volume 6 (Season 7), Inside Look, Commentary, Notes About Nothing, Sony Pictures Home Entertainment, November 21, 2006.

Seinfeld Volume 7 (Season 8), Inside Look, Commentary, Notes About Nothing, Sony Pictures Home Entertainment, June 5, 2007.

Seinfeld Volume 8 (Season 9), Inside Look, Commentary, Notes About Nothing, Sony Pictures Home Entertainment, November 6, 2007.

StarCam interview with Jason Alexander at CSA 27th Annual Artois Awards, September 26, 2011.

Websites

Internet Movie Database (IMDb), imdb.com

Kennykramer.com

Lawrencewatson.com

Menupages.com

Originalsoupman.com

Petermehlman.com

Seinfeld-fan.net

Seinfeld official site, Sonypictures.com/tv/shows/seinfeld

Seinfeldscripts.com

Urbandictionary.com

Index

THE FAQ SERIES

Prices, contents, and availability
subject to change without notice.